YOUNG CHILDREN IN CONTEXT

YOUNG CHILDREN
IN CONTEXT
Impact of
Self, Family and Society
on Development

Edited by

CAVEN S. MCLOUGHLIN, Ph.D.

and

DOMINIC F. GULLO, Ph.D.

CHARLES C THOMAS • PUBLISHER
Springfield • Illinois • U.S.A.

Published and Distributed Throughout the World by

CHARLES C THOMAS • PUBLISHER
2600 South First Street
Springfield, Illinois 62717

ISBN 0-398-05059-7

Library of Congress Catalog Card Number: 84-8892

Printed in the United States of America
SC-R-3

Library of Congress Cataloging in Publication Data

Main entry under title:

Young children in context.

Bibliography: p.
Includes index.
1. Child development—Addresses, essays, lectures.
2. Home and school—Addresses, essays, lectures.
3. School environment—Addresses, essays, lectures.
4. Handicapped children—Addresses, essays, lectures.
I. McLoughlin, Caven S.   II. Gullo, Dominic F.
LB1115.Y58   1984   305.2'3   84-8892
ISBN 0-398-05059-7

CONTRIBUTING AUTHORS

Editors and Chapter Contributors

Caven S. Mcloughlin, Ph.D.
Kent State University
Educational Psychology

Caven S. Mcloughlin is an Assistant Professor in the College of Education, Kent State University. His current primary responsibility is in the preparation of school psychologists with an early childhood specialty. He is Editor-in-Chief for *School Psychology International Journal* and associate editor for several other professional publications. Dr. Mcloughlin is particularly interested in single subject design methodologies, behaviorally based interventions for young children, the use of parents as behavior change agents, the impact of legislation and litigation upon education, and cross-cultural studies in child development. He was educated at the graduate level in both the USA and England.

Dominic F. Gullo, Ph.D.
Kent State University
Early Childhood Education

Dominic F. Gullo is an Associate Professor of Early Childhood Education. He has an interdisciplinary training background in developmental psychology and education, specializing in the development of the very young child, zero to five years old. His teaching and research interests include language and cognitive development as well as the ways in which different social and physical environments facilitate or hamper a child's development. Currently, he is involved in researching the effects of how adults' expectations of infant development ultimately affect the subsequent development of the child. Dr. Gullo is a reviewer and contributor to various developmental and educational journals, and is the co-founder of the *Midwestern Society for Research in Lifespan Development.*

Chapter Contributors

Nicholas J. Anastasiow, Ph.D.
Professor, Hunter College; and
Head of Human Development Area Programs in Educational Psychology
Graduate Center
City University of New York

Nicholas J. Anastasiow obtained his doctoral degree from Stanford University and completed post-doctoral work at Columbia College of Physicians and Surgeons. He has had extensive experience in universities and public school settings. He has also written extensively, particularly on language development of children who reside in poverty. He is a Fellow of the American Psychological Association and has presented at national and international symposia on the infant-at-risk, and the continuing phenomenon of adolescent pregnancies. He is currently involved in establishing child development courses for junior high school students.

Raquel Bild, Ph.D.
Miami Institute of Psychology
Caribbean Center for Advanced Studies

Raquel Bild is Academic Dean of the Miami Institute of Psychology, of the Caribbean Center for Advanced Studies. She is a licensed psychologist in the State of Florida, and has worked extensively in psychotherapy with children and their families. She has presented many papers and workshops in the areas of family therapy, acculturation, behavioral medicine, and working with Hispanic clients. She is a member of the American Psychological Association, the Florida Psychological Association, and is Past-President of the South Florida Association of Hispanic Psychologists.

Mary Jo Cherry, Ph.D.
Villa Maria College

Mary Jo Cherry serves as Associate Dean for the College of Education, a cooperative program of Villa Maria College and

Cannon University in Erie, Pennsylvania. Dr. Cherry is an Associate Professor of education, and is responsible for program design and teaching in the fields of early childhood and elementary education. Her most recent research and study has focused on the growth and development of infants and toddlers, especially in the area of social development. She has been instrumental in designing and implementing parent-infant-toddler programs in which parents and children share playtime in a center setting.

Douglas H. Clements, Ph.D.
Kent State University
Department of Early Childhood Education

Douglas H. Clements is an Assistant Professor of Early and Elementary Education at Kent State University. Previously, he was a kindergarten teacher for five years. His interests include the differential effects of scheduling on kindergartners, preschool children's concepts of number, and the use of computers with young children. Concerning the last of these, he is conducting research to determine the differential effects of computer assisted instruction vs. computer programming in Logo on young children's development. He is the author of *Computers in Early and Primary Education* (1985) concerning the application of computers to early childhood education.

Evelyn Diaz, M.A.
Miami Institute of Psychology
Caribbean Center for Advanced Studies

Evelyn Diaz is Director of the Specialized Training Institute at Miami-Dade Community College. She received her masters in educational psychology from New York University and is currently working towards her doctorate in clinical psychology at the Miami Institute of Psychology. Ms. Diaz's professional interests include acculturation, cultural differences, psychological stress and coping behavior. She has completed numerous research projects on cultural aspects of behavior and has worked extensively with minority group populations. She is a student affiliate of the American Psychological Association, the National Hispanic Psychological Association and the South Florida Association of Hispanic Psychologists.

J. Bradley Garner, M.S.Ed.
Mid-Eastern Ohio Special Education Regional Resource Center

J. Bradley Garner is a school psychologist by training and experience. His efforts are primarily directed toward the development of integrated educational options for children labeled severely handicapped. Mr. Garner has great interest in the philosophical frameworks which guide the development and implementation of service delivery options for persons with handicaps. He has worked as a teacher, administrator, coordinator of federal projects, and as a consultant to various agencies and organizations in the public and private sectors. He is currently a consultant with the Mid-Eastern Ohio Special Education Regional Resource Center.

Michael E. Lamb, Ph.D.
University of Utah
Departments of Psychology, Psychiatry, and Pediatrics

Michael E. Lamb is currently Professor of Psychology, Psychiatry, and Pediatrics and Adjunct Professor of Family and Consumer Studies at the University of Utah. His research is concerned with social and emotional development, particularly in infancy and early childhood, and he has published extensively on this topic. Several of his recent research projects have been concerned with the effects of varying patterns of child care (both intracultural and cross-cultural) on development in early childhood. He is the author or editor of several books including *The Role of the Father in Child Development* (1976, 1981), *Nontraditional Families* (1982), *Sibling Relationships* (1982), *Development in Infancy* (1981), and *Socialization and Personality Development* (1982).

Philip J. Lazarus, Ph.D.
Florida International University

Philip J. Lazarus is an Associate Professor and the Director of the School Psychology Training Program at Florida International University. He received his baccalaureate degree from Tulane University and his doctoral degree from the University of Florida. Dr. Lazarus has published and presented extensively in the area of psychological assessment and intervention with children and serves on the editorial board of *Psychology in the*

Schools. Dr. Lazarus is senior editor of *Psychoeducational Evaluation of Children with Low Incidence Handicaps* (1985). In addition to his teaching responsibilities, Dr. Lazarus maintains a practice in clinical and school psychology.

Michele A. Paludi, Ph.D.
Kent State University
Department of Psychology

Michele A. Paludi received her Ph.D. in experimental psychology from the University of Cincinnati. Her major area of concentration is life-span developmental psychology. She teaches undergraduate and graduate courses in this area as well as in the development of gender role identity. Dr. Paludi has published research in the psychological and structural factors affecting the achievement behavior of women: Achievement orientation, expectancy of success, sex discrimination in educational settings, mentoring, and attitudes about women's abilities and roles. In addition, Dr. Paludi has been conducting psychometric research with tests of preschoolers' knowledge of sex-determined role standards and sex-role preferences. She is currently designing a behaviorally based measure of preschoolers' sex-role preference.

Brenda Y. Terrell, Ph.D.
Case Western Reserve University
Department of Communication Sciences

Brenda Y. Terrell is an Assistant Professor in the Department of Communication Sciences at Case Western Reserve University. She received the B.S. in Speech Pathology from the University of Tennessee, Knoxville, and the M.A. in Speech Pathology from Memphis State University. Before receiving the Ph.D. in communication disorders from the University of Pittsburgh, she served as a speech-language pathologist and clinical instructor in a university/community speech and hearing clinic. Her areas of primary interest are cognition and language development and disorders, with a particular focus on infant and preschool populations. Most recently her research interest has been in the relationship between play and language in normal and language-impaired children.

Valora Washington, Ph.D.
Howard University
School of Human Ecology

Valora Washington is a child development specialist with research interests in early childhood specialization, in crosscultural development, and in social policy. Her present research includes a community needs assessment, and an investigation of the effectiveness of parent involvement, in Project Head Start. As a postdoctoral Congressional Science Fellow for the *Society for Research in Child Development* in 1981–1982, Dr. Washington worked as a Legislative Assistant for a member of the U.S. Senate. She has also served as a faculty member of the Bush Institute on Children and Social Policy at the University of North Carolina at Chapel Hill. Dr. Washington received her graduate and undergraduate degrees from Indiana University and Michigan State University, respectively. She now serves as Assistant Dean and Associate Professor at Howard University, Washington, DC.

M. Jeanne Wilcox, Ph.D.
Kent State University
School of Speech Pathology and Audiology

M. Jeanne Wilcox is an Associate Professor in the School of Speech Pathology and Audiology at Kent State University. She received her B.A. in Speech Pathology and Linguistics from Kansas State University and earned her M.A. and Ph.D. from Memphis State University. Her primary areas of interest include normal and disordered child language development with a special emphasis on severely handicapped infants and young children.

CONTENTS

xi

YOUNG CHILDREN IN CONTEXT

PART I

PERSONAL ECOLOGY

CHAPTER 1

ECOLOGICAL PERSPECTIVES ON THE DEVELOPMENT OF THE YOUNG CHILD

CAVEN S. MCLOUGHLIN AND DOMINIC F. GULLO

INTRODUCTION

In recent years our attention has shifted away from studying child behavior as isolated instances affected only by the inherited potential of the child, to studying the child as a member of an ecological system. Ecology can be defined as "the study of the relation of organisms or groups of organisms to their environment" (Moos, 1976, p. 9). In this manner *environment* must be viewed more broadly than the physical suround, rather environment must be viewed as everything that is internal and external to the organism itself. It is the *process* of one's adjustment to this environment that is the contemporary focus of child, and is the focus of this book.

> The life of an organism . . . is inescapably bound up with the conditions of the environment which comprise not only topography . . . but other organisms and then activities as well . . . all organisms are engaged in activities which have as their logical conclusion adjustment to the environment. (Hawley, 1950, p. 3)

Bronfenbrenner (1977) hypothesized that behavior is the result of the interaction among four categories of environment. The first category is the macrosystem. This represents one's culture—a set of values, beliefs, mores, customs. In turn, these are transmitted from generation to generation and influence the perception, motivation and meaning of one's life experiences. The second category is the exosystem which consists of the social structure within which one lives. The exosystem has a more immediate effect on behavior and is represented by such as interpersonal relationships established in the community, family, workplace and political arena.

The third category is the microsystem which Bronfenbrenner asserts to be the most important and influential in affecting day-to-day behavior. The microsystem represents everyday events that one experiences at home, school, church, or at the workplace. This aspect of the ecological system has characteristics such as time, place, action, participants and role. Finally, the mesosystem represents the interrelationship among and between any of the microsystems. For example, behavior at school or the workplace is interrelated to the behavior at home, and so on.

In this book the focus will be how the child's ecology, that is, factors pertaining to self, family and society, impact on normal and abnormal development. Additionally, we focus on specific ecological factors which seem to facilitate or hamper development as well as ways of evaluating it.

CHAPTER OVERVIEW

The book is organized into three sections. First considered is the child's individual or personal ecology. This includes the development of thinking and problem solving, the acquisition of communicative competence in social endeavor through language, the development of differences in patterns of acquired behavior in young boys and girls, and observations on the prospects for young handicapped children in our society. The theoretical perspectives in Chapter 2 are dually Information Processing and Piagetian. Chapter 3 places great emphasis on understanding the acquisition of complex linguistic structures in the context of the interpersonal communicative setting. The fourth chapter describes similarities and differences between boys and girls, particularly in terms of cognitive ability and achievement, and addresses the influences on the development of gender role identity. Chapter 5 deals with the plight of the young handicapped child and advocates for a radically changed philosophy concerning the worth of the damaged child. The implications of deficits in the major domains are considered, and model characteristics are postulated for an ideal early childhood program for the handicapped child.

Section Two moves from the consideration of skill or repertoire development in the individual, to the wider perspective of the child in family and social contexts. The social milieu of the child *inter*personally as well as *intra*personally is addressed. The focus moves from the development of social relationships in the context of peers (Chapter 6), to the impact of family variables upon development (Chapter 7). Separately considered are the influences of the contemporary cultural "melting pot" (Chapter 8); television, computers and other modern teaching modes (Chapter 9); and, the role of politics, public policy and lobby efforts on childrens' behalf (Chapter 10).

The final section of the book both considers issues in evaluating the young child in context, and means of optimizing the facilitation of children's development.

CHANGING VIEWS OF CHILDHOOD

It is important to identify and recognize changes in society's views of children through the centuries, for as our views of childhood have changed, so too have our ways of studying them.

De Mause (1974) identifies four distinct phases of society's views of childhood. In the first phase there was no apparent conception of childhood. Up until the 4th century A.D., which De Mause calls the *infanticide mode,* children were often offered as sacrifices to pagan gods. Those born with obvious handicapping conditions often were destroyed. From the 4th to the 13th centuries, the *abandonment mode,* unwanted children were simply left on the hillsides to die. It is not clear whether these practices were a method of population control, a status symbol, or were reflective of the economic crises of the era.

In the second phase in the history of childhood there was an emergence of the notion of childhood as a special period of life. This occured between the 14th and 17th centuries and De Mause terms this phase the *ambivalent mode.* Due to high infant mortality "the general feeling was that one had several children in order to keep just a few. Before they are old enough to bother you, you will have lost half of them or perhaps all of them" (Aries, 1962, p. 38). For this and associated economic reasons parents often were reluctant to become emotionally attached to their children.

Perhaps the most influential view of children of this period came from the philosopher, John Locke, who in an advice manual to parents stated that "children should be used to submit their desires, and go without their longings, even from the cradle" (Locke, 1690, reprinted 1824). Locke compared the child's mind to that of a blank slate (*tabula rasa*) upon which messages could be etched by society. Reward and punishment were the instruments used to impress knowledge and habits on the child.

In the third phase, parents began to feel responsibility for the child's soul. De Mause calls this the *intrusive mode*. During the 18th century, children, like adults, were held accountable for their deeds and misdeeds. One consequence of this was that punishment was as equally harsh on children as adults. By contrast, Rousseau (1762, reprinted 1911) saw the child as neither good nor bad until the experiences of reward and punishment, administered by the adults in society, could influence their development. Rousseau wrote, "God makes all things good; man meddles with them and they become evil" (1762). He was the first to postulate the concept of stages in childhood.

Finally, the fourth phase in the history of childhood is the *socialization mode*. In this phase De Mause sees parents as becoming responsible for the training of children. With this view comes the recognition of children's independence. This view of childhood coincided with the enactment of child labor laws and compulsory education in the beginning of the 19th century, and lasted through the middle of the 20th century. Out of this movement grew the belief that experiences in the early years shape later behaviors. The beginning of the scientific study of children was also an outgrowth of this period. The information acquired from empirical research in child development contributed to a rapidly changing view of the child in contemporary society. De Mause argues that we are leaving the *socialization mode* and now entering the *helping mode*. In the *helping mode* it is assumed that the "child knows better than the parent what it needs at each stage of life, and fully involves both parents in the child's life as they work to empathize with and fulfill the expanding particular needs" (De Mause, 1974, p. 52).

CONTEMPORARY PERSPECTIVES

While recent advances in knowledge about stages in children's development have spurred new understanding of the facts, processes and nature of childrens' progress towards adulthood, what is sometimes underestimated are the effects of societal expectations as a driving force for those changes. Peoples' beliefs about the nature of childhood, the experiences they provide, their notions of the optimal conditions for child development, and their attempts to fashion a society suitable for children, all provide important indicators about what adults value in a society for their progeny. As far as terminology is concerned, *society* is generally thought of as the aggregation of individuals who live together in an organized population, while *socialization* is the process by which a child's roles in the society is transmitted (LeVine, 1973).

THE INFLUENCE OF CULTURE

Since this book deals primarily with the child, this first chapter has placed focus upon the cultural milieu into which the child is thrust. Undoubtedly, the child is influenced by the culture in which he or she is raised. It may sound trite, but it is certainly true, that the things children learn are centrally dependent on their environment. Equally certainly, the social scientist is caused to study *particular* aspects of the child's existence by similar sets of societal and cultural expectations. Researchers invariably begin with an agenda for discovery. This agenda should not be thought of as a preselection of the results, but is more of a predisposition to find particular results if they are embedded in the arena where the study is to be performed. In that sense, then, the researcher sets the agenda, specifically, for *which results* may be discovered. It is in this way that research becomes shaped by the cultural expectations of researchers.

To understand the child-in-context requires both an understanding of the child, and of the context. It is important to recall that while an investigator of young children may *directly* influence or bias a child's actions, for example, by heavy-handed involvement in the child's play, an equally important *indirect* bias can occur through the nature of questions posed in the research. Therefore, the early childhood researcher can be equally as influential as the individual who offers intervention—and both are part of the child's context.

Culture means different things to different people. As with so many terms in the social sciences, *culture* has both a popular and scientific overlay. Kroeber and Kluckhohn (1952) for example, record over 160 varying definitions of the term in the literature. The first scientific uses were by nineteenth century anthropologists who defined culture as that "complex whole which includes knowledge, belief, art, morals, law, custom, and any other capabilities and habits acquired by man as a member of society" (Keesing, 1965, p. 1). These "capabilities" were not seen wholly as the individual's own work, but were the result of the rich heritage conveyed both by informal as well as formal education (Lowie, 1937).

Since culture is learned, then it is axiomatic that it must be taught (or at least be *teachable*). Such teaching does not, of course, have to be intentional or planned. Perhaps the greater part of the learning that characterizes the child's rapidly developing knowledge-base is that which is informal. Contemporary usage of *culture* implicates the "existing body of customary behavior, attitudes, values and products of a given people" (Henderson & Bergan, 1976, p. 6). Yet, as these writers remind, "culture does not simply *consist* of those things—it also *induces* these behaviors in new members of the culture" (original emphases, p. 6). It is this 'induction' of the young into the society, alongside the 'inducing' of behavior which are the themes of the book.

According to Zigler and Berman (1983) findings from research are only imperfectly related to practice. Even advances to knowledge discovered in meritorious early childhood intervention programs are not readily generalized to other programs. These writers characterize the work of childhood interventionists in terms of *experimentation* and *gradual* development. Emphases have shifted, sequentially since the 1960s, from the deficit model (which saw the lower socioeconomic classes as automatically deprived, depraved or disadvantaged), to a focus on intelligence and its heritability, to the concept of "critical period" (an optimal or sensitive temporal window for specific skill development), and the spirit of optimism signalled in the "Head Start" program. This nationwide intervention program encapsulizes the idea verbalized by President Lyndon Johnson "that a few weeks of effort could wipe out the past and future effects of impoverished life circumstances" (Zigler & Berman, 1983, p. 898).

Current societal trends, or at least trends in demographics, have disturbing implications for children. For example, the proportion of children living in poor, single parent family settings has risen sharply, even though the the total number of children has declined (Zigler & Muenchow, 1984). Politics may be *the* new element of the context in which children live, for the government of the day has sweeping powers to extend, enhance, or remove existing services for children. Over the past decade, federal spending on children and families has declined in real terms. Eligibility thresholds for the receipt of child-related benefits have risen to crowd out a larger percentage of needy children from aid. Thus, the perspective for those children who are most in need remains bleak. There are no legitimate reasons to anticipate that the demographic trends towards increasing numbers of working single parent mothers will be reversed, or even hold stable. The future is likely to become bleaker.

All contemporary theories of child development of merit acknowledge that children's development results from the influences of both biological and environmental factors. Even though there is some disagreement as to the degree of influence that each of these forces discharge, their impact is found largely through their interaction rather than in unitarity. This book is given to exploring the environmental context in which the child is located. The child is viewed sequentially both as an individual, and in terms of membership in the environments of the family and the immediate social setting. This is, then, an attempt at viewing the child from both *individual* and *holistic* perspectives.

REFERENCES

Aries, P. (1962). *Centuries of childhood.* New York: Vintage Books.
Bronfenbrenner, U. (1977). Toward an experimental ecology of human development. *American Psychologist, 32,* 513–531.

De Mause, L. (1974). The evolution of childhood. In L. De Mause (Ed.), *The history of childhood.* New York: The Psychohistory Press.

Hawley, A. (1950). *Human ecology.* New York: Ronald Press.

Henderson, R. W., & Bergan, J. R. (1976) *The cultural context of childhood.* Columbus, OH: Merrill.

Keesing, F. M. (1965) *Cultural anthropology: The science of custom.* New York: Appleton-Century.

Kroeber, A. L., & Kluckhohn, C. (1952) *Culture: A critical review of concepts and definitions.* New York: Vintage Books.

LeVine, R. A. (1973) *Culture, personality, and socialization.* Chicago: Aldine.

Locke, J. (1690, 1824) Some thoughts concerning education, 1690. In *The works of John Locke.* London: Charles Baldwin. Reprinted 1824.

Lowie, R. H. (1937) *The history of ethnological theory.* New York: Holt, Rinehart and Winston.

Moos, R. H. (1976). *The human as context.* New York: Wiley.

Rousseau, J. J. (1762, 1911). *Emile as on education.* [Barbara Foxley, Trans.] London: Dent. (Originally published, 1762).

Zigler, E., & Berman, W. Discerning the future of early childhood intervention. *American Psychologist, 38*(8), 894–906.

Zigler, E., & Muenchow, S. (1984) How to influence policy affecting children and families. *American Psychologist, 39*(4), 415–420.

CHAPTER 2

DEVELOPMENTAL CHANGES IN CHILDREN'S THINKING

DOMINIC F. GULLO

Cognitive development is a difficult process to define. Traditionally, cognition has referred to products of the human mind. Terms such as knowledge; consciousness; intelligence; thinking; imagining; creating; generating plans, strategies, and ideas; reasoning, problem solving, and inferring have been used to refer to cognition. Less cerebral in nature are such activities as organized motor movement and social cognition, including language. It is difficult to exclude any of these when defining cognition. If one were to list all the psychological processes that cognition reflected upon, one would have to ask "What psychological process *cannot* be described as cognitive in some nontrivial sense, or do *not* implicate cognition in some trivial degree? The answer is that mental processes habitually intrude themselves into virtually *all* human psychological processes and activities" (Flavell, 1977a, p. 2).

In this chapter cognitive development in young children will be discussed from two different but complementary points of view. The first perspective that will be discussed will be the information processing perspective. This theory of cognitive development was developed by psychologists who drew comparisons between how computers operate and how the mind functions (Broadbent, 1958). These psychologists argued that both humans and computers use logic and rules in processing information from their environment. Old rules may be refined and new rules added as the child obtains more information through interaction with the environment (Fodor, 1972). Information processing is comprised of the interactive processes of attention, perception, memory, thinking and problem solving.

13

The second perspective of cognitive development in young children discussed will be the adaptation model of Piaget. Piaget views cognitive development as biological adaptation to the environment (Flavell, 1977a). This is achieved through the two complementary processes of assimilation and accommodation. Assimilation refers to the process whereby children incorporate aspects of their environment into their existing knowledge. The end result of assimilation may be either a thought or physical action. Accommodation, on the other hand, refers to the process whereby the child changes existing knowledge to fit the demands of the environment. Both of these processes are achieved through interaction with physical objects in the environment as well as with other individuals.

The final section of this chapter will discuss factors affecting cognitive development in young children. These will include both personal and environmental factors.

INFORMATION PROCESSING

In the information-processing view, mental activity stems from the processing of information from the environment (Ellis & Hunt, 1983; Klahr & Wallace, 1975; Siegler, 1983). In this view the environment contains an event which, in turn, contains information that an individual can detect and understand. The child's success in detecting and understanding the information contained in the environmental event will depend on how efficiently and completely the information is processed. The information is processed in the following stages: attention, perception, memory, thinking, and problem solving (Yussen & Santrock, 1982). How efficiently or completely the information is processed, or if it is processed at all, will determine the nature of the response to the event. This may include no response at all. Each of the stages in information processing will now be discussed.

Attention

Attention may be defined as the process of noticing an event or "tuning in" to sensory information. Before children *can* respond to an environmental event, they must first recognize that the event exists. Jackson, Robinson, and Dale (1976) describe five factors which will determine the focus and duration of a young child's attention.

First, young children attend to information that they can discriminate. This factor relies on the premise that children cannot attend to that which they cannot see or hear. It is important, therefore, that the adult remain cognizant of the fact that often the child cannot, from their point of view, see and/or hear things in the same manner that the adult does. Thus, the child may respond in a manner that the adult does not expect, or not respond at all to what the adult *presumes* the child is paying attention.

Second, children seem to be more attentive at some times than at others. At the same time, some children are simply more attentive than others all the time. Factors which seem to affect attention are fatigue, overexcitedness, or distress. A child who is in one of these states may have difficulty attending.

Third, the physical qualities and background of an event may influence whether a child will attend to that event. Size, shape, complexity, and loudness are all event characteristics which affect attention. The more intense each of these characteristics is for any event, the greater the likelihood that it will be attended to.

Fourth, there is greater likelihood that an event will be attended to if it has meaning for the child. Children learn that not only do entire events have meaning but that within an event there are aspects which contain important information, while other aspects of the event may be ignored (Pick, 1965; Pick, Christy, & Frankel, 1972).

Fifth, attention will be determined by the way it fits into the child's existing knowledge of the world's events. Children tend to pay attention to events which are slightly unfamiliar or novel (Kagan, 1972; Piaget, 1963).

Changes in the ability to pay attention continue beyond the early years and into the sixth and seventh year of life (Yussen & Santrock, 1983). These changes in the ability to attend have an effect in the child's ability to extract information from their environment (Hagen & Hale, 1973; Pick, Frankel, & Hess, 1976).

Perception

Once children have noticed or attended to an environmental event, they must make some sense out of it. Perception may be defined as the cognitive process whereby one recognizes and interprets meaning from that which was picked up by the sensory receptors (Mussen, Conger, & Kagan, 1979; Yussen & Santrock, 1982).

According to Mussen et al. (1979), the major goal of the perception process is to understand environmental events, and to match what is perceived to some cognitive unit already present in the child. These environmental events include: (a) Physical objects that are static in nature (e.g., house, table); (b) events that are dynamic in nature and occur over time (e.g., a dog chasing a bone as opposed to a dog bringing a newspaper); (c) two-dimensional representations of three-dimensional events; (d) symbolic representations of events (e.g., words, numbers, language); and (e) body sensations (e.g., increased heartbeat and muscle tension).

There are many developmental changes in perception throughout childhood. As children mature, they acquire more knowledge about the world leading to more efficient use of perception. As they becomes more knowledgeable about information contained in environmental events, less information or less redundancy is required to perceive them. Gollin (1962) investigated how much information was required by individuals at different ages in order for them to identify objects from line drawings. He showed his subjects five sets of incomplete line drawings of objects. Each set had less information or was more incomplete in its depiction of the object than the other, although the objects depicted in each set were the identical object. Gollin found that the amount of information required to recognize the object was directly related to age. The younger the subject, the more information was required.

As children grow older, they also change in how physical characteristics of objects are perceived. Objects in the environment have many physical properties, e.g., size, shape, color. Which one of these properties of the object is the most salient feature for the child? It has been conjectured that different children have different propensities as to which feature will be the most salient to them (Odom, 1978). That is, there seem to be individual differences in preference of these features for individual children.

In the same view, it has also been shown that younger children have a more holistic perception of objects (Kemler, 1982; Kember & Smith, 1979). That is, younger children, when asked to classify objects, tend to group objects according to some overall idea of sameness rather than looking at underlying dimensions. The reverse is true for older children. For example, younger children might group objects that are the same color but differ on shape and size. An older child will group according to all dimensions. That is, any objects of the same size, shape, and color will go into the same group. Young children seem unable to make these finer perceptual discriminations, and are unable to discriminate on more than one feature at a time.

Finally, perception changes with experience. That is, the more experiences a child has, the more meaning the perception of that event will have for the child. Much evidence for this has been found in transcultural research. In our culture children have many experiences interpreting two-dimensional events. Children who either lack this type of experience (Hochberg & Brook, 1962) or who are from cultures where this type of experience was not available normally to them (Hudson, 1960, 1967; Mundy-Castle, 1966) had difficulty in recognizing the meaning of common objects or events represented in two dimensions.

Memory

Now that environmental events have been detected and interpreted, in this section the manner in which the event is stored and recalled will be discussed.

Memory is defined as the retention of information over time (Yussen & Santrock, 1982). Memory can be described as two types. In one type of memory, information is processed and stored only temporarily for immediate use. This is called short-term memory (STM). This type of memory is useful in aiding one to perform everyday activities. We need STM to help retain ideas as we go about our daily activities. STM may last from a few seconds to a minute. Studies have shown that STM across a wide spectrum of ages in childhood remains similar (Cole, Frankel, & Sharpe, 1971; Kail, 1979).

A second type of memory, called long-term memory (LTM), is a process whereby information may be stored and retrieved for up to a lifetime. It is in LTM that one stores information and experiences about the world that will be drawn upon for daily use, or from time to time, over a long period of time. Yussen and Santrock (1982) indicated that the greatest developmental differences occur in LTM or in shifting information from STM to LTM. They delineate four processes believed responsible for shifting information: (a) rehearsal, (b) elaboration, (c) organization, and (d) categorizing. Each of these processes will be discussed.

In *rehearsal* a child may repeatedly respond to a stimulus. This repetition, a form of rehearsal, has been shown to increase the likelihood that something will be remembered. It has been shown that older children will rehearse in this way silently and spontaneously; however, younger children need to be encouraged to do this (Flavell, Beach, & Chinsky, 1966; Ornstein, 1978).

Another way of trying to remember information just perceived is to *elaborate* on it. This may be done by trying to associate the new information with an already familiar experience. This technique has been shown to be used more by older children than younger ones. Yussen and Santrock (1982) maintain that elaboration is a more advanced skill than rehearsal; however, they suggest that there is a great deal of overlap between the two processes.

Organization is the process whereby information is remembered by "chunking" it into smaller units or "bits" (Miller, 1956). For example, a telephone number or social security number is remembered by grouping sets of digits rather than trying to remember individual numbers in a particular sequence.

Finally, it has been shown that information is more easily remembered if it is divided into meaningful *categories* (Kail, 1979; Mandler, 1967). If, however, there are too many categories or if the categories are too abstract, this process will not be as helpful for remembering.

Although research indicates developmental differences in memory patterns among children, strengths and weaknesses in these patterns may also be due to the type of response used to measure memory (Jackson et al., 1976). Recognition, recall, and reconstruction are three different ways to measure memory; each will yield different findings. Jackson et al. (1976) delineate four points that may determine whether a young child is likely to remember information:

1. Children are more likely to remember information if it is familiar, meaningful, and contains an internal organization of its own.
2. Children are more likely to remember information when they have been actively involved with the material that is to be remembered.
3. Children are more likely to remember information if they have had repeated exposure to the material to be remembered.
4. Children are more likely to remember information if the information is of interest to them and draws their attention.

Thinking

The next step in information processing is thinking. Mussen et al. (1979) describe this process as the means whereby a child reflects on the information being processed in order to assess and evaluate it before responding. Some children act quickly and accept the first hypothesis they produce. These children we call impulsive. Others take a longer time to consider the merits of any hypothesis they generate, oftentimes rejecting an hypothesis they consider to be of poor quality. These children we call reflective. This difference among children is already evident by the age of six. Additionally, this trait appears to be consistent within an individual across problem types and is stable over time (Kagan, 1965). Differences between impulsive and reflective children appears to stem from differences in concern for minimizing error. In order to avoid error, some children take longer to consider alternative hypotheses; others are far less concerned and respond quickly without evaluating the accuracy of their hypothesis.

Problem Solving

According to Yussen and Santrock,

> Problem solving is processing information to fulfill a major goal. Attention, perception, remembering, and drawing inferences (thinking) may all occur rather quickly as the child examines the information . . . problem solving usually occurs over an extended period of time . . . it directs us to the particular information we will process and governs the manner in which the information is processed. (1982, p. 236)

There are, according to Yussen and Santrock (1982), four components to problem solving which account for how children solve problems and how this ability changes over time. These four components are: (a) Problem identification, (b) planning the approach, (c) monitoring the progress, and (d) checking solutions. Children become better problem solvers as they become more knowledgeable about the world around them, build a repertoire of strategies with which to solve tasks, and become more knowledgeable about their own cognitive activity.

In summary, information processing is the means through which one becomes tuned in to, interprets, and acts on the information in their environment. The final response to the initial stimulus (information) changes over time as the child develops and their ability to attend to, interpret, remember, and reflect on environmental events and changes. In the next section Piaget's adaptation model of cognitive development will be discussed.

PIAGET'S THEORY OF COGNITIVE DEVELOPMENT

Piaget views human cognition as biological adaptation of an organism to a complex environment. In this section Piaget's views on how this is accomplished will be discussed. First, the factors necessary for development will be discussed, followed by an explanation of some Piagetian terminology used to explain the basic structure of his theory. Following this will be a brief description of what occurs in each of Piaget's stages of cognitive development. Incorporated into the discussion of the various aspects of Piaget's theory of cognitive development will be factors which distinguish the child's thinking from that of the adult's. These include assimilation, accommodation, object permanence, egocentricity, and operations. Appendix A presents a glossary of Piagetian terms.

Developmental Factors in Cognitive Growth

Piaget and his associates view cognitive development as the interrelation and interplay among the following four factors: maturation, physical experience, social experience, and equilibration (Inhelder, Sinclair, & Bovet, 1974). Each of these factors will be discussed below.

Maturation

Piaget explains that children universally progress through stages of cognitive development in exactly the same order. However, it is well established that the rate at which children will progress through the stages may differ. One factor which influences the rate of development is the genetic potential of each individual (Phillips, 1975). Thus, according to Piaget, maturation refers to the influence of genetic inheritance on development.

Physical Experience

Experience of the environment interacts with one's genetic potential in two ways (Piaget & Inhelder, 1969). In physical experience proper, a child interacts with the physical properties of his or her world to discover various properties of it. For instance, a child learns that objects are hard or soft, liquid or solid, breakable or unbreakable, heavy or light, and so on, by manipulating them. By interacting in this manner, the child has to start to make internalized comparisons of these physical events in their environment.

Another type of physical experience is what Piaget calls logico-mathematical experience. In this type of physical experience the child gains knowledge not from the physical experience itself, but rather from reflecting on it. The child learns indirectly that relations that are apparent in one physical experience can also be applied to other experiences. An important aspect of this type of knowledge is that it contains logical rules that can be applied to any objects (Gallagher & Reid, 1981).

Social Experience

Social experience, the third developmental factor in cognitive development, is the knowledge one gains by interaction with people. This includes social relationships, education, language, and culture (Gallagher & Reid, 1981). As with maturation, the specific social milieu of particular children may affect the rate at which they progresses through the stages of cognitive development. Social experience also makes it possible for the child's thinking to become more flexible and understand events from others' points of view.

Equilibration

As has been stated previously, neither maturation nor experience alone (physical or social) can explain the sequential nature of development or the different rates at which development progresses across individuals. It is equilibration which coordinates all other factors (Piaget & Inhelder, 1969). Equilibration is a self-regulatory process whereby children constantly adapt to the environment until they reach a state of equilibrium. When children enter into a situation where they are confronted with an incongruent cognitive experience, they will adapt to it by assimilating or accommodating, thus restoring balance or equilibrium. (Assimilation and accommodation as mechanisms of adaptation will be discussed fully in the next section.) This process protects children from being overloaded with more stimuli than they can adapt to through assimilation or accommodation. Equilibrium is a self-regulating mechanism whereby the child can determine the rate at which new cognitive knowledge will be acquired (Osborn & Osborn, 1983).

In the next secion, some of the basic structures in Piaget's theory of cognitive development will be discussed.

The Structure of Piaget's Theory

Figure 1 illustrates the model of Piaget's theory that will be discussed in this section. Scheme, structure, function, organization, and adaptation will be defined and discussed in terms of how they are interrelated in the overall theory.

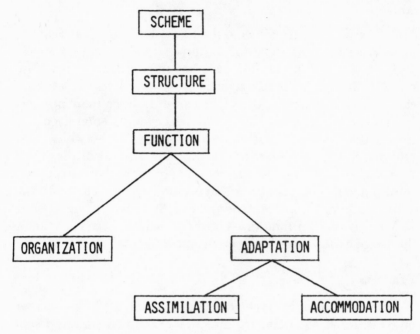

Figure 2-1. Structure of Piagetian Theory.

Scheme

According to Piaget, schemes are the basic units of cognitive structure (Brainerd, 1978). They represent a group of cognitive structures that are organized according to common features of environmental events. The child gains these through maturation and/or experience. An important characteristic of schemes is that they are *organized* patterns of behavior (Osborn & Osborn, 1983). A scheme can be likened to a blueprint. That is, it represents a plan for action. The action can either be cognitive in nature (e.g., mental category for dog or other animals) or physical (e.g., action plan to reach and grasp). As the child gains experiences in the world and matures, lines may be added to the blueprint, thus changing ideas and actions. The following aspects of Piaget's theory will explain more fully how this is accomplished.

Structure

Cognitive structure refers to the form or pattern that behavior takes in each of the stages of cognitive development (Brainerd, 1978). Each stage of development has in it an inherent unique manner of behavior. These structures are completely abstract and cannot be directly measured. One can only infer their presence from what the specific behaviors in each developmental stage have in common. In essence, structures are those entities which separate qualitative characteristics of thinking at each of the stages. The child's schemes are interpreted through their structures, resulting in an overt behavior that is uniquely characteristic of the child's stage of cognitive development. Structural changes occur as a result of equilibration—children change their behavior as they have experiences in the environment.

Functions

According to Brainerd (1978), cognitive functions are directions or goals which determine the direction of cognitive development. Piaget maintains that cognitive functions remain constant during the course of development. Cognitive functioning can be thought of as principles of intellectual development that are present regardless of age. They are simply principles that maintain that behavior will occur. There are two cognitive functions, according to Piaget, that are present in all individuals. These are organization and adaptation. Each will now be given consideration.

Organization. Organization may be defined as an integration of schemes. This accounts for the fact that there is some degree of sameness in cognitive behavior over time (Brainerd, 1978). Organization refers to the tendency for individuals to systematically organize their structures into a coherent system. For example, at birth and for a time after, the infant can either look at or grasp an object. With maturation and experience the infant learns that s/he can integrate these structures into a meaningful (reach-grasp) organization.

Adaptation is the complement of organization. It is through the process of adaptation that an individual adapts to the environment. It is, presumably, by this process that discontinuities in development occur across individuals. Adaptation is itself divided into two aspects, assimilation and accommodation.

In *assimilation* the individual takes the incoming information and tries to fit it into one of his or her existing scheme. This can occur in either a physical or psychological behavior. For example, when young children begin to learn how to catch a ball, their behaviors are limited. That is, they have only one scheme that is used for this reason. When given the opportunity to catch a ball, the child is likely to use the same "catching" behavior regardless of the size of the ball or the direction from which it is coming. Thus, the child has assimilated all various sizes of balls into a single scheme for "catching."

Psychologically speaking, when the child learns the concept "ball," therefore obtaining a scheme for it, the scheme is very limited in its scope. The child's scheme for ball may contain only one salient attribute for ball, for example, round. Thus, whenever the children see a round object, they will assimilate it into their scheme for ball. Thus, an orange, grapefruit, or spherical Christmas tree ornament may all be represented by the same scheme. Therefore, the child may treat the orange, grapefruit, or ornament like a ball and try to throw, bounce, or roll them.

Along with physical and social experience, maturation allows the child to adjust schemes to fit the demands of the environment. This process is called *accommodation*— it is how schemes become organized and change over time.

Consider, for a moment, the "catching ball" example. As children have more experience with various-sized balls, they begin to recognize that the reaching and catching posture of the hands and arms must adjust to the size and direction of the oncoming ball. Likewise, physical maturation must progress sufficiently to allow this to happen.

In the same manner, children's psychological schemes for ball will change and new schemes will be added when they are given feedback from others. If the child calls an orange a ball, an adult may provide feedback in the form of correction. Thus, children may add some discriminating feature to the scheme for ball that will distinguish it from orange. They may also discover this on their own when they find out that the orange does not bounce.

These two processes, assimilation and accommodation, continually function until equilibration is achieved.

Stages of Cognitive Development

In this section a brief description of each of the stages of cognitive development will be discussed. It should be noted that for each stage only the major characteristics will be discussed. The reader is referred to Flavell (1963); Ginsburg and Opper (1978); Phillips (1975); and, Piaget and Inhelder (1969) for excellent detailed overviews of Piaget's stages of cognitive development. During the discussion of each of the stages, particular concepts will be elaborated upon. These concepts are *object permanence, egocentricity, operations,* and *conservation.* It is precisely these characteristics which create differences between child and adult thinking.

Piaget postulates that there are stages of cognitive development. The order of these stages is invariant across all individuals. It is only the rate of development that may be accelerated or decelerated dependent upon physical and social experiences that the individual has. Piaget's major stages, and the approximate age for these stages, are: *sensorimotor* (0-2 years), *preoperational* (2-7 years), *concrete operations* (7-11 years), and *formal operations* (12 and older).

Sensorimotor Period

The sensorimotor period is the time when the infant learns to integrate perceptual with motor skills. It is a time of exploration and discovery—exploration of the environment and self and discovery that objects and events in the world are permanent and separate from one's self. The sensorimotor period is divided into six substages.

1. *Reflexive stage (0-1 month).* During the reflexive stage, the infant assimilates the world into its reflex schemes. Grasping, sucking, vocalization, and orienting both visually and auditorially are among the reflex behaviors that in later stages the infant will accommodate to environmental events. That is, adaptation through modification of these behaviors will bring the infant to equilibration as they become more knowledgeable about events in their environment.

2. *Primary circular reaction (1-4 months)*. A circular reaction can be defined as first "stumbling upon some experience as a consequence of some act, and second, . . . trying to recapture the experience by reenacting the original movements again and again in a kind of rhythmic cycle" (Flavell, 1963, p. 93).

A circular reaction is inherently reinforcing, thus circular. The purpose of circular reactions is to provide the means of adapting behavior. The primary circular reaction is one in which self-investigation becomes the ultimate end. They are acts which center in on the infant's own body and are comprised mainly of the former reflexes exercised in the first stage. Examples of primary circular reactions are such as grasping hands, sucking fingers, and watching feet.

3. *Secondary circular reactions (4-8 months)*. Actions now move away from the infant's body to the outside environment. Now the infant begins to explore the world, using the same primary circular reactions but now on objects in the environment. Infants begins to make simple associations between their actions and the effect they have on objects in the environment. Object permanence begins to take form by the end of this period.

Object permanence refers to the ability to understand that objects exist separate from one's own actions upon them. Putting it succinctly, it is self-world differentiation. Prior to object permanence, infants behave according to the addage, "out of sight—out of mind." Object permanence develops as the child's brain matures and through repeated sensory and motor actions in the environment. Piaget believes that object permanence is necessary before thinking and problem solving can take place, for without it there would be no mental images of objects and events. The classic manner in which Piaget tested for object permanence involved showing a child an object, hiding the object under a cloth, then watching to see if the child would search for the hidden object. Piaget found that although object permanence begins at the end of the third substage of the sensorimotor period, its development is not complete until the end of the sixth substage.

4. *Coordination of secondary schemes (9-12 months)*. As noted earlier, new behaviors are formed from existing ones. It is during this fourth substage that infants begin to combine and coordinate

secondary circular behaviors as they gain repeated experiences in their environment. The result is new patterns of behavior. The infant learns new ways to interact with the environment and to solve problems. For example, the infants may learn to reach for an object they see and grasp it. In the same manner, the infant may learn, with that object, to reach for or hit another object that is just out of reach.

5. *Tertiary circular reactions (12–18 months)*. The key word describing the nature of this substage is "novelty." The infant learns to create new and novel events by executing old behaviors in new ways. It is the first attempt on the part of the infant to learn the cause-effect nature of behaviors. It is during this substage that the infant achieves great delight out of throwing, dropping, or banging objects to see what happens. Exploration and curiosity are at the heart of an infant's motivation, aided by the fact that they now can walk.

6. *Invention of new means (18–24 months)*. Piaget sometimes refers to this substage as the beginning of true thought. There is now evidence that action patterns are internalized and elementary problem solving begins. The child begins to show elementary signs of logic and insight. The infant can now quickly come to a decision without a lot of trial-and-error practice that was necessary in earlier substages. Deferred imitation and pretend play become evident during this substage and the child's language is developing rapidly. By the end of the sixth substage, object permanence is fully developed. This means that the child now understands that an object exists even after it has been hidden from sight or moved by hidden displacement.

Preoperational Period.

The preoperational period is characterized by the child's lack of mental operations in performing certain cognitive tasks. In this manner, the preoperational period is somewhat negative in that it generally describes children in terms of what they *cannot* do rather than what they *can* do. Four factors characterize preoperational thought: egocentricity, centration, irreversibility, and static thought.

Egocentricity. Piaget and Inhelder (1956) describe the child's thinking in the preoperational stage as egocentric. Egocentricity "denotes a cognitive state in which the cognizer sees the world from a single point of view—his own" (Flavell, 1963).

Flavell (1977b) posited that there are two levels of visual perspective taking (egocentricity): Level 1—the child knows *what* another sees but not necessarily *how* he sees it; Level 2—requires knowledge of both the *what* and *how* components. Piaget and Inhelder (1956) used the "Three Mountain Task" to support their view of egocentric thought. In this task children were asked to visualize how a doll would view a three-dimensional model of a mountain scene from different vantage points. The child was asked to select from an array a photograph which depicted the doll's view. Results of their study showed that children younger than seven tended to depict their own points of view when choosing the photograph. Piaget and Inhelder's "Three Mountain Task" represents Level 2 perspective taking.

A number of other studies examined preoperational children's ability to coordinate visual perspectives in less complex tasks. In one group of studies children were asked to rotate a visual display to be commensurate with another person's perspective of a duplicate display (Borke, 1972; Fishbein, Lewis, & Keiffer, 1972). In other studies children were asked to hide toy figures to obscure their view from someone having a different visual vantage point than their own (Flavell, Shipstead, & Croft, 1978; Hobson, 1980; Hughes, 1975) or to identify objects that someone could see from a different visual perspective (Gullo & Bersani, 1983). In each of these studies the child had only to identify *what* another person saw, thus making it a Level 1 perspective-taking task. In each of these studies it was shown that children as young as three could make nonegocentric choices. Greater success on these later tasks appeared to be due to the reduced number of visual cues needed to be interpreted by the child in order to make the correct choice.

These studies seem to indicate that what we interpret children's cognitive abilities to be will depend to a great extent on how we go about testing for them. This has been one of the most common criticisms of Piaget's work—that he was too limited in his method of testing his hypotheses. The reader is referred to Donaldson (1978) for a more indepth discussion of this and other criticisms of Piaget's work.

Centration. Centration is a characteristic of preoperational thought whereby the child focuses in on or attends to one salient attribute of an object or an activity at a time. At the same time, the child will neglect or have difficulty becoming aware of other attributes of these objects or activities. For example, a child may focus or "center" on the four-legged attribute of a dog when forming a scheme for dog. The result will be that the child will call any fourlegged animal a dog. Different children appear to be attracted to different attributes and these will be the ones they will tend to center in on.

Reversibility. The third characteristic of the preoperational child's thinking is that it is irreversible. This is the inability to understand that certain operations can be reversed, and that the end result will be the same as where you began. The inability to mentally reverse a process affects children's sequential or serial thinking. Likewise it affects their ability to conserve quantities. Conservation will be discussed more fully in the section, *Concrete Operational Period.*

Static Thought. Finally, children's preoperational thinking is said to be static. That is, they tend to center in on the present state of an object and are mentally unable to visualize the process whereby the object was transformed to that state. Dynamic thought characterizes the ability to carry out this mental operation. In one manner of speaking, reversibility and dynamic thought are complementary operations. The former represents a backward mental operation while the latter represents one that is forward moving.

Centration, irreversibility and static thought all contribute to the egocentric nature of the child at this stage. In the following stage the child will become operational, and thinking becomes more like that of the adult. Concrete and formal operations stages will now be discussed as a means to see where the child is headed; but because this age level is not the focus of this book, they will not be dealt with in as much detail as prior stages.

Concrete Operational Period

In the stage of concrete operations children are now able to mentally use operations to mediate between themselves and their environment. "Operations can be defined as an internalized set of actions which permit the youngster to do mentally what he has previously done physically. Operations conform to the rules of logical thought and, as the child grows older, these cognitive operations become more advanced and more sophisticated" (Osborn & Osborn, 1983, p. 32).

According to Brainerd (1978), the best single indicator that a children have passed from preoperations to concrete operations is their ability to conserve. Inhelder and Sinclair, two of Piaget's associates, contend that conservation may be viewed as "the main symptoms of a budding system of operational structures" (1969, p. 3.).

Conservation. Conservation is defined as the child's ability to understand that two quantities which start as equal, remain equal, even if one of the quantities undergoes an irrelevant perceptual deformation (Brainerd, 1978). An irrelevant perceptual deformation is any physical transformation of a quantity which does not involve addition or subtraction.

A standard test of conservation would include showing the child two quantities that are equal in amount and perceptually identical. For example, the child might be shown two identical glasses containing equal amounts of a colored liquid. At this point equivalence is established by asking the child if one glass has more liquid than the other or if they are both the same. Once equivalence has been established, one of the quantities is transformed perceptually but nothing will be added to or subtracted from the original quantity. In the example used here, one glass of colored liquid would be poured into another container that is taller but narrower than the original. In this manner the water level will appear higher than in the remaining original container. Equivalence is once again established between the amounts of liquid contained in the remaining original glass and the new taller but narrower glass.

The preoperational child will probably maintain that the taller glass has more liquid in it than the original glass. This child is unable to conserve. The concrete operational child will say that both glasses contain equal amounts of liquid. This is an example of the ability to conserve because the child can perform the mental operations of *reversibility* ("just pour it back to the other glass and it will be the same again") and *dynamic thought* (the child no longer *centers* in on the present state of the quantity but can mentally perform the process to see that nothing has been added to or subtracted from the original amount).

Although conservation is the most highly acknowledged concept that is acquired during concrete operations, the acquisition of mental operations also affect children's thinking regarding other abilities. These include relational concepts, classification concepts, and number concepts.

Formal Operational Period

The period of formal operations signals the child's passage to more "adult-like" thinking. Children's thinking now becomes freed from the concrete world and takes on characteristics that are more abstract in nature. Their cognitive skills involve an increased ability to use logic and to come to conclusions using deductive reasoning. They are no longer egocentric and can, therefore, approach problems from many points of view. The world is no longer dichotomously viewed as black or white, good or bad, right or wrong. The child is now able to see that something can be good or bad depending on the circumstances. The child's thinking now reflects more of the attitudes, values, and beliefs that will later lead them to an adult approach to life.

FACTORS CONTRIBUTING TO DIFFERENCES IN COGNITIVE DEVELOPMENT

The chapter has discussed two complementary views on how cognition develops and changes over time in children. In this final section, factors which influence cognitive development in general will be discussed briefly. In many instances, other chapters in this book will address these factors more completely. The reader is referred to these chapters for a more indepth discussion.

Personal Factors

The obvious factor to be considered here is simply genetic inheritance. It has been stated previously in this chapter that children who are born with more native intelligence will develop cognitively at a rate faster than those with less intelligence, all other factors equal.

Another, less obvious personal factor is gender. Although it has never been shown that one sex has a greater capacity for cognitive growth, it has been shown that there are differences between the sexes which lead to greater measured capacity of particular cognitive tasks (see Chapter 4 for a complete discussion of this topic). As is suggested, any differences in cognitive development between the sexes is most likely due to socialization rather than genetic differences.

Finally, it has been shown that birth order may affect cognitive development (Dinkmeyer & Dreikurs, 1963). According to this theory, birth order and sibling relations shape the child's life, and affects the way the child adapts to the environment. This may also be influenced by differential parental attention.

Cultural Differences

It is hypothesized that cultural differences affecting cognitive development mainly stem from differences in childrearing practices between socioeconomic low- and middle-class parents (Hess & Shipman, 1968). Chilman (1966) reports that the following are some of the characteristics of lower-class parents which may lead to lower measured cognitive ability in their children when compared to middle-class children:

- They provide limited freedom for exploration during infancy and early childhood years;
- They provide fewer long-range goals for their children;
- There is a greater tendency for educational and occupational failure;
- They provide limited verbal interaction experiences for their children; and
- They have authoritarian attitudes in childrearing.

Just as there is no simple explanation for elucidating what is cognitive development or how it progresses, so, too, the factors affecting its development intermesh. As such, there is no way to isolate any particular variable as having a causal effect or enhancing or diminishing one's chances for development. As we become more knowledgeable about the process of cognition, we will better understand those variables affecting it. In this manner we will be able to know which ones we have control over and can change for the benefit of the child, and which ones over which we have no control. For more insights into these notions the reader is referred to the final section of this book which discusses evaluating and facilitating the child's development.

REFERENCES

Borke, H. (1972). Piaget's mountain task revisited: Changes in the egocentric landscape. *Developmental Psychology, 1,* 240–243.

Brainerd, C. (1978). *Piaget's theory of intelligence.* Englewood Cliffs, NJ: Prentice Hall.

Broadbent, D. E. (1958). *Perception and communication.* Elmsford, NY: Pergamon Press.

Chilman, C. (1966). *Growing up poor.* Washington, DC: Welfare Administration Publication, No. 13.

Cole, M., Frankel, F., & Sharpe, D. (1971). Development of free recall learning in children. *Developmental Psychology, 4,* 109–123.

Dinkmeyer, R., & Driekurs, R. (1963). *Encouraging children to learn.* Englewood Cliffs, NJ: Prentice Hall.

Donaldson, M. (1978). *Children's minds.* Glasgow, Scotland: Fontana.

Ellis, H. C., & Hunt, R. R. (1983). *Fundamentals of human memory and cognition.* Dubuque, IA: W. C. Brown.

Fishbein, H. D., Lewis, S., & Keiffer, K. (1972). Children's understanding of spatial relations: Coordination of perspectives. *Developmental psychology, 1,* 21–33.

Flavell, J. (1963). *The developmental psychology of Jean Piaget.* New York: D. Van Nostrand.

Flavell, J. (1977a). *Cognitive development.* Englewood Cliffs, NJ: Prentice Hall.

Flavell. J. (1977b). The development of knowledge about visual perspectives. *Nebraska Symposium on Motivation,* Lincoln, NE: University of Nebraska Press, 25, 43–76.

Flavell, J., Beach, D., & Chinsky, J. (1966). Spontaneous verbal rehearsal in a memory task as a function of age. *Child Development, 37,* 283–299.

Flavell, J., Shipstead, S., & Croft, K. (1978). Young children's knowledge about visual perspectives: Hiding objects from others. *Child Development, 49,* 1208–1211.

Fodor, J. (1972). Some reflections on L. S. Vygotsky's *Thought and language. Cognition, 1,* 37–45.

Gallagher, J., & Reid, D. (1981). *The learning theory of Piaget and Inhelder.* Monterey, CA: Brooks/Cole.

Ginsburg, H., & Opper, S. (1978). *Piaget's theory of intellectual development: An introduction.* Englewood Cliffs, NJ: Prentice Hall.

Gollin, E. S. (1962). Factors affecting the visual recognition of incomplete objects: A comparative investigation of children and adults. *Perceptual and Motor Skills, 15,* 583–590.

Gullo, D. F., & Bersani, C. (1983). Effects of three experimental conditions of preschool children's ability to coordinate visual perspectives. *Perceptual and Motor Skills, 56,* 675–678.

Hagen, J. W., & Hale, G. A. (1973). The development of attention in children. In A. D. Pick (Ed.), *Minnesota Symposia on Child Psychology* (Vol. II). Minneapolis: University of Minnesota Press.

Hess, R., & Shipman, V. (1968). Maternal influences on early learning: The cognitive environments of urban preschool children. In R. Hess & R. Bear (Eds.), *Early learning.* Chicago: Aldine.

Hobson, R. P. (1980). The question of egocentrism: The young child's competence in the coordination of perspectives. *Journal of Child Psychology and Psychiatry, 21,* 325–331.

Hochberg, J., & Brook, V. (1962). Pictorial recognition as an unlearned ability: A study of one child's performance. *American Journal of Psychology, 2,* 154–160.

Hudson, W. (1960). Pictorial depth perception in subcultural groups in Africa. *Journal of Social Psychology, 52,* 183–208.

Hudson, W. (1967). The study of pictorial perception among unacculturated groups. *International Journal of Psychology, 2,* 90–107.

Hughes, M. (1975). Egocentrism in preschool children. Unpublished doctoral dissertation, Edinburgh University. [Cited in M. Donaldson (1978). *Children's Minds.* Glasgow: Fontana, 13–16.]

Inhelder, B., & Sinclair, H. (1969). Learning cognitive structures. In P. H. Mussen, J. Langer, & M. Covington (Eds.), *Trends and issues in developmental psychology.* New York: Holt, Rinehart & Winston.

Inhelder, B., Sinclair, H., & Bovet, M. (1974). *Learning and the development of cognition.* Cambridge, MA: Harvard University Press.

Jackson, N. E., Robinson, H. B., & Dale, P. S. (1976). *Cognitive development in young children.* Washington, DC: National Institute of Education.

Kagan, J. (1965). Individual differences in the resolution of response uncertainty. *Journal of Personality and Social Psychology, 2,* 154–160.

Kagan, J. (1972). Do infants think? *Scientific American,* 226–774.

Kail, L. J. (1979). *Memory development in children.* San Francisco: Freeman.

Kemler, D. G. (1982). Classification in young and retarded children: The primacy of overall similarity relations. *Child Development, 53,* 768–779.

Kember, D. G., & Smith, L. B. (1979). Is there a developmental trend from integrality to separability in perception? *Journal of Experimental Child Psychology, 26,* 498–507.

Klahr, D., & Wallace, J. G. (1975). *Cognitive development: An information processing view.* Hillsdale, NJ: Erlbaum.

Mandler, G. (1967). Organization and memory. In K. W. Spence & J. T. Spence (Eds.), *The psychology of learning and motivation* (Vol. 1). New York: Academic Press.

Miller, G. A. (1956). The magical number seven, plus or minus two: Some limits on our capacity for processing information. *Psychological Review, 63,* 81–97.

Mundy-Castle, A. C. (1966). Pictorial depth perception in Ghanain children. *International Journal of Psychology, 1,* 290–300.

Mussen, P. H., Conger, J. J., & Kagan, J. (1979). *Child development and personality.* New York: Harper and Row.

Ornstein, P. (1978). *Memory development in children.* Hillsdale, NJ: Erlbaum.

Osborn, K., & Osborn, J. (1983). *Cognition in early childhood.* Athens, GA: Education Associates.

Phillips, J. L. (1975). *The origins of intellect: Piaget's theory.* San Francisco: Freeman.

Piaget, J. (1963). *The origins of intelligence in children.* New York: Norton Library.

Piaget, J., & Inhelder, B. (1956). *The child's conception of space.* London: Routledge & Kegan Paul.

Piaget, J., & Inhelder, B. (1969). *The psychology of the child* (H. Weaver, trans.). New York: Basic Books.

Pick, A. D. (1965). Improvement of visual and tactual form discrimination. *Journal of Experimental Psychology, 69,* 331–339.

Pick, A. D., Christy, M. D., & Frankel, G. W. (1972). A developmental study of visual selective attention. *Journal of Experimental Child Psychology, 14,* 166–175.

Pick, A. D., Frankel, D. G., & Hess, V. L. (1976). Children's attention: The development of selectivity. In E. M. Hetherington (Ed.), *Review of child development* (Vol. 5). Chicago: University of Chicago Press.

Siegler, R. S. (1983). Information processing approaches to development. In P. H. Mussen (Ed.), *Handbook of child psychology: History, theories, and methods,* Vol.1. New York: Wiley.

Yussen, S. R., & Santrock, J. W. (1982). *Child development: An introduction.* Dubuque, IA: W. C. Brown Co.

APPENDIX A
PIAGETIAN CONCEPTS

Definitions of Piagetian Terms

Scheme — An organized pattern of behavior. It involves action on the part of the child. Refers to the structure underlying the child's overt actions.

Cognitive Structure — Organized properties of intelligence which are inferred from behavior. Examples: schemes, mental operations.

Assimilation — The taking in of sensory information or experiences. The child relates what he perceives to his existing knowledge and understanding.

Accommodation — Changes in behavior which result from variations in the environment that demand modification of the existing scheme.

Symbolic Function — Capacity of the child to form mental symbols which stand for or represent absent things or events. Based on actions, imitations, and later thoughts.

Horizontal Decalage — The child is at different stages of development with regard to problems involving similar mental operations. Example: different ages at which conservation of number, continuous quantity, volume occurs.

Vertical Decalage — Refers to hierarchically arranged gaps or lags between action and thought. Example: what child learns action-wise at age seven is restructured into thought at age 11.

Terms Related to the Preoperational Period

Egocentrism — Child cannot take the role of or see the viewpoint of another. He believes that everyone thinks the same way and the same things that he does. Always present during the attainment and use of any new cognitive structure. Inhibits accommodation.

Centration — The child fixes his attention on a limited perceptual aspect of the stimulus and is unable to explore all aspects of the stimulus. Its opposite is decentration.

Transformation—Refers to the ability of the child to focus exclusively on the elements in a sequence of changes or successive states rather than on the process by which one state is changed to another. Focus moves from event to event but doesn't integrate the events into a whole.

Coordination—The ability to use all dimensions simultaneously and relate the changes in these dimensions to the transformations performed.

Reversibility—The ability of the child which enables him to follow a line of reasoning back to where it started. Example: the child knows the starting and stopping points of a falling pencil. He is able to draw the points in between.

Reciprocity—A type of reversibility in which the child cancels the differences between the dimensions of the stimuli by balancing one difference against the other.

Conservation—The conceptualization that the amount or quantity of matter stays the same regardless of any changes in shape or position.

Conservation Tasks

Kinds of

Number—Child's ability to recognize that the number property of a set remains invariant despite irrelevant changes. Usually attained between 5 and 6 years.

Continuous Quantity—Child recognizes that pouring liquid from one container to another does not increase or decrease the amount of liquid. 6 to 7 years.

Substance—Child's ability to recognize that changing the shape doesn't alter the amount of matter involved. 7 to 8 years.

Weight—Child's ability to recognize that weight remains the same despite changes in shape. 9 to 10 years.

Volume—Child's ability to recognize that the amount of water displaced remains the same despite changes in the shape of the displacing substance. 11 to 12 years.

Area—Child's ability to recognize that the amount of area remains the same despite the addition of buildings, figures, etc. to that area. 7 to 8 years.

Phases

1. The child does not recognize that the numbers, quantity, etc. remain the same despite the transformations which take place.
2. The child recognizes that the amounts are equal but fails to conserve. Judgment is based on perceptual properties.
3. The child conserves. He may give the following reasons.
   a. If liquid is returned to the original container, you would have the same amount.
   b. Haven't added anything or taken anything away. Known as the identity explanation.
   c. What you lost in height was gained in width; therefore, the amounts are equal. Known as compensation or reciprocity explanation.

Ages of attainment of each conservation task vary within and among cultures. Development is continuous and gradual. The same child is not always at the same stage of development for each task. There are different levels of achievement in regard to problems calling for similar mental operations.

CHAPTER 3

CHILD LANGUAGE BEHAVIOR: THE ACQUISITION OF SOCIAL COMMUNICATIVE COMPETENCE

M. JEANNE WILCOX AND BRENDA Y. TERRELL

S ocial communicative competence can generally be described as the ability to convey effectively and efficiently an intended message to a receiver. As such, this ability requires not only knowledge of the conventional communicative code (i.e., linguistic competence), but also knowledge pertaining to socially appropriate communicative behavior. In recent years, various language specialists have attempted to describe behavior and knowledge comprising social communicative competence (e.g., Bates, 1976; Hymes, 1971; Prutting, 1982; Prutting & Kirchner, 1983; Wilcox & Davis, in press; Wilcox and Webster, 1980). As the results of various investigations have emerged it has become clear that the acquisition of linguistic structures can best be understood in the context of the interpersonal communicative setting.

Several questions arise in the attempt to describe children's acquisition of social communicative competence. First it is necessary to gain an understanding of the *whats* of social communicative competence. In other words, what must a child attain in order to be regarded as a socially competent communicator? A second question pertains to the *hows;* more specifically, how might a child go about acquiring the necessary information? One aspect of the *how* obviously involves cortical processing that cannot be directly described. However, through systematic observations of children in various settings it is possible to hypothesize the various factors that may be necessary, or facilitative, to the attainment of social communicative competence. In this chapter we will initially describe the basic parameters of social communicative competence. Following this, we shall attempt to describe a) *when* children seem to acquire aspects of this communicative competence, and b) *how,* in the sense of necessary or facilitative conditions, this competence is acquired.

PARAMETERS OF
SOCIAL COMMUNICATIVE COMPETENCE

Various investigators have identified context as the key to understanding social communicative competence (e.g., Prutting, 1982; Wilcox & Davis, in press). Essentially, context can be viewed as the primary determiner of *how* as well as *what* symbols are to be used in communication. The term "context" is rather broad and ambiguous. For purposes of communication there are three components to keep in mind. These include *linguistic* context, *paralinguistic* context, and *extralinguistic* context. Definitions, as well as the relative influences of these contextual components, are considered in the following section. It would appear that two basic abilities pertaining to the manipulation and understanding of context are important to for understanding and describing social communicative competence. Wilcox and Davis (in press) have discussed these abilities as a) the consideration of context when encoding and decoding messages, and b) the utilization of contextual information so as to appropriately initiate and sustain communicative interactions.

Context when Encoding and Decoding Messages

The ability to consider context when encoding and decoding messages means that an individual must be able to integrate available contextual information such that, when messages are being sent or received, an accurate interpretation can be achieved. As mentioned previously, contextual information is available from three sources; linguistic, paralinguistic, and extralinguistic.

Linguistic Context

Linguistic context is composed of verbal behavior. Prutting (1982) has defined linguistic context and its role in communication as "prior, co-occurring, and post verbal behavior used in composing and interpreting communication" (p. 125). Thus, what has been said, or what is being said, plays a role in the way in which a communicator will encode (compose) and decode (interpret) a message. For example, consider the following exchange:

"The bank is closed today."

"Oh, did you try to go there?"

In this exchange it is not necessary for the second speaker to specify what is meant by "there." Such specification would be regarded as redundant, or given, as the destination (bank) serves as information that is already known to both speakers. Thus, the second speaker's message was influenced, in its encoding, by the preceding linguistic context.

Paralinguistic Context

Paralinguistic context occurs in conjunction with linguistic context and is comprised of forms of behavior that are produced during verbal efforts. Prutting and Kirchner (1983) have referred to these types of behavior as the trappings surrounding a verbal production. Specific paralinguistic conventions include intonation, stress, vocal quality, rate of speech, and juncture (i.e., brief pauses).

Paralinguistic conventions serve various purposes in communication. They are often employed to convey information relative to emotional state, either intentionally or unintentionally (Laver & Trudgill, 1979). For example, in English, anger is frequently associated with a harsh vocal quality, elevated intonation and increased loudness; nervousness is frequently associated with an increased rate of speech. In the same line, paralinguistic behaviors such as rate (fast-slow) and intensity (loud-soft) are paired with specific personality traits as well as persons' judgments of personality traits (Brown, Strong, & Rencher, 1974; Markel, Phillis, Vargas & Howard, 1972; Smith, Brown, Strong & Rencher, 1975).

Paralinguistic conventions are also used in communication for purposes of specifying new information, correct interpretation of lexical items, and message intents. Relative to specification of new information, consider the following sentences:

"Elaine made the *meatballs*."

"*Elaine* made the meatballs."

In the first sentence, the speaker has assumed that the listener already knows that Elaine made something but does not know what she made. With the second sentence, the speaker has assumed that the listener already knows that someone made the meatballs but does not know that Elaine made them. In each of the examples *stress* is used to indicate the new information.

Stress as well as juncture are often used for purposes of disambiguating lexical items. For example, in the sentence "That's a hot dog," stress as well as juncture will determine if *hot dog* is to be interpreted as a frankfurter or a warm canine. In terms of message intents, intonation can frequently serve as a key identifier. For example, consider the sentence "Is it time to leave?" In this sentence word order (i.e., copula inversion) as well as intonation signal that the intent is a question. However, it would also be possible to say "It is time to leave?" wherein the rising intonation, by itself, will signal that the message intent is a question.

Extralinguistic Context

Extralinguistic context, which is probably the most potent contextual variable governing communicative behavior, is also the most difficult to specifically delineate. It can be regarded as potent in that it usually governs *what* message is communicated, *how* a message is communicated, and *when* a message is communicated. It is difficult to delineate the specific parameters of extralinguistic context as they frequently vary across and even within cultures (Brown & Fraser, 1979). For example, some cultures regard eye contact during communication as a signal indicating interest, whereas others may regard direct eye contact as rude.

Several investigators have described parameters of extralinguistic context (e.g., Brown & Fraser, 1979; Prutting & Kirchner, 1983; Wilcox & Davis, in press). Wilcox and Davis have defined extralinguistic context as that which is neither verbal or vocal in nature. They have described it as consisting of nonverbal elements that include the purpose, setting, and participants associated with a communicative exchange.

Purpose. A purpose, which can be viewed as the motive in communication, may be depicted in terms of the general activity type and the subject matter of an activity type (Brown & Fraser, 1979). Exemplary activity types might include sporting events, teaching, shopping, conversing with a friend, or a meeting. A given activity type also can be further specified in terms of subject matter, for example, a meeting might occur for purposes of discussing any number of different things. Different activities have different goals and the appropriate communicative behavior will vary as a function of these goals. For example, one's communicative behavior would be quite different in a corporate board meeting by comparison with a chat with an old friend.

Setting. The extralinguistic parameter referred to as setting includes physical (e.g., place) as well as temporal (e.g., time) variables. A setting, in and of itself, will usually have little influence on communicative behavior. Exceptions might include such as using hushed tones in a church, or talking louder in order to be heard in a large crowd of people. The influences of setting are most apparent when they interact with the purpose of communication. For example, given the topic of baseball, one's views on the subject might be expressed quite differently at an actual baseball game than they would in a class devoted to informing participants as to how the game is played.

Participants. The participants in a communicative interaction comprise the final aspect of extralinguistic context. Influential aspects relative to participants include shared knowledge, the physical orientation of the participants to each other, movements and gestures produced by participants, and the perceived role of each of the participants. In terms of shared knowledge, communication between people depends largely on the degree to which they share knowledge of a conversational topic, as well as knowledge of appropriate social communicative conventions (e.g., gaze behavior, use of polite forms).

The physical orientation of participants refers to actual positions. Depending upon the purpose, as well as setting of communication, participants may be facing each other, standing side-by-side, or back-to-back. Variance is also found in terms of distance maintained between participants. Although various investigators have found linguistic correlates of physical orientation (Moscovici & Plon, cited in Brown and Fraser, 1979) there are also affective correlates of physical orientation. For example, positive affect is frequently associated with less distance between participants.

Movements produced by participants can also convey varying forms of information. Movements may be postural in nature (e.g., leaning forward and backward) or differentiated (e.g., movements associated with the arms, hands, legs, and feet as well as facial expressions and gaze direction). All of these movements may be communicative in nature. For example, a forward lean accompanied by nodding of one's head frequently signals interest as well as comprehension to a speaker. Certain movements are sometimes described as gestures, and as such, may be used to support or replace verbal behavior.

Perceptions of participants' roles in a communicative interaction comprises the final aspect of extralinguistic context. Role perception can be explained at two levels. One is individually based and pertains to a person's need or desire to identify with a given group that may be either socially/culturally based, or occupationally based. Depending upon the desire for identification with a certain group, a speaker may adopt a style that contain lexical, syntactic, as well as paralinguistic features that are characteristic of a particular group. The second level of role perception concerns social relationships between communicators. In this sense, significant factors are each participant's perceived relationship to the other participants. Communicative variations have been observed as a function of familiarity of participants, kinship of participants, and perceived authority of participants (Brown & Fraser, 1979).

The Application of Context:
Initiating and Sustaining Communication

Once contextual information has been coded, it serves as a guideline for engaging in socially appropriate communicative interactions. Such appropriateness involves a variety of verbal and nonverbal behavior. Basically, one must be able to get a receiver's attention and then maintain it for the amount of time required to convey an intended message. Typically initiation is comprised of nonverbal behaviors such as eye contact and body position. For example, a potential sender may look at, then lean or walk toward a potential receiver. In some cases this nonverbal behavior may be supplemented by verbal behavior such as saying the potential receiver's name. Once attention has been obtained there are various conventions that are observed for purposes of sustaining an interaction. These include a) observance of turn-taking procedures, b) distinguishing between given and new information, and c) effectively conveying intended information.

Turn-Taking Procedures. The major goal of turn-taking conventions is to ensure that smooth interchanges will occur in a conversation (Prutting & Kirchner, 1983). Such smooth interchanges are accomplished in the following way. First, turns should be related to as previous turns (i.e., incorporate the same topic). If a topic is to be changed, relatedness still applies in that the previous topic is acknowledged, a termination signal is sent, and a new topic is introduced (e.g., "Oh, yes, I understand. You know, that reminds me of something else. . . . "). A second aspect of turn-taking pertains to feedback that should be provided to a speaker. Specifically, feedback should be provided so as to indicate that a message was either accurately received (e.g., "yes," "really," "oh my") or not understood (e.g. "What?"). Third, speakers should be able to repair turns in which a listener has indicated that the message was not understood. Finally, there should be a minimal overlap of turns (e.g. interruptions).

Given/New Distinctions. Paralinguistic as well as linguistic behaviors are used to signify that which serves as given information and that which serves as new information (MacWhinney & Bates, 1978; Prutting & Kirchner, 1983). Specific behavior includes stress, pronominalization, ellipses, initialization, and use of indefinite and definite articles.

As noted previously, stress is frequently used to indicate new information. Pronominalization refers to instances in which a referent can be identified from a pronoun (e.g., "Merle bought a new horse. He says he's faster than any of his others"). Ellipsis is used in situations in which information is given and basically means that given information can be deleted (e.g., "What is the snake doing?" "Hissing"). Initialization means that given information is stated before new information (e.g., "You know, the wallpaper I was planning to buy; well it's on sale now"). Finally, indefinite articles are used to signal new information (e.g., "I want a car"), while definite articles are used to convey given information (e.g., "I want the car").

Conveying Intended Messages. The final aspect of sustaining communication involves the ability to effectively convey intents that are appropriate in a given context. Intents, which are also referred to as speech acts, include among others, requests, questions, assertions, confirmations, protesting, agreeing, warning, and congratulating. The effective production of a desired intent requires linguistic as well as paralinguistic proficiency (e.g., auxiliary inversion and rising intonation for conveying a yes/no question). It is also important that an intent be appropriate to express in a given context. In this sense, coding of extralinguistic context is also important. For example, one would produce a request as opposed to an order, when communicating with a person perceived as having authority over the speaker.

ESTABLISHING SOCIAL COMMUNICATIVE COMPETENCE

As mentioned previously, social communicative competence requires knowledge pertaining to a conventional communicative code as well as knowledge of appropriate social interactive behaviors. In the first section of this chapter we have described the variables governing linguistic behavior in interpersonal communicative settings. At this time we shall turn to issues pertain to children's acquisition of the necessary skills.

We view language and communication as social phenomena that in children can be conceptualized as evolving from interpersonal interactions. As the discipline of child language has moved from a formalist to a more functionalist perspective (Bates & MacWhinney, 1979; 1982), there has been a greater interest in the development of communication outside the bounds of linguistic structures. In the process of applying this newer orientation, investigators have speculated not only that social communicative competence is more basic than linguistic competence, but that it is the development of interactionally based nonlinguistic communication which serves as the foundation for the development of linguistic structures.

The outgrowth of language from this basic interactional structure is the focus of this section of the chapter. We shall specifically discuss caregiver/infant interactional systems, the interactional/ contextual basis of prelinguistic communication, the emergence of early words in the interpersonal setting, and the ways in which context and interaction facilitate the development of syntax and discourse abilities necessary for social communicative competence.

As theoreticians and researchers have investigated aspects of socio-communicative development, terminology and concepts from speech act theory (Austin, 1962; Searle, 1965) have been adapted for use. In Austin's proposals regarding the functions and contents of utterances, he suggested three types of speech acts: Perlocutions, illocutions, and locutions. These acts also represent the three components of any utterance. In relating these concepts to the development of linguistic and socio-communicative competence, Bates, Camaioni and Volterra (1975) have proposed that each of the three components represent a separate stage in the ontogeny of communication. The perlocutionary stage or period appears first and is followed by the illocutionary and locutionary periods, respectively. The beginning of the illocutionary phase is marked by the appearance of children's intentional but not yet verbal communications, such as gestures. When children begin using words the locutionary phase of development has begun.

Traditionally, the locutionary phase of development has been viewed as the beginning of language development. As such it has served as the starting point for various investigations of children's language development. However, as child language specialists have examined earlier phases of children's communicative interactions (i.e., perlocutionary and illocutionary) it has become clear that a large amount of information important to the use of verbal behavior is acquired prior to children's actual use of words.

The First Interaction

The perlocutionary phase of development corresponds to that period during infancy when behavior demonstrated by an infant has a communicative effect upon adults in the environment, yet. there is no actual communicative intent on the part of the infant. Although these behaviors are not intended as communication by the infant, they appear to effect an adult in much the same way as do words in later phases of development. Essentially, the foundations for the development of word production systems are based in the acquisition of social communicative skills established through early primary caregiver/infant interactions (e.g., Brazelton, 1982; Bruner, 1977).

The necessary social communicative skills may be viewed as deriving from the quality of moment-to-moment social interchanges, occurring during infancy (Snow, 1981; Tronick, 1982). These social interchanges, originating in infancy, continue throughout life, with the early interactions setting the tone for the developmental process. The optimal social interchange, that is, one which is linked with the achvement of skills required for successful socio-communicative interactions, is one in which successful regulation of joint interactions occurs (Brazelton, 1982; Bruner, 1977; Tronick, 1982).

The term *joint regulation* takes on meaning in a dyadic context and means that each member of an interaction learns to influence and be influenced by the other. Successful joint regulation occurs when dyadic participants share directional tendencies. This means that each member of an interaction must be able to understand the other's intents and goals and respond in a reciprocal fashion.

An infant begins to learn about regulation from birth in the context of the caregiver/infant interaction. In these early interactions, *affective behavior* serves as the primary regulatory focus. The caregiver/infant affective system controls regulation while the affective state of each member serves as that which is actually regulated. A caregiver must be able to appropriately interpret an infant's cues and provide a related responses. This response, in turn, influences the original signal produced by the infant.

Initially, an infant's affective state and regulatory messages are

undifferentiated and basically convey either "stop" or "continue."
Eventually, with the assistance of the caregiver, the infant's affective system and subsequent regulatory cues become more differentiated and are paired with intentional communication. Als (1982)
has outlined the development of an infant's regulatory system.
The specific component steps are as follows:

1. Regulation of physiological (e.g., breathing) and motoric
   (e.g., smoothness and complexity of movement) systems.
2. Regulation of state (e.g., sleep, drowsy, alert).
3. Coordinated regulation of physiological systems, motoric
   systems, and state.
4. Regulation of play dialogue with caregiver.
5. Regulation of object play with caregiver.
6. Coordinated regulation of object play and play dialogue
   with caregiver.

As can be seen, regulation initially focuses upon an infant's
physiological and motoric systems and is then gradually extended
to the environment. The role of a caregiver in an infant's emerging regulatory system can be viewed as that of an organizer. As the
organizer, the caregiver assists infant development by providing
stabilization and gradual expansion of behavior. For example, a
caregiver may engage an infant in play dialogue, maintain this for
a short time, and then introduce a rattle. The goal in this example
would be coordinated object play and play dialogue.

These early caregiver/infant interactions can be characterized
in terms of an affective feedback loop in which each partner
continues to learn about the other. Since an infant is quite
clearly preverbal, it is through affective messages that each
partner conveys information to the other. For example, when
an infant cries in a manner that is perceived as distress, a
typical caregiver response might include soothing vocalizations
and gentle touch; all of which are designed to convey a calm,
positive affect. There must be an appropriate interplay of caregiver/
infant affect in order to achieve a jointly regulated interchange.
An "appropriate interplay of affect" requires that caregiver/
infant dyads share the same affective directional tendencies.
For example, a caregiver should lower the stimulation level

when an infant is clearly sending a "stop" message.

In order to share directional tendencies, a caregiver must be able to interpret an infant's cues. Obviously a caregiver's ease and ability with interpreting infant cues is an evolving process. However, reasonably on-target interpretations are important as it is the caregiver's ability to attribute meaning to infant behavior that is believed to eventually enable an infant to associate that meaning with his or her own behavior (Tronick, 1982). Snow (1981) maintains that only through the knowledge that the infant's behavior has consistent and predictable effects on the environment can an infant come to an understanding of the "notion of signal . . . the first stage in developing the ability to communicate" (p. 197).

Interaction and context are crucial to communication during infancy. It is the interaction between a caregiver or another adult and an infant that makes this perlocutionary phase communicative. If a caregiver does not attend and respond to behavior of an infant, there is no communication. It is the combination of context and infant behavior that structures meaning for a caregiver. As caregivers come to recognize behavior that an infant demonstrates relative to particular activities or contexts, the behavior takes on signal value for the caregiver. An infant demonstrates anticipatory responses that become meaningful for a caregiver and in turn, may serve as signals for the performance of certain actions or other behavior (Brunner, 1977). The caregiver then responds by making performance of these activities possible (e.g. giving an infant a bottle or toy). This infant behavior-caregiver response cycle develops into a type of circular reaction that begins to take on communicative dimensions.

Expanding the Interactional Base: Intentions

In the previous section, which focused upon caregiver/infant interactions, a key component included consistent environmental responses to infant behavior, or the ability to interpret infant cues. Because particular behavior of an infant has consistent effects upon the environment, the infant eventually comes to perform certain behavior with the aim (i.e., intent) of gaining these predictable ends. When a child begins to evidence these *communicative intentions*, the illocutionary period of development has begun.

Bates et al. (1975) proposed that this period begins when a child recognizes an adult as a possible actor or agent in the environment. With this recognition, a child begins to engage in gestural and vocal behaviors with the intent of having an adult perform some action or attend to some aspect of the environment. A child's intent to communicate is marked by his/her attention to an adult, where in the previous phase this attention was absent. A child, who upon being unable to retrieve a ball that has rolled out of reach, looks toward an adult while still reaching for the ball, evidences an illocutionary stage behavior. If the adult is inattentive or fails to respond, the child may use a vocalization to gain attention, and generally will persist in the attempt to communicate.

Communicative intentions have been accorded a significant role in the development of social communicative competence. Ingram (1974) has maintained that the increasing number and variety of communicative intentions may be more reflective of developmental changes during the early periods than are lexical or structural changes. Halliday (1975) has proposed seven communicative functions/intentions as universals and suggests that the appearance of these functions is a necessary, and possibly sufficient condition for transition from a child's "own protolanguage into the mother tongue" (p. 82). The specific functions (which are listed below) were derived from Halliday's observations of a child's prespeech communicative interactions.

1. *Instrumental,* in which language is used to satisfy material needs.
2. *Regulatory,* in which language is used to control actions of other persons.
3. *Interactional,* in which language is used to establish and maintain contact with other persons.
4. *Personal,* in which language is used to inform others of one's own behavior.
5. *Heuristic,* in which language is used to explore and obtain explanations about the environment.
6. *Imaginative,* in which language is used to create a pretend environment.
7. *Informative,* in which language is used to give information to someone whom it is believed did not possess the information.

Overall, Halliday has suggested that children learn, and with prespeech communicative forms, convey the above meanings (excepting the *informative*) well before they have a conventional verbal means of expressions. These social meanings then provide the foundation for the later expression of conventional language forms. The informative function, which emerges significantly later than the others, is the function that indicates a child is using language in the adult sense, or engaging in true language.

As child language specialists have come to recognize the importance of prespeech communicative functions, various taxonomies have been developed for purposes of delineating communicative intentions expressed by children (see Chapman, 1981 for a review of these systems). Further, various investigators have attempted to determine an order of emergence for communicative intentions (e.g., Bates et al., 1975; Bates, Camaioni, & Volterra, 1979; Carpenter, Mastergeorge & Coggins, 1981; Dore, 1974; Halliday, 1975).

Carpenter, Mastergeorge and Coggins (1981) conducted a longitudinal investigation of six children, with a focus on identifying an order of emergence of preverbal communicative intentions. The children were observed from 8 to 15 months of age and their communicative behaviors were coded with the system devised by Coggins and Carpenter (1981). The system included the following intentions: Request for information, protest, request for action, request for object, comment on action, comment on object, and answering.

Protest, as an intention, was the first to emerge. This intent was shown by each of the children at the beginning of the investigation, indicating that its emergence occurred prior to eight months. The developmental order of other intentions was as follows: Request for action, request for object, comment on action, comment on object, and answering. None of the children evidenced use of the request for information category during the course of the investigation.

The intentions observed by Carpenter et al. were expressed with three different modes; gesture alone, gesture plus vocalization, and verbal behavior. A developmental order was also determined for these modes of expression. At the earliest level, gesture alone, and gesture plus vocalization were the primary modes of expression. At approximately ten months the use of gesture alone showed a decline with a corresponding increase in the use of gesture plus vocalization. Gesture plus vocalization continued to be the primary means of expressing the communicative intentions at the end of the study; however, verbal behavior began to be used at approximately 13 months.

Words and Structures

We have previously described how the contingent responding of the perlocutionary period served as the foundation for the intentional communication of the illocutionary period. In the same line it appears that the communicative intentions of the illocutionary period serve as the framework for the use of words as children are entering the locutionary period (Carpenter et al., 1981; Halliday, 1975). The appearance of words in the previously nonlinguistic communication frames of the illocutionary period would seem to indicate that the first words produced by a child function as more than labels for objects and events in the environment.

Carter (1975; 1978) has suggested that an adult model plays a strong role in determining the first words that children use in expressing their intentions. In a longitudinal investigation of a single child, Carter traced the evolution of words in eight different and distinct categories of communicative behavior. The child first expressed communicative intentions through the use of specific gestures. These gestures were later accompanied by word-like signals which appeared to serve intentional functions; these were labeled sensorimotor morphemes. During this period specific vocalizations were used to express different functions (e.g., /m/—initial vocalizations accompanied the child's reach for objects, and /b/—initial vocalizations accompanied gestures which indicated his rejection of an object). Environmental conditioning through the input of the mother appeared to play a significant role in determining the sensorimotor morpheme, as well as the words that the child later used to express these functions. The /m/ plus gesture, indicating desire for an object, was the precursor of "more" and "mine" in these communicative frames.

Context continues to play an important role during children's single word productions. Specifically, it influences what aspect of an event a child will encode, and it is used by an adult in decoding single word messages of children. Greenfield and her colleagues (Greenfield, 1978; Greenfield & Smith, 1976; Greenfield & Zukow, 1978) have maintained that it is the association between the single word produced and the nonlinguistic context that serves as the precursor for the notion of given/new information. The given information for the single word user is in the context and therefore is not expressed.

Gradually children's single word productions are expanded and expressed as elementary structures. Scollon (1979), upon analyzing transcripts of a child during the single and early two-word period, found the beginnings of syntax in the single-word period. Through the production of "vertical structures," the child in this investigation was able to construct syntactically appropriate utterances, one word at a time, across successive turns in conversation. Some of these vertical structures appeared not to differ significantly from the successive single-word utterances described by Bloom (1973). Frequently, in producing vertical structures, the child appeared to use an adult utterance to build a verbal construction. For example:

Child: "Kimby."
Adult: "What about Kimby?"
Child: "Hiding."
Adult: "Hiding? What's hiding?"
Child: "Balloon." (Scollon, 1979; p. 220–221)

Scollon found that the vertical constructions did not disappear once the child began producing two word constructions. Rather, they appeared to serve as a vehicle for moving the child into the production of more complex structures. Schwartz, Chapman, Prelock, Terrell, and Rowan (in press) also explored children's use of vertical structures. They elicited vertical structures from children in the single word phase of development by inserting adult utterances between successive child utterances. This procedure was continued across ten experimental sessions. Results indicated that the children exposed to vertical structures produced more word combinations at the end of the experimental sessions than did those comprising a matched control group. Schwartz et al. concluded that the vertical structures had a facilitative effect upon the children's syntactic development.

Other factors that may have a *facilitative* effect upon children's syntactic development pertain to environmental communicative input, that is, adult language addressed to children in conversational interactions. Several investigators (e.g., Brown, 1968; Brown, Cazden & Bellugi, 1969) have proposed that mothers' use of questions facilitates children's acquisition of specific aspects of grammar. Brown suggested that through the use of what he termed "occasional questions," mothers cued their children's attention to the form and function of certain grammatical constructions. Expansions and recasts of children's utterances (i.e., providing new syntactic information while maintaining the child's semantic content of prior utterances) have also been shown to effect syntactic development. Through experimental manipulation of adult responses to child utterances, Nelson, Carskaddon and Bonvillian (1973) and Nelson (1976), determined that children acquired forms that had been presented to them through recasting.

Wilcox (1984), following a detailed review of the adult input literature, summarized those variables that have been found to exert positive influences on children's language acquisition. She identified three adult-interactive strategies. The first strategy relates to expansions; specifically, she suggested that adult comments about child utterances should be in the form of expansions that preserve a child's semantic intent. For example, if a child says "doggie sleep," an adult might respond with something like "the doggie is sleeping in the chair." A second strategy pertained to synchrony of an adult with a child's level. Wilcox maintained that children verbally gain the most when the adult is in cognitive as well as verbal synchrony with them. She suggested that a way to facilitate such synchrony was by allowing a child to select the topic of join attention (i.e., adult-child). Thus, a child is encouraged by an adult to direct the activity or interaction. The third strategy relates to adult feedback to child utterances. Specifically, Wilcox suggested that children will derive maximum benefit from input that responds to the *truth value,* rather than the linguistic accuracy of their utterances. For example, if a child says "doggie sleep" an adult response responding to truth value would be something along the lines of "yes, the doggie is sleeping." Essentially, the adult confirms that the message sent by the child has been received.

Appropriate Use of Verbal Structures

In addition to linguistic content and structures, children must also learn the rules for the appropriate expression of their linguistic structures in conversation. These rules, which were the focus of the first section of this chapter, have only begun to be examined in terms of children's communicative development. Hence, although children's acquisition of conversational rules has begun to receive considerable attention, specific information concerning development is still somewhat sketchy.

Children acquire conversational conventions not through observation of, but through participation in communicative interactions. One aspect of conversational competence that has received considerable attention is children's turn-taking abilities. Snow (1977) proposed that mothers use a "conversational model" in interacting with the infants, and that the use of this conversational mode facilitates the child's acquisition of turn-taking abilities. Snow noted that during the earliest interactions, mothers appear to accept any response from their infants as their turn. Mothers' requirements for appropriate turns, however, become more stringent as their children become capable of more communicative behavior.

Ervin-Tripp (1979) examined children around the age of two, when they appear to be conversationally less sophisticated, in the sense that they are generally incapable of managing interruptions in the conversational flow. She reported that such young children do evidence the ability to reply to adjacency pairs. An adjacency pair is defined as two utterances, occurring across speakers in conversation, in which the first utterance elicits the second utterance (Sachs, Schegloff, and Jefferson, 1974). Included among the adjacency pairs that young children reply to are greetings, yes-no questions, competence questions, control questions, commands, and offers.

Children also evidence their knowledge and understanding of the conventions of turn-taking and conversational structure through their use and responses to contingent queries. A contingent query is a question that is embedded in a larger stretch of conversation, and is addressed to the immediately prior speaker. Speakers utilize queries for purposes of obtaining specific clarifying information. When presented with a contingent query the previous speaker is obligated to respond; failure to respond results in conversational breakdown.

Children's use and responses to contingent queries have been studied extensively (Gallagher, 1977; 1981; Garvey, 1975; 1977; Wilcox & Webster, 1980). Garvey proposed that children acquire knowledge of the contingent query through participating in and as a part of the process of conversational interactions. Gallagher as well as Wilcox and Webster have found that even children as young as 17 months demonstrate the ability to respond to the contingent query, thereby indicating their awareness of the obligation to respond. Gallagher additionally found that adults were sensitive to children's levels of competence. Those queries which required complex responses more often were directed to children who demonstrated the ability to respond to them, than to children who did not.

Although children evidence the ability to take their turns in conversation, Kaye and Charney (1981) suggested that much of the continuity in conversation seems to result from a participating adult's behavior. These investigators found that mothers, when interacting with their two-year-old children, produced more "turn-abouts" than did their children. A turnabout was described as a communicative behavior that both responded to and required a response from the other participant. Although the children produced both responsives and mands (i.e., behavior which expects a response), they tended not to do such within the same turn. Hence, the children's behavior did not maximally contribute to the continuation of the conversational interactions.

Questions also appear to function as a device by which adults ensure that children take their conversational turns. A consistent finding across several studies is that mothers use lots of questions in their interactions with children (e.g., Newport, 1977; Snow, 1972). It is likely that the use of questions is related to their facilitative effects in eliciting response from children. Olsen-Fulero and Conforti (1983) analyzed sixty minutes of interaction of 11 mother-child dyads in which the children ranged in age from two and one-half to three years. Comparison of maternal questions and declaratives indicated that 56% of the questions elicited response from the children, while only 16% of the declarative statements resulted in children's responses.

Helfrich-Miller (1983) examined mothers in interactions with their three-year-old children. She reported that the mothers appeared to be actively teaching turn-taking, construction of conversational interactions, and other aspects of socio-communicative competence. An example of this active teaching strategy is as follows:

Mother: "Backup and we'll load it up."
Mother: "Are you the guy for the wood?"
Mother: "You're supposed to tell me."
Mother: "Backup and pick up the wood."
Child: "Came to pick up the wood."
Mother: "Well, back it up Jack. Okay, get going."

(Helfrich-Miller, 1983; p. 4)

In the preceding example, in order for the conversational interaction to continue successfully, the second utterance produced by the mother requires a response from the child. When no response seems to be forthcoming from the child, the mother states to him, in a rather exact fashion, that he should take his conversational turn. After this instruction the mother repeats the utterance which preceded the child's "dropping of the conversational ball." The child then appropriately takes his turn, and the interaction continues.

Another important variable for smooth conversational flow pertains to relatedness of turns, or conversational cohesion. Bloom, Rocissano and Hood (1976) investigated the developing conversational abilities of children between the ages of 21 and 36 months, relative to the children's use of such contingent speech. They concluded that children's use of contingent (or related) responses increases developmentally. Children exhibiting an average of two words per sentence used contingent speech approximately 50% of the time while children with an average sentence length of four and one-half words used such speech 73% of the time. However, as Bloom et al. examined only verbal behavior they may have underestimated the children's communicative abilities. In a study of children at the one word phase of language development, Prelock, Messick, Schwartz and Terrell (1981) classified both verbal and nonverbal behavior and found that the children were able to sustain a topic of conversation across at least three turns. This finding indicates that even at the early stages of communicative development, children may possess conversational abilities beyond their linguistic abilities to express them.

As noted in the initial section of this chapter, distinctions relative to given versus new information also contribute to the continuity and coherency of conversational behavior. Given or new distinctions may be made through both linguistic and nonlinguistic means. Children appear to be aware of these distinctions at very early stages of development (Lucas & Bacharach, 1983), but appear not to learn all the rules for linguistic expression until later in development (Maratsos, 1974).

Pronominalization and definite articles are two linguistic devices used to code given information that have received some investigative attention. Lucas and Bacharach (1983) examined topicalization in children ranging in age from three to five years. They found that pronominalization was increased in both groups of children when the topic had been made explicit by a previous speaker (i.e., established as given information). Maratsos (1974) studied definite and indefinite article use in children ranging in age from three to nine years. He determined that although all children made distinctions in their use of the two forms, the younger children did not always consider their listener's perspective when making their choices. For these young children, it appeared to be sufficient that they had a definite referent in mind which made use of the definite article appropriate, even if that use did not assist the listener in selecting the appropriate referent.

A final aspect that will be considered with respect to children's appropriate use of their linguistic behavior relates to children's sensitivity to the extralinguistic parameter referred to as participants. One parameter pertaining to participants that has received some attention is the use of polite forms of address. Bates (1976) determined that children at the age of 34 months were able to discriminate polite forms of address. However their sociolinguistic awareness of variation in conventions (i.e., variation as a function of participants) was not well developed at that time.

Another parameter relating to participants concerns the ability to adapt one's communicative patterns to varying listeners. As children become socially competent language users they demonstrate the ability to vary the style of their communication relative to the characteristics of their listeners. Shatz and Gelman (1973) found that even prior to the time when children can take the listener's perspective, as determined by tests of egocentrism, they evidence the ability to modify their speech styles in accordance with listener characteristics. Specifically their four-year-olds spoke differently when describing a game to two-year-olds, than they did to adults or to other four-year-olds. They spoke more directly and simply to the two-year-olds than they did to the adults, and they used more questions in talking with the adults than they did with any of the children.

The acquisition of stylistic differences may develop through children's observations of adults' interactions with them, in contrast to adults' interactions with more competent communicators. Because children observe adults in communication with partners who are not children, and also with children other than themselves, comparative observations are possible. Further, young children also observe older children in conversational interactions, and therefore are able to observe style modifications in these interactions. Gleason (1973) reported an investigation of family interaction during dinner time. Not only did the parents show style modifications as they spoke to different children, but the older children made style modifications in speaking to their younger siblings. Hence, children have numerous opportunities to observe more competenct communicators making speech style modifications on the basis of differences in their listeners.

SUMMARY AND CONCLUSIONS

In this chapter we have discussed children's language behavior as a system of social communicative competence. We have presented language acquisition as a process by which children integrate social as well as linguistic knowledge. Basically we are maintaining that children's linguistic behavior can best be understood when observed and described in the context of interpersonal communicative interactions. After outlining the parameters of social communicative competence we attempted to create a picture of the development of the skills necessary for this competence. We believe that the process begins at birth, in the context of caregiver/infant interactions. Subsequent development can then be viewed as a gradual expansion and modification of these early interactive patterns.

REFERENCES

Als, H. (1982). The unfolding of behavioral organization in the face of biological violation. In E. Tronick (Ed.), *Social interchange in infancy: Affect, cognition and communication.* Baltimore: University Park Press.

Austin, J. (1962). *How to do things with words.* Cambridge: Harvard University Press.

Bates, E. (1976). *Language in context.* New York: Academic Press.

Bates, E., Camaioni, L., & Volterra, V. (1975). The acquisition of performatives prior to speech. *Merrill-Palmer Quarterly.* 21. 205–244.

Bates, E., Camaioni, L., & Volterra, V. (1979). The acquisition of performatives prior to speech. In E. Ocks & B. Achieffelin (Eds.), *Developmental pragmatics.* New York: Academic Press.

Bates, E. & MacWhinney, B. (1979). A functionalist approach to the acquimsition of grammar. In E. Ochs & B. Schieffelin (Eds.), *Developmental pragmatics.* New York: Academic Press.

Bates, E. & MacWhinney, B. (1982). Functionalist approaches to grammar. In L. Gleitman & E. Wanner (Eds.), *Language acquisition: The state of the art.* New York: Cambridge University Press.

Bloom, L. (1973). *One word at a time: The use of single-word utterances before syntax.* The Hague: Mouton.

Bloom, L., Rocissanno, L., & Hood, L. (1976). Adult-child discourse: Developmental interaction between information processing and linguistic knowledge. *Cognitive Psychology.* 8. 521–552.

Brazelton, T. (1982). Joint regulation of neonate-parent behavior. In E. Tronick

(Ed.), *Social interchange in infancy: Affect, cognition, and communication*. Baltimore: University Park Press.

Brown, R. (1968). The development of wh-questions in child speech. *Journal of Verbal Learning and Verbal Behavior.* 7. 279–290.

Brown, R., Cazden, C., & Bellugi, U. (1969). The child's grammar from I to III. In J. Hill (Ed.), *The Second Annual Minnesota Symposium on Child Psychology.* Minneapolis: University of Minnesota Press.

Brown, P. & Fraser, C. (1979). Speech as a marker of situation. In K. Scherer & H. Giles (Eds.), *Social markers in speech.* Cambridge: Cambridge University Press.

Brown, B., Strong, W., & Rencher, A. (1974). Fifty four voices from two: The effects of simultaneous manipulations of rate, mean fundamental frequency, and variance of fundamental frequency on ratings of personality from speech. *Journal of the Acousitical Society of America.* 55. 313–318.

Brunner, J. (1977). Early social interaction and language acquisition. In H. Schaffer (Ed.), *Studies in mother-infant interaction.* London: Academic Press.

Carpenter, R., Mastergeorge, A., & Coggins, T. (1981). The acquisition of communicative intentions in infants. Unpublished manuscript, University of Washington.

Carter, A. (1975). The transformation of sensorimotor morphemes into words: A case study of the development of "more" and "mine." *Journal of Child Language.* 2. 233–250.

Carter, A. (1978). From sensorimotor vocalizations to words: A case study of the evolution of attention-directing communication in the second year. In A. Locke (Ed.), *Action, gesture and symbol: The emergence of language.* London: Academic Press.

Coggins, T. & Carpenter, R. (1981). The communicative intention inventory: A system for observing and coding children's early intentional communication. *Applied Psycholinguistics.* 2. 235–252.

Chapman, R. (1981). Exploring children's communicative intents. In J. Miller, *Assessing language production in children: Experimental procedures.* Baltimore: University Park Press.

Dore, J. (1974). A pragmatic description of early development. *Journal of Psycholinguistic Research.* 3. 343–350.

Ervin-Tripp, S. (1979). Children's verbal turn-taking. In E. Ochs & B. Schieffelin (Eds.), *Developmental pragmatics.* New York: Academic Press.

Gallagher, T. (1977). Revision behaviors in the speech of normal children developing language. *Journal of Speech and Hearing Research.* 20. 303–318.

Gallagher, R. (1981). Contingent query sequences within adult-child discourse. *Journal of Child Language.* 8. 51–62.

Garvey, C. (1975). Requests and responses in children's speech. *Journal of Child Language.* 2. 41–63.

Garvey, C. (1977). The contingent query: A dependent act in conversation. In M. Lewis & L. Rosenglum (Eds.), *Interaction, conversation, and the development of language.* New York: Wiley.

Gleason, J. (1973). Code switching in children's language. In T. More (Ed.), *Cognitive development and the acquisition of language.* New York: Academic Press.

Greenfield, P. (1978). Informativeness, Presupposition, and semantic choice in single-word utterances. In N. Waterson & C. Snow (Eds.), *The development of communication.* London: Wiley.

Greenfield, P. & Smith, J. (1976). *The structure of communication in early development.* New York: Academic Press.

Greenfield, P. & Zukow, P. (1978). Why do children say what they say when they say it?: An experimental approach to the psychogenesis of presupposition. In K. Nelson (Ed.), *Children's Language, Volume I.* New York: Gardner Press.

Halliday, M. (1975). *Learning how to mean: Explorations in the development of language.* New York: Elsevier.

Hymes, D. (1971). Competence and performance in linguistic theory. In R. Huxley & E. Ingram (Eds.), *Language acquisition: Models and methods.* New York: Academic Press.

Ingram, D. (1974). Stages in the development of one-word utterances. *Papers and Reports in Child Language Development.* Palo Alto: Stanford University Press.

Kaye, K. & Charney, R. (1981). Conversational assymmetry between mothers and children. *Journal of Child Language.* 8. 35–49.

Laver, J. & Trudgill, P. (1979). Phonetic and linguistic markers in speech. In K. Scherer & H. Giles (Eds.), *Social Markers in Speech.* Cambridge: Cambridge University Press.

Luszcz, M. & Bacharach, V. (1983). The emergence of communicative competence: Detection of conversational topics. *Journal of Child Language.* 10. 623–637.

MacWhinney, B. & Bates, E. (1978). Sentential devices for conveying givenness and newness: A cross-cultural developmental study. *Journal of Verbal Learning and Verbal Behavior.* 17. 539–558.

Maratsos, M. (1974). Preschool children's use of definite and indefinite articles. *Child Development.* 45. 446–455.

Nelson, K. (1976). Facilitating children's syntax acquisition. *Developmental Psychology.* 13. 101–107.

Nelson, K., Carskaddon, G., & Bonvillian, J. (1973). Syntax acquisition: Impact of experimental variation in adult verbal interaction with the child. *Child Development.* 44. 497–504.

Newport, E. (1977). Motherese: The speech of mothers to young children. In N. Castellan, D. Pisoni, & G. Potts (Eds.), *Cognitive theory, Volume 2.* Hillsdale, N.J.: Lawrence Erlbaum.

Olsen-Fulero, L. & Conforti, J. (1983). Child responsiveness to mother questions of varying type and presentation. *Journal of Child Language.* 10. 495–520.

Prelock, P., Messick, C., Schwartz, R., & Terrell, B. (1981, June). *Mother-child discourse during the one-word stage.* Paper presented at the Second Annual Wisconsin Symposium on Research in Child Language Disorders, Madison, Wisconsin.

Prutting, C. (1982). Pragmatics as social competence. *Journal of Speech and Hearing Disorders.* 47. 123–133.

Prutting, C. & Kirchner, D. (1983). Applied pragmatics. In T. Gallagher & C. Prutting (Eds.), *Pragmatic assessment and intervention issues in language.* San Diego: College-Hill Press.

Rees, N. (1978). Pragmatics of language: Applications to normal and disordered language development. In R. Schiefelbusch (Ed.), *Bases of language intervention.* Baltimore: University Park Press.

Sacks, H., Schegloff, E., & Jefferson, G. (1974). A simplest systematics for the organization of turn-taking for conversation. *Language.* 50. 696–735.

Schwartz, R., Chapman, K., Prelock, P., Terrell, B., & Rowan, L. (In press). Facilitation of early syntax through discourse structure. *Journal of Child Language.*

Scollon, R. (1979). A real early stage: An unzippered condensation of a dissertation on child language. In E. Ochs & B. Schieffelin (Eds.), *Developmental pragmatics.* New York: Academic Press.

Searle, J. (1969). *Speech acts: An essay in the philosophy of language.* Cambridge: Cambridge University Press.

Shatz, M. & Gelman, R. (1973). The development of communication skills: Modification in the speech of young children as a function of the listener. *Monographs of the Society for Research in Child Development.* 5 (Serial No. 38).

Snow, C. (1972). Mother's speech to children learning language. *Child Development.* 43. 549–565.

Snow, C. (1977). The development of conversation between mothers and babies. *Journal of Child Language.* 4. 1–22.

Snow, C. (1981). Social interaction and language acquisition. In P. Dale & D. Ingram (Eds.), *Child language: An international perspective.* Baltimore: University Park Press.

Tronick, E. (Ed.). (1982). *Social interchange in infancy: Affect, cognition, and communication.* Baltimore: University Park Press.

Wilcox, M. (1984). Developmental language disorders: Preschoolers. In A. Holland (Ed.), *Language disorders in children.* San Diego: College-Hill Press.

Wilcox, M. & Davis, G. (In press). *Pragmatics, PACE, and adult aphasia.* San Diego: College-Hill Press.

Wilcox, M. & Webster, E. (1980). Early discourse behavior: An analysis of children's responses to listener feedback. *Child Development.* 51. 1120–1125.

CHAPTER 4

SEX AND GENDER SIMILARITIES AND DIFFERENCES AND THE DEVELOPMENT OF THE YOUNG CHILD

MICHELE A. PALUDI

Acquisition of a sex-role identity is a fundamental component in the personality development of children. Mowrer(1950) summed up its importance in the following manner: "personal normality presupposes that an individual has assimilated not only those values and ideals which are regarded as necessary and proper for all persons, but also those values and ideals which are uniquely appropriate to one's sex-role, as a man or as a woman" (p. 615). Kagan(1964) attributed the importance of sex-role identity to its central directive function in aiding the development of the child's definition of self and his or her subsequent behavioral choices. And, Duvall(1967) cited the achievement of a sex-role identity as a major developmental task of early childhood.

TERMINOLOGY

The construct of sex-role identity is often used in a parsimonious way to describe a complex developmental process. The child's acquisition of sex-role identity has been thought to include at least the following: sex-role preference, sex-role adoption, and sex-role identification. *Sex-role preference* refers to the desire to adopt the behavior associated with either men or women, or the perception of such behavior as more desirable or preferable(Brown, 1956b; Lynn, 1959). Sex-role preference is operationally defined on the basis of preferential responses of children to objects, activities, and figures that are typical of one sex in contrast to the other sex. Children's sex-role preference is typically measured by the stan-

66

dard or alternate version of the *IT Scale for Children*(Brown, 1956a). In recent years, children's sex-role preferences have been assessed by one of several new instruments which avoid the methodological constraints of the IT Scale. Among these newer measures are the *Sex-Role Learning Index* (Edelbrock & Sugawara, 1978) and the *Children's Sex-Role Preference Scale* (Paludi, 1982).

Sex-Role Adoption refers to a child's overt behavior which is characteristic of a given sex, not to stated preferences *per se*. It is the activities in which the child participates in rehearsing and practicing the characteristic modes of behavior of the preferred sex-role(Lynn, 1959). Sex-role adoption has been measured by observing children's behavior in their daily activities at home and at the nursery or preschool(e.g., Connor & Serbin, 1977).

Sex-Role Identification is the automatic, unconscious, culturally determined behavior of a particular sex-role(Lynn, 1959). Unlike sex-role preference and sex-role adoption, sex-role identification is more difficult to measure, as there are more steps between the observable characteristics of the person and the construct inferred. In addition, the importance of unconscious factors increases, thus increasing the difficulties of the measurement process and the specification of appropriate external criteria for validation(Constantinople, 1973). However, attempts have been made to measure children's sex-role identification through projective techniques, such as figure drawings(e.g., Datta & Drake, 1968; Heinrich & Triebe, 1972; Tolor & Tolor, 1974).

Sex-Role Typing is the process by which children acquire the motives, values, and behaviors appropriate to either males or females in a specific culture. Sex-typed behavior is the degree to which a child has incorporated these motives, values, and behaviors. *Masculinity* and *femininity* are sex-specific subdivisions of sex typed (e.g., the number of items from a sex-role typing questionnaire that a child has incorporated). A highly masculine male and a highly feminine female are highly sex-typed. Feminine males and masculine females are *cross-sex-typed;* they have incorporated a sex-role standard which is in the opposite direction from his or her biological sex. Typically, measures of sex-typing and cross-sex-typing elicit artificial bipolar characteristics inasmuch as they have been treated as opposite poles of a single bipolar continuum (e.g., *California Psychological Inventory, Minnesota Multiphasic Personality Inventory*). When masculinity and femininity are measured independently, they are found to be orthogonal; i.e., masculinity and femininity are present in varying degrees in both males and females. The Bem *Sex Role Inventory*(Bem, 1974) and the *Personal Attributes Questionnaire* (Spence & Helmreich, 1972) yield the categories of masculinity, femininity, androgyny (the incorporation of both masculine and feminine traits within an individual) and undifferentiated (the incorporation of neither masculine and feminine traits).

SEX VS. GENDER

A major obstacle to understanding and interpreting sex-role research is the terminology. The various usages of the term sex-role is by no means clear. In different contexts the term "sex-role" can be used to describe the child's preference for certain activities or hobbies or the child's actual behavior in the school classroom or home. In that researchers have not defined the various components of sex-role identity in the same way, it should come as no surprise to find zero or relatively weak correlations among the various measures of sex-role identity. Furthermore, there are a variety of psychometric problems associated with these measures, especially in the areas of reliability and construct validity. Finally, researchers have tended to use the term *sex* interchangeably as both a dependent and an independent variable (Unger & Denmark, 1975). When used as a dependent variable, it is assumed that sex is derived from cultural experiences. As an independent variable it is implied that sex is biologically determined by the hormonal, chromosomal, and morphological structure of the organism. This distinction may prove to be a disadvantage, however, for researchers studying cognitive differences between males and females since the explanation concerns the interaction between the psychological and physiological mechanisms. The differentiation between the terms may eventually lead to greater clarity in interpreting research in the area of children's sex-role typing.

METHODOLOGICAL CONSTRAINTS

First, when sex and gender differences are found, they are only averages. There is considerable overlap in the psychological characteristics of males and females in all of the skills to be discussed in this chapter. Some males are represented in the upper quartile on measures of "feminine" personality characteristics, some females are represented in the upper quartile on "masculine" personality characteristics.

Second, much of the research on sex and gender differences is, in reality differences of white, middle-class American children. Margaret Mead's (1935) classic studies of three New Guinea tribes informed Americans of a very important fact: not every society has the same masculine and feminine roles as ours. Research by Barry, Bacon, and Child (1957) found differential socialization practices for males and females in several nonliterate cultures. Stereotypic gender role socialization was associated with an economy which placed a high premium on superior strength. Within the United States, children from the lower socioeconomic class acquire a gender role identity at an earlier age than do children from the middle or upper classes (Pope, 1953; Rabban, 1950). Intercultural research presents evidence to counter the argument that gender differences are the result of biological forces.

Third, there is substantial evidence that biases exist in selecting subjects for research. In particular, males are used more frequently as subjects than females. In some entire areas of research (e.g., achievement motivation; aggression), only male subjects have typically been used. It appears likely that the choice of subjects is influenced by the kind of behavior the researcher is investigating. When experimenters study a stereotyped "masculine" behavior (e.g., aggression), they are not likely to include females as subjects. The major problem with this kind of bias is that it leads to a psychology of male behavior rather than human behavior.

Fourth, experimenter and observer effects are common. With children, female experimenters obtain better results, while with adult subjects male experimenters get better performance. Furthermore, since the majority of psychological research has been conducted by men, it seems possible that the results might have been very different had the research been conducted by women. One of the major problems in research in children's gender role typing is that it is almost impossible for experimenters and observers to be unaware of or "blind" to the sex of subjects. An observer's report may be influenced by subjective judgments about the subject's sex. For example, Condry and Condry (1976) asked college students to view a videotape of a nine-month-old infant's reaction to several situations. Some students were told the infant was a boy; others were told the infant was a girl. When the infant showed a strong reaction to a jack-in-a-box, students were more likely to label the response as anger when the child was a "boy" and fear when the child was believed to be a "girl." Similar findings are obtained when subjects are asked to "imagine" an infant rather than viewing one, suggesting that differences are in the mind as well as the eye of the beholder.

Lastly, differences between males and females have news value; similarities between the sexes do not. Therefore, there tends to be a bias in reporting research: only statistically significant differences tend to get reported. Very few researchers weigh their results according to magnitude of difference between the sexes or to sample size or quality of the difference. Maccoby and Jacklin(1974) noted instances of direct pressure to keep results which do not agree with an accepted view out of published papers, reviews, and textbooks. Maccoby and Jacklin evaluated over 1600 published studies from January 1966 to Spring 1973. They listed a study as indicating a sex difference if the statistical analysis yielded a probability value of .05 or less. The difference was listed as a trend if the probability value was between .05 and .10. Statistical analyses yielding a probability value greater than .10 was listed as not revealing a sex difference. From their review, Maccoby and Jacklin listed only four well documented differences between males and females: males excel in visual-spatial ability and quantitative ability and they are more aggressive than females. Females excel in verbal ability.

In the section that follows, a discussion of these and other sex and gender similarities and differences will be presented. In this discussion, the interweaving of biological factors and cultural pressures on gender role typing will be highlighted.

PHYSIOLOGICAL SEX SIMILARITIES AND DIFFERENCES

Male Vulnerability. Males are more vulnerable to most every type of physical disease, environmental insult, and developmental difficulty. This greater male vulnerability holds true from conception to old age, and the death rate for American males is higher than that for females in every decade of life(Sherman, 1971). Approximately 140 males are conceived for every 100 females. By the end of the prenatal period however, there is a significant loss in male concepti: the ratio of males to females at birth is 105 to 100(Reinisch, Gandelman, & Spiegel, 1979). A higher proportion of males than females are spontaneously aborted (Bell, Weller, & Waldrop, 1971). The incidence of a variety of congenital defects, for example, anoxia (the lack of oxygen due to the infant's being slow to begin breathing) is greater among male infants. In addition, males are more vulnerable to childhood diseases. For example, pneumonia, influenza, measles, polio, diphtheria, and whooping cough occur significantly more often in males. Eight times as many boys die of pneumonia (Stott, 1966). Bayley(1966) noted that boys were more frequently affected (in terms of duration of ill effects and retardation of growth) than girls by the atomic bombing of Nagasaki and Hiroshima.

The finding that male fetuses are more vulnerable to problems during pregnancy and childbirth has been interpreted in one of two ways: (1) The basic pattern of fetal development is female. Males have to undergo an additional process during gestation and this change from a female to a male pattern of differentiation increases the likelihood that some process will go wrong, and (2) females have additional genetic protection with respect to any aspect of development affected by a gene on the X chromosome since they have two X chromosomes while males have one.

Throughout the elementary school years, boys are overrepresented among children who have speech, behavior, and learning disorders. Approximately twice as many boys as girls exhibit articulatory errors; three times as many boys as girls stutter(Bentzen, 1963). In addition, the incidence of reading problems is almost five times more prevalent in boys than in girls(Knopf, 1979). Mental retardation is also higher among males than females: 1.3

to 1 for mild retardation; 2 to 1 for severe retardation. Furthermore, more male than female children have autism, hyperactivity, enuresis, and nightmares (Knopf, 1979). The ratio of boys to girls who are referred to mental health practitioners for behavior or emotional problems is 2 to 1. This pattern continues throughout adolescence and adulthood: males have a higher rate of schizophrenia, delinquency, suicide, and academic underachievement.

Physical Size. Female infants are more mature at birth than are males. One basis for this maturation rate is the finding that girls' bones are farther along in the hardening process at birth(Flory, 1936). Researchers have also looked for sex differences in the maturity of the nervous system at birth. Witelson and Pallie(1973), for example, examined the brains of ten infants who died at birth. They found that the temporal planum was larger in the left cerebral hemisphere than the right, as is true in adults. This difference reflects the specialization of the left side of the brain for linguistic functions. Witelson and Pallie found the size discrepancy in *both* male and female infants in about the same degree. Their results therefore suggest that no pronounced sex difference exists in the readiness of the neonate's brain for language acquisition.

Females mature between two and two-and-a-half years faster than males. Their skeletal development at birth is approximately one month ahead of males. At adolescence, girls' development is three years in advance of boys': they reach puberty sooner. Height remains equal for both boys and girls until age seven, when girls become taller than boys. This difference reverses at age ten: boys become taller. As a group, males are stronger and heavier than females after puberty. The greater height and weight of males gives them an advantage in sports and occupational activities which require weight, height, and physical strength. In many cultures, however, girls and women do heavy physical labor (e.g., carry plows in their hands, heavy baskets on their heads).

Many of the physiological systems develop at the same rate in boys and girls. For example, no consistent differences have been observed in the average age of onset of certain developmental tasks: eruption of teeth, walking, sitting up, or thumb-and-forefinger grasping(Bayley, 1965).

The issue of sex differences in maturation rate has implications for educational policy. For example, given the research that indicates that girls mature faster, should they be allowed to begin elementary school at an earlier age? It is important to recognize that rates of growth of various functions may be independent. Bayley (1956) pointed out that the rate of growth of stature was unrelated to the rate of intellectual development. Therefore, the fact that girls' bones solidify faster than boys' bones gives no indication about their readiness for school.

There is evidence to suggest however, that early maturational differences may produce effects that are evident long after the maturational differences have disappeared. For example, sex-related differences in infant irritability may later contribute to a parent-child relationships pattern that would result in girls being less aggressive and resistive than boys.

INTERPERSONAL BEHAVIOR AND TEMPERAMENT

Activity Level. Boys have a higher basal metabolism rate than girls. Boys, however, do not necessarily have more surplus energy to expend. Boys may need additional food to sustain their level of activity.

During infancy, males spend more time awake than do females. Throughout their first three years of life boys and girls appear to be about equally active. Jacklin and Maccoby(1978) observed children in their homes and laboratory playrooms in order to get a record of the distance they cover in the course of their play, amount of squirming while getting dressed, and the amount of splashing and movement while being bathed. Results consistently show differences in activity level for individual toddlers, however, the differences are very seldom significantly related to the child's sex. Both boys and girls are more active when playing on trampolines, swings, and jungle-gyms than while playing with crayons or blocks.

Dependency. "Dependence" is a rather complex term to translate into operational terms that can be measured. Researchers have used the following as definitions of dependence: amount of touching and/or eye contact between children and their mothers, the amount of acting-up a child does to attract adult attention; compliance; and the amount of assistance requested from an adult. During the preschool age, there are no differences between boys and girls in proximity, touching, or resistance to separation from parents or other adults.

Goldberg and Lewis (1969) concluded that prolonged physical contact between children and their parents may lessen children's drive to explore, master their environment, and become independent. Mothers in their study did not treat male and female babies alike. Mothers of twelve-week-old girls looked at and talked to their infants more than did mothers of boys. Boys, however, received more hugs and touches. At six months of age, however, the reverse was true. Girls received more verbal and visual attention and physical contact. Lewis (1972) described mothers as granting their infant boys a three month grace period, followed by expecting their sons to become less dependent.

Neither boys nor girls are more likely to choose to be with others rather than alone during stressful situations. There is no evidence to suggest that boys are more susceptible to peer compliance and conformity than girls.

Fear and Anxiety. No difference between male and female children has been observed in their response to fearful stimuli and test anxiety. Boys and girls react similarly when their parents leave the room, and they cry equally often. When self-report measures and teachers' ratings are obtained, however, girls tend to be more fearful than boys. It appears that the conflicting results can be attributed to girls being more willing than boys (who are under pressure not be "sissies") to admit anxiety and fear.

Nurturance. It is commonly believed that females at all ages are warm, cheerful, and helpful toward other people. These qualities are supposed to equip females for future social roles of babysitter, wife, and mother. In actuality, there are very few studies concerning nurturant behavior in children. In addition, there is little research on the responses of adult men to children. Even in cultures where women's participation in the labor force is required and/or encouraged (e.g., the Israeli Kibbutzim, Soviet Union, China, Sweden), childcare is provided in facilities almost exclusively staffed by women. Among American children, no differences have been observed between males and females in nurturant and altruistic behavior. Whiting and Edwards (1973) collected data on children's nurturant behavior in six cultures: Kenya, Okinawa, India, the Philippines, Mexico, and the United States (New England). No sex difference in nurturance was observed in children aged three to six. However, seven-year-old girls often helped and gave emotional support to others more than did boys. This difference was obtained when the observational data was combined from all six cultures. Within each culture, however, girls and boys did not differ in nurturance or helpfulness.

Aggression. Aggression is usually defined as one individual's intention to hurt another for its own sake or for the desire to control this person. Maccoby and Jacklin(1974) reported that in every culture in which males and females differ in aggressiveness, males are the more aggressive. Males of all ages engage in more physical aggression, verbal aggression, play aggression, and fantasy aggression. This difference between males and females appears as soon as children begin to play with each other (approximately two to three years); it continues through adulthood(Wolman, 1978). Girls are not submissive. They do not withdraw or yield under attack. Furthermore, the victims of male aggression among children are usually boys.

Compliance. Girls, preschool age or younger, tend to comply more frequently and sooner to adults' requests and demands than boys. There is no difference between boys and girls, however, in compliance to pressure from peers who try to dominate them.

Dominance. In children's playgroups, dominance is associated with "toughness" for boys and girls. "Tough" boys dominate other boys and girls. Boys appear to make more attempts at dominance than girls do in same-sex playgroups. Fights occur most often between two children who have not settled the issue of who is dominant (Strayer, 1977). Boys try to dominate adults more than girls do. Whiting and Whiting (1973; 1975) defined the term "egoistic dominance" as the dominance interactions in which pressure is exerted on another individual for the actor's benefit, not for the target's benefit. In five out of six cultures the Whitings studied, boys exhibited more egoistic dominance than girls. Edwards and Whiting (1977) also observed more egoistic dominance from boys in African villages. Girls exhibited more attempts to control another child's behavior for safety.

Relationships with Parents. Observations of children in a variety of situations suggest that differences exist in the quality of boys' and girls' interactions with both parents. For example, boys are more resistive than girls to the teaching and training efforts of their parents. Boys are also more likely than girls to make counter-demands and demand their mother's attention. This difference has been observed in children as young as ten months of age. Observations of children in their own homes indicate that one- or two-year-old boys engage in activities forbidden by parents: climbing on furniture, pulling at curtains, touching dangerous and fragile objects (Minton, Kagan, & Levine, 1971; Smith & Daglish, 1977) more than girls.

Intercultural comparisons also suggest differences between boys and girls in their orientation toward parents. Edwards and Whiting(1977) found girls in African cultures to be more likely than boys to approach their mothers sociably, wanting to play with them, and offering to help them. Boys, on the other hand, approached their mothers with egoistic demands. In summary, the relationship between mothers and sons was more likely to focus on disciplinary issues; the interaction between mothers and daughters took the form of shared activities.

Researchers (e.g., Rutter, 1970) have observed that boys' and girls' relationships with their parents change in different ways when the family is under stress. Girls show delayed effects during their adolescence (e.g., shyness); in childhood, boys become hard to control under family stress, such as divorce by developing coercive cycles with their parents.

COGNITIVE ABILITY AND ACHIEVEMENT

Verbal Ability. From the initial establishment of speech until puberty, boys and girls perform quite similarly in verbal ability. This includes combining words into sentences, picture vocabulary, and mean length of utterance. Until puberty, girls perform better than boys only in underprivileged populations. After puberty, girls excel in productive and receptive language, comprehension of written material, logical relations, verbal creativity, grammar, punctuation, and spelling. This superiority continues through adulthood.

Quantitative Ability. Young children do not differ in quantitative ability. Early school-aged girls and boys are equally able to understand numerical concepts and operations. In studies with disadvantaged children, girls perform better than boys. At puberty, however, boys begin to outperform girls in quantitative skills. Boys take more math courses than girls do. In addition, boys score higher on mathematical aptitutde and achievement tests. This superiority is maintained throughout adulthood. More girls than boys are "math anxious"; they worry about mastering quantitative concepts and seeming unfeminine if they do (Tobias, 1976).

Creativity. Creativity is usually defined as the ability to produce novel and unique ideas. On creativity tests which involve a degree of verbal fluency, girls seven years of age and older perform better than their male peers. However, on nonverbal tests of creativity, neither sex does better than the other.

Visual-Spatial Ability. Spatial ability is a difficult concept to define; it has been measured in several ways. In visual spatial abilities measured by tasks unrelated to analytic processes, males outperform females only after puberty. Until age eight, no differences have been observed. From ages eight to puberty, inconsistent results have been obtained. No differences between boys and girls have been found in studies that deal with nonvisual spatial ability.

On tests of disembedding (e.g., *Embedded Figures Test; Rod and Frame Test*), there is no consistent trend in performance in early childhood. Male superiority emerges at puberty and continues into adulthood. However, males do not do better than females on nonvisual tasks that require disembedding, for example an auditory disembedding test that requires them to attend to one voice and block out another (reported in Maccoby & Jacklin, 1974).

Learning and Memory. No differences between boys and girls have been observed in a variety of learning processes: paired-associates learning, conditioning, probability learning, learning through imitation, discrimination learning with reversal or non-reversal shifts. Furthermore, neither boys nor girls has a superior memory capacity or superior ability in the storage or retrieval of material.

Achievement Motivation. When achievement motivation is measured by grades in school, girls (and also women) have a higher achievement motive than boys (and men) since they get better grades. When achievement motivation is assessed projectively, differences between males and females are common. For example, females show a high level of achievement whether in an "achievement arousal" condition or not. Males, on the other hand, exhibit a high achievement motive when aroused by reference to their aptitude for intelligence and leadership. Girls are no more likely than boys to achieve in order to reach social goals, such as approval. Furthermore, research on the "fear of success" component of achievement motivation does not indicate that young girls are more fearful in this way(Jackaway, 1974; Paludi & Fankell-Hauser, 1984; Romer, 1975).

Self-Concept. There is no evidence to suggest that girls have a lower self-concept and self-esteem than boys. It is true however, that girls (and women) are less confident about their ability to perform well on intellectual tasks. Girls are also more likely to attribute their successes (especially on "masculine" tasks) to luck whereas boys explain their achievements by ability(Etaugh & Ropp, 1976; Paludi, Hrabowy, Johnson, & McNeer, 1984). Girls are more likely to attribute their failure to lack of ability whereas boys attribute failure to external causes (e.g., poor teacher; unfair test).

In addition, boys are more defensive about their performances; girls, however, disclose their weaknesses. In self-report measures, middle-childhood aged boys see themselves as higher on dominance, power, and strength than girls see themselves. Girls are more likely to see their positive qualities in prosocial interpersonal skills(e.g., cooperativeness). Thus, boys and girls have a more favorable self-concept in their own arena; their overall self-esteem is similar.

STABILITY OF SEX AND
GENDER SIMILARITIES AND DIFFERENCES

In their longitudinal Fels Institute Study, Kagan and Moss(1962) reported that children's gender role typing was predictive of adult behavior when the childhood behavior was congruent with culturally-determined standards for males and females. Thus, childhood aggression was predictive of adult aggression for men, but not for women. Similarly, childhood dependency was predictive of this adult behavior in women, but not in men. When childhood behaviors conflicted with role standards, more socially appropriate behavior was substituted in adulthood. For example, tantrums and aggression in girls were associated with intellectual competitiveness in women; passivity and dependence in boys were correlated with noncompetitiveness and social apprehension in men.

SUMMARY

From this review, it can be seen that several aspects of cognitive and personality processes of boys and girls are quite alike. When discrepancies are noted, they are usually small and based on average group behavior. Boys and girls and men and women overlap in personality traits and abilities, as they overlap in physical attributes. Many girls delight in aggressive games, and many boys prefer verbal games and activities (e.g., crossword puzzles). Many individual girls prove difficult for their parents to control; many individual boys are easy-going. The differences between boys and girls are fewer and less dramatic than most parents and teachers believe.

A chronological summary of sex and gender similarities and differences based on Maccoby and Jacklin's (1974) review is presented in Appendix A. Well documented differences between males and females include the following: males are more aggressive than females; males excel in quantitative and visual-spatial ability; females excel in verbal ability. Research has been inadequate to test whether or not there are differences in activity level, fear, dominance, compliance, and nurturance. In several areas of functioning there are clearly no differences between boys and girls: self-esteem, achievement motivation, memory. Furthermore, most differences between males and females are not consistently observed until late childhood and puberty. Block(1978) has criticized Maccoby and Jacklin for being overly conservative in their compilation of the research. Block argued that there are more differences between boys and girls than Maccoby and Jacklin noted. These differences may likely emerge in the characteristics lacking any consistent results to date (e.g., compliance, nurturance).

The fact that there are more similarities between boys and girls than there are differences should not imply that being a male is no different from being a female. Girls and women see the world differently from boys and men. They make different decisions and have different experiences. They perceive situations differently. From a fairly young age, boys and girls prefer different toys, television programs, and books. Girls report on paper-and-pencil personality measures that they think of themselves as different from boys. This may set the stage for a self-fulfilling prophecy: when girls think they are different from boys, in some ways they may actually be different.

Where do children's perceptions of masculinity and femininity come from? There is no one-to-one correspondence between perceptions and actual behavior. If so, how do these perceptions continue to persist? And, what are the origins of the well documented differences between boys and girls? The factors which influence the development of perceptions of masculinity and femininity and sex differentiation will be explored in the next section. Specifically, three major classes of factors will be discussed: hormonal, social, and cognitive.

FACTORS INFLUENCING CHILDREN'S ACQUISITION OF A GENDER-ROLE IDENTITY

Hormonal

The sex hormones appear to be critical during two phases of development: the prenatal and the pubertal phases(Petersen, 1979). During the prenatal period, there is a point at which the male embryo receives increased androgen (male hormone). This increase is what produces the development of male physical characteristics. If androgen is not present during this phase, the fetus develops as a female, despite it being genetically *XY.* Similarly, a genetically female fetus (*XX*) may develop into a physical male if androgen is added during this critical phase(Money, 1971). Thus, prenatal hormone differences can explain physical differences between boys and girls. Can it account for any cognitive or personality characteristic? The answer is "yes" with respect to aggression (Phoenix, Goy, & Resko, 1969). Male hormones administered prenatally to genetically female monkeys and other primates lead to more aggression and rough-and-tumble play. Similar results have been noted with humans. Ehrhardt and Money (1967) and Ehrhardt and Baker(1974) studied girls with adrenogenital syndrome (Note 1). These girls are typically born with masculinized external genitalia which range from an enlarged clitoris to the presence of a penis and an empty scrotum. These are corrected surgically and girls have to receive continued cortisone therapy after birth. If these girls are not treated with the hormone, they will exhibit further masculinization at puberty: lowered voice and facial hair. No development of the breasts is present; menstruation and ovulation do not occur.

Compared with normal girls, adrenogenital syndrome girls consider themselves, and are rated by others, as more aggressive, less interested in playing with dolls and more interested in playing with boys, not girls (Ehrhardt & Baker, 1974). There is no evidence to suggest that these girls have more advanced cognitive skills than normal girls, however.

There is some indication that prenatal exposure to excess estrogen may negatively influence visual-spatial skills and positively affect verbal skills in males with an androgen insensitivity syndrome (Note 2) and male pseudohermaphrodites (Note 3). Furthermore, Dalton (1968) found that pregnant women who had been exposed to prenatal progesterone was positively related with the children's school performance and to teachers' ratings of performance in mathematics, English, and verbal reasoning.

Petersen (1979) argued that at some critical prenatal period, appropriate levels of hormones set potentials for hemispheric specialization. Hormone levels are activated at puberty and produce the stereotypic male who is better at visual-spatial relations and the female who excels in verbal skills. Petersen proposed that more mature boys and girls would be better at spatial abilities than verbal skills; would be androgenized in physical appearance and have right-hemispheric dominance. Furthermore, boys and girls better at verbal skills would appear physically to be more masculine and feminine and have left-hemispheric dominance. The strength of this predisposition would vary from child to child, depending on social experiences.

Social Influences.

Parents. Systematic attempts to communicate sex-typed behaviors in boys and girls begin in earliest infancy. Rubin, Provenzano, and Luria(1974) interviewed the parents of 15 newborn boys and 15 newborn girls within the first 24 hours of birth. Although male and female babies did not differ in birth weight, length, or Apgar neonatal activity scores, daughters were significantly more likely than sons to be described as little, beautiful, cute, weak, and petite. Sons were characterized as firm, larger-featured, alert, strong, and hardy. Fathers made more extreme and stereotyped judgments of their newborns than did mothers. Fathers' descriptions were based only on their viewing their child through a display window in the hospital nursery, mothers had held and fed the neonates.

Parents of older children report that boys and girls have distinct personalities. For example, Canadian parents interviewed by Lambert, Yackley, and Hein(1971) said that boys were rougher, more active, noisier, more mechanically minded, more competitive, and more likely to defend themselves than girls. Parents said girls were cleaner and neater, more reserved, quieter, better mannered, more likely to cry, and more helpful at home.

Do parents act on their attitudes? Pressures on boys and girls to act in certain ways are unequal. More flexibility is granted to girls. There is less pressure for girls than boys to conform to sex-appropriate standards: "tomboys" are tolerated; "sissies" rejected. Almost all parents encourage some sex-typed behavior in their children. For example, parents buy more trucks than dolls for boys and more dolls than trucks for girls.

Will, Self, and Datan(1976) asked mothers of infants to play with a six-month-old child to determine which of three toys—a doll, a train, or a fish—the mothers would offer to the child. In some conditions, the child was introduced as "Adam" and wore blue pants. To other mothers the child was named "Beth" and wore a pink dress. Although mothers reported that they did not perceive any differences between boys and girls at six months old, they were sex-typed in their toy choices for the baby. The women who thought the child was a girl most often offered "her" a doll to play with. Women who believed the child was a boy frequently offered "him" a train. Women also smiled more when they thought they were holding a girl. Mothers did not seem to be aware of this differential treatment.

Seavey, Katz, and Zalk's(1975) results also attest to the differential responses made by adults to boys and girls. Nonparents also interact differentially in terms of toy choice and physical handling, with the same infant as a function of the sex label used or its absence (Rytting & Carr, 1978).

Rebelsky and Hanks(1971) found parents interacted more with male rather than female infants. In addition, consistent trends have been found in what parents respond to in their children. Both mothers and fathers respond more frequently to large muscle movements in boys than in girls(Moss, 1967). Furthermore, girls are treated as though they are more fragile than boys(Minton, Kagan, & Levine, 1971). Parents are also more apprehensive about girls' well being than about that of boys(Pederson & Robson, 1969). Boys are handled more roughly than girls and are more commonly engaged in aggressive play (Yarrow, Rubenstein, & Pedersen, 1971).

Parents are concerned that their sons prefer appropriate sex-typed activities. Lansky(1967) asked parents of preschool and kindergarten children a series of hypothetical questions, such as "if a boy had a choice between playing with a toy shaving kit and playing with a toy cosmetic kit, how would his father feel if his son wanted to play with the toy shaving kit?" Mothers and fathers both responded more negatively to opposite-sex choices by boys than by girls. Most parents were neutral about opposite-sex choices in girls.

Fling and Manosevitz(1972) asked parents a similar set of questions about activities they thought appropriate, encouraged, or discouraged for their son or daughter. They observed that both mothers and fathers were more concerned about cross-sex choices for their sons than for their daughters. Furthermore, fathers were more likely to encourage "appropriate" gender-role choices in their sons, whereas mothers were more likely to encourage "appropriate" choices in daughters. Thus, each parent was primarily concerned with the appropriate preferences of the same-sex child and both parents were concerned about inappropriate choices expressed by their son.

Hartley (1959) hypothesized that gender-role identity for boys is seldom defined positively as something the boy should do, but more often negatively as something he should not do, and that these negative sanctions are frequently enforced by punishment. It has even been concluded that the basic developmental task of girls is learning how not to be a baby, and the basic developmental task of boys is learning how not to be a girl(Emmerich, 1959). Lynn(1969) argued that an additional difficulty in boys' development of a masculine gender role identity is the necessary shift from their initial identification with their mother to identification with their father. This transition together with the greater demands for conformity and harsher prohibitions used in gender role training of boys makes the acquisition of an identity more stressful for boys than for girls. Hartley(1959) indicated that eight-to-eleven-year-old boys expressed great anxiety about maintaining the masculine role. Their anxiety verged on panic at being "caught" in the performance of "feminine" activities. This apprehension was not expressed by girls. These behaviors are extremely widespread and have apparently not changed significantly despite the re-evaluation of gender roles now taking place in many segments of society(Paludi, Geschke, Smith, & Strayer, in press).

Father Absence. A significant variable in the study of parental socialization effects on the child's acquisition of a gender role identity is father absence. In most research on father-absence, the father was away at war or absent due to occupational demands, divorce, or death. Hetherington(1966) and McCord, McCord, and Thurber(1962) investigated father absence due to separation, desertion, and divorce. These studies indicated that some disruption in acquiring a masculine identity existed in these boys. They tended to be less aggressive in doll play situations, have father fantasies similar to girls and are more dependent than boys whose fathers are living in the home. Boys deprived of the influence of their fathers develop "compensatory masculinity," which involves both masculine and feminine behaviors exhibited in an inconsistent manner. These sex(gender)-role problems are more severe if the separation occurred at or before the age of five.

In girls, some cognitive deficits have been reported, as have difficulties in male-female relationships(Hetherington, 1972). These latter disturbances appeared as either excessive sexual anxiety and shyness or promiscuous sexual behavior and inappropriately aggressive behavior with male peers. The former of these patterns was more often characteristic of girls whose fathers had died. The latter pattern described girls whose parents were divorced. Therefore, both groups of father-absent girls experienced general anxiety in their relationships with men; they adopted different strategies for coping with the anxiety. Hetherington also found that these girls had little if any chance to resolve some negative feelings toward their fathers and later projected them unto their husbands.

Maternal Employment. Maternal employment influences children's perception of gender roles. When both parents are employed outside the home, their roles may be perceived as quite similar. In addition to the maternal employment, the father may take part in childrearing and household tasks. Banducci(1967), Nye and Hoffman(1963) and Stein(1973) found maternal employment to be related to higher educational and occupational goals in children. Daughters of working mothers also perceived woman's role as involving freedom of choice and satisfaction. Moreover, these girls had higher self-esteem and wished to combine a family and career life after marriage(Baruch, 1972). Achievement striving was also likely to be characteristic of women whose parents reinforced and encouraged achievement efforts and who were reared in a dual-career family. These women viewed their relationship with their parents as closer, warmer, more sharing, and more supportive than other women(Hennig & Jardim, 1977; Paludi & Fankell-Hauser, 1984).

Sons of employed mothers perceive a smaller difference between women and men in terms of warmth and expressiveness than do sons of unemployed mothers(Broverman, Vogel, Broverman, Clarkson, & Rosenkrantz, 1972). This finding, in conjunction with the research cited earlier suggest that the stereotypic conceptions of gender roles are not immutable.

Teachers. Serbin and O'Leary(1975) trained experimenters to record exactly how and when preschool teachers spoke to the children. Their results indicated that teachers rewarded the boys for being aggressive. Teachers responded over three times as often to boys who misbehaved as to girls who misbehaved. When teachers reprimanded girls, it was briefly, softly, and out of other children's hearing. When they scolded the boys, however, it was loud and called attention to the boys' naughtiness. The loud reprimands inspired the boys to be more disruptive.

In addition, teachers reinforced girls for being dependent. They responded more often to girls when they were nearby than when they were farther away. In contrast, teachers encouraged the boys to do independent work. Teachers paid more attention to boys. Boys were twice as likely as girls to get tangible rewards for academic work.

Serbin and O'Leary argued that the teachers' encouragement of boys' aggressiveness explains why more boys than girls have reading problems: boys' rowdiness prevents them from paying attention when they should. Girls, who are praised for remaining close to their teachers, learn more easily to read, but not to solve problems independently.

Teachers in Serbin and O'Leary's study were not aware that they were treating girls and boys differently. Neither were the personnel at a nursery school Joffe(1974) observed. Although teachers reported having an egalitarian philosophy toward children, they perpetuated stereotypic differences between the sexes. For example, the teachers and the mothers who assisted them complimented girls when they wore dresses, not when they wore pants. They seldom complimented the boys on their apparel. However, boys were praised for defending themselves in a fight, despite the fact the school had a rule against fighting.

Lee and Gropper(1974) concluded that teachers prefer both boys and girls to be conforming, orderly, and dependent. Boys, therefore, have pressure upon them to accomodate to a pupil role which is in conflict with their own gender role. Girls have pressure on them not to deviate from their own role.

Children see their female teachers performing their tasks in an achievement oriented and competent manner. Therefore the gender role stereotyping obvious in teachers' behavior is full of mixed messages about appropriate behavior for males and females. In recent years, there has been some evidence to suggest that male teachers have a positive effect on boys in their classes, with no negative one on girls. For example, Lee and Wolinsky(1973) observed that boys liked male teachers better than female teachers. There is some intercultural evidence to suggest that the high incidence of reading problems among boys is reduced by having male teachers. It is believed that male teachers reinforce the idea that learning is male-appropriate. In Japan, for example, reading problems are distributed equally between girls and boys(Janis, Mahl, Kagan, & Holt, 1969). In Germany, boys excel in reading (Preston, 1962). This finding has been replicated in the United States(Shinedling & Pederson, 1970) and in England(Brimer, 1969) when boys are being taught by male teachers.

Guttentag and Bray(1976) designed a non-sexist school curriculum for kindergarteners, fifth, and ninth graders. For six weeks, children read stories, saw movies, acted out plays, and wrote book reports on equality between males and females. Women and men from a variety of occupations gave presentations to the classes about their career and family life. Guttentag and Bray also taught the teachers to be aware of subtle forms of differential treatment. Unfortunately, the non-sexist curriculum failed. Most boys became more rigid and stereotyped in their views of women and women's place. More girls than boys accepted the egalitarian attitudes. Furthermore, most of the teachers were not enthusiastic about changing students' attitudes about masculinity and femininity.

Children's Books. Books for preschool children, grammar-school readers, and textbooks in science and social studies are primarily populated by males. *Women on Words and Images*(1972) surveyed 134 children's readers from fourteen publishers. Their study found that boys and men in the readers monopolized highly valued traits: bravery, achievement, curiosity, perseverance. Girls and women were portrayed as fearful, incompetent, and easily excitable in a minor crisis. Girls and women were most often shown at home rather than at work or outdoors. When females were involved in the story, most things happened to them as a result of chance; factors outside of their control. Males' own actions contributed to their good fortune. This finding is consistent with the increasing external locus of control noted for females. The differential treatment of males and females in children's readers becomes more stronger through the school years(Saario, Jacklin, & Tittle, 1973).

Publishers report a variety of explanations for the portrayals of males and females in their books. A common explanation is that the books describe reality; that females live more routine, less adventurous lives than males. This clearly ignores the statistics which indicate that more than half of all women with pre-school age children work outside the home. Another explanation surrounds the belief that because boys are surrounded by females (mothers and teachers), they do not have good male role models. In addition, because boys have a more difficult time learning how to read, they need some additional motivation of seeing themselves in adventurous situations. Whatever the explanation, the fact remains that active, competent, achievement-oriented male models do not have to exist at the expense of active, competent, achievement-oriented females. An annotated list of non-sexist children's stories and books is presented in Appendix B.

Television. In a representative study, Sternglanz and Serbin (1974) viewed and analyzed gender roles in children's shows. Their results indicated that children's programs present disproportionate numbers of male and female actors with a stereotyped repertoire of activities and occupations. Males were typically shown being rewarded for engaging in exciting, behaviors; females were ignored.

Streicher(1974) content analyzed cartoons and found that females were less numerous, played fewer lead roles, made fewer appearances, and had fewer lines than males. Furthermore, female characters held fewer positions of responsibility; were portrayed as less skillful, less active, more babylike.

Vogal(1970) and Bernabei(1974) found little difference between commercial and public broadcasting networks in their portrayal of males and females. Even Sesame Street had a sex-ratio problem. Vogal reported a 2:1 male to female ratio in the roles on the educational program. A few years later, after protest from feminist groups, the ratio had risen to 2.5:1. When animated characters are added to these statistics, the male to female ratio would be even higher.

Cognitive

During childhood, when some differences in behavior between males and females appear, children are beginning to form concepts about their own identity: their sense of being an individual of a given sex and the understanding of the implications of this fact. A complete understanding of what it means to be a boy or a girl occurs gradually. Children refer to themselves as boys or girls without comprehending that these labels imply belonging to a group who share the label and that the labels are permanent attributes. Most young children believe the sex of an individual would change if the person's hair, clothes, and activities were transformed. Children achieve sex constancy by the time they are seven years old. Emmerich, Goldman, Kirsh, and Sharabany(1976) drew an analogy between sex constancy and the conservation of size, weight, and quantity. They believe that sex constancy is achieved with other types of conservation as part of the transition from Piaget's (1952) preoperational to the concrete operational stage of thinking. Therefore, cognitive maturity has much to do with children understanding that a person's sex remains the same despite transformations in hair, clothes, or other physical attributes.

Developmental patterns of a gender role identity differ for boys and girls. For example, when asked what sex they would like to be, a majority of children from as young as three years state a preference for their own sex(Abel & Sahinkaya, 1962; Parsons, cited in Frieze, Parsons, Johnson, Ruble, & Zellman, 1978). But girls are more likely to express a desire to be boys than boys to be girls. In addition, while children of both sexes prefer interacting with same-sex peers, girls are more likely to report friendships with boys than vice versa(Fagot & Patterson, 1969; Kohlberg & Zigler, 1967). Ferguson and Maccoby(1966) observed that at the age of ten boys preferred the activities associated with their own gender role more than did girls. Bem and Lenney's(1976) research suggests that the greater preference by males for sex-appropriate activities continues into college age. Their male subjects chose "masculine" over "feminine" activities even when they were told they would be paid more for performing feminine activities.

Such findings, in conjunction with earlier ones reported by

DeLucia (1963), Hartup and Zook (1960) and Rabban (1950) suggest that both boys and girls are stereotyped at nursery school age, and beginning at age four boys become increasingly more gender typed than girls. Boys typically select "masculine" jobs such as police officer, scientist, cowboy, while girls choose nurturant, traditionally "feminine" occupations such as nurse or secretary (Beuf, 1974, Garrett, Ein, & Tremaine, 1977). Boys are more likely to avoid sex-inappropriate activities and prefer sex-appropriate ones.

One explanation of these results is that girls perceive Western culture to be male-oriented, with greater esteem, privileges, and status accorded to the masculine role. Children form stereotypes to help them understand their world. Stereotypes along the dimensions of prestige, power, strength, competence, and size are among the earliest to develop (Kohlberg, 1966). Since cultural ideologies attribute to men a greater amount of these valued characteristics, it is not surprising that girls are more ambivalent than boys about their gender-role identity.

In addition, children attach positive and negative values to perceptual cues. Children express an unmistakable preference for large things. It is difficult to convince a three-or-four-year-old child that the biggest present is not always the best present. This may predispose children to attribute greater power and status to men. Therefore, differences between men and women in height and strength may underlie the greater valuing of males than females (Kohlberg, 1966). For children, as well as adults, height is associated with physical attractiveness, perceived power, and actual occupancy of positions of power (Frieze, Parsons, Johnson, Ruble, & Zellman, 1978). This tendency to associate value with size might set the stage for children's universal conclusion that men are better than women, and therefore what men do is better than what women do.

CONCLUDING REMARKS: IS ANDROGYNY THE ANSWER?

The explanations for the observed differences between boys and girls are more complex than may be initially apparent. From the brief overview of factors contributing to the observable differences, the analysis is not as simple as "boys are this way" and "girls are that way." Some of the differences have biological origins which are then accentuated by a variety of social influences: the media, educational system, and parents. Biological factors and behavior interact. Therefore, a child's sex is not only a biological fact, it is a social fact as well. People react in specific ways that depend on a child's sex. Rubin, Provenzano, and Luria (1974) have shown that stereotypes even influence adults' perceptions of newborn infants. Parents provide distinctive or "canalized" environments for boys and girls. This runs the gamut from buying the children distinctive toys and clothes to decorating the child's room differently (Rheingold & Cook, 1975). Gender-role information from children's teachers, books, and television is also high stereotypic.

Boys develop a masculine gender-role identity earlier and more consistently than girls develop a feminine identity. Furthermore, gender-appropriate behaviors are more narrowly defined for boys than for girls. However, the masculine role commands a higher status in this culture. Hence, perceived higher status may encourage boys to gender-appropriate toys and activities so as to be perceived as more attractive. This may also influence girls toward preferring some masculine activities as well. Thus, not only are there consistent and persistent cultural stereotypes related to boys and girls, these stereotypes are systematically biased in favor of boys; masculine qualities are more highly valued than are feminine ones. These stereotypes begin very early, as early as preschool age (Paludi, Geschke, Smith, & Strayer, in press). The information children receive from the socialization agents is consistent and highly stereotyped through puberty.

Maccoby and Jacklin (1974) suggest that children begin to incorporate these various stereotypes into their own cognitions of gender during the early years of childhood. Parents' and teachers' beliefs sometimes become self-fulfilling prophecies. By adolescence, differences in the behavior of boys and girls are noticeable. This contributes to the difficulty in separating actual differences from stereotype or cultural myth.

Stereotypes about male/female differences in behavior however, are not highly correlated with children's actual behavior. Stereotypes do not accurately reflect social reality. They are representations of cultural inventions which are woven around biological facts. In actuality, girls are more competent than the stereotype implies and boys are more expressive and nurturant than the stereotype suggests. The stereotypes do affect behavior in important ways. For example, children (as well as adults) rate stories presumably written by male authors as better written and more valuable than the identical stories with a female author's name (Etaugh & Rose, 1975; Paludi & Strayer, 1983).

The constancy of individual children's maintaining gender role stereotypes is not very great (Mischel, 1966). A girl who plays at one moment with dolls is very likely to play with "sex neutral" or "masculine" activities the next time she is observed (Sears, Rau, & Alpert, 1965). As they mature, children's behavior increasingly depends on context. For example, adolescent males and females are both more likely to behave in sex-typed ways when on a date than when alone. Not all of the stereotypes constituting masculine and feminine behavior for children hold true for adults. There is no evidence to date to suggest that highly sex-typed children become highly sex-typed adults.

Currently, androgyny is being hailed as the exemplar for childrearing and teaching children. Androgyny implies an integration of positive masculine and feminine traits in a single person. Such individuals would be expected to be maximally effective in a wide range of situations because they would not be constrained by stereotypic masculine or feminine behaviors. Bem's (1975) research supports the effectiveness of adult androgynous individuals. Stein and Bailey (1973) confirmed a similar finding in children. They argued that androgynous children were high in achievement and creativity. These children expanded their behavioral repertoire so as to include personality and cognitive characteristics of both sexes.

Similar results were obtained with children who are undifferentiated (possessing neither weak nor strong masculine or feminine traits). However, it should be remembered that there are many psychometric constraints in the measurement of various aspects of children's gender identity. Therefore it is unclear whether children's superior achievement and creativity are attributed to their androgynous or undifferentiated personalities or are simply artifacts of the measuring instruments (Nash, 1979).

Moreover, cultural lag is an important contributor to the dilemma of what is actually being measured by tests of children's acceptance of masculinity and femininity. For example, responses given to the *IT Scale for Children* by Brown's (1956b) normative sample in the 1950s may have reflected, in part, actual differences in preferences at that time. It is evident that item content does interact in tests of masculinity and femininity. However, it is still unclear as to how to control for their effects (Constantinople, 1973).

It is also unclear as to the impact of androgyny on children's interpersonal relations. Being highly sex-typed is related to popularity among peers. Moreover, it is an important aspect of self-esteem. The question remains to be answered whether androgynous children would be able to maintain their status in the peer group and have a favorable self-concept.

Finally, androgynous childrearing and school curricula will not, by themselves, change the inequality between boys and girls. Androgyny should not be used as a substitute for social change. Instead of socializing children to exhibit both "masculine" and "feminine" behaviors, it would be to society's advantage to value *all* positive behaviors, regardless of their appropriateness for one sex or the other. Consequently, all children would be allowed flexibility in behaving, without incurring strong social sanctions.

REFERENCES

Abel, H., & Sahinkaya, R. (1962). Emergence of sex and race friendship preferences. *Child Development, 33,* 939–943.

Banducci, R. (1967). The effect of mother's employment on the achievement, aspirations, and expectations of the child. *Personnel and Guidance Journal, 46,* 263–267.

Barry, H., Bacon, M., & Child, I. L. (1957). A cross-cultural survey of some sex differences in socialization. *Journal of Abnormal and Social Psychology, 55,* 327–332.

Baruch, G. K. (1972). Maternal influences upon college women's attitudes toward women and work. *Developmental Psychology, 6,* 32–37.

Bayley, N. (1956). Individual patterns of development. *Child Development, 27,* 45–74.

Bayley, N. (1965). Comparisons of mental and motor test scores for ages 1–15 months by sex, birth order, race, geographical location, and education of parents. *Child Development, 36,* 380–411.

Bayley, N. (1966). Developmental problems of the mentally retarded child. In

I. Philips (Ed.), *Prevention and treatment of mental retardation* (pp. 85–110). New York: Basic Books.

Bell, R. Q., Weller, G. M., & Waldrop, M. F. (1971). Newborn and preschooler: Organization of behavior and relations between periods. *Monographs of the Society for Research in Child Development, 36*, (1–2, Serial No. 142).

Bem, S. L. (1974). The measurement of psychological androgyny. *Journal of Clinical and Consulting Psychology, 42*, 155–162.

Bem, S. L. (1975). Sex-role adaptability: One consequence of psychological androgyny. *Journal of Personality and Social Psychology, 31*, 634–643.

Bem, S. L., & Lenney, E. (1976). Sex typing and the avoidance of cross-sex behavior. *Journal of Personality and Social Psychology, 33*, 48–54.

Bentzen, F. (1963). Sex ratios in learning and behavior disorders. *American Journal of Orthopsychiatry, 33*, 92–98.

Bernabei, R. (1974). *Can you tell me how to get to Sesame Street?* Columbus, OH: Ohio State University.

Beuf, A. (1974). Doctor, lawyer, household drudge. *Journal of Communication, 24*, 142–145.

Block, J. H. (1978). Another look at sex differentiation in the socialization behaviors of mothers and fathers. In F. Wenmark & J. Sherman (Eds.), *Psychology of women: Future direction of research*. New York: Psychological Dimensions.

Brimer, M. A. (1969). Sex differences in listening comprehension. *Journal of Research and Development Education, 3*, 72–79.

Broverman, I. K., Vogel, S. R., Broverman, D. M., Clarkson, F. E., & Rosenkrantz, P. S. (1972). Sex-role stereotypes: A current appraisal. *Journal of Social Issues, 28*, 59–78.

Brown, D. G. (1956a). *The IT Scale for Children*. Missoula, MT: Psychological Test Specialists.

Brown, D. G. (1956b). Sex-role preference in young children. *Psychological Monographs, 70*, (14, Whole No. 421).

Condry, J., & Condry, S. (1976). Sex differences: A study in the eye of the beholder. *Child Development, 47*, 812–819.

Connor, J. M., & Serbin, L. A. (1977). Behaviorally based masculine and feminine activity preference scales for preschoolers: Correlates with other classroom behaviors and cognitive tests. *Child Development, 48*, 1411–1416.

Constantinople, A. (1973). Masculinity-femininity: An exception to a famous dictum? *Psychological Bulletin, 80*, 389–407.

Dalton, K. (1968). Ante-natal progesterone and intelligence. *British Journal of Psychiatry, 144*, 1377–1382.

Datta, L., & Drake, A. (1968). Examiner sex and sexual differentiation in preschool children's figure drawings. *Journal of Projective Techniques and Personality Assessment, 32*, 397–399.

DeLucia, L. (1963). The toy preference test: A measure of sex-role identification. *Child Development, 34*, 107–117.

Duvall, E. M. (1967). *Family development*. New York: Lippincott.

Edelbrock, C., & Sugawara, A. I. (1978). Acquisition of sex-typed preferences in preschool-aged children. *Developmental Psychology, 14*, 614–623.

Edwards, C. P., & Whiting, B. (1977). *Sex differences in children's social interaction.* Unpublished manuscript, Ford Foundation.

Ehrhardt, A. A., & Baker, S. W. (1974). Fetal androgens, human central nervous system differentiation and behavior sex differences. In R. C. Friedman, R. M. Richart, & R. L. Vande Wiele (Eds.), *Sex differences in behavior.* New York: Wiley.

Ehrhardt, A. A., & Money, J. (1967). Progestin-induced hermaphroditism: I.Q. and psychosexual identity in a study of ten girls. *Journal of Sex Research, 3*, 63–100.

Emmerich, W. (1959). Young children's discriminations of parent and child roles. *Child Development, 30*, 403–419.

Emmerich, W., Goldman, K. S., Kirsh, B., Sharabany, R. (1976). *Development of gender constancy in economically disadvantaged children.* Report of the Educational Testing Service, Princeton.

Etaugh, C., & Ropp, J. (1976). Children's self-evaluation of performance as a function of sex, age, feedback, and sex type task label. *The Journal of Psychology, 94*, 115–122.

Etaugh, C., & Rose, S. (1975). Adolescents' sex bias in the evaluation of performance. *Developmental Psychology, 11*, 663–664.

Fagot, B. I., & Patterson, G. R. (1969). An in vivo analysis of reinforcing contingencies for sex-role behaviors in the preschool child. *Developmental Psychology, 1*, 563–568.

Ferguson, L. R., & Maccoby, E. E. (1966). Interpersonal correlates of differential abilities. *Child Development, 37*, 549–571.

Fling, S., & Manosevitz, M. (1972). Sex-typing in nursery school children's play interests. *Developmental Psychology, 7*, 146–152.

Flory, C. D. (1936). Ossepus development in the hand as an index of skeletal development. *Monograph of the Society for Research in Child Development, 1*, (96–97).

Frieze, I. H., Parsons, J. E., Johnson, P. B., Ruble, D. N., & Zellman, G. L. (1978). *Women and sex roles: A social psychological perspective.* New York: W. W. Norton.

Garrett, C. S., Ein, P. L., & Tremaine, L. (1977). The development of gender stereotyping of adult occupations in elementary school children. *Child Development, 48*, 507–512.

Goldberg, S., & Lewis, M. (1964). Play behavior in the year-old infant: Early sex differences. *Child Development, 40*, 21–31.

Guttentag, M., & Bray, H. (1976). *Undoing sex stereotypes.* New York: McGraw-Hill.

Hartley, R. E. (1954). Children's concepts of male and female roles. *Merrill-Palmer Quarterly, 6*, 83–91.

Hartup, W. W., & Zook, E. A. (1960). Sex-role preferences in three-and-four-year-old children. *Journal of Consulting Psychology, 24*, 420–426.

Heinrich, P., & Triebe, J. K. (1972). Sex preferences in children's human figure drawings. *Journal of Personality Assessment, 36,* 263–267.

Hennig, M., & Jardim, A. (1977). *The managerial woman.* New York: Anchor/Doubleday.

Hetherington, E. M. (1966). Effects of paternal absence on sex-typed behaviors in Negro and White preadolescent males. *Journal of Personality and Social Psychology, 4,* 87–91.

Hetherington, E. M. (1972). Effects of father-absence on personality development in adolescent daughters. *Developmental Psychology, 7,* 313–326.

Jackaway, R. (1974). Sex differences in the development of fear of success. *Child Study Journal, 4,* 71–79.

Jacklin, C. N., & Maccoby, E. E. (1978). Social behavior at 33 months in same-sex and mixed-sex dyads. *Child Development, 49,* 557–569.

Janis, I. L., Mahl, G. F., Kagan, J., & Holt, R. R. (1969). *Personality: Dynamics, development, and assessment.* New York: Harcourt Brace Jovanovich.

Joffe, C. (1974). Sex role socialization and the nursery school: as the twig is bent. *Journal of Marriage and the Family, 42,* 353–358.

Kagan, J. (1964). Acquisition and significance of sex-typing and sex-role identity. In M. Hoffman & L. W. Hoffman (Eds.), *Review of child development research: Vol. 1,* (pp. 137–169). New York: Russell Sage.

Kagan, J., & Moss, H. A. (1962). *Birth to maturity: A study in psychological development.* New York: Wiley.

Knopf, I. J. (1979). *Childhood psychopathology.* Englewood Cliffs, NJ: Prentice Hall.

Kohlberg, L. A. (1966). A cognitive-developmental analysis of children's sex-role concepts and attitudes. In E. E. Maccoby (Ed.), *The development of sex differences.* Stanford, CA: Stanford University Press.

Kohlberg, L. A., & Zigler, E. (1967). The impact of cognitive maturity on the development of sex-role attitudes in the years 4 to 8. *Genetic Psychology Monographs, 75,* 89–165.

Lambert, W. E., Yackley, A., & Hein, R. N. (1971). Child training values of English Canadian and French Canadian parents. *Canadian Journal of Behavioral Science, 3,* 217–236.

Lansky, L. M. (1967). The family structure also affects the role model: Sex-role attitudes in parents of preschool children. *Merrill-Palmer Quarterly, 13,* 139–150.

Lee, P. C., & Gropper, N. B. (1974). Sex-role culture and educational practice. *Harvard Educational Review, 44,* 369–410.

Lee, P. C., & Wolinsky, A. L. (1973). Male teachers of young children. *Young Children, 28,* 342–353.

Lewis, M. (1972). Culture and gender roles: There's no unisex in the nursery. *Psychology Today, 5* (May), 54–57.

Lynn, D. B. (1959). A note on sex differentiation in the development of masculinity and femininity. *Psychological Review, 64,* 126–135.

Lynn, D. B. (1969). *Parental and sex-role identification.* Berkeley, CA: McCutchan Publishing Corporation.

Maccoby, E. E., & Jacklin, C. N. (1974). *The psychology of sex differences.* Stanford, CA: Stanford University Press.

McCord, J., McCord, W., & Thurber, E. (1962). Some effects of paternal absence on male children. *Journal of Abnormal and Social Psychology, 64,* 361–369.

Mead, M. (1935). *Sex and temperament in three primitive societies.* New York: Morrow.

Minton, C., Kagan, J., & Levine, J. A. (1971). Maternal control and obedience in the two year old. *Child Development, 42,* 1873–1894.

Mischel, W. (1966). A social learning view of sex differences in behavior. In E. E. Maccoby (Ed.), *The development of sex differences.* Stanford, CA: Stanford University Press.

Money, J. (1971). Sexually dimorphic behavior, normal and abnormal. In N. Kretchmer & D. N. Alcher (Eds.), *Environmental influences on genetic expression: Biological and behavioral aspects of sexual differentiation.* Washington, DC: U.S. Government Printing Office.

Moss, H. A. (1967). Sex, age, and state as determinants of mother-infant interaction. *Merrill-Palmer Quarterly, 13,* 19–36.

Mowrer, O. H. (1950). *Learning theory and personality dynamics.* New York: Ronald.

Nash, S. C. (1979). Sex role as a mediator of intellectual functioning. In M. A. Wittig & A. C. Petersen (Eds.), *Sex related differences in cognitive functioning: Developmental issues.* New York: Academic Press.

Nye, F. I., & Hoffman, L. W. (1963). *The employed mother in America.* Chicago: Rand McNally.

Paludi, M. A. (1982, March). The Children's Sex-Role Preference Scale: Construction of a measuring instrument. Paper presented at the Biennial Meeting of the Southwestern Society for Research in Human Development, Galveston, TX.

Paludi, M. A., & Fankell-Hauser, J. (1984, April). An idiographic approach to the study of women's achievement striving. Paper presented at the Second International Interdisciplinary Congress Conference on Women, The Netherlands.

Paludi, M. A., Geschke, D., Smith, M., & Strayer, L. A. (in press). Toward the development of a measure of preschoolers' knowledge of sex-determined role standards. *Child Study Journal.*

Paludi, M. A., Hrabowy, I., Johnson, V., & McNeer, A. E. (1984, May). Children's causal attributions for success and failure on sex-appropriate and sex-inappropriate tasks. Paper presented at the Midwestern Society for Research in Life-Span Development, Akron, OH.

Paludi, M. A., & Strayer, L. A. (1983, June). What's in an author's name? Differential evaluations of successful performance as a function of author's name. Paper presented at the National Women's Studies Association, Columbus, OH.

Pedersen, F. A., & Robson, K. S. (1969). Father participation in infancy. *American Journal of Orthopsychiatry, 39,* 466–472.

Petersen, A. C. (1979). Hormones and cognitive functioning in normal development. In M. A. Wittig & A. C. Petersen (Eds.), *Sex related differences in cognitive functioning: Developmental issues.* New York: Academic Press.

Phoenix, C. H., Goy, R. W., & Resko, J. A. (1969). Psychosexual differentiation as a function of androgenic stimulation. In M. Diamond (Ed.), *Reproduction and sexual behavior.* Bloomington, IN: Indiana University Press.

Piaget, J. (1952). *The origins of intelligence in children.* New York: International Universities Press.

Pope, B. (1953). Socio-economic contrasts in children's peer culture prestige values. *Genetic Psychology Monographs, 48,* 157–220.

Preston, R. C. (1962). Reading achievement of German and American children. *School and Society, 90,* 350–354.

Rabban, M. (1950). Sex-role identification in young children in two diverse social groups. *Genetic Psychology Monographs, 42,* 81–158.

Rebelsky, F., & Hanks, C. (1971). Fathers' verbal interaction with infants in the first three months of life. *Child Development, 42,* 63–68.

Reinisch, J. M., Gandelman, R., & Spiegel, F. S. (1979). Prenatal influences on cognitive abilities: Data from experimental animals and human endocrine syndromes. In M. A. Wittig & A. C. Petersen (Eds.), *Sex related differences in cognitive functioning: Developmental issues.* New York: Academic Press.

Rheingold, H. L., & Cook, K. U. (1975). The contents of boy's and girl's rooms as an index of parents' behavior. *Child Development, 46,* 459–463.

Romer, N. (1975). The motive to avoid success and its effects on performance in school-age males and females. *Developmental Psychology, 11,* 689–699.

Rosaldo, M. Z. (1974). Women, culture, and society: A theoretical overview. In M. Z. Rosaldo & L. Lamphere (Eds.), *Women, culture, and society.* Stanford, CA: Stanford University Press.

Rubin, J. Z., Provenzano, F. J., & Luria, Z. (1974). The eye of the beholder: Parents' views on sex of newborns. *American Journal of Orthopsychiatry, 43,* 720–731.

Rutter, M. (1970). Sex differences in children's response to family stress. In E. J. Anthony & C. Koupernik (Eds.), *The child in his family.* New York: Wiley.

Rytting, M. B., & Carr, J. P. (1978, May). The effect of gender information on interaction between infants and adults in a general population. Paper presented at the Annual Meeting of the Midwestern Psychological Association, Chicago.

Saario, T., Jacklin, C. N., & Tittle, C. K. (1973). Sex-role stereotyping in the public schools. *Harvard Educational Review, 43,* 386–404.

Sears, R. R., Rau, L., & Alpert, R. (1965). *Identification and child rearing.* Stanford: Stanford University Press.

Seavey, C. A., Katz, D. A., & Zalk, S. R. (1975). Baby X: The effect of gender labels on adult responses to infants. *Sex Roles, 1,* 103–109.

Serbin, L. A., & O'Leary, K. D. (1975, December). How nursery schools teach girls to shut up. *Psychology Today, 9,* 56–58.

Sherman, J. (1971). *On the psychology of women: A survey of empirical studies.* Springfield, IL: Thomas.

Shinedling, M. M., & Pederson, D. M. (1970). Effects of sex of teacher and student on children's gains in quantitative and verbal performance. *Journal of Psychology, 76,* 79–84.

Smith, P. K., & Daglish, L. (1977). Sex differences in parent and infant behavior in the home. *Child Development, 48,* 1250–1254.

Spence, J. T., & Helmreich, R. (1972). The attitudes toward women scale. *JSAS Catalog of Selected Documents in Psychology, 2,* 66.

Stein, A. H. (1973). The effects of maternal employment and educational attainment on the sex-typed attributes of college females. *Social Behavior and Personality, 1,* 111–114.

Stein, A. H., & Bailey, M. M. (1973). The socialization of achievement orientation in females. *Psychological Bulletin, 5,* 345–366.

Sternglanz, S. H., & Serbin, L. A. (1974). Sex role stereotyping in children's television programs. *Developmental Psychology, 10,* 710–715.

Stott, D. H. (1966). *Studies of troublesome children.* London: Tavistock.

Strayer, F. F. (1977). Peer attachment and affiliative subgroups. In F. F. Strayer (Ed.), *Ethological perspectives on preschool social organization.* Memo de Recherche #5, Universite du Quebec, A Montreal, Department of Psychologie.

Streicher, H. W. (1974). The girls in cartoons. *Journal of Communication, 4,* 125–129.

Tobias, S. (1976, September). Math anxiety: Why is a smart girl like you counting on your fingers? *Ms., 5,* 56–59.

Tolor, A., & Tolor, B. (1974). Children's figure drawings and changing attitudes toward sex roles. *Psychological Reports, 34,* 343–349.

Unger, R. K., & Denmark, F. L. (Eds.), (1975). *Woman: Dependent or independent variable.* New York: Psychological Dimensions.

Vogal, S. (1970). *Sesame Street and sex-role stereotypes.* Pittsburgh, PA: KNOW.

Whiting, B. B., & Edwards, C. P. (1973). A cross-cultural analysis of sex differences in the behavior of children aged three through eleven. *Journal of Personality and Social Psychology, 91,* 171–188.

Whiting, B. B., & Whiting, J. W. M. (1973). Altruistic and egoistic behavior in six cultures. In L. Nader & T. W. Maretzki (Eds.), *Cultural illness and health: Essays in human adaptation.* Washington, DC: American Anthropological Association.

Whiting, B. B., & Whiting, J. W. M. (1975). *Children of six cultures.* Cambridge, MA: Harvard University Press.

Will, J. A., Self, P. A., & Datan, N. (1976). Maternal behavior and perceived sex of infant. *American Journal of Orthopsychiatry, 46,* 135–139.

Witelson, S. F., & Pallie, W. (1973). Left hemisphere specialization for language in the newborn: Neuroanatomical evidence of asymmetry. *Brain, 96,* 641–646.

Wolman, B. B. (Ed.), (1978). *Psychological aspects of gynecology and obstetrics.* Oradell, NJ: Medical Economics

Women on Words and Images. (1972). *Dick and Jane as victims: Sex stereotyping in children's readers.* Princeton, NJ.

Yarrow, L. J., Rubenstein, J. L., & Pedersen, F. A. (1971). Dimensions of early stimulation: Differential effects of infant development. Paper presented at the meeting of the Society for Research in Child Development.

REFERENCE NOTES

Note 1

An autosomal recessive gene causes this adrenogenital syndrome. It is a metabolic disorder in which the adrenal gland secretes excessive amounts of adrenal androgens instead of the adrenal hormone cortisol in response to ACTH (adrenocorticotrophic hormone) from the pituitary.

Note 2

These are genetic males who cannot utilize either endogenous or exogenous androgen since its absorption is blocked at the cellular level.

Note 3

These genetic males had an insufficient production of androgen in utero.

APPENDIX A

CHRONOLOGICAL SUMMARY OF SEX AND GENDER SIMILARITIES AND DIFFERENCES*

INTERPERSONAL BEHAVIOR AND TEMPERAMENT

	Age Of Children				
Characteristic	Birth–3 Years	3–6 Years	6–9 Years	9–12 Years	12 Plus Years
Activity Level	No difference	Boys more active *only* in groups of other boys	Inconsistent results; when difference is found, boys are more active	Inconsistent results	Poor data
Dependency Proximity Seeking Toward Parents	No difference	No difference	No difference	No difference	—
Proximity Seeking Toward Peers	Boys slightly more likely to "tag along"	Boys "tag along" more	Poor data	Poor data	—
Fear and Anxiety	No difference	No difference; girls may *report* more fear and timidity	Girls report more fears and are rated as more fearful by parents and teachers. Observational data indicates no differences between boys and girls.		

*Maccoby and Jacklin's (1974) review was the primary source for this summary with updating from more recent research cited in this chapter.

INTERPERSONAL BEHAVIOR AND TEMPERAMENT (Continued)

Characteristic	Age Of Children				
	Birth–3 Years	3–6 Years	6–9 Years	9–12 Years	12 Plus Years
Nurturance	Inconsistent data; nurturance rare at this age	No difference	Inconsistent data from laboratory; girls across cultures have responsibility for younger children		Little data; males may be as nurturant as females toward newborns
Aggression	Boys more aggressive than girls	Boys more aggressive than girls	Boys more aggressive	Boys more aggressive	Boys and men more aggressive than girls and women
	— Males are both the aggressors and victims of aggression more often —				
Compliance	Girls more compliant to parents' requests and demands	Girls more compliant to teachers' and other adults' requests	Inconsistent results	No consistent difference	No consistent difference
Dominance	In nursery school, boys seen as "tougher" than girls	Egoistic dominance exhibited more by boys	Inconsistent data, perhaps boys are more dominant	Perhaps boys are seen as more dominant	Perhaps boys and men; poor data
Relationships with Parents	Boys more likely to demand their caretakers' attention	Boys engage in activities forbidden by parents	Boys' relationship with parents focus on disciplinary concerns		Poor data

COGNITIVE ABILITY AND ACHIEVEMENT

Characteristic	Birth–3 Years	3–6 Years	6–9 Years	9–12 Years	12 Plus Years
Verbal Ability	No clear difference	No clear difference	No difference except among underprivileged populations where girls excel in verbal tasks		Girls and women perform better on a variety of verbal tasks
Quantitative Ability	–	Among underprivileged populations girls are better at counting	Inconsistent results	Inconsistent results	Boys and men perform better on quantitative tasks
Creativity					
Verbal	–	No difference	Girls better	Girls better	Girls and women better
Nonverbal	–	No difference	No difference	No difference	No difference
Visual-Spatial Ability	–	No difference	Inconsistent results	Inconsistent results	Boys and men better
Learning and Memory	–	No difference	No difference	No difference	No difference
Achievement Motivation					
Grades	–	Girls obtain better grades	Girls better	Girls better	Girls better
Projective Tests	–	Probably no difference	No difference	No difference	Boys and men have a higher achievement motive when aroused by reference to their intelligence and leadership ability
Self-Concept					
Confidence in Task Performance	–	No difference	Inconsistent data	Boys more confident	Boys and men are more confident
General Self-Esteem	–	No difference	No difference	No difference	Inconsistent results

APPENDIX B

Annotated List of Non-Sexist Children's Stories and Books[1]

Works cited here include fiction and non-fiction recommended for children preschool age to age 14. For more complete bibliographies, consult the following texts:

Adell, J., & Klein, H. D. 1976. *A guide to non-sexist children's books.* Chicago, IL: Academy Press.

Bracken, J., & Wigutoff, S. (1981) *Books for today's young readers: An annotated bibliography of recommended fiction for ages 10-14.* Old Westbury, NY: The Feminist Press.

The following organizations offer a variety of resources and materials on non-sexist childrearing and non-sexist teaching:

Action for Children's Television (ACT)
46 Austin Street
Newtonville, MA 02160

American Family Society
P.O. Box 9873
Washington, D.C. 20015

American Federation of Teachers
The Women's Rights Committee
1012 Fourteenth Street, N.W.
Washington, D.C. 20005

American Library Association
Committee on the Status of Women
50 East Huron Street
Chicago, IL 60611

---

[1]Prepared with the assistance of Nancy Caldwell.

American Parents Committee
1346 Connecticut Avenue, N.W.
Suite 310
Washington, D.C. 20036

Center for the Study of Women and Sex Roles
33 West 42nd Street
Room 1400
New York, NY 10036

Change for Children
2588 Mission Street
Room 226
San Francisco, CA 94110

Children's Book Council
175 Fifth Avenue
New York, NY 10010

Children's Foundation
1420 New York Avenue, N.W.
Suite 800
Washington, D.C. 20005

Feminist Book Mart
162-11 Ninth Avenue
Whitestone, NY 11357

Feminist Press
P.O. Box 334
Old Westbury, NY 11568

Lollipop Power
P.O. Box 1171
Chapel Hill, NC 27514

Ms. Magazine
370 Lexington Avenue
New York, NY 10017

National Education Association
1201 Sixteenth Street
Washington, D.C. 20036

National Institute of Education
The Office of Education
400 Maryland Avenue, S.W.
Washington, D.C. 20202

National Organization for Girls and Women in Sports
1900 Association Drive
Reston, VA 22091

National Organization for Women
425 13th Street, N.W.
Suite 1048
Washington, D.C. 20004

Public Action Coalition on Toys
38 W. 9th Street
New York, NY 10011

Resource Center on Sex Roles in Education
1156 Fifteenth Street
Washington, D.C. 20005

Sex Equality in Guidance Opportunities
1607 New Hampshire Avenue, N.W.
Washington, D.C. 20009

Women's Action Alliance
370 Lexington Avenue
New York, NY 10017

Women's Equity Action League
National Press Building
Washington, D.C. 20045

Women on Words and Images
P.O. Box 2163
Princeton, NJ 08540

Preschool Through Third Grade

Diana and her rhinoceros by Edward Ardizzone. N.Y.: Walck, 1964.
Diana nurses an ailing rhinoceros escaped from the zoo. When armed men come to take the animal back to the zoo, Diana turns them away.

Boys and girls, girls and boys by Eve Merriam. N.Y.: Holt, Rinehart & Winston, 1972.

Children from a variety of ethnic backgrounds play in an atmosphere free of sex-determined role standards.

Mommies at work N.Y.: Scholastic Book Services, 1971.

Mothers are depicted doing jobs stereotypically considered for fathers only.

Womenfolk and fairy tales edited by Rosemary Minard. Boston: Houghton Mifflin, 1975.

A collection of fairy tales devoid of the poor fair maiden being "awaken" by the wealthy handsome prince.

The queen who couldn't bake gingerbread by Dorothy Van Woerkom. N.Y.: Knopf, 1975.

A king and a queen have to make mutually compromised choices. The king wants his wife to bake gingerbread; she can't. The queen wants her husband to play the slide trombone; he can't. So the king learns to bake gingerbread and the queen learns to play the slide trombone.

Ruby! by Amy Aitken. Scarsdale, N.Y.: Bradbury, 1979.

Ruby wants to change her routine life. She imagines the excitement and fame she will receive when she becomes an author, movie star, and President of country.

There was nobody there by Barbara Bottner. N.Y.: Macmillian, 1978.

A young girl wakes up during the night and believes she's all alone. She imagines herself in many adventures, including landing on the moon, arriving at the North Pole, and shipping out to sea.

The terrible thing that happened at our house by Marge Blaine. N.Y.: Parents' Magazine, 1975.

A young girl's mother returns to her teaching position. The daughter described what happened at their home when this occurred. Things weren't so bad when everyone cooperated and kept to their schedules.

Cranberry mystery by Wende Devlin and Harry Devlin. N.Y.: *Parents' Magazine*, 1978.

Several antiques begin disappearing in Cranberry port. The townspeople become worried. Maggie's courage, independence, and quick thinking lead to the solution of the mystery.

Amy for short by Laura Joffee Numeroff. N.Y.: Macmillian, 1976.

Amy and Mark are best friends. Amy begins to grow taller than Mark and she's concerned about their remaining friends.

Hurray for Captain Jane! by Sam Reavin. N.Y.: *Parents' Magazine*, 1971.

At a party, Jane wins a bar of soap, a bag of jellybeans, and a waxed paper sailor's cap. While bathing, Jane fantasizes that the water in the tub is the ocean and she is the captain of an ocean liner.

Hester the Jester by Ben Shecter. N.Y.: Harper & Row, 1977.

Hester's father is a jester. She wants to be one too, but girls can't be jesters. One day, Hester's father cannot make the King laugh. Hester is given the opportunity and succeeds. She is then permitted to be a Knight and a King.

Let's paint a rainbow by Eric Carle. N.Y.: Philomel, 1983.

Painters—a man and a woman—teach colors and numbers to young readers.

Just us women by Jeanette Caines. N.Y.: Harper & Row, 1983.

A spirited black girl and her aunt take off on an event-filled car trip together.

Fourth Through Seventh Grade

Kick a stone home by Doris Buchanan Smith. N.Y.: Crowell, 1974.

Sara is a shy 15-year-old girl who wants to be a veterinarian. She enjoys being on the football, baseball, or basketball team more than going to school. She begins to meet people and learns friendship. She gains more confidence and learns to be herself.

The witness by Dorothy Uhnak. N.Y.: Simon & Schuster, 1968.

A plainclothes woman on the policeforce solves case after case, one involving a murder in a street demonstration.

Nothing is impossible: The story of Beatrix Potter by Dorothy Aldis. N.Y.: Atheneum, 1969.

This book depicts the early life of the world renowned author and illustrator of books for children.

I'm nobody, who are you? The story of Emily Dickinson by Edna Barth. N.Y.: Seabury, 1971.

Several of Dickinson's poems are presented in this book along with her biography. Emphasis is placed on her great strength of character and enthusiasm for life.

Women who win by Francene Sabin. N.Y.: Random House, 1975.

The lives of 14 women athletes are depicted. The book deals with the athletes' skill as well as the personal and societal blocks which confronted their success.

Julie of the wolves by Jean Craighead George. N.Y.: Harper & Row, 1972.

The book describes an Eskimo girl who inadvertently wanders into wolf territory and learns self-reliance.

Naomi by Bernice Rabe. Nashville: Nelson, 1975.

Naomi is a farm girl in Missouri in the late 1930s. She rejects the custom of girls 14 being married and decides to become a physician.

Girls are equal too by Dale Carlson. N.Y.: Atheneum, 1975.

Adolescent girls are told what they can expect from life and what mature women are like. A discussion of The Women's Movement is presented.

Law and the new woman by Mary McHugh. N.Y.: Franklin Watts, 1975.

This book is one in a series of guides to the professions for adolescent girls. A description is given on law schools, corporate, public, and private law practices. There is a presentation on combining a law career with family life.

The boy who wanted a baby by Wendy Lichtman. Old Westbury, N.Y.: The Feminist Press, 1983.

Dan is a twelve year old boy who enjoys camping and bicycling. He dreams of giving birth: "that's amazing, really amazing, to have a whole living person inside you. You'd never get lonely."

Seafaring women by Linda Grant DePauw. Boston: Houghton Mifflin, 1983.

This book includes a collection of biographies of women who were traders, sea captains, pirates, and whalers from the Fifth century B.C. to the present.

Embers: Stories for a changing world by Ruth S. Meyers and Beryle Banfield. Old Westbury, N.Y.: The Feminist Press, 1983.

This book is an anthology of poems and stories with a message against discrimination because of race, sex, or disability. Historical figures are emphasized, Harriet Tubman, Jeannette Rankin, among them.

CHAPTER 5

THE YOUNG HANDICAPPED CHILD: PHILOSOPHICAL BELIEFS AND PRAGMATIC ACTIONS

J. BRADLEY GARNER

There are several perspectives from which one can determine the ways in which a society perceives and meets the needs of its individual members or collective groups of its citizens. The first of these perspectives focuses upon the prevailing beliefs and assumptions used as criteria for judging the value of societal members or groups (e.g., potential, productivity, social status, sex, racial, ethnic, religious membership, financial status, etc.). Second, collections of beliefs and assumptions are generally interwoven to form a philosophical framework for societal actions and reactions in relation to the demands of the environment. The relationship between beliefs/assumptions, and philosophies is generally interactive in nature. That is, the fabric of the philosophies held by a person or a society is constantly changing as beliefs are challenged in the course of day-to-day activity. Third, the philosophies valued by a society directly impact upon the quality and quantity of services that are available to meet the unique needs of its citizens. This can include the nature and thrust of research (e.g., which research questions are important enough to be funded or even asked), and the definition of those societal members who qualify for, or are deemed worthy of, the varied supportive and remedial services that may be required to facilitate growth, development, and independence. A high degree of congruence should exist between the components of this interdependent triad (i.e., beliefs/assumptions, philosophies, services). In that this is true, services provided reflect the concern of a society for its citizens.

There are at least two types of discrepancies that can adversely

111

affect the relationship between a society's beliefs, assumptions, philosophies, and the services provided to its citizens. The first type of discrepancy involves a social climate in which certain societal members are devalued and, therefore, considered to be unworthy of extensive societal services (Wolfensberger, 1972). This phenomenon has been observed frequently in relation to persons labeled as handicapped. The second type of discrepancy centers on the concept of *progressive status quoism*. This concept, originally discussed by Farber (1968) and later by Gold (1980), is evidenced by two simultaneous events: (a) A society claims that it is trying to solve a pressing social problem, and (b) no real effort is being made in response to that identified problem. Each of these discrepancies affect the quality and quantity of services available to young handicapped children. It is proposed that these children and their dilemma best represents the disparity between society's stated good intentions and the availability of actual service delivery options.

ISSUES OF SURVIVAL AND SERVICES

From primitive times, young handicapped children often have been subjected to precarious levels of treatment and service (Filler, 1983; Hewett & Forness, 1977; Wolfensberger, 1972). Today, debates brew over the advisability of withholding medical treatment from severely handicapped infants to the extent of facilitating their early death. These debates focus upon the quality of life and a societal perception that persons labeled as severely handicapped invariably face a life of adversity, require costly medical care, and constitute a perpetual burden to their families and society. The significance of this issue is not to be understated. Approximately 14% of all neonatal deaths are estimated to be related to the withholding of medical treatment (Duff & Campbell, 1973). Numerous reviews of the literature have summarized the ethical, medical, and moral issues considered germane to this controversy (Affleck, 1980; Cohen, 1981; Powell, Aiken, & Smylie, 1982; Wolfensberger, 1980). What kinds of conclusions can be drawn regarding society's perception and value of potentially handicapped infants? Decisions appear to be made relative to beliefs, assumptions, and philosophies despite modern technological developments (e.g., amniocentesis, neonatal care).

Another area of concern relative to young handicapped children is the availability of early intervention services (Campbell, 1982; Hayden, 1979). Public Law 94-142, the *Education for All Handicapped Children Act of 1975*, is frequently touted as the cornerstone of opportunity for the handicapped child. However,

> for the handicapped preschooler this law is a flawed mandate. Many of these children will not see the inside of a classroom or a school until age five or six. Many of them will lose precious time for learning, for overcoming or reducing the limitations that their disabilities impose, because the free appropriate public education mandated in the law is inconsistent with the law or the educational practice in their States for children of their age, and thus does not apply to them. (Cohen, Semmes, & Guralnick, 1979, p. 279)

Programs for young handicapped children are permissive under existing federal legislation. Currently each state is required to provide education and related services to *all* handicapped children between the ages of six and eighteen years of age. Services to handicapped children below the age of six may be possible, but only where stipulated by state law.

Services available to handicapped children have been summarized and analyzed in a report published by the United States General Accounting Office (1981). This report indicates that only sixteen states mandate services for handicapped children in the three to five year range. Twenty-two states mandate services for handicapped children in the four to five year range, and twelve states mandate services for handicapped children at the age of six years. Only five states have enacted mandates for serving handicapped children at birth. On a composite basis only 2.6% of the estimated three to five year old population are receiving special educational services through the public schools. This statistic becomes significant when compared with the fact that 7.8% of the estimated six to seventeen year old population are receiving special education through the public schools. This discrepancy indicates that although each state is required to identify and evaluate handicapped children of all ages, educational services are being provided only as statutorily required by federal law.

Hayden (1979) offers a possible explanation for the paucity of public school programs for the young handicapped child:

> A basic problem is that children's needs do not fit our budgets. Do we really want to know just how good or bad a job we are doing, or do we want to continue to offer excuses and raise questions that detract attention from our piecemeal, too-little-too-late, penny-wise-and-pound-foolish, exclude-rather-than-include approach to solving these problems? (p. 514)

Our society does not appear to value the fate of the young handicapped child, at least to the extent of providing the resources necessary to support a network of early intervention programs. There are several reasons for this phenomenon. First, many parents and public agencies are not aware of the fact that the public schools are responsible for the identification and assessment of all handicapped children beginning at birth. Second, young handicapped children are typically not referred to, or evaluated by, public school personnel. Limited data, therefore, exists in the public realm to establish the need for intervention programs. Prevalence data is available for review by public school administrators. However, unless these children are systematically brought to the attention of the public schools and formally identified as handicapped, service systems will not be implemented. Third, many young handicapped children are served by agencies that are not formally affiliated with the public schools (e.g., Easter Seals, Association for Retarded Citizens, United Cerebral Palsy Association). These agencies provide extensive services and often are somewhat reluctant to identify specific children for a school district. Finally, many public school systems may *not want to know* if young handicapped children are residing within their districts. Inevitably, knowledge of numbers would lead to a requirement that services be provided. Based upon current practices, it appears that young handicapped children have not been systematically deemed worthy of extensive societal services.

FACTORS ADVERSELY AFFECTING DEVELOPMENT: IDENTIFYING THE YOUNG CHILD WITH HANDICAPS

The disciplines of psychology, education, and medicine collaboratively have documented the sequence of developmental milestones typical to the majority of children (Cohen, Gross, & Haring, 1976; Flavell, 1977; Gesell, 1940; Goldstein, 1964; Kagan & Moss, 1962; Piaget, 1952). These sequences outline expected patterns of growth and skill acquisition in such areas as gross motor, fine motor, receptive language, expressive language, self-care, cognitive, and social development. Statistically derived developmental data have been generated in each of these areas to denote the chronological age at which given skills are generally demonstrated or mastered (e.g., standing alone at 11 months, speaking in nearly complete sentences at 48 to 60 months, tieing shoes at 72 months). Several prominent test developers have organized these developmental competencies into standardized, norm-referenced assessment instruments (Bayley, 1969; Cattell, 1940; Frankenburg, Dodds, & Fandal, 1975; Terman & Merrill, 1973; see Chapter 11). Traditionally, the young child's performance on standardized developmental assessment instruments, as compared to chronological agemates, has served as the primary criterion for distinguishing those considered *normal* and those labeled as *handicapped.*

Despite the apparent simplicity and logic of comparing a young child's developmental status with established norms, the resulting conclusions (e.g., the severity or implication of identified handicapping conditions) and decisions (e.g., types of interventions needed) must be developed and validated with great vigilance. This caveat was delineated by Horowitz (1978) as follows:

Detection of abnormality is not always simple. Some children show deviant development that is not necessarily abnormal. Some children seem to have developmental problems that turn out to be quite temporary. It is important to be cautious in deciding that there is a problem that is to be labeled as abnormal.... There are ... instances in which the label of abnormality results from a lack of knowledge about cultural and social definitions of what is normal and what is abnormal in different subcultures in out society. (p. 21)

Within the past few years, various classification systems have evolved as a means to categorize and communicate the types of handicapping conditions experienced by young children (*Education for All Handicapped Children Act of 1975;* Kirk, 1972; Quay, 1973). These classification systems have, perhaps, provided a mechanism to generate demographic data regarding the prevalance of various handicapping conditions and, therefore, a numerical case for the establishment of corresponding services (Gallagher, Forsythe, Ringelheim, & Weintraub, 1975). Such classification systems, for the most part, have lead to the widespread practice of using *stereotypical decision statements* to refer to the needs of young children (Garner, 1980). For example, it is not uncommon to overhear professionals as they make programming recommendations based upon the label attached to the child (e.g., "Children with autism need...," "Children who are mentally retarded should receive services in...," etc.). Professionals often tend to ignore the principle of individual differences, exacerbate the stigmata attached to being labeled as handicapped, view the child as merely a member of a categorical group and, thereby, limit expectations for the young child's potential as a learner (Galloway & Chandler, 1978; Gold, 1980; Wolfensberger, 1972).

Another factor that confuses the process of identifying the needs of young children is the extensive use of adjectives to clarify the severity of a handicapping condition. The confusion surrounding the use of adjectives to clarify the nature of a handicapping condition was well illustrated by Safford (1978). Safford cites the work of Davis and Silverman (1970), who use the terms *slight, mild, marked, severe,* and *extreme* to define the severity of a hearing impairment. The same type of graded system has been used by professionals in the field of mental retardation who refer to individuals as being *mildly* mentally retarded, *moderately* mentally retarded, *severely* mentally retarded, and *profoundly* mentally retarded (Grossman, 1977).

Professionals continue to debate the advisability of maintaining and refining a system which categorizes the needs of young children in accord with the severity of their identified handicapping conditions (Burton & Hirshoren, 1979; Sontag, Certo, & Button, 1979). Perhaps the best analysis of this dilemma was formulated by Gold (1981). Gold proposed that if society is to use the terms moderate, severe, and profound to refer to the severity of a person's handicap, then the same should be done to refer to a person's perceived level of normality (e.g., persons who are moderately normal, people who are severely normal, etc.). Labeling systems are primarily intended for the convenience of professionals. The needs of young children may be misrepresented by the attachment of a categorical label to identified learning difficulties (Hobbs, 1975).

An alternative to labeling is a focus on the difficulties that young children may experience in six major areas of development: (a) sensory deficits, (b) communication and language disorders, (c) motor impairments, (d) cognitive deficits, (e) behavioral and motivational difficulties, and (f) health-related difficulties. It is acknowledged that individual children may experience difficulties in one, two, or a combination of as many as six of these developmental areas. Intervention is based upon the young child's identified area(s) of difficulty, the potential interaction of identified difficulties, and their relationship to the young child's developmental context (Kirk, 1972; Quay, 1973).

Sensory Deficits

Sensory deficits in young children include varying degrees of difficulty with vision, hearing, or both. The eyes and the ears are the primary gateways through which initial and ongoing interactions with the environment are facilitated. Visual difficulties in young children may be the result of many varied types of dysfunctions such as refractive errors, astigmatism, amblyopia, cataracts, glaucoma, retinitis pigmentosa, macular degeneration, and retinal detachment (DuBose, 1979a). The interaction between an identified visual handicap and a young child's overall development can also adversely affect the young child's cognitive (Frailberg, 1968; Higgins, 1973; Piaget & Inhelder, 1969), motor (Frailberg, 1977), language (Warren, 1977), and social development (Hewett & Forness, 1977).

The existence of a hearing impairment in young children can be the result of congenital or adventitious events (Davis & Silverman, 1970). The type of hearing loss that the child experiences is critical. *Conductive hearing losses* are the result of malformations or difficulties in the outer or middle ear (e.g., wax build up, foreign objects, fluid build up in the eustachian tube) preventing a clear transmission of sound waves to the inner ear. These hearing losses can generally be treated medically, or through the use of amplification. *Sensorineural hearing losses* are the result of defects in the inner ear or the auditory nerve. This type of hearing loss is difficult to treat with medical or surgical procedures, and amplification may not be totally effective (Cox & Lloyd, 1976). The young child with a hearing impairment may have difficulties with language, cognitive, and social development (DuBose, 1979b).

Communication and Language Disorders

Bricker (1983) distinguished the difference between communication and language in the following manner:

The terms *communication* and *language* are often incorrectly interchanged. *Communication* is more inclusive. It encompasses all behavior generally used for transfer of information, be it social or informative, between a sender and receiver. There is controversy about the parameters of communication ... but for our purposes, *communication* is any gestural, vocal, or facial-body response used to control another's behavior or convey information. *Language* is a form of communication based on a referential or representational system. That is, language is a formal system that uses symbols, generally words, to stand for objects, people and events ... (original emphases, p. 269)

Obviously, the development of communication and language is a complex process. Developmental difficulties with communication and language are the most prevalent of all handicapping conditions (United States General Accounting Office, 1981). This statistical reality is based upon the fact that that these disorders can occur in isolation or in combination with other handicapping conditions (Garwood, 1979).

The young child with communication and language disorders is at a distinct disadvantage in acquiring the skills involved in negotiating social contexts, expressing personal needs and wants, and developing and demonstrating cognitive competencies (Cromer, 1981; Uzgiris, 1981). The enhancement of communication and language should be a critical component of intervention programs for young children (Bricker, 1983; Coggins & Sandall, 1983).

Motor Impairments

Stone (1977) cogently described the effects of motor impairments on the child as follows:

A child's motor functioning affects other areas of functioning. A child whose oral mechanism is seriously motorically involved may not have the motor patterns necessary for developing oral expressive language. His ability to move his limbs independently of each other reduces the opportunities for early sensorimotor learning experiences. He may be deprived experiences to facilitate his cognitive development. Inability to independently move and relate to people may drastically impair social and emotional development. These are examples of problems that occur with the child whose only disability is severe motor impairment. Compound that involvement with blindness, deafness, or mental deficiency, and the above problems multiply. (p. 83)

Motor impairments can include a wide variety of neurological disorders (e.g., cerebral palsy, spina bifida) and musculoskeletal conditions (e.g., muscular dystrophy, arthritis, ostogenesis imperfecta) (Langley, 1979). The presence of motor impairments in young children can also have an adverse effect upon cognitive (Robinson, 1982), social, and language development (Campbell, 1983; Langley, 1979). Many of the adverse effects of motor impairments can be reduced through interdisciplinary planning and programming (Campbell, 1982; Campbell, Clegg, & McFarland, 1982), medical and therapeutic interventions (Campbell, 1983), and the use of adaptive and therapeutic devices (Bergen & Colangelo, 1982; Campbell, McInerney, & Middleton, 1982).

Cognitive Deficits

Many efforts have been made to operationalize the development of cognitive skills in young children (Piaget, 1952; Robinson & Robinson, 1983; Uzgiris & Hunt, 1975). Despite these efforts, the measurement of cognitive skills has, in practice, come to be associated with one outcome: Performance on an individualized intelligence test (Garner, in press). Young children who perform their chronological agemates on these measures are typically given the label mentally retarded, and a qualifying adjective (e.g., trainable, educable, severe, profound) as a means of clarifying their inabilities in cognitive pursuits.

There are several cautions that must be exercised when evaluating, analyzing, or interpreting the cognitive development of young children. First, standardized measures of intelligence have been shown to have a low level of predictive validity when used with young children (McCall, 1979; Zelazo, 1982). In other words, poor performance by the young child on a standardized test of intelligence may not be a valid index of future difficulties. Second, young children who experience language, motor, sensory, or social impairments may be penalized on evaluation instruments administered in a traditional fashion (Garner, in press; Zelazo, 1982). For these children, poor test performance may be more a function of their difficulties with providing a verbal response or manipulating test stimuli than a deficit in cognitive functioning. Third, the detrimental effects of being labeled mentally retarded may have a life-long effect on the opportunities and levels of expectation afforded the young child (Gold, 1980; Wolfensberger, 1972).

The cognitive skills and competencies of the young child are certainly worthy of development and enhancement. These skills affect many other areas of the child's adaptation to the environment (Robinson, 1982). Further, models of intervention have been developed for facilitating the acquisition of cognitive skills in young children (Robinson & Robinson, 1983). If cognitive deficits are to be identified as an area of instructional need for the young child, professionals should exercise great caution in categorizing such deficits through the use of "lethal labels" (Mercer, 1972).

Behavioral and Motivational Difficulties

Behavioral and motivational difficulties are the most complex to delineate and define. This phenomenon, to a large extent, is due to the fact that the parameters of *normal* behavioral repertoires are relative in nature. Behavior such as social withdrawal, social aggression, or noncompliance can be operationally defined. However, the social contexts in which these behavioral definitions are to be exercised additionally must be described (Hewett & Forness, 1977; Kauffman, 1979).

Behavioral and motivational difficulties in young children are those maladaptive forms of behavior that significantly interfere with the child's involvement in home, school, and community functioning. Such a definition is relative when considering a child below the age of five who spends a majority of time within the home and family context. The emphasis placed on a young child's display of behavioral and motivational difficulties may largely be a function of several factors: (a) The resiliency of the parents in relating to the child's needs, (b) the impact of the extended family on the parents and their responsibilities in child rearing, and (c) the willingness of the family to alter routines and responsibilities as a means of meeting the child's behavioral needs (Kauffman, 1979).

Health-Related Difficulties

Young children with chronic medical problems may, to varying degrees, be prevented from experiencing many of the developmental activities that are typically associated with childhood (e.g., active play experiences in the neighborhood, socialization in a variety of environments). Chronic medical difficulties in young children can result in isolation, rejection, and exclusion. The degree of isolation may be dependent upon the nature of the health problem, the attitude of the parents toward the illness, the degree of necessity for extended hospitalizations, and the degree of mobility and activity permitted. Each of these factors affects the young child as development proceeds. Further, these events will affect the young child's adjustment to extended environments such as the school and the community.

The medical complications that can affect young children have been well described in the professional literature (Bleck & Nagel, 1982; McCubbin, 1983). Despite the availability of these resources, professionals may still tend to approach the young child with, for example, cancer or sickle-cell disease with a certain degree of fear and trepidation. Effective programming for the young child with health-related difficulties must include provisions for ongoing communication between the home, the school and medical personnel (McCubbin, 1983). This communication network can serve to provide a mechanism for monitoring the young child's health status, transmitting information relative to effective home and school management strategies, and reassuring parents and school personnel as to the child's overall adjustment.

THE YOUNG HANDICAPPED CHILD
AS A MEMBER OF THE FAMILY

Much has been written regarding the impact of a handicapped child on the family (Gabel, McDowell, & Cerreto, 1983; Turnbull & Turnbull, 1978). Historically, the effect of the birth of a handicapped child has been viewed as precipitating a grieving process similar to that experienced at the death of a loved one (Cohen, 1962; Farber, 1968; Olshansky, 1962). The sequence of events in this grieving process has been conceptualized to include mourning, shock, denial and hope, grief, anger, guilt, and finally, adaptation (Gabel, McDowell, & Cerreto, 1983). Distressingly, much of the professional literature reflects a rather patronizing view of parents who have handicapped children. The emphasis in this literature is on strategies for helping parents to reconcile their guilt feelings, accept the child, or work through the grieving process. Such generalizations tend to categorize and stereotype parents in much the same way that handicapped persons have traditionally been categorized and stereotyped.

Being the parent of *any* child is, at times, stressful and demanding. The handicapped child may bring added stress to the family, but the stresses and experiences of all parents are more alike than they are different. To fully understand the effect that a handicapped child can have on the family, professionals must look beyond the traditional teachings of guilt, loss, and rejection. The parents of handicapped children, like every other inhabitant of this planet, have a complex set of needs, interests, and aspirations. To fully understand the needs of parents who may have a handicapped child, professionals must learn to remember that parents are *people* first.

CHARACTERISTICS OF A QUALITY INTERVENTION PROGRAM FOR THE YOUNG HANDICAPPED CHILD

Quality is critical when developing service options for the young child with handicaps. Efforts must be made to assure that services are developed in accord with certain programmatic criteria (Campbell, 1982). Five critical criteria include: (a) A goal structure based upon the principle of normalization, (b) the provision of opportunities to engage in longitudinal interactions with nonhandicapped peers, (c) a focus on providing parents and the family with needed support and training so as to facilitate the growth of the child, (d) an interdisciplinary approach to planning and programming, and (e) a data-based system for determining the effectiveness of intervention strategies.

A Goal Structure for Early Intervention Services

Intervention programs for young children should have two main objectives: (a) To reduce and remove the stigma of the child's handicap, and (b) to enhance the competence of the child in relation to the demands of the environment (Galloway & Chandler, 1978). These two goals are derived from the *competence/deviance hypothesis* originated by Gold (1980). The competence/deviance hypothesis, simply stated, proposes that the more competence a person has, the more deviance will be tolerated in that person by others. Programming efforts with young children must be directed toward reducing the stigmata attached to being labeled as handicapped while, at the same time, enhancing the child's competencies in relation to the demands of the environment. This emphasis will increase probabilities for the child to be effectively integrated into the mainstream of society. Many early childhood programs have been modeled on this philosophy (Apolloni & Cooke, 1978; Bricker, 1978; Campbell, 1982; Safford, 1978; Vincent, Salisbury, Walter,

Brown, Grunewald, & Powers, 1980). Services are available from birth with a goal to facilitate entry into normalized, integrated, public school programs.

> the major purpose of early childhood/special education services should be to teach handicapped children the skills necessary to function in as many of the current but more importantly future environments that are available to normal children as is possible. This goal should serve to direct curriculum development, instructional methodology, and program evaluation. This goal should be set for all handicapped children, including the severely handicapped. Implementing this goal implies that the skills necessary to succeed in the normal school environments are effectively documented. Implementing this goal also implies that changes in early childhood/special education and in school age environments will be undertaken. (Vincent, Salisbury, Walter, Brown, Grunewald, & Powers, 1980, p. 307)

The Provision of Services in Integrated Settings

Involvement in integrated settings which include nonhandicapped age peers is critical to the definition of quality in early intervention services. Gilhool and Stutman (1978) clarify the reason for such a position:

> If a child can come to school at all, even to a self-contained class in a handicapped-only center, he can come to a self-contained class in a normal school. Any teaching technique that can be used in a self-contained class can be used in a self-contained class in a regular school building. There are few if any legitimate teaching strategies which require the complete isolation of a child from interaction with other children. (p. 215)

This type of involvement in integrated settings provides a mechanism for modeling age-appropriate behaviors (e.g., language, social behaviors, etc.), raises the expectations of instructional personnel with regard to child performance, provides a nonthreatening method for teaching nonhandicapped children about those who experience handicaps, and eliminates the stigmata that can be attached to a segregated program. Strategies for facilitating integrated program options for young handicapped children have been well documented (Apolloni & Cooke, 1978; Galloway & Chandler, 1978; Fredericks, Baldwin, Grove, Moore, & Riggs, 1978; Safford, 1978; Vincent & Broome, 1977).

A Family Focus

Early intervention services for young handicapped children should have a family focus that includes a number of common characteristics (Bristol & Gallagher, 1982; Campbell, 1982). Training parents to become effective trainers of their own children, including parents in the decision-making process, advising parents of their rights and responsibilities in relation to future school environments, and providing support for the family in interactions with other public agencies, their own extended families, and the community at large are important components (Anastasiow, 1981; Bricker & Casuso, 1979; Filler, 1983; Garner, 1980; Turnbull, 1983). Effective early intervention programs must include provisions for effective involvement of the young handicapped child's parents and siblings. The reason for actively including parents in the intervention process was, perhaps, best described by Cansler, Martin, and Valand (1975) in the following observation: "Work with a child and you foster a year's growth. Work with a parent, and you enhance the family for life" (p. 5).

Interdisciplinary Planning and Programming

Children identified as handicapped during the preschool years are typically those with multiple handicaps or additional chronic medical conditions (Beck, 1977) where an interdisciplinary approach to planning and programming becomes critical. By implementing interdisciplinary strategies, professionals can both gain and share expertise within the context of a team approach. The interdisciplinary team provides a forum for problem identification, the development and implementation of child-centered intervention strategies, and the documentation of child progress (Campbell, 1982).

Implementation of an interdisciplinary team planning and programming process is directed toward one outcome: The demonstration of newly acquired skills and competencies by the young handicapped child. The realization of this outcome is dependent upon several factors including: (a) An effective team approach which integrates the theoretical and philosophical orientations of various professional disciplines, (b) a commitment to documented child progress as the measure of program effectiveness, (c) integral involvement of the child's parents as the providers of information and as members of the decision-making team, and (d) flexibility in team operation as related to the individualized needs of the child (Albano, Cox, York, & York, 1981; Campbell, 1982; Fewell, 1983; Hart, 1977).

Data-Based Educational Decision Making

The documentation of skill acquisition by the young handicapped child is the ultimate measure of effective early intervention services (see Chapter 11). To realize this goal, service providers must design and deliver individualized learning experiences related to the child's needs. However, systems must be implemented for monitoring the child's progress toward achieving instructional goals. This monitoring process, simply stated, involves:

(a) Collecting baseline data which illustrates the child's level of performance prior to intervention (e.g., consistency or frequency of correct responses to verbal directions, duration of sustained effort on assigned activities),

(b) systematically collecting child performance data during the intervention process,

(c) analyzing derived data to determine if the child is making progress toward identified instructional goals, and

(d) modifying the intervention program (e.g., changing the mode of presentation, the consequences for correct or incorrect responses, the instructional materials, etc.) as indicated by the child's performance data (Haring, Liberty, & White, 1980; Snell, 1983).

THE COURSE OF FUTURE EVENTS:
NEEDED TRENDS AND REQUIRED ACTIONS

If young handicapped children are to be afforded access to early intervention services, societal perceptions and commitments must be changed. As in all other areas of human pursuit, the process of change often occurs slowly and with varying degrees of resistance. Efforts directed toward altering societal commitments to young handicapped children must include the orchestration of several critical initiatives including:

(a) Systematically documenting the costs and benefits of early intervention within those media formats used by the general public (e.g., newspapers, television),

(b) marketing "stories" about individual children who benefited from early intervention programs,

(c) a continuation of research and dmonstration efforts within a variety of service delivery settings (e.g., public schools, nursery and day care programs),

(d) the establishment of a legislative coalition representing the needs of young handicapped children, and

(e) the provision of information to the parents of young handicapped children (e.g., where services currently exist, who to talk with to facilitate the development of new programs).

The professional literature contains many eloquent arguments for the expansion of early intervention services. However, the problem is that *professionals have only convinced each other* that these services are a viable component of a comprehensive support system for young handicapped children. The general public, the legislative decision makers, and the administrators of human service agencies have yet to be convinced. The success of these initiatives can not be measured by the number of pages published on early intervention, or the number of presentations delivered at national conventions. The only criterion for success is the availability of vastly improved service delivery options. The time for rhetoric has long passed. Action and results are the order of the day.

REFERENCES

Affleck, G. G. (1980). Physicians' attitudes toward discretionary medical treatment of Down's Syndrome infants. *Mental Retardation, 18,* 79–81.

Albano, M. L., Cox, B., York, J., & York, R. (1981). Educational team for students with severe and multiple handicaps. In R. York, W. Schofield, D. J. Donder, & D. L. Ryndak (Eds.), *The severely and profoundly handicapped child* (pp. 23–33). Urbana, IL: Illinois State Board of Education.

Anastasiow, N. J. (1981). Early childhood education for the handicapped in the 1980's: Recommendations. *Exceptional Children, 47*(4), 276–282.

Apolloni, T. J., & Cooke, T. P. (1978). Integrated programming at the infant, toddler, and preschool levels. In M. J. Guralnick (Ed.), *Early intervention and the integration of handicapped children and nonhandicapped children* (pp. 147–166). Baltimore, MD: University Park Press.

Bayley, N. (1969). *Bayley Scales of Infant Intelligence.* New York: Psychological Corporation.

Beck, R. (1977). Interdisciplinary model: Planning distribution and ancillary input to classrooms for the severely/profoundly handicapped. In E. Sontag, N. Certo, & J. Smith (Eds.), *Educational programming for the severely and profoundly handicapped* (pp. 397–404). Reston, VA: Council for Exceptional Children.

Bergen, A. F., & Colangelo, C. (1982). *Positioning the client with central nervous system deficits.* Valhalla, NY: Valhalla Rehabilitation Publications.

Bleck, E. E., & Nagel, D. A. (1982). *Physically handicapped children: A medical atlas for teachers* (2nd ed.). New York: Grune and Stratton.

Bricker, D. D. (1978). A rationale for the integration of handicapped and nonhandicapped preschool children. In M. J. Guralnick (Ed.), *Early intervention and the integration of handicapped and nonhandicapped children* (pp. 3–26). Baltimore, MD: University Park Press.

Bricker, D. D. (1983). Early communication: Development and training. In M. Snell (Ed.), *Systematic instruction of the moderately and severely handicapped* (2nd ed.) (pp. 269–288). Columbus, OH: Merrill.

Bricker, D. D., & Casuso, V. (1979). Family involvement: A critical component of early intervention. *Exceptional Children, 46*(2), 108–115.

Bristol, M. M., & Gallagher, J. J. (1982). A family focus for intervention. In C. T. Ramey & P. L. Trohanis (Eds.), *Finding and educating high-risk and handicapped infants* (pp. 137–162). Baltimore, MD: University Park Press.

Burton, T. A., & Hirshoren, A. (1979). The education of severely and profoundly retarded children: Are we sacrificing the child for the concept? *Exceptional Children, 45*(8), 598–602.

Campbell, P. H. (1982). Individualized team programming with infants and young handicapped children. In D. P. McClowry, A. M. Guilford, & S. O. Richardson (Eds.), *Infant communication: Development, assessment, and intervention* (pp. 147–186). New York: Grune and Stratton.

Campbell, P. H. (1983). Basic considerations in programming for students with movement difficulties. In M. Snell (Ed.), *Systematic instruction of the moderately and severely handicapped* (2nd ed.) (pp. 168–202). Columbus, OH: Merrill Publishing Co.

Campbell, P. H., Clegg, K. J., & McFarland, L. (1982). Measuring motor behavior. In M. Stevens-Dominguez & K. Stremel-Campbell (Eds.), *Ongoing data collection for measuring child progress* (pp. 59–90). Monmouth, OR: Western States Technical Assistance Resource.

Campbell, P. H., McInerney, W., & Middleton, M. (1982). *A manual of augmented sensory feedback for training severely handicapped students.* (Available from Children's Hospital Medical Center of Akron, Akron, Ohio)

Cansler, D. P., Martin, G. H., & Valand, M. C. (1975). *Working with families.* Chapel Hill, NC: Kaplan.

Coggins, T. E., & Sandall, S. (1983). The communicatively handicapped infant: Application of normal language and communication development. In S. G. Garwood & R. R. Fewell (Eds.), *Educating handicapped infants: Issues in development and intervention* (pp. 165–215). Rockville, MD: Aspen.

Cohen, L. (1981). Ethical issues in withholding treatment from severely handicapped infants. *Journal of The Association for the Severely Handicapped, 6*(2), 65–67.

Cohen, M., Gross, P., & Haring, N. G. (1976). Developmental pinpoints. In N. G. Haring & L. J. Brown (Eds.), *Teaching the severely handicapped* (Vol. 1) (pp. 35–110). New York: Grune and Stratton.

Cohen, P. C. (1962). The impact of the handicapped child on the family. *Social Casework, 42,* 137–142.

Cohen, S., Semmes, M., & Guralnick, M. J. (1979). Public Law 94-142 and the education of preschool handicapped children. *Exceptional Children, 45*(4), 279–285.

Cox, B. P., & Lloyd, L. L. (1976). Audiologic considerations. In L. L. Lloyd (Ed.), *Communication assessment and intervention strategies* (pp. 123–194). Baltimore, MD: University Park Press.

Cromer, R. F. (1981). Reconceptualizing language acquisition and cognitive development. In R. L. Schiefelbusch & D. D. Bricker (Eds.), *Early language: Acquisition and intervention* (pp. 51–138). Baltimore, MD: University Park Press.

Davis, H. & Silverman, S. R. (1970). *Hearing and deafness* (3rd ed.). New York: Holt, Rinehart, & Winston.

DuBose, R. R. (1979a). Working with sensorily impaired children, Part I: Visual impairments. In S. G. Garwood (Ed.), *Educating young handicapped children: A developmental approach* (pp. 323–360). Germantown, MD: Aspen.

DuBose, R. R. (1979b). Working with sensorily impaired children, Part II: Hearing impairments. In S. G. Garwood (Ed.), *Educating young handicapped children: A developmental approach* (pp. 361–398). Germantown, MD: Aspen.

Duff, R. S., & Campbell, A. G. N. (1973). Moral and ethical dilemmas in the special care nursery. *New England Journal of Medicine, 289*(17), 890–894.

Education for All Handicapped Children Act of 1975, Rules and Regulations, *Federal Register,* August 23, 1977.

Farber, B. (1968). *Mental retardation: The social context and social consequences.* New York: Houghton Mifflin.

Fewell, R. R. (1983). The team approach to infant education. In S. G. Garwood & R. R. Fewell (Eds.), *Educating handicapped infants: Issues in development and intervention* (pp. 299–320). Rockville, MD: Aspen.

Filler, J. W. Jr. (1983). Service models for handicapped infants. In S. G. Garwood & R. R. Fewell (Eds.), *Educating handicapped infants: Issues in development and intervention* (pp. 369–381). Rockville, MD: Aspen.

Flavell, J. (1977). *Cognitive development.* New York: Prentice-Hall.

Frailberg, S. (1968). Parallel and divergent patterns in blind and sighted infants. *Psychoanalytic Study of the Child, 23,* 264–300.

Frailberg, S. (1977). *Insights from the blind.* New York: Basic Books.

Frankenburg, W. K., Dodds, J., & Fandal, A. (1975). *Denver Developmental Screening Test: Reference manual* (Rev. ed.). Denver: LADOCA Project and Publishing Foundation.

Fredericks, H. D., Baldwin, V., Grove, D., Moore, W., & Riggs, C. (1978). Integrating the moderately and severely handicapped preschooler into a normal day care setting. In M. J. Guralnick (Ed.), *Early intervention and the integration of handicapped and nonhandicapped children* (pp. 191–206). Baltimore, MD: University Park Press.

Gabel, H., McDowell, J., & Cerreto, M. C. (1983). Family adaptation to the handicapped infant. In S. G. Garwood & R. R. Fewell (Eds.), *Educating handicapped infants: Issues in development and intervention* (pp. 455–493). Rockville, MD: Aspen.

Gallagher, J. J., Forsythe, P., Ringelheim, D., & Weintraub, F. (1975). Funding patterns and labeling. In N. Hobbs (Ed.), *Issues in the classification of children* (Vol. 2) (pp. 432–462). San Francisco: Jossey-Bass.

Galloway, C., & Chandler, P. (1978). The marriage of special and generic early education services. In M. J. Guralnick (Ed.), *Early intervention and the integration of handicapped and nonhandicapped children* (pp. 261–287). Baltimore, MD: University Park Press.

Garner, J. B. (1980). *Educational evaluation and decision making process: A forum for parent/professional interaction.* (Available from Mid-Eastern Ohio Special Education Regional Regional Resource Center, Cuyahoga Falls, Ohio)

Garner, J. B. (in press). Intelligence testing or testing intelligently: Implications for persons labeled as handicapped. *School Psychology International.*

Garwood, S. G. (1979). Language and language disorders in young children. In S. G. Garwood (Ed.), *Educating young handicapped children: A developmental approach* (pp. 233–260). Rockville, MD: Aspen.

Gesell, A. (1940). *Gesell Developmental Schedules.* New York: Psychological Corporation.

Gilhool, T. K., & Stutman, E. A. (1978). Integration of handicapped students. In *Developing criteria for the evaluation of the least restrictive environment provision* (pp. 191–227). Washington, D.C.: Bureau of Education for the Handicapped.

Gold, M. W. (1980). *Did I say that?* Champaign, IL: Research Press.

Gold, M. W. (1981, November). *Whatever I feel like talking about in November.* Paper presented at the meeting of The Association for the Severely Handicapped, New York, NY.

Goldstein, H. (1964). Social and occupational adjustment. In H. A. Stevens, & R. Heber (Eds.), *Mental retardation: A review of research* (pp. 214–258). Chicago: University of Chicago Press.

Grossman, H. J. (1977). *Manual on terminology and classification in mental retardation.* Washington, DC: American Association on Mental Deficiency.

Haring, N. G., Liberty, K. A., & White, O. R. (1980). Rules for data-based strategy decisions in instruction programs: Current research and instructional implications. In W. Sailor, B. Wilcox, & L. Brown (Eds.), *Methods of instruction for severely handicapped students* (pp. 159–192). Baltimore, MD: University Park Press.

Hart, V. (1977). The use of many disciplines with the severely and profoundly handicapped. In E. Sontag, N. Certo, & J. Smith (Eds.), *Educational programming for the severely and profoundly handicapped* (pp. 391–396). Reston, VA: Council for Exceptional Children.

Hayden, A. H. (1979). Handicapped children, age birth to three. *Exceptional Children, 45,* 510–517.

Hewett, F. M., & Forness, S. R. (1977). *Education of exceptional learners.* Boston, MA: Allyn & Bacon.

Higgins, L. C. (1973). *Classification in congenitally blind children.* New York: American Foundation for the Blind.

Hobbs, N. (1975). *The futures of children: Categories, labels, and their consequences.* San Francisco: Jossey-Bass.

Horowitz, F. D. (1978). Normal and abnormal development. In K. E. Allen, V. A. Holm, & R. L. Schiefelbusch (Eds.), *Early intervention: A team approach* (pp. 3–26). Baltimore, MD: University Park Press.

Kagan, J., & Moss, H. A. (1962). *Birth to maturity: A study in psychological development.* New York: Wiley.

Kauffman, J. (1979). Emotional disorders in young children. In S. G. Garwood (Ed.), *Educating young handicapped children: A developmental approach* (pp. 449–471). Germantown, MD: Aspen.

Kirk, S. A. (1972). *Educating exceptional children* (2nd ed.). Boston: Houghton Mifflin.

Langley, M. B. (1979). Working with young physically handicapped children: Part B, educational programming. In S. G. Garwood (Ed.), *Educating young handicapped children: A developmental approach.* Germantown, MD: Aspen.

McCall, R. (1979). The development of intellectual functioning in infancy and the prediction of later IQ. In J. Osofsky (Ed.), *Handbook of infant development* (pp. 707–741). New York: Wiley.

McCubbin, T. (1983). Routine and emergency medical procedures. In M. Snell (Ed.), *Systematic instruction of the moderately and severely handicapped* (2nd ed.) (pp. 148–165). Columbus, OH: Merrill.

Mercer, J. (1972, April). IQ: The lethal label. *Psychology Today,* p. 44.

Olshansky, S. (1962). Chronic sorrow: A response to having a mentally defective child. *Social Casework, 43,* 190–192.

Piaget, J. (1952). *The origins of intelligence in children.* New York: International Universities Press.

Piaget, J., & Inhelder, B. (1969). *The psychology of the child.* New York: Basic Books.

Powell, T. H., Aiken, J. M., & Smylie, M. A. (1982). Treatment or involuntary euthanasia for severely handicapped infants: Issues of philosophy and public policy. *Journal of The Association for the Severely Handicapped, 6*(4), 3–10.

Quay, H. (1973). Special education: Assumptions, techniques, and evaluative criteria. *Exceptional Children, 40,* 165–170.

Robinson, C. C. (1982). Questions regarding the effects of neuromotor problems on sensorimotor development. In D. D. Bricker (Ed.), *Intervention with at-risk and handicapped infants: From research to application* (pp. 233–246). Baltimore, MD: University Park Press.

Robinson, C. C., & Robinson, J. H. (1983). Sensorimotor functions and cognitive development. In M. Snell (Ed.), *Systematic instruction of the moderately and severely handicapped* (2nd ed.) (pp. 227–266). Columbus, OH: Merrill.

Safford, P. L. (1978). *Teaching young children with special needs.* St. Louis, MO: Mosby.

Snell, M. (1983). Developing the IEP: Selecting and assessing skills. In M. Snell (Ed.), *Systematic instruction of the moderately and severely handicapped* (2nd ed.) (pp. 76–112). Columbus, OH: Merrill.

Sontag, E., Certo, N., & Button, J. E. (1979). On a distinction between the education of the severely and profoundly handicapped and a doctrine of limitations. *Exceptional Children, 45*(8), 605–616.

Stone, C. (1977). Motor skills. In N. G. Haring (Ed.), *Developing effective individualized education programs for severely handicapped children and youth* (pp. 58–90). Washington, DC: Bureau of Education for the Handicapped.

Terman, L. M., & Merrill, M. A. (1973). *Stanford-Binet Intelligence Scale.* Boston, MA: Houghton Mifflin.

Turnbull, A. P. (1983). Parent professional interactions. In M. Snell (Ed.), *Systematic instruction of the moderately and severely handicapped* (2nd ed.) (pp. 18–43). Columbus, OH: Merrill.

Turnbull, A. P., & Turnbull, H. R. III (1978). *Parents speak out: Views from the other side of the two way mirror.* Columbus, OH: Merrill.

United States General Accounting Office (1981). *Disparities still exist in who gets special education.* Washington, DC: United States General Accounting Office.

Uzgiris, I. C. (1981). Experience in the social context. In R. L. Schiefelbusch & D. D. Bricker, (Eds.), *Early language: Acquisition and intervention* (pp. 139–168).

Uzgiris, I. C., & Hunt, J. McV. (1975). *Assessment in infancy: Ordinal scales of psychological development.* Urbana, IL: University of Illinois Press.

Vincent, L. J., Broome, K. (1977). A public school service delivery model for handicapped children between birth and five years of age. In E. Sontag,

N. Certo, & J. Smith (Eds.) *Educational programming for the severely and profoundly handicapped* (pp. 177-188). Reston, VA: Council for Exceptional Children.

Vincent, L. J., Salisbury, C., Walter, G., Brown, P., Grunewald, L., & Powers, M. (1980). Program evaluation and curriculum development in early childhood/ special education: Criteria of the next environment. In W. Sailor, B. Wilcox, & L. Brown (Eds.), *Methods of instruction for severely handicapped students* (pp. 303-328). Baltimore, MD: Paul R. Brookes Publishers.

Warren, D. (1977). *Blindness and early childhood development.* New York: American Foundation for the Blind.

Wolfensberger, W. (1972). *The principle of normalization in human services.* Toronto, Canada: National Institute on Mental Retardation.

Wolfensberger, W. (1980). A call to wake up to the beginning of a new wave of euthanasia of severely impaired people. *Education and Training of the Mentally Retarded, 15,*

Zelazo, P. R. (1982). Alternative assessment procedures for handicapped infants and toddlers: Theoretical and practical issues. In D. D. Bricker (Ed.), *Intervention with at-risk and handicapped infants: From research to application* (pp. 107-128). Baltimore, MD: University Park Press.

PART II

FAMILY AND SOCIETAL ECOLOGY

CHAPTER 6

THE DEVELOPMENT
OF SOCIAL RELATIONSHIPS

MARY JO CHERRY

Man is by nature a social animal. From the beginning, he enters into a social network. . . . [which] becomes the context in which his personality, cognition, and social development are embedded" (Lewis, Young, Brooks, & Michalson, 1975, p. 28). This social milieu includes a broad spectrum of relationships, usually beginning with interactions between the child and parents, broadening to include other family members, and gradually admitting peers as part of the context. It is on the development of social relationships with peers that this chapter is focused.

It is difficult to address the nature of social development within the confines of a single chapter, even if one limits discussion to peer interaction, as entire books have been devoted to this topic (Bronson, 1981; Lewis & Rosenblum, 1975; Rubin & Ross, 1982; Webb, 1977). However, highlights of progression can be noted, and the reader can expand upon information offered by pursuing references cited. Thus, this chapter is written to provide merely a glimpse of the growing body of data which addresses the factors affecting the development of social relationships with one's peers.

Although most individuals spend some time alone, they are also involved in many social relationships. The importance of peer interactions was noted by Yarrow (1975), when she suggested that

> Peers are the life of people—not only of children. . . . [an] individual is likely to be with near-age mates for very considerable portions of his time and for very widely varying relationships. . . . closeness to some peer(s) and acceptance by one's peers are potent factors in the well-being of the individual. (p. 299)

The study of the development of this ability to interact effectively with peers and form relationships with them, therefore, is an important task.

SOCIAL COMPETENCE

The ability to interact competently with other human beings is a requirement for successful participation in society (O'Malley, 1977). Individuals must develop concepts of themselves as effective social beings involved in reciprocal relationships, in which one not only influences but also is influenced by other human beings. Although individuals learn much about the world by themselves, many things must be learned with the help of others. Much of human development, therefore, is social in nature, and a great deal of the understanding of social phenomena is acquired during direct experience and interaction with other human beings.

White (1979) suggests that social competence includes "skills or abilities in getting along with other people" (p. 2). Individuals must acquire behaviors which will allow them to act in a manner acceptable to other members of their society, and this involves narrowing their range of behaviors to the established societal norms. The process of becoming socially competent is a lifelong endeavor, with its roots grounded in the interactions of the young child both with peers and adults.

The ability to "share perspectives and coordinate actions and reactions with others" (Damon, 1979, p. 208) is but one social skill involved in successful interpersonal relationships. This ability begins to develop at an early age as the infant relates with adults and peers. Moore (1979) suggests that the ability to predict social outcomes will improve as the skills of perceiving others' moods and assessing their motives gradually develop. The results of these experiences will include the formation of social concepts such as friendship, rivalry, and fairness; the understanding of which are necessary for effective social interaction.

Since social interaction is a basic part of all adult human lives, the ability to relate competently with others is an important characteristic one must acquire. Evidence from the studies of nonhuman primates suggests that early peer relations play an important role in social development (Harlow & Harlow, 1965), and studies of humans suggest that there is a critical period for acquiring social skills which occurs during the early years of life and involves peers as well as adults (Blurton-Jones, 1967; Greif, 1977; White, 1969).

Dimitrovsky (1970) suggests a sequence of social development through which all children pass, progressing from treatment of peers as things, to enjoyment of another's presence with little interest in direct interaction, and, eventually, to the ability to cooperate and express the need for their companionship. It is during these stages that the child is able to rehearse the life roles and social skills essential for adult functioning (McCandless & Hoyt, 1961; Reese & Lipsitt, 1970).

EFFECTIVE COMMUNICATION

An important aspect of interpersonal interaction is the ability to communicate ideas effectively. In fact, it has become apparent that "optimal human development depends to a large degree on the development of communication" (Bullowa, Fidelholtz, & Kessler, 1975, p. 253).

Communication is a purposeful process which includes all exchanges, verbal and nonverbal, in which messages are transmitted among persons. One of the primary purposes of communication is to affect others in some way and, ultimately, to produce a response from them. When this process results in a sufficient understanding of meaning by both parties, effective communication is said to have occurred.

Communicating with others is a social affair which begins during infancy. Verbal and nonverbal techniques for influencing others are learned at an early age through interaction. These then become processes which can be used quite easily. The young child learns to communicate effectively with others through parent-child contacts, as well as during interactions with agemates. Since the techniques employed and messages shared with adults are not necessarily similar to those involved in peer communication, peer relationships become an essential part of the child's development. Hartup (1977) suggests that optimal social development occurs when opportunities are provided for interaction with individuals of like social and cognitive capabilities.

EARLY PEER RESEARCH

A growing number of studies have addressed the beginnings of the processes involved in learning from and with others. Although young children, especially those under the age of two to three years, have seldom been considered social beings (except for the mother-infant relationship), evidence is beginning to dispel the notion that the youngest members of humanity are incapable of interacting socially with each other. Rather than revealing that young children possess few socially related behaviors, studies are uncovering the existence of a complex system of peer interaction that progresses from treatment of peers as objects, to indirect interaction during parallel play, and finally to direct contact with one's peers.

During the early decades of this century, several researchers studied the social development of the very young (Bridges, 1933; Maudry & Nekula, 1939). The results of these studies suggested that peer interaction does occur at an early age and that it has an important effect upon the child's social development.

An early study by Parten (1932) analyzed the social participation of children as young as two years of age during free-play in a nursery school setting. Results suggested that the youngest children tended to play alone or were involved in parallel play, with the amount of peer interaction increasing as the children's ages increased. In a recent study of parallel play, it is suggested that this type of involvement provides the basis of social development. Children are often seen to become involved in side-by-side play with the same materials, and have been observed exchanging objects and showing them to one another (Eckerman & Whatley, 1977).

In an attempt to discover trends of social and emotional growth during the early stages of development, Bridges (1933) recorded detailed observations of the behavior of infants and toddlers. Although social development began in relation to adults, and interest in peers began later and progressed slowly until the age of nine months, more rapid social development occurred during the second year of life.

Following these early attempts to study peer behavior, few studies of social development were reported until recently. The apparent lack of interest in this area of study can be attributed to several factors, primary among them being the rise of psychoanalysis, with its emphasis on mother-infant relationships as the basis for all social-emotional development, and the influence of Piagetian theory which stresses the egocentric nature of the young child and, therefore, suggests the restriction of the child's ability to meaningfully interact with others (Arnold, 1979; Lewis et al., 1975; Mueller & Vandell, 1979). Apolloni and Cooke (1975) further note that very early peer behavior has been ignored since few opportunities for social interaction with peers have been provided.

The rise in the number of young children placed in group care settings seems to have sparked an interest in the study of peer relations among young children. Observational techniques and data-collection processes have been improved, and the development of social relations among young peers is again receiving attention (Brooks, 1974; De Stefano, 1976; Mueller & Vandell, 1979).

STAGES OF EARLY PEER ENCOUNTERS

As noted previously, Piagetian theory could be interpreted so as to deny the existence of peer relations among the very young. Several studies, however, have focused efforts on identifying the existence of peer relationships among young children, and the developmental changes which occur in these interactions. Mueller and Lucas (1975) identified stages of development in peer relations which occur during the sensorimotor period. Stage I is characterized by object centered contact during which time the young child is effective in interacting with inanimate objects but not with peers. Transition to Stage II shows the appearance of an active seeking and desiring by the child to receive contingencies from others, but these encounters are still limited to simple actions which are merely imitative interchanges in which children exchange turns but not roles. Finally, the third stage involves rule complementarity in which the toddlers perform reciprocal or intercoordinated actions such as offering and receiving. Thus, social interaction among peers does progress during the first two years of life.

Eckerman, Whatley, and Kutz (1975) provide further support for the position that infants and toddlers can, indeed, interact with peers. Their findings suggested that all children interacted both with the toys provided and their peers, with the frequency of peer interaction increasing with age. Involvement progressed from distant watching and smiling to more direct involvement and physical contact. Social involvement through play with one's peers increased as the children grew older.

Similar results were found by Finkelstein, Dent, Gallacher, and Ramey (1978) who observed infants and toddlers attending daycare programs. Study of the social behaviors observed revealed that older children were more likely to be involved in social relationships with peers than were younger children, and that children in both groups were more successful at interaction with their peers when some type of object-centered contact was involved. As the children grew older, a substantial amount of time was spent in social encounters with their agemates.

Increases in the quantity of interactions with peers are accompanied by changes in the nature of the involvement. Becker (1977) found that infants involved in play-sessions in their homes gradually increased the complexity of their peer-oriented behavior and the degree of social engagements, suggesting that exposure to the stimulating behavior of another infant causes a change in the child's interactive behavior. Verbal interaction during peer encounters has also been shown to increase with age (Mueller, Bleier, Krakow, Hegedus, and Cournoyer, 1977), particularly during the third year of life.

The frequency of peer contacts continues to increase as children progress through the preschool years, and the nature of these interactions also changes. Ferguson (1971) suggests that "the means of initiation are more and more verbal rather than physical or material" (p. 120). Garvey and Hogan (1973) found that preschool-aged children not only engaged in sustained interactions, but many of these engagements included talk which became the primary focus of their relationship. Contact with a peer, therefore, is increasingly achieved and maintained through the use of speech.

The duration of the peer interactions of preschoolers and kindergarten-aged children increases, and contacts expand from ones which are dyadic in nature to small group gatherings where three or more children are able to engage successfully in social relations. Friendships with peers begin to form at this time. Damon (1979) suggests that preschoolers and young children consider as friends the playmates and/or peers with whom they attend school. Positive interchanges such as the giving and sharing of objects tend to establish friendships, while negative encounters such as the refusal to share usually terminate the relationship. Seldom are these friendships stable, as children make and break ties dependent upon the immediate context within which the relationship has developed. Thus, social interactions among young peers are still tender and subject to frequent change, although growing in complexity, duration, and number.

VISUAL REGARD

Prior to actual physical contact, infants initiate interaction with others through visual regard. Studies of mother-infant interaction (Stern, 1974) have noted the importance of dyadic gazing in initiating and sustaining conditions for social behavior. Further support for the necessity of reciprocal attention for interaction to occur is offered by Finkelstein et al. (1978), for they propose that eye-to-eye contact may act as the stimulus for the continuation of interaction. Sustained periods of mutual visual attention appear to serve as important roots of social behavior, with this development apparently beginning during mother-infant contacts (Mueller & Vandell, 1979).

Several studies have found that a dominant activity of toddlers in dyadic or group situations is that of watching their peers (Bronson, 1975; Eckerman et al., 1975; Mueller, 1979). Given a setting which allows toddlers the freedom of many choices, as many as 60 percent of observations indicate visual regard, rather than physical contact, as the toddler's activity.

Most researchers, although acknowledging the occurrence of watching by peers, tend to exclude it from any discussion of social interaction. Mere gaze behavior does not fulfill requirements for inclusion in the category of true social responsiveness in most toddler peer studies. Extended visual regard of peers is usually seen as an exploratory activity, similar to what the infant does with any novel or interesting object.

However, Mueller (1979) suggests that gaze behavior may hold more information regarding early stages of social development than once considered. He showed that sixteen month old children watched toys more than people, and they focused their attention on an active peer more often than on the normally inactive teacher. "Looks" at people were brief when compared with visual regard of objects. He hypothesizes that if toddlers' visually directed gazes mirror their thought, then visual attention may provide an index of the child's preoccupation. He notes further that gazes, although not specific to a peer's social potential, do suggest some awareness of the peer's presence. Social encounters may emerge from this increasing awareness and interest.

Research by Cherry (1982) also revealed gaze behavior among toddlers during conflict with peers. The majority of toddler gazes were directed toward the peer with whom interaction was occurring. It appeared that the toddlers wished to remain aware of strategies that peers might use against them, thus attempting to control what was being watched. The directed-watching by toddlers appeared to be a strategy accompanying and/or supplementing the toddlers' actual movements, which helped the child control the interpersonal behavior.

Thus, it seems possible that gaze behavior directed toward one's peer may precede and supplement overt movements. Watching one's peer may set the stage for future direct contact, almost as if the young child needs to survey the situation prior to making an attempt to interact.

VARIABLES AFFECTING PEER INTERACTION

Studies of peer interaction have focused on various factors which effect the development of social relationships among young children. These factors include peer experience, degree of familiarity, group size, situational factors, and behavioral setting. Of these, two of the most important are "experience and familiarity with peers" and "situational factors." These factors will be discussed at this point in the chapter.

Experience and Familiarity with Peers

One variable considered by the research is the effect that the amount of peer interaction has upon peer relationships. Mueller and Brenner (1977) observed playgroups comprised of twelve- and sixteen-month-old children, and found that the more peer-experienced toddlers (even if slightly younger chronologically than the inexperienced children) showed a higher frequency of more complicated, coordinated social behaviors in their interactions, and produced significantly more sustained interaction sequences.

The degree of familiarity among peers involved in studies also proved to affect social interaction. Mueller and Brenner (1977) have shown that, although unacquainted toddlers could just as often elicit single responses to social initiations, familiar toddlers more often could sustain the interchange. More positive social interaction has also been observed among long-acquainted peers (Rubenstein & Howes, 1976).

The effect of familiarity with one's peers, upon the type of interchanges which occur, has also been studied with preschool children. Doyle (1982) found that play among acquainted three-year-olds was more often social in nature (associative and co-operative) than was play in situations involving unfamiliar mates. Factors that were affected positively in the presence of a familiar peer included "frequency of social overtures, amount of social interaction, and complexity of toy play during this social interaction" (p. 238). Doyle suggests that the more positive and complex nature of social relations among acquainted peers may warrant more frequent contact with familiar children, rather than constant changes in peer group composition.

Four-year-olds studied by Schwarz (1972) also displayed a positive reaction to the presence of a familiar peer as compared with situations involving an unacquainted child or time spent alone. Preschoolers exhibited more positive affect, were more motile, and talked more to each other when a familiar child was in their presence. Schwarz suggests further that "the presence of an attached peer has a distress-inhibiting effect" on the preschool-aged child (p. 282).

It appears that social relations among young children are influenced by the degree of familiarity shared among peers. Although interaction occurs among strangers, the nature of the relations is positively affected when the children interacting are acquaintances.

Situational Factors

As mentioned previously, the early stages of the development of peer relations involve inanimate objects in the environment (Mueller & Lucas, 1975). Bronson (1975) notes that whether the encounters among toddlers are agonistic (socially aggressive) or prosocial, it is evident that objects play a central role in mediating the interaction. Approximately half of all the prosocial behaviors observed in her study revolved around agemate-toy combinations, while the majority of social conflicts also centered around objects.

Further support for the prominence of object involvement in early peer relations is found in studies by Mueller (1979) in which more than 90 per cent of all the social peer interactions of one-year-old children in dyads occurred during an object-centered contact. It is suggested that children are drawn into contact by reciprocal interaction with physical materials, and that these object-focused contacts provide the beginnings of peer social relations (Mueller & Brenner, 1977).

The effects of both the presence and absence of toys on peer interactions among peers of one- or two-year-olds were studied by Eckerman and Whatley (1977). Although interactions occurred under circumstances involving either toy presence or toy absence, the nature of these encounters differed. When no toys were available, the children often contacted one another through smiles, gestures, and imitations of each other's actions. The encounters changed when toys were present, as the children showed and exchanged the play objects with each other and became involved in parallel play with similar play materials. Toys, therefore, appeared to be used as vehicles for certain types of social interactions.

The social relationships of preschool-aged peers are also affected by factors within the environment. Preschoolers studied by Shure (1963) exhibited more solitary play in the block and games areas of the nursery school, while the "most complex social interactions occurred most often in the doll corner. . . . and half of the play in the block area was of this complex quality" (p. 987). Shure notes that the physical proximity of peers to each other may affect the nature of their contacts.

It appears that the physical environment, and the objects within it, have an impact on the social performance of young children. Both the quantity and quality of peer interactions are affected.

THE GROWTH OF AGGRESSION WITH PEERS

Both positive and negative encounters among infant/toddler peers have been reported, with both types of interactions increasing with age (Eckerman et al., 1975; Mueller & Vandell, 1979). However, positive encounters continue to exceed negative interactions. Conflict occurs predominantly when an object (toy) is involved (Bronson, 1975; Cherry, 1982), and when only the target child possesses an object of interest at the onset of the interaction (Cherry, 1982; Rogers, 1977).

Cherry (1982) found the nature of social conflicts of toddler peers to be complex and varied, focusing upon situations involving a small object and most often occurring between near-age peers. Toddlers tended to use movements which decreased distance between self and the desired object and/or increased the distance between the peer and this object. Actions were supplemented by gaze behaviors, and verbalizations used were predominantly negative in nature.

As with the younger child, positive affect tends to predominate in peer interactions among preschool and kindergarten children (Walters, Pearce, & Dahms, 1957). However, aggressive acts do occur. Aggressive social interactions among preschool children appear to be affected by a child's own personality and by the characteristics of the environment. Kohn (1966) found that young children of kindergarten age create their own environment; for, "a hostile child is the recipient more frequently of hostile activity from others than is the unhostile child" (p. 99). Muste and Sharpe (1947) discovered more aggressive activities in a more controlled nursery school than in the freer nursery school they studied. It appears, therefore, that one needs to consider the nature of the environment as well as the unique personal characteristics of the child when attempting to understand the reasons for aggressive behavior during interactions with peers.

IMPLICATIONS AND RECOMMENDATIONS

It is clear from this research that young children do, indeed, interact with each other, and benefit from situations which allow social relations to develop and grow. Even the youngest members of society appear to possess the ability to communicate with their peers, and studies reveal that they also have an interest in doing so. It seems reasonable, therefore, to suggest that parents and educators should provide opportunities for young children to spend time with each other.

The need for stimulation from and interaction with adults by young children is well-established. Studies have shown that the adult-child relationship is important for the positive growth of the child. However, peer interaction also is needed to facilitate positive social development. As Michalson, Brooks, and Lewis (1975) note:

> The peer social context is quite different from the more pervasive caregiver milieu where the adult guides, directs, and controls. In contrast, peers are relatively equal in terms of their social skills, the capacity to formulate and carry out their goals, and the extent of their socialization. In this social context, infants not only mutually socialize each other, but they have a better chance at successfully affecting one another. (p. 6)

It appears, then, that what young children learn from peers differs in nature from those messages transmitted to them by their adult caregivers. Children need both peers and adults to facilitate competence in relating with others.

The increase in day-care centers, nursery and preschools, and playgroups suggests that earlier opportunities for children to interact with peers is being provided. Young peers need time to develop the skills of interaction, whether of a positive or negative nature, and group settings in which they play provide opportunity for this growth in social relations. Not only must adults provide opportunities for children to interact, but environments which encourage the children to interact must also be designed. Children need ample opportunity for free play, especially in the block and housekeeping corners of the classroom where children most often become involved in group play. Less structured environments where group activity is facilitated, appear more appropriate for the growth of social relationships.

Learning to deal with social conflict is also a necessary part of one's social development. Occasions will arise when messages and desires will not be accepted amicably by one's peers. These misunderstandings and upsets among young children are inevitable. Guidance must be provided so that children will learn socially accepted means of settling disputes. Adult intervention may be warranted at times, but children should also be permitted to attempt settlements on their own. Parents and educators might facilitate children's understanding of conflict and modes used to settle disputes with stories and role-play situations. Children must be allowed the opportunity to learn from each other, and unless physical harm is feared, are probably best left to deal with peers without adult intervention. Cherry (1982) found that even children as young as toddler-age desire independence in working through problems with their peers. Although gazes were directed toward parents and teachers by both the initiators of the conflicts and the target children, most strategies used by the children involved actions which were independent of adult aid or the seeking of this aid by the child. Review of the outcomes of adult interventions during toddler peer conflicts revealed an inconsistent success by the adults at mediating the problems, with no method being found consistently successful or helpful. Learning to deal with conflict is as important for the healthy social growth of the child as the ability to establish positive, meaningful relationships with one's peers.

Adults must be able to interact competently with their peers in both their professional and personal lives. This ability should be fostered from a young age, allowing the young child time to develop the capacity to relate socially with agemates. Adults can set the stage for this growth by providing ample opportunities for young peers to interact. Young children definitely need other young children for healthy social development.

Further study of this area of human growth and development is warranted. As the age at which children enter group settings increasingly becomes younger, it is important that caregivers understand the factors which influence the social development that occurs among peers. Parents are also asked to study the necessity of peer relationships among young children so that a well-rounded environment might be provided for the young child. If adults are to experience success in relationships with peers, it seems only natural that the roots of these social encounters (i.e., social relationships among young peers) be studied, understood, and fostered. It is time for society to realize that children help each other grow and develop.

REFERENCES

Apolloni, T., & Cooke, T. P. (1975). Peer behavior conceptualized as a variable influencing infant and toddler development. *American Journal of Orthopsychiatry*, 45(1), 4–17.

Arnold, M. R. (1979). Early child-child communication. *Theory into Practice*, 18(4), 213–219.

Becker, J. M. T. (1977). A learning analysis of the development of peer-oriented behavior in nine-month-old infants. *Developmental Psychology*, 13(5), 481–491.

Blurton-Jones, N. (1967). An ethological study of some aspects of social behavior of children in nursery school. In D. Morris (Ed.), *Primate ethology*. London: Weidenfeld and Nicholson.

Bridges, K. M. B. (1933). A study of social development in early infancy. *Child Development*, 4, 36–49.

Bronson, W. C. (1975). Developments in behavior with age mates during the second year of life. In M. Lewis & L. A. Rosenblum (Eds.), *Friendship and peer relations*. New York: Wiley.

Bronson, W. C. (1981). *Toddlers' behaviors with agemates: Issues of interaction, cognition, and affect*. Norwood, NJ: Ablex.

Brooks, J. (1974). *Social perception and peer group interaction in infancy: Final report*. Princeton, NJ: Educational Testing Service. (ERIC Document Reproduction Service No. ED 100 527)

Bullowa, M., Fidelholtz, J. L., & Kessler, A. R. (1975). Infant vocalization: Communication before speech. In T. R. Williams (Ed.), *Socialization and communication in primary groups*. Chicago: Aldine.

Cherry, M. J. (1982). A naturalistic inquiry of the social conflicts of toddler peers.

Dissertation Abstracts International, 42, 3005A. (University Microfilms No. 81-28, 485)

Damon, W. (1979). Why study social-cognitive development? *Human Development, 22,* 206–211.

De Stefano, C. T. (1976). Environmental determinants of peer social behavior and interaction in a toddler playgroup. *Dissertation Abstracts International, 36,* 5861B–5862B. (University Microfilms No. 76-11, 691)

Dimitrovsky, L. (1970). Social development in children. In J. R. Davitz & S. Ball (Eds.), *Psychology of the educational process.* New York: McGraw-Hill.

Doyle, A. (1982). Friends, acquaintances, and strangers: The influence of familiarity and ethnolinguistic background on social interaction. In K. H. Rubin & H. S. Ross (Eds.), *Peer relations and social skills in childhood.* New York: Springer-Verlag.

Eckerman, C. O., & Whatley, J. L. (1977). Toys and social interaction between infant peers. *Child Development, 48*(4), 1645–1656.

Eckerman, C. O., Whatley, J. L., & Kutz, S. L. (1975). Growth of social play with peers during the second year of life. *Developmental Psychology, 11*(1), 42–49.

Ferguson, L. R. (1971). Origins of social development in infancy. *Merrill-Palmer Quarterly, 17*(2), 119–137.

Finkelstein, N. W., Dent, C., Gallacher, K., & Ramey, C. T. (1978). Social behavior of infants and toddlers in a daycare environment. *Developmental Psychology, 14*(3), 257–262.

Garvey, C., & Hogan, R. (1973). Social speech and social interaction: Egocentrism revisited. *Child Development, 44,* 562–568.

Greif, E. B. (1977). Peer interactions in preschool children. In R. A. Webb (Ed.), *Social development in childhood: Day-care programs and research.* Baltimore: Johns Hopkins Univ. Press.

Harlow, H. F., & Harlow, M. K. (1965). The affectional systems. In A. M. Schrier, H. F. Harlow, & F. Stollnitz (Eds.), *Behavior of non-human primates* (Vol. 2). New York: Academic Press.

Hartup, W. W. (1977). Peer relations: Developmental implications and interaction in same- and mixed-age situations. *Young Children, 32*(3), 4–13.

Kohn, M. (1966). The child as a determinant of his peers' approach to him. *The Journal of Genetic Psychology, 109,* 91–100.

Lewis, M., & Rosenblum, L. A. (Eds.). (1975). *Friendship and peer relations.* New York: Wiley.

Lewis, M., Young, G., Brooks, J., & Michalson, L. (1975). The beginning of friendship. In M. Lewis & L. A. Rosenblum (Eds.), *Friendship and peer relations.* New York: Wiley.

Maudry, M., & Nekula, M. (1939). Social relations between children of the same age during the first two years of life. *Journal of Genetic Psychology, 54,* 193–215.

McCandless, B., & Hoyt, J. (1961). Sex, ethnicity, and play preferences of preschool children. *Journal of Abnormal Social Psychology, 62,* 683–685.

Michalson, L., Brooks, J., & Lewis, M. (1975, April). *Peers, parents, people: Social relationships in infancy.* Paper presented at the meeting of the Eastern Psychological Association, New York City.

Moore, S. G. (1979). Social cognition: Knowing about others. *Young Children, 34*(3), 54–61.

Mueller, E. (1979). (Toddlers + toys) = (An autonomous social system). In M. Lewis & L. A. Rosenblum (Eds.), *The child and its family.* New York: Plenum Press.

Mueller, E., Bleier, M., Krakow, J., Hegedus, K., & Cournoyer, P. (1977). The development of peer verbal interaction among two-year-old boys. *Child Development, 48*(1), 284–287.

Mueller, E., & Brenner, J. (1977). The origins of social skills and interaction among playgroup toddlers. *Child Development, 48*(3), 854–861.

Mueller, E., & Lucas, T. (1975). A developmental analysis of peer interaction among toddlers. In M. Lewis & L. A. Rosenblum (Eds.), *Friendship and peer relations.* New York: Wiley.

Mueller, E., & Vandell, D. (1979). Infant-infant interaction. In J. D. Osofsky (Ed.), *Handbook of infant development.* New York: Wiley.

Muste, M. J., & Sharpe, D. F. (1947). Some influential factors in the determination of aggressive behavior in preschool children. *Child Development, 18,* 11–28.

O'Malley, J. M. (1977). Research perspective on social competence. *Merrill-Palmer Quarterly, 23*(1), 29–43.

Parten, M. B. (1932). Social participation among pre-school children. *Journal of Abnormal and Social Psychology, 27,* 243–269.

Reese, H., & Lipsitt, L. (1970). *Experimental child psychology.* New York: Academic Press.

Rogers, P. P. (1977). Two year old's use of objects in peer interaction. *Dissertation Abstracts International, 37,* 4120B–4212B. (University Microfilms No. 77-03, 113).

Rubenstein, J., & Howes, C. (1976). The effects of peers on toddler interaction with mother and toys. *Child Development, 47*(3), 597–605.

Rubin, K. H., & Ross, H. S. (Eds.). (1982). *Peer relationships and social skills in childhood.* New York: Springer-Verlag.

Schwarz, J. C. (1972). Effects of peer familiarity on the behavior of preschoolers in a novel situation. *Journal of Personality and Social Psychology, 24*(2), 276–284.

Shure, M. B. (1963). Psychological ecology of a nursery school. *Child Development, 34,* 979–992.

Stern, D. N. (1974). Mother and infant at play: The dyadic interaction involving facial, vocal, and gaze behaviors. In M. Lewis & L. A. Rosenblum Eds.), *The effect of the infant on its caregiver.* New York: Wiley.

Walters, J., Pearce, D., & Dahms, L. (1957). Affectional and aggressive behavior of preschool children. *Child Development, 28*(1), 15–26.

Webb, R. A. (Ed.). (1977). *Social development in childhood: Day-care programs and research.* Baltimore: Johns Hopkins Univ. Press.

White, B. L. (1969). Child development research: An edifice without a foundation. *Merrill-Palmer Quarterly, 15,* 47–58.

White, B. L. (1979). A review of current research on social competence. *The Center for Parent Education Newsletter, 1*(5), 1-5.

Yarrow, M. R. (1975). Some perspectives on research on peer relations. In M. Lewis & L. A. Rosenblum (Eds.), *Friendship and peer relations.* New York: Wiley.

CHAPTER 7

FAMILY INFLUENCES ON THE DEVELOPMENT OF THE YOUNG CHILD

MICHAEL E. LAMB

There occurred an explosion of interest in the 1970s in the socialization and socioemotional development in infancy. This returned to prominence an issue that had fallen from favor in the preceding decades. Like the research and theorizing that dominated the earlier era of concern with this topic, most of the attention within the 1970's was on the family, since many of the more important aspects of socialization were believed to take place early in life, when extrafamilial experiences were few. Thus, it was with parental—especially maternal—influences that psychologists became concerned.

To make their models concise and their hypotheses testable students of socialization made a number of simplifying assumptions about the sorts of families in which children were being raised. Prominent among these was the assumption that "normal" socialization took place in the context of a two-parent family in which the father assumed responsibility for financial support while mother eschewed involvement in employment in order to assume responsibility for the care of children, home, and family. This simplifying assumption was never wholly satisfactory, because it failed to accord attention to the many families which violated the supposed norm.

Moreover, this "model" of the family has become increasingly unsatisfactory as the number of families which deviate from this standard has continued to mount. Mothers are currently employed outside the home in the majority of American families, and the continuing rise in divorce rates means that many children spend at least part of their childhood in single-parent homes.

Unfortunately, psychologists have only recently recognized that the "average" or "traditional" American family is no longer normative. Hence, we must consider the effects of various family forms more systematically and more carefully than in the past. Additionally, this realization has been achieved slowly, and there have been few studies designed to explore the effects of these changing family forms. Scholars have been satisfied to assume that any deviations from traditional patterns of childcare must have adverse consequences.

The goal of this chapter is to review the available evidence concerning the effects of the alternative forms of family and childcare arrangements on the development of young children. First to be reviewed is how socialization proceeds in traditional two-parent families (where mother is caretaker and father is breadwinner). Attention then focuses on three major deviations from the traditional pattern: (a) maternal employment and the increased use of out-of-home care, (b) increased paternal participation in childcare, and (c) divorce/single parenthood. Since we still have only a sketchy understanding of the way in which these different family arrangements affect child development, it is often necessary to speculate about the effects of these deviations on the basis of our knowledge concerning socialization in traditional families.

SOCIALIZATION IN TRADITIONAL FAMILIES

The first section briefly summarizes the current understanding of maternal and paternal influences on development in infancy. The initial consideration is the formation of infant-parent attachments: To whom do infants form attachments? And, why? Are there sex differences in the patterns of infant-parent interaction? Then, the focus turns to individual differences in the security of infant-parent attachment: What factors affect these? What long-term effects, if any, do they have on child development? How can we assess the quality of relationships?

To Whom Do Attachments Form? Infants apparently become attached to those people who have been available to them extensively and consistently during the first six to eight months of life (Ainsworth, 1973; Rajecki, Lamb, & Obmascher, 1978). Thus, it seems that *mere exposure* is the most important factor determining to whom infants form attachments. Presumably, although it is not yet certain, it is also important that adults and infants interact, with the adults responding to the infants' signals appropriately and providing for some of their needs (e.g., for contact comfort).

In most societies, mothers assume the primary, if not the sole responsibility for infant care. It is their faces that infants are most likely to see when they are alert. Mothers are likely to pick up and comfort infants when they are distressed, and feed them when they are hungry. By virtue of their mothers' consistent availability and responsiveness, one would expect infants to form primary attachments to them, as indeed most infants seem to do (Lamb, 1980). From around six to eight months, infants begin to respond differentially to separations from their mothers (Stayton, Ainsworth, & Main, 1973), and they begin to retreat to their mothers when alarmed by the appearance of strangers or by other stressful circumstances. Mothers are better able to soothe their infants than other women (Ainsworth, 1973).

Less self-evident is the fact that most infants in traditional western cultures form attachments to fathers (Lamb, 1977c; Schaffer & Emerson, 1964) or consistent substitute caretakers in others (Fox, 1977). This occurs at about the same time as they form attachments to their mothers, even though the amount of time infants spend interacting with their fathers is substantially less than the time spent with their mothers (Lamb & Stevenson, 1978). Infants appear to easily discern both mothers and fathers from strangers (Lamb, 1977a, 1977c, 1980). They seek proximity, contact, and comfort from their fathers with the same intensity and frequency as from their mothers, without apparent preference (Lamb, 1976b, 1977a). By the end of the first year, however, the situation changes somewhat. Although infants continue to show no preference for either parent in familiar or stress-free situations, they begin to turn preferentially to their mothers when distressed (Lamb, 1976e). This tendency is still evident at 18 months of age (Lamb, 1976a), but appears to have disappeared by 24 months (Lamb, 1976c).

Sex of Child Differences. A rather different shift in preference occurs in the stress-free home environment during the second year of life. Although parents respond preferentially to newborns of their own sex (Parke & Sawin, 1980), these preferences diminish during the early part of the first year. There are no major sex differences in the behavior of either parents or infants throughout most of the first year, but the situation changes by the second year (Lamb, 1977c; Pedersen, Cain & Anderson, 1980).

Starting around the first birthday if not before, fathers begin to pay greater attention to sons than to their daughters, and apparently as a result, boys start to focus their attention and proximity/contact-seeking behaviors on their fathers (Lamb, 1977a, 1977b). By the end of the second year, all but one of the boys in one small longitudinal study were showing marked and consistent preferences for their fathers on a number of attachment behavior measures (Lamb, 1977b). Girls were much less consistent: by age two, some preferred their mothers, some their fathers, and some neither parent. This is consistent with other evidence suggesting that parents are initially less concerned about establishing sex-appropriate behavior in daughters than in sons (cf. Lamb, 1976d, 1981).

A similar pattern of sex differences was not observed in a sample of Swedish mothers, fathers, and first-borns (Lamb, Frodi, Hwang, & Frodi, in press; Lamb, Frodi, Hwang, Frodi, & Steinberg, 1982) and in a group of kibbutz-dwelling Israeli families, neither mothers nor fathers showed clear preferences for first-born children of their own sex (Lamb, Sagi, Lewkowicz, Shoham, & Estes, 1982; It is not clear whether these findings reflect sampling or cultural variations, but the preferential treatment of same-sex infants does seem to be quite widespread.

Sex of Parent Differences. Attachment figures are by definition sources of protection and comfort (Bowlby, 1969), so infants' preferences for their mothers when distressed, alarmed, or frightened are especially pertinent in defining mothers as the primary attachment figures. However, mothers are not preferred in all circumstances and for all types of interaction. Rather, mothers and fathers engage in different types of interaction with their infants, and come to represent different types of experiences.

As primary caretakers, mothers are much more likely to engage in caretaking routines than are fathers. On the other hand, fathers are relatively more likely than mothers to play with their infants, and the play itself is likely to be more unpredictable and physically stimulating than is mothers' play (Lamb, 1976b, 1977c; Belsky, 1979; Power & Parke, 1982). Infants respond more positively to play bids from their fathers (Lamb, 1977c) and through 30 months, prefer to play with their fathers when given a choice (Clarke-Stewart, 1978). Boys continue to show this preference through four years of age, whereas girls switch to a preference for their mothers between two and four years of age (Lynn & Cross, 1974).

Individual Differences in Parent-Infant Attachments. It is widely believed that the responsiveness or unresponsiveness of adults influences the quality or "security" of attachment relationships. Ainsworth and her colleagues reported that when mothers were sensitively responsive to their infants during the first year of life, their infants formed secure attachments to them. When the mothers were insensitive, insecure relationships result (Ainsworth, Blehar, Waters, & Wall, 1978). As yet, no one has asked whether the same factors account for individual differences in the security of infant-father and infant-mother attachments.

To assess individual differences in the quality of infant-adult attachments, Ainsworth and Wittig (1969) devised a laboratory procedure, the *Strange Situation,* which permitted researchers to observe how infants organize their attachment behaviors around attachment figures when they are distressed. The primary focus in the Strange Situation is on the infant's responses to reunion with the attachment figure following two brief separations. Securely attached infants behave in the manner predicted by ethological attachment theory. They use their parents as secure bases from which to explore, especially in the preseparation episodes, and they attempt to reestablish interaction (often by seeking proximity or contact) when reunited with their parents following the brief separations. Some insecurely attached infants are labeled "avoidant" because they actively avoid their parents when reunited; others are called "resistant" because they respond to reunion with angry ambivalence, both seeking contact/interaction and rejecting it when it is offered.

Ainsworth's reports concerning the consistent relationship between early parental behavior and infant behavior in the Strange

Situation have elicited a great deal of attention, particularly in light of evidence that the patterns of behavior observed in the Strange Situation are *characteristic of the relationship rather than the infant.* That is, the same infants may behave differently with their mothers and fathers (Lamb, 1978b; Lamb, Hwang, Frodi, & Frodi, 1982; Main & Weston, 1981; Grossman, Grossman, Huber, & Wartner, 1981) and that the patterns of behavior can be remarkably stable over time (Connell, 1976; Waters, 1978).

ALTERNATIVE FAMILY FORMS

The preceding section focused on the processes and outcomes of socialization in traditional two-parent families. As previously noted, such families are decreasing in incidence as the number of novel family forms increase. The most recent estimates suggest that only 23% of the households in the United States now fit the traditional pattern with father as sole breadwinner and mother at home caring for one or more children (Pleck, 1983; Pleck & Rustad, 1980). There are three major ways in which contemporary families tend to deviate from the traditional norm: Maternal employment, increased paternal participation, and divorce/single parenthood. The goal of the following section is to describe both the ways in which socialization processes may be changed by these nontraditional family conditions, and their likely or demonstrated effects on child development.

MATERNAL EMPLOYMENT AND OUT-OF-HOME CARE

An increasing number of women choose to, or feel they have to remain in paid employment after the birth of their children. By 1978, 50% of the women in the United States and 44% of the women-with-husbands were in the paid labor force. The proportion of married women who are employed is expected to rise to 57% by 1995 (Glick, 1979). Employment rates are not substantially lower for married mothers in intact families than for women in general. For economic reasons, employment rates are even higher among single mothers and black mothers, whether single or married (Glick & Norton, 1979). In 1979, 52% of the mothers of school-aged children (six to 17 years old) and 36% of the mothers of infants and preschool-aged children were employed (Glick & Norton, 1979). Clearly, *most* American children now grow up in families where both parents, or the single-resident parent, are employed outside the home (see Lamb, 1982b for a critical review of the literature concerned with the effects of maternal employment on child development).

At this stage in the chapter the focus will be on evidence concerning the effects of maternal employment on the security of infant-mother attachment. Research of this topic is of particular importance because of the long-term implications on the security of attachment, and because of the widespread assumption that maternal employment is certain to have more deleterious effects on infants than on children of any other age. Unfortunately, developmental psychologists and educators have felt so confident about this assumption that there have been relatively few empirical studies executed to support this claim. Further, most of them have separately considered the effects of maternal employment and of alternative care even though these conditions generally co-occur.

Maternal Employment. Concerns about the effects of alternative (extrafamilial) care on socioemotional development were initially stimulated by evidence concerning the harmful effects of major maternal separations on child development. For example, of importance were the studies of maternal separations resulting either from hospitalization or institutionalization (Bowlby, 1951; Robertson & Bowlby, 1952; Schaffer, 1958; Schaffer & Callender, 1959; Spitz & Wolf, 1946).

Initial reports suggested that the reactions of young children to major separations are extremely alarming. Children show a phase of active protest immediately following separation, then a phase of withdrawal and apathy, and finally a phase involving either detachment or anxious attachment (Bowlby, 1969, 1973; Yarrow, 1964). However, children's reactions to hospitalization or institutionalization are influenced by a number of other factors apart from the separation experience alone (Yarrow, 1964). These factors include the quality of the institution, the number of substitute caretakers, duration of the separation, and the age of the child.

Consequently, although major separations clearly place children at risk, it cannot be assumed that adverse effects are inevitable.

Despite these limitations, several developmentalists have concluded that *any* separation in the early years may weaken the attachment relation to the mother and/or make the child less secure and trusting (eg. Blehar, 1975). During the last decade, however, theorists have come to question the analogy between institutionalization and daily supplementary care. In fact, most of the research shows that day care and/or maternal employment *need not* have harmful effects on children.

Although Hock (1980) reported no significant effects of maternal employment on the security of infant-mother attachment in the Strange Situation, three recent studies suggest the likelihood of increased insecure (especially avoidant) attachment relationships when the mothers of young infants are employed (Owen, Chase-Lansdale, & Lamb, 1982; Thompson, Lamb, & Estes, 1982; Vaughn, Gove, & Egeland, 1980). Although none of these studies considered maternal employment in the context of alternative care characteristics, their findings nonetheless highlight a number of factors that need to be taken into account when assessing the effects of maternal employment. Most importantly, maternal employment does not necessarily have adverse effects on the infant-mother attachment. Taken together, these studies show that about half of the children whose mothers were employed have secure attachments, compared to the usual rate of 65%.

Mothers' attitudes and circumstances, along with the quality of alternative care, determine whether secure or insecure relationships will result. This was demonstrated quite clearly by Owen et al. (1982) who found that infants who were securely attached had mothers who valued parenthood highly, whereas those who were insecurely attached had mothers who tended to value work highly and parenthood less. When mothers valued parenthood highly, they tended to have securely attached infants—*regardless of whether or not they were employed.* This suggests that maternal employment is a less important determinant of the security of attachment than is mother's attitudes and values. This is important because it underscores the inappropriateness of the assumption that employed mothers constitute a homogenous group. Clearly, one can only understand the effects of maternal employment when taking into account the attitudes, values, motivations, and circumstances of both employed and unemployed mothers, and stop viewing them as homogenous groups.

Further, Thompson et al. (1982) showed that although maternal employment was associated with attachment insecurity, there was an even clearer relationship between maternal employment and *changes* in the security of attachment. In other words, mothers' return to work appeared to affect the interaction between mothers and infants, but these effects could be both positive and negative. In some cases, maternal employment seemed to make insecure relationships into secure ones; in other families, the reverse occurred. Again, therefore, we need to consider not only *whether* mothers work, but *why* they work. Presumably, if mothers dislike being home and feel more fulfilled when employed, then the return to employment may have positive rather than negative effects.

In summary, the evidence suggests that whereas maternal employment has a fairly clear-cut effect on the sex-role attitudes of boys and girls, the effects of the quality of parent-child relationships are less consistent. These effects filter down indirectly to impact upon the child's psychological adjustment. Their presence and nature depend on a number of factors—including the values and attitudes of the mothers, their spouses, and the members of their social networks. Presumably, effects also differ depending on the types of non-maternal care to which children are exposed. The evidence currently available demonstrates that—contrary to popular belief—maternal employment does not necessarily have harmful effects on child development. In fact, the effects may in many circumstances be beneficial.

Effects of Extrafamilial Care on Parent-Child Relationships. In addition to parental attitudes and motivations, the *quality of the care* obtained when the child is not with the mother affects her reaction to employment. Unfortunately, although there have been several studies concerned with the effects of extrafamilial care, the quality of care has not been considered. Instead, focus has been on whether or not day care affects child development. The first attempt to compare the effects of nonparental and home care was completed by Caldwell, Wright, Honig, and Tannenbaum (1970), who studied two groups of 2½-year-old children, half attending a high-quality day-care facility and the others raised at home. No differences were revealed between the day-care and home-care children on any of the measures of child-mother, child-other, and mother-child interactions.

In a widely cited study, Blehar (1974) then compared 20 two- and three-year-old children receiving full-time group day care with 20 home-reared children of similar ages. The children were observed with their mothers in Ainsworth's Strange Situation, and Blehar reported disturbances in the day care children's attachments. More specifically, the two-year-olds exhibited "detachment-like behavior" (i.e., avoidance), and the three-year-old children exhibited "anxious, ambivalent attachment behaviors." These older children were reported to explore less, were more distressed by separation and sought more proximity to and contact with their mothers upon reunion than did the home-care controls.

Since these findings seemed to confirm that day care had effects similar to long-term separation, several investigators attempted to replicate Blehar's study. Portnoy and Simmons (1978), for instance, compared three groups of 3½- to four-year-old children. Despite the fact that they used the same observational procedure they found no significant group differences in attachment patterns. In another attempt Moskowitz, Schwarz and Corsini (1977) compared a group of 3½-year-old children who had approximately six months of day-care experience with a matched group of home-reared controls. This study was (in contrast to Blehar's) designed to minimize experimenter bias. Moskowitz et al. did find that day-care children showed less distress than the home-reared children in the latter parts of the Strange Situation. Apart from this, the two groups were not different on any other measures, including those of attachment behavior to their mothers. Several other attempts to replicate Blehar's findings with both two- and three-year-olds have also been unsuccessful (Barahal, 1977; Brookhart & Hock, 1976; Cornelius & Denney, 1975; Doyle, 1975; Ragozin, 1977, 1980; Roopnarine & Lamb, 1978).

In Cochran's (1977) Swedish study, mother-child separations were observed in the home rather than in the laboratory. Cochran reported that the center- and home-reared children responded very similarly to brief separations. Fewer than 60% of the children in both groups followed their mothers toward the door, and fewer than 35% cried when their mothers left. Kagan, Kearsley, and Zelazo (1978) also found that children reared at home did not cry more or less when separated from their mother in a laboratory situation than did those who had been in day care.

Roopnarine and Lamb (1978) adopted a somewhat different strategy when comparing day care with home-reared children. Three-year-old children were observed in the Strange Situation immediately prior to enrollment in day care and again three months later. When comparing this group to another group of children, matched in all respects except for the fact that their parents had no plans to enroll them in day care, they found that the day-care children were more concerned about the brief separations than were the home-care children. After three months of day care, however, these group differences had disappeared. Roopnarine and Lamb (1980) later replicated these findings, showing that group differences in responses to separation were greater in pre-enrollment than in post-enrollment assessments. Thus, they urged that researchers turn attention from group comparisons to studies in which initial differences are related to effects of substitute care.

Relationships with Caretakers. Instead of studying reactions to brief separations, several researchers have asked whether children in substitute care develop attachment-like relationships with caretakers, and if so, how these relationships compare with mother-child relationships. In one such study, Ricciutti (1974) found that children responded more positively to the approach of their regular caretakers than to the approach of strangers. These children also became less upset when left alone with their mothers, indicating that the relationships to mothers were more important than those to either strangers or familiar caretakers. Later, Farran and Ramey (1977) observed 23 children interacting with their mothers and teachers and reported that the children showed an overwhelming preference for proximity to and interaction with their mothers. Similar results were also found in a Norwegian study (Martinson, Smorvik, & Smith, 1977).

Cummings (1980) compared reactions to irregular caretakers,

regular caretakers, and mothers. In the day-care setting, the children revealed a preference for regular over irregular caretakers. In the unfamiliar surroundings of the laboratory, however, the children rarely approached caretakers, preferring instead to spend time in the proximity of their mothers; they were often upset when left alone with one of the caretakers. Finally, home observations of parents and two- to three-year-old children in Clarke-Stewart's (1980) detailed study revealed no differences either in the behavior of parents or children. In all, even though no one has yet attempted to describe the nature of the relationship between the child and the caretaker, it seems that the enrollment of children in day care does *not* lead to the replacement of the mother by the caretaker as the child's primary object of attachment.

Supplementary Care Effects on Relationships-with-Others. In another line of research, interactions with unfamiliar adults have been studied, but here consistent group differences between home-reared and center-reared children have not been found. Schwarz et al. (1974), for example, reported that day-care children were more aggressive (both physically and verbally) toward adults and generally less cooperative than were home-reared children. This finding, however, was not replicated in two other studies (Macrae & Herbert-Jackson, 1976; Lay & Meyer, 1972). McCutcheon and Calhoun (1976) showed that increased interaction with peers led day-care children to interact less with adults.

In an earlier study, Raph, Thomas, Chess, and Korn (1964) reported that negative behavior toward teachers varied depending on the amount of prior group experience. In two other studies, home-reared and family-day-care-reared children were found to interact (Finkelstein & Wilson, 1977) and to verbalize (Cochran, 1977) with their caretakers more than day-care children. Day-care children, on the other hand, were found to interact more with unfamiliar adults than did children in the other groups. Since none of these studies used standardized measures it is difficult to appraise or compare their findings. Clarke-Stewart (1980) found that two- to three-year-old children in alternative care settings were more compliant, prosocial and socially competent than children being raised at home, who appeared "more attached" to their mothers. Those in family day care fell between those in centers and those cared for exclusively at home. However, none of these studies involved pretest assessments, making interpretation of the findings difficult at best.

Surprisingly little attention has been paid to the effects of day care on peer relationships, even though children in group care settings typically have more experience with peers than do home-reared children. Becker (1977) reported that regular contact with peers increased peer competence, but none of her subjects were in alternative care. Schwarz et al. (1974) reported that center-reared children were more aggressive than home-reared agemates. However, these effects appear to be culture-specific since similar effects are not observed in China (Kessen, 1975) or in the USSR (Bronfenbrenner, 1970). Unfortunately, no researchers have systematically examined the effects of alternative care on peer competence using standardized measures of known reliability and validity in a pretest-posttest design.

Research Limitations. There are several respects in which the research on the effects of substitute care is severely limited. First, many of the studies have focused upon optimal, university-affiliated childcare programs, in which there is a high staff-child ratio and a curriculum for tutoring cognitive, emotional and social development. The care provided in these settings is probably not representative of the care most children receive, which makes the generalization of findings questionable.

Second, most studies have involved only a single post-enrollment assessment, without any assessment of long-term effects. Moore (1975) and Cochran (1977) examined longer-term outcomes, but in Moore's study, family instability was confounded with type of early care, and many of Cochran's subjects changed group status, making it hard to interpret evidence regarding long-term effects. Thus, we really have no relevant information on this concern.

The third limitation is that many of the published studies have not matched the family backgrounds of children in the different groups, even though families using extrafamilial care may differ in important respects from families who rear their children at home (Hock, 1976).

Fourth, the overwhelming majority of studies have been carried out in the U.S.A. which limits the generalizability of the reported findings. Further research in other settings is important not only for what it tells us about children in these countries, but also because the study of diverse cultures helps us to identify *general* processes of development as distinct from those that are unique to a *specific* culture.

The fifth concern is that most studies investigating socioemotional effects of nonparent care have focused on group day-care centers. Scant attention has been given to family day-care homes. This is important because family day-care is a much more common type of substitute care than is enrollment in a day-care center. Even though family day-care also involves separation from the parents, care is provided by a single adult in a home setting, and the number of peers is smaller than in day-care centers. Thus, the effects of family day-care and center day-care are likely to be different.

Despite evidence that children form attachment bonds to their fathers, researchers have not investigated the effects of extrafamilial care on father-child relationships. This is also a limitation. For, progress toward understanding early socioemotional development requires an acknowledgement that infants are socialized in the context of a complex, multidimensional social system, and this means that broader assessments of the effects of substitute care are essential.

Seventh, previous studies have assessed only selected aspects of the child's socioemotional development using laboratory assessments whose ecological and predictive validity is questionable. Researchers have yet to assess multiple aspects of socioemotional development using ecologically and predictively valid measures.

Finally, researchers have sought only to compare *groups* of children usually with the goal of determining whether substitute care is good or bad for children. This fails to recognize that what is good for one child or one family may be bad for another. What is now needed are studies that explore the effects of different types of early rearing experiences on children whose socioemotional characteristics differ initially. Only in this way will we get a more differentiated understanding of the ways in which different experiences can affect early socioemotional development. We also need studies in which the quality of extrafamilial care is related to measures of the children's adjustment. While it seems reasonably safe to predict that poor quality care will have adverse consequences the relevant research has yet to be done.

INCREASED PATERNAL PARTICIPATION

As in the case of maternal employment, day care, and single parenthood, developmentalists have expressed concern about the implications of increased paternal involvement. This is particularly so when this leads fathers to be as involved, or more involved, as their wives. Psychoanalysts have been especially clear about the need for fathers to avoid extensive involvement in "feminine activities" such as caretaking, lest they allegedly "confuse children" and deny them a more psychologically distant figure to help them separate and individuate (Cath, Gurwitt, & Ross, 1982). Others have expressed concern that fathers' effectiveness as sex-role models will be compromised and their children's psychological adjustment will be threatened. Although the empirical evidence is lacking, these concerns are probably not warranted.

First, there is no reason to believe that father needs to be the person who helps the child through the process of separation-individuation in the second year of life. Nor are there reasons to believe that women are any better qualified than men to serve as primary caretakers. Second, there is no reason to believe that men are viewed as less masculine by their children when they become extensively involved in child care. Indeed, Lamb's research in Sweden showed that there were distinctive differences between maternal and paternal behavioral styles *regardless* of the parents' relative involvement in child care (Lamb, Frodi, Hwang, Frodi, & Steinberg, 1982; Lamb, Frodi, Frodi, & Hwang, 1982). Third, even if the parents' gender roles are blurred in role-reversed or role-sharing families, there is no reason to believe that the child's sense of gender identity and personal adjustment will be affected. There is, in fact, no relationship between traditionality of gender role and security of gender identity. Fourth, one could argue that in our more egalitarian contemporary world, it is advantageous for children to develop androgynous gender roles rather than an exclusively traditional masculine and feminine role (see Chapter 4 for a consideration of this topic).

The few available empirical studies concerned with increased paternal involvement in child care have involved job sharing or temporary role reversal. As noted earlier, the mother-child relationship appears to have a greater impact on most aspects of socioemotional development. This is presumably because mothers typically serve as primary caretakers and socialization agents. If this is true, then one would expect the relative importance of the father-child relationship to increase in parallel with an increase in the extent of paternal involvement. However Lamb's recent research in Sweden failed to show this. There was no relationship between the degree of paternal involvement and the predictive validity of the infant-mother and infant-father attachment relationships (Lamb, Hwang, Frodi, & Frodi, 1982). Likewise, the degree of paternal involvement was unrelated to the children's patterns of preferences (Lamb, Frodi, Hwang, & Frodi, in press).

Studies of older children have yielded different results. Russel's (1982a, 1982b) highly involved fathers reported that they felt much closer to their children as a result of their role sharing or role reversal (but unfortunately no effects on the children were assessed). Radin reported that increased paternal involvement has positive effects on the locus of control and academic achievement of preschoolers (Radin, 1982; Radin & Sagi, 1982). Children with highly involved fathers, like those with employed mothers, had less stereotyped attitudes regarding male and female roles.

In a later study of Israeli fathers in which Sagi employed Radin's measures, similar but stronger results were reported (Sagi, 1982; Radin & Sagi, 1982). Presumably, the effects on sex-role attitudes occurred because the role-sharing parents provided less stereotyped models with which their children could identify, and they also encouraged their children to have egalitarian attitudes. The effects on intellectual performance may reflect fathers' traditional association with achievement and occupational advancement, or it could reflect the benefits of having extensive stimulation from two highly involved and relatively competent parents.

Attempts to explain increased paternal participation usually identify two factors associated with extensive paternal involvement—Maternal employment, and unusually high or low involvement by the fathers' own fathers. Much more attention has been devoted to the relationship between maternal employment and paternal involvement. It is widely suggested in both the popular and professional literature that maternal employment affects family life through a redistribution of the family work load. When mothers/wives are employed, the essential argument goes, their husbands start to play a greater role in child care and housework.

The empirical evidence, however, suggests that men do *not* do much more housework and child care when their wives are employed than when their wives are full-time homemakers and mothers. The results of a recent national time-use survey revealed that the increased male involvement in child care associated with maternal employment were negligible (Pleck, 1983).

The fact that absolute levels of paternal involvement increase so little when mothers are employed is rather surprising, given the widespread claims that men today *want* to be more involved in child care than were their own fathers (Sheehy, 1979). Perhaps such men are only espousing these values because currently they are socially approved, or perhaps our social and economic system is still too rigid to permit men to assume a greater role in childcare without risking great personal and professional costs. At first glance, this seems unlikely, since the provision of paid paternal leave with a guarantee of reemployment at or above the preleave level has induced remarkably few eligible fathers to request even small amounts of paternal leave (at least in Sweden; Lamb & Levine, 1983). On the other hand, the attitudes of peers and employers may still inhibit fathers from seeking parental leave, as may the attitudes that men have internalized during years of living in a sex-stereotyped society. It is also possible, but highly equivocal, that men are biologically designed to be less interested and competent in child care than are women.

Other than maternal employment and institutional practices, discussions of paternal participation often identify the earlier involvement of the father's own father as a key determinant for the level of involvement. Some have asserted that fathers become highly involved in their attempt to compensate for the limited involvement of their own fathers (Gersick, 1975; Mendes, 1976) whereas others have argued that highly involved fathers themselves had unusually involved fathers, who they attempt to emulate (Manion, 1977). One recent study of Israeli fathers provided clear support for the *identification* hypothesis: Highly involved fathers reported that their own fathers had been unusually involved in child care (Sagi, 1982; Radin & Sagi, 1982). There is little empirical support for the *compensation* hypothesis.

Summary

Considerably more research is needed before we will fully understand the effects of increased paternal involvement. Based on the available evidence, however, we can discount popular fears that the personal adjustment and gender identity of children will be seriously disturbed if their fathers assume an extensive role in raising their children. It is true that many of Russell's (1982a, 1982b) subjects returned to more traditional lifestyles when they had the opportunity, but none of the children in these or any of the other studies reported here appeared to suffer adverse consequences. Several researchers are currently engaged in studies designed to explore the effects of these nontraditional child-rearing styles on children, so we should be much better informed a few years from now.

DIVORCE AND SINGLE PARENTHOOD

Of the alternative family forms considered in this chapter, single parenthood is the one about which there is most reason for concern. Of further concern is the fact that the number of single-parent families has risen dramatically over the last few decades. National statistics now suggest that about a third of the children in the United States will spend some portion of their childhood in a single-parent family (Glick & Norton, 1979). For 90% of them, the single parent will be their mother. Unfortunately, none of the studies on this topic have involved infants and very young children, so we may only speculate about the effects on young children.

To the extent that they do not have a spouse to supplement their parenting efforts, single mothers and fathers are essentially in a similar predicament, with lack of supervision and control over children being possible consequences. Furthermore, in all single-parent families one major sex-role model is absent. Many single mothers also lack the training and experience to obtain satisfying and financially rewarding jobs, so they are likely to be in less-favorable economic circumstances than single fathers. Social isolation is commonly experienced by both divorced parties, but may be especially acute for mothers whose social network was largely defined by their ex-husband's work associates. For all of these reasons, single mothers may often be in worse straits than single fathers.

As long as these social and economic stresses remain, single parents are likely to be less effective, consistent and sensitive as parents. This, in turn, is likely to distort their relationships with their children and have adverse effects on their children's psychological adjustment regardless of the children's ages. We cannot yet say what proportion of the adverse effects of father absence would be eliminated *if* single mothers could count on less financially stressful circumstances and were less isolated from social networks. We do know, however, that increasing numbers of women combine working with mothering, and consequently these women retain independent sources of income and access to social networks. Divorce is substantially less stressful and disruptive for these women (Hetherington, 1979) than for previously unemployed single mothers. However, marital dissolution is inherently stressful for almost all people making temporary disturbances of psychological functioning almost inevitable (Hetherington, Cox, & Cox, 1978).

There have been numerous studies of children raised by single mothers and substantially fewer studies of single fathers (for reviews see Lamb, 1976d, 1981; Biller, 1976, 1981). Although researchers now question whether the absence of a male model satisfactorily accounts for the observed effects, it is fairly clear that children (especially boys) raised by single mothers are "at risk." Boys raised by single mothers are more likely than those from two-parent families to be less "masculine," more psychologically maladjusted, to be delinquent, hyper- or hypo-aggressive and to perform more poorly at school (see reviews by Radin, 1981; Shinn, 1978; Biller, 1981; Lamb, 1981). Although the evidence is not clearcut, it seems that these effects become *exaggerated* when the father absence begins *early* in the children's lives.

Girls, too, may reveal deficits in their ability to interact with males, although these effects may not become evident prior to adolescence, even when the fathers' absence occurred much earlier (Hetherington, 1972). The availability of alternative male models (e.g., stepfathers, older brothers, uncles, grandfathers) can reduce the adverse effects on sex-role development although few substitute relationships can match the intensity of close father-child relationships (Biller, 1974).

Interestingly, the only available comparative study of single fathers indicated that girls adapted more poorly than boys did in the care of single fathers (Santrock & Warshak, 1979; Santrock, Warshak, & Elliott, 1982). This is consistent with evidence suggesting that fathers are embarrassed when called upon to purchase clothing for, and to discuss menstruation and sexuality with, their pubescent daughters. This is likely to be especially problematic for single fathers (Fox, 1978; Hipgrave, 1982). Together with the results of studies concerned with the children of single mothers, these findings tentatively suggest that single parents are more successful raising children of the same than of the opposite sex, but we need further documentation of this fact.

Although most social scientists seem to consider single fathers to be in an especially invidious position because they typically have to assume sole parental responsibility without adequate warning or preparation, in some respects (and *on average*) today's single fathers are more likely than single mothers to succeed in meeting the extensive demands placed on them. This is because they comprise a highly selected and self-motivated group, simply because popular and judicial skepticism regarding their motivation and ability ensures that they have to fight to obtain custody. Typically, mothers gain custody by default. In addition, society either tolerates or expects single fathers to work full time, and to employ others to assist in child and home care. Whereas, both of these circumstances would be viewed as indices of incompetence on the part of single mothers.

Despite this, the potential for deviant outcomes among the children of single mothers and fathers is considerably greater than with any of the other nontraditional family forms. As Eleanor Maccoby (1977) has said:

> "Childrearing is something that many people cannot do adequately as single adults functioning in isolation. Single parents need time off from parenting, they need the company of other adults, they need to have other voices joined with theirs in transmitting values and maturity demands to their children" (p. 17).

The socialization process *need* not fail, of course. Its success depends on the availability of emotional, practical, and social supports for single parents and their children.

Three other issues must also be mentioned for this chapter to be complete. First, marital disharmony appears to have more deleterious effects, especially on boys, than does divorce and father absence (Block, Block, & Morrison, 1981; Lamb, 1977d; Rutter, 1972). It is conceivable, therefore, that some of the "effects of single parenthood" may be consequences of the marital hostility that *preceded* divorce, rather than of the divorce and *subsequent* period of single parenthood. Thus, if our goal is to minimize the psychological damage to developing children, single parenthood may be the more desirable of the realistic alternatives where an unstable family with marital disharmony exists.

Second, psychological father absence (which occurs when fathers are seldom available to their children) and actual father absence have *qualitatively similar effects* on sex-role development (Blanchard & Biller, 1971). Likewise, distant or hostile fathers and absent fathers have qualitatively similar (though *quantitatively* different) effects on moral development (Hoffman, 1970). These findings again imply that single parenthood may not have less desirable consequences than the alternative arrangement.

Finally, it is important not to exaggerate the ill effects of divorce or single parenthood. Even though many studies demonstrate statistically significant group differences between children in single- and two-parent families, many of the individuals in the groups do not deviate from the norm. In other words, we must not let the evidence of development problems in *some* children of divorce lead us to unfounded statements about the assumed *inevitable* effects of divorce.

CONCLUSION

There is substantial evidence that experiences within the family have a major impact on the social, personality, and intellectual development of young children. Of course, socializing agents outside the family—television, peers, teachers, for example—also affect development, and later experiences can either reverse or accentuate the effects of earlier experiences. What we can confidently state is that there is no evidence of "sensitive" or "critical" periods during which specific experiences have irreversible effects on subsequent development. Nevertheless, it is reasonable to conclude that children who have good and rewarding early relationships within the family are probably at an advantage relative to those whose initial experiences are less satisfactory.

It is also clear that the socializing experience differs when children are raised in families that deviate from the two-parent, traditional norm, and that the differences indeed affect children's development. We are still in need of investigations designed both to identify the effects more precisely and to define the processes by which these effects are mediated. However, we already know enough to underscore some of the points made earlier.

First, there is *no justification* for assuming that any family forms that deviate from the traditional form necessarily have harmful consequences. In fact, some of these deviant styles—for example, those involving maternal employment—have what may be seen as *positive effects* on children. Second, we must be careful to distinguish between the objective description of findings or effects and the subjective evaluation of those findings. It is one thing to say that girls whose mothers are employed are less stereotypically feminine; a value judgment is involved if we then describe this effect as either desirable or undesirable.

Because societal attitudes change over time, the same "deviant" family form may have different effects in different historical epochs or in different social contexts. For example, maternal employment was, in the 1950s, viewed very negatively; three decades later, maternal employment is the normative practice. It is now the unemployed mother who often must cope with questions about how she can be fulfilled if she is "only a mother." Maternal employment is thus likely to have had different effects in the 1950s and the 1980s.

Finally, we need to remember that families do not exist in isolation. They are embedded in and influenced by a wider social context. Consequently, both the attitudes and values of others affect the behavior of parents, and thus directly and indirectly affect their children.

REFERENCES

Ainsworth, M. D. S. (1973). The development of infant-mother attachment. In B. M. Caldwell & H. N. Ricciuti (Eds.), *Review of child development research* (Vol. 3). Chicago: Univ. of Chicago Press.

Ainsworth, M. D. S., & Wittig, B. A. (1969). Attachment and exploratory behavior of one-year-olds in a strange situation. In B. M. Foss (Ed.), *Determinants of infant behavior* (Vol. 4). London: Methuen.

Ainsworth, M. D. S., Blehar, M. C., Waters, E., & Wall, S. *Patterns of attachment.* Hillsdale, NJ: Erlbaum.

Barahal, R. M. (1977). *A comparison of parent-infant attachment and interaction patterns in day care and non day care family groups.* Unpublished doctoral dissertation, Cornell University.

Becker, J. N. T. (1977). A learning analysis of the development of peer-oriented behavior in nine-month-old infants. *Developmental Psychology, 13,* 481–491.

Belsky, J. (1979). Mother-father-infant interaction: A naturalistic observational study. *Developmental Psychology, 15,* 601–607.

Biller, H. B. (1974). *Paternal deprivation: Family, school, sexuality and society.* Lexington, MA: Heath.

Biller, H. B. (1976). The father and personality development: Paternal deprivation and sex-role development. In M. E. Lamb (Ed.), *The role of the father in child development.* New York: Wiley.

Biller, H. B. (1981). Father absence, divorce, and personality development. In M. E. Lamb (Ed.), *The role of the father in child development* (rev. ed.). New York: Wiley.

Blanchard, R. W., & Biller, H. B. (1971). Father availability and academic performance among third grade boys. *Developmental Psychology, 4,* 301–305.

Blehar, M. C. (1974). Anxious attachment and defensive reactions associated with day care. *Child Development, 45,* 683–692.

Blehar, M. (1975). Anxious attachment and defensive reactions associated with day care. In U. Bronfenbrenner & M. A. Mahoney (Eds.), *Influences on human development.* New York: Holt, Rinehart & Winston.

Block, J. H., Block, J., & Morrison, A. (1981). Parental agreement-disagreement on childrearing orientations and gender-related personality correlates in children. *Child Development, 52,* 965–974.

Bowlby, J. (1951). *Maternal care and mental health.* Geneva, Switzerland: WHO.

Bowlby, J. (1969). *Attachment and loss* (Vol. 1) *Attachment.* New York: Basic Books.

Bowlby, J. (1973). *Attachment and loss* (Vol. 2). *Separation: Anxiety and anger.* New York: Basic Books.

Bronfenbrenner, U. (1970). *Two worlds of childhood.* New York: Simon & Schuster.

Brookhart, J., & Hock, E. (1976). The effects of experimental context and experiential background on infants' behavior toward their mothers and a stranger. *Child Development, 47,* 333–340.

Caldwell, B. M., Wright, C. M., Honig, A. S., & Tannenbaum, J. (1970). Infant day care and attachment. *American Journal of Orthopsychiatry, 40,* 397–412.

Cath, S. Gurwitt, A., & Ross, J. (1982). *Fatherhood: Developmental and clinical perspectives.* Boston: Little Brown.

Clark-Stewart, K. A. (1978). And daddy makes three: The father's impact on mother and young child. *Child Development, 49,* 466–478.

Clarke-Stewart, K. A. (1980). Observation and experiment: Complementary strategies for studying day care and social development. In S. Kilmer (Eds.), *Advances in early education and day care.* Greenwich, CT: JAI Press.

Cochran, M. M. (1977). A comparison of group day and family childrearing patterns in Sweden. *Child Development, 48,* 702–707.

Connell, D. B. (1976). *Individual differences in attachment behavior.* Unpublished doctoral dissertation, Syracuse Univ.

Cornelius, S. W., & Denney, N. W. (1975). Dependency in day-care and home-care children. *Developmental Psychology, 11,* 575–582.

Cummings, M. E. (1980). Caregiver stability and day care. *Developmental Psychology, 16,* 31–37.

Doyle, A. B. (1975). Infant development in day care. *Developmental Psychology, 11,* 655–656.

Farran, D. C., & Ramey, C. T. (1977). Infant day care and attachment behavior toward mothers and teachers. *Child Development, 48,* 1112–1116.

Finkelstein, M., & Wilson, K. (1977, March). *The influence of day care on social behavior toward peers and adults.* Paper presented to the Society for Research in Child Development, New Orleans.

Fox, G. L. (1978, October). *The family's role in adolescent sexual behavior.* Paper presented to the Family Impact Seminar, Washington, DC.

Fox, N. (1977). Attachment of kibbutz infants to mother and metapelet. *Child Development, 48,* 1228–1239.

Gersick, K. (1975). *Fathers by choice: Characteristics of men who do and do not seek custody of their children following divorce.* Unpublished doctoral dissertation, Harvard Univ.

Glick, P. C. (1979). Future American families. *COFU Memo, 2*(3), 2–5.

Glick, P. C., & Norton, A. J. (1979). Marrying, divorcing, and living together in the U.S. today. *Population Bulletin, 32,* whole number 5.

Grossman, K. E., Grossman, K., Huber, F., & Wartner, U. (1981). German children's behavior towards their mothers at 12 months and their fathers at 18 months in

Ainsworth's Strange Situation. *International Journal of Behavioral Development, 4,* 157–181.

Hetherington, E. M. (1972). Effects of father-absence on personality development in adolescent daughters. *Developmental Psychology, 7,* 313–326.

Hetherington, E. M. (1979). Divorce: A child's perspective. *American Psychologist, 34,* 851–858.

Hetherington, E. M., Cox, M., & Cox, R. (1978). The aftermath of divorce. In J. P. Stevens & M. Matthews (Eds.), *Mother/child, father/child relationships.* Washington, DC: National Association for the Education of Young Children.

Hipgrave, T. (1982). Childrearing by lone fathers. In R. Chester, P. Diggory, & M. Sutherland (Eds.), *Changing patterns of child bearing and childrearing.* London: Academic.

Hock, E. (1976). *Alternative approaches to childrearing and their effects on the mother-infant relationship* (Final report, Grant No. OCD-409). Washington, DC: Office of Child Development, Department of Health, Education and Welfare.

Hock, E. (1980). Working and nonworking mothers and their infants: A comparative study of maternal caregiving characteristics and infant social behavior. *Merrill-Palmer Quarterly, 26,* 79–101.

Hoffman, M. L. (1970). Moral development. In P. H. Mussen (Ed.), *Carmichael's manual of child psychology* (3rd ed.), Vol. 2. New York: Wiley.

Kagan, J., Kearsley, P., & Zelazo, P. (1978). *Infancy: Its place in human development.* Cambridge, MA: Harvard Univ. Press.

Kessen, W. (1975). *Child care in China.* New Haven: Yale Univ. Press.

Lamb, M. E. (1976). Effects of stress and cohort on mother- and father-infant interaction. *Developmental Psychology, 12,* 435–443. (a)

Lamb, M. E. (1976). Interactions between eight-month-old children and their fathers and mothers. In M. E. Lamb (Ed.), *The role of the father in child development.* New York: Wiley. (b)

Lamb, M. E. (1976). Interactions between two-year-olds and their mothers and fathers. *Psychological Reports, 36,* 447–450. (c)

Lamb, M. E. (1976). Parent-infant interaction in eight-month-olds. *Child Psychiatry and Human Development, (7),* 56–63. (d)

Lamb, M. E. (1976). The role of the father: An overview. In M. E. Lamb (Ed.), *The role of the father in child development.* New York: Wiley. (e)

Lamb, M. E. (1976). Twelve-month-olds and their parents: Interaction in a laboratory playroom. *Developmental Psychology, 12,* 237–244. (f)

Lamb, M. E. (1977). The development of mother-infant and father-infant attachments in the second year of life. *Developmental Psychology, 13,* 637–648. (a)

Lamb, M. E. (1977). The development of parental preferences in the first two years of life. *Sex Roles, 3,* 495–497. (b)

Lamb, M. E. (1977). Father-infant and mother-infant interaction in the first year of life. *Child Development, 48,* 167–181. (c)

Lamb, M. E. (1977). The effects of divorce on children's personality development. *Journal of Divorce, 1,* 163–174. (d)

Lamb, M. E. (1978). Qualitative aspects of mother- and father-infant attachments. *Infant Behavior and Development, 1,* 265–275.

Lamb, M. E. (1980). The development of parent-infant attachments in the first two years of life. In F. A. Pedersen (Ed.), *The father-infant relationship: Observational studies in a family setting.* New York: Praeger Special Studies.

Lamb, M. E. (1981). Paternal influences on child development: An overview. In M. E. Lamb (Ed.), *The role of the father in child development* (rev. ed.). NY: Wiley.

Lamb, M. E. (1982) Maternal employment and child development: A review. In M. E. Lamb (Ed.), *Nontraditional families: Parenting and child development.* Hillsdale, NJ: Erlbaum.

Lamb, M. E., Frodi, A. M., Frodi, M., & Hwang, C.-P. (1982). Characteristics of maternal and paternal behavior in traditional and nontraditional Swedish families. *International Journal of Behavioral Development, 5,* 131–141.

Lamb, M. E., Frodi, A. M., Hwang, C.-P., Frodi, M., & Steinberg, J. (1982). Mother- and father-infant interaction involving play and holding in traditional and nontraditional Swedish families. *Developmental Psychology, 18,* 215–221.

Lamb, M. E., Frodi, M., Hwang, C.-P., & Frodi, A. M. (in press). Effects of paternal involvement on infant preferences for mothers and fathers. *Child Development.*

Lamb, M. E., Hwang, C.-P., Frodi, A., & Frodi, M. (1982). Security of mother- and father-infant attachment and its relation to sociability with strangers in traditional and nontraditional Swedish families. *Infant Behavior and Development, 5,* 355–367.

Lamb, M. E., & Levine, J. A. (1983). The Swedish parental insurance policy: An experiment in social engineering. In M. E. Lamb & A. Sagi (Eds.), *Fatherhood and family policy.* Hillsdale, NJ: Erlbaum.

Lamb, M. E., Sagi, A., Lewkowicz, K., Shoham, R., & Estes, D. (1982, June). *Security of infant-mother, -father, and -metapelet attachments in kibbutz-reared infants.* Paper presented to the Denver Psychobiology Research Group Retreat, Estes Park CO.

Lamb, M. E., & Stevenson, M. B. (1978). Father-infant relationships Their nature and importance. *Youth and Society, 9,* 277–298.

Lay, M. Z., & Meyer, W. J. (1972). *Effects of early day-care experiences on subsequent observed program behaviors.* Unpublished progress report, Syracuse Univ.

Lynn, D. B., & Cross, A. R. (1974). Parent preferences of preschool children. *Journal of Marriage and the Family, 36,* 555–559.

Maccoby, E. E. (1977, September). *Current changes in the family and their impact upon the socialization of children.* Paper presented to the American Sociological Association, Chicago.

Macrae, J. W., & Herbert-Jackson, E. (1976). Are behavioral effects of infant day care program specific? *Developmental Psychology, 12,* 269–270.

Main, M. B., & Weston, D. R. (1981). Security of attachment to mother and father: Related to conflict behavior and the readiness to establish new relationships. *Child Development, 52,* 932–940.

Manion, J. (1977). A study of fathers and infant caretaking. *Birth and the Family Journal, 4,* 174–179.

Martinson, H., Smorvik, D., & Smith, L. (1978) Effects of presence of mother versus preschool teacher on the behavior of infants in a strange situation. *Scandinavian Journal of Psychology, 19,* 159–162.

McCutcheon, B., & Calhoun, K. (1976). Social and emotional adjustment of infants and toddlers to a day care setting. *American Journal of Orthopsychiatry, 46,* 104–108.

Mendes, H. (1976). Single fatherhood. *Social Work, 21,* 308–312.

Money, J., & Ehrhardt, A. A. (1972). *Man and woman, boy and girl.* Baltimore: Johns Hopkins Univ. Press.

Moore, T. W. (1975). Exclusive early mothering and its alternatives: The outcomes to adolescence. *Scandinavian Journal of Psychology, 16,* 255–272.

Moskowitz, D., Schwartz, J., & Corsini, D. (1977). Initiating day care at three years of age: Effects on attachment. *Child Development, 48,* 1271–1276.

Owen, M. T., Chase-Lansdale, P. L., & Lamb, M. E. (1982). *Mothers' and fathers' attitudes, maternal employment, and the security of infant-parent attachment.* Unpublished manuscript.

Parke, R. D., & Sawin, D. B. (1980). The family in early infancy: Social interactional and attitudinal analyses. In F. A. Pedersen (Ed.), *The father-infant relationship: Observational studies in the family setting.* NY: Praeger Special Studies.

Pedersen, F. A., Anderson, B., & Cain, R. (1980). Parent-infant and husband-wife interactions observed at age five months. In F. A. Pedersen (Ed.), *The father-infant relationship: Observational studies in the family setting.* NY: Praeger Special Publications.

Pleck, J. H. (1983). Husbands' paid work and family roles: Current research issues. In H. Lopata & J. H. Pleck (Eds.), *Research in the interweave of social roles,* (Vol. 3), *Families and jobs.* Greenwich, CT: JAI.

Pleck, J. H., & Rustad, M. (1980). *Husbands' and wives' time in family work and paid work in the 1975-76 study of time use.* Unpublished manuscript, Wellesley College.

Portnoy, F., & Simmons, C. (1978). Day care and attachment. *Child Development, 49,* 239–242.

Power, T. G., & Parke, R. D. (1982). Play as a context for early learning: Lab and home analyses. In L. M. Laosa & I. E. Sigel (Eds.), *Families as learning environments for children.* NY: Plenum.

Radin, N. (1981). The role of the father in cognitive, academic, and intellectual development. In M. E. Lamb (Ed.), *The role of the father in child development* (rev. ed.). NY: Wiley.

Radin, N. (1982). Primary caregiving and role-sharing fathers. In M. E. Lamb (Ed.), *Nontraditional families: Parenating and child development.* Hillsdale, NJ: Erlbaum.

Radin, N., & Sagi, A. (1982). Childrearing fathers in intact families in Israel and the U.S.A. *Merrill-Palmer Quarterly, 28,* 111–136.

Ragozin, A. S. (1977, March). *Attachment behavior of day care and home-reared children in a laboratory setting.* Paper presented to the Society for Research in Child Development, New Orleans.

Ragozin, A. S. (1980). Attachment behavior of day care children: Naturalistic and laboratory observations. *Child Development, 51,* 409–415.

Rajecki, D. W., Lamb, M. E., & Obmascher, P. (1978). Toward a general theory of infantile attachment: A comparative review of aspects of the social bond. *Behavioral and Brain Sciences, 1,* 417–463.

Raph, J. B., Thomas, A., Chess, S., & Korn, S. J. (1964). The influence of nursery school on social interactions. *American Journal of Orthopsychiatry, 38,* 144–152.

Ricciuti, H. (1974). Fear and development of social attachments in the first year of life. In M. Lewis & L. A. Rosenblum (Eds.), *The origins of fear.* NY: Wiley.

Robertson, J., & Bowlby, J. (1952). Responses of young children to separation from their mothers. *Courrier de Centre International de L Enfance, 2,* 131–142.

Roopnarine, J. L., & Lamb, M. E. (1978). The effects of day care on attachment and exploratory behavior in a strange situation. *Merrill-Palmer Quarterly, 24,* 85–95.

Roopnarine, J., & Lamb, M. E. (1980). Peer and parent child interaction before and after enrollment in nursery school. *Journal of Applied Developmental Psychology, 1,* 77–81.

Russell, G. (1982). Shared-caregiving families: An Australian study. In M. E. Lamb (Ed.), *Nontraditional families: Parenting and child development.* Hillsdale, NJ: Erlbaum (a)

Russell, G. (1982). *The changing role of fathers.* St. Lucia, Queensland: Univ. of Queensland Press. (b)

Rutter, M. (1972). *Maternal deprivation reassessed.* Harmondsworth, England: Penguin.

Sagi, A. (1982). Antecedents and consequences of various degrees of paternal involvement in childrearing: The Israeli project. In M. E. Lamb (Ed.), *Nontraditional families: Parenting and child development.* Hillsdale, NJ: Erlbaum.

Santrock, J. W., & Warshak, R. A. (1979). Father custody and social development in boys and girls. *Journal of Social Issues, 35,* 112–125.

Santrock, J. W., Warshak, R. A., & Elliott, G. L. (1982). Social development and parent-child interaction in father-custody and stepmother families. In M. E. Lamb, (Ed.), *Nontraditional families: Parenting and child development.* Hillsdale, NJ: Erlbaum.

Schaffer, H. R. (1958). Objective observations of personality development in early infancy. *British Journal of Medical Psychology, 31,* 174–183.

Schaffer, H. R., & Callender, W. (1959). Psychological effects of hospitalization in infancy. *Pediatrics, 24,* 528–539.

Schaffer, H. R., & Emerson, P. E. (1964). The development of social attachments in infancy. *Monographs of the Society for Research in Child Development, 29,* serial number 94.

Schwartz, J. D., Strickland, R. G., & Krolick, G. (1974). Infant day care: Behavioral effects at preschool age. *Developmental Psychology, 10,* 502–506.

Sheehy, G. (1979). Introducing the postponing generation. *Esquire, 92*(4), 25–33.

Shinn, M. (1978). Father absence and children's cognitive development. *Psychological Bulletin, 85,* 295–324.

Spitz, R. A., & Wolf, K. M. (1946). Anaclitic depression. *Psychoanalytic Study of Child, 2,* 313–342.

Stayton, D. J., Ainsworth, M. D. S., & Main, M. B. (1973). The development of separation behavior in the first year of life: Protest, following and greeting. *Developmental Psychology, 9,* 213–225.

Thompson, R. A., Lamb, M. E., & Estes, D. (1982). Stability of infant-mother attachment and its relationship to changing life circumstances in an unselected middle class sample. *Child Development, 53,* 144–148.

Vaughn, B., Gove, F., & Egeland, B. (1980). The relationship between out-of-home care and the quality of infant-mother attachment in an economically disadvantaged sample. *Child Development, 51,* 1203–1214.

Waters, E. (1978). The reliability and stability of individual differences in infant-mother attachment. *Child Development, 49,* 483–494.

Yarrow, L. J. (1964). Separation from parents during early childhood. In M. L. Hoffman & L. W. Hoffman (Eds.), *Review of child development research* (Vol. 1). NY: Russell Sage Foundation.

CHAPTER 8

MULTICULTURAL INFLUENCES ON THE DEVELOPMENT OF THE YOUNG CHILD

PHILIP J. LAZARUS AND RAQUEL BILD AND EVELYN DIAZ

Child development is increasingly seen as the confluence of many interelated, changing systems and subsystems including the biological, social, cultural, and historical (Bronfenbrenner, 1977; Draguns, 1979; Laboratory of Comparative Human Cognition, 1979; R. A. Le Vine, 1979; Looft, 1973; Tapp, 1981). No single discipline or technique by itself can solve the complex problems in the study of child development, albeit in one or more cultures. Kluckhohn and Murray (1948) observed more than thirty years ago that psychiatrists, psychologists, sociologists, social workers, educators, biologists, and anthropologists have long been preoccupied with the relation of the child to society. More recently, Tapp (1981) called for the use of cross-cultural, cognitive, interactive (bio-social) and life span developmental strategies for mapping the range and universality of personality development.

Within the last decade the need for cross-disciplinary and/or cross-cultural research strategies for the assessment of personality formation has been emphasized (Brislin, Lonner & Thorndike, 1973; Butcher & Pancheri, 1976; R. A. Le Vine, 1973; Looft, 1973; Manaster & Havighurst, 1972; Munroe & Munroe, 1975; Price-Williams, 1974, 1975; Triandis, 1972; Triandis, Malpass & Dadidson, 1972, 1973). During the same period there was a call for more comparative cross-cultural child development research (R. A. Le Vine, 1970). As stated by Tapp, "social scientists interested in personality, culture and behavior began addressing the importance of using cross-disciplinary paradigms beyond the traditional parameters of psychology and anthropology"

(1981, p. 345). Any contemporary book on child development needs to include cross-cultural research, and psychologists and educators need to be aware of the ways that a culture can influence behavior.

MULTICULTURAL FACTORS ON NORMAL CHILD DEVELOPMENT

The major focus of this chapter is the examination of the multicultural factors that influence the course of child development — both normal and abnormal. Emphasis is given to landmark studies in anthropology and more recent research in cross-cultural psychology. Specifically, cross-cultural child-rearing practices are discussed. As noted by Escovar and Lazarus, "the study of comparative child-rearing patterns offers a wide breadth of information about the social, cultural and psychological development of children" (1982, p. 143). This information can help specify what aspects of child development are culturally bound and what aspects are reflections of general human development (Lazarus & Escovar, 1981).

This chapter emphasizes how differences in child rearing practices across cultures influence the nature and course of personality development in young children. As previously mentioned, it is the confluence of changing systems and subsystems that help determine the child development process. We focus our discussion toward the *cultural* determinants of child development. However, one needs to be mindful that biological, historical, geographical, political, economic, and social determinants all interact to influence the developmental process. Because all these determinants interactively influence child development; it is impossible at times to separate those forces that are cultural from the total milieu. Therefore, when these determinants interact, the interaction is discussed.

It is our position that the development of the young child can only be understood within the context of the culture. Factors which shape the personality of the young child include: (a) the nature of the instrumental competencies within a given culture,

(b) the position of the parents within society, (c) the degree and type of control exerted by parents over their children, (d) the expression of parental warmth and affection, and (e) the values inculcated in children by their parents. It is these factors that are highlighted within this chapter. Furthermore, the nature and impact of stress within a given culture plays a significant part in determining the nature and incidence of childhood psychopathology; this feature receives attention in the concluding section. It should be noted that all the psychological processes (such as cognition, memory, emotion, perception, motivation, and language) are influenced by the culture. However, it is beyond the scope of this chapter to address how the culture influences these psychological processes. Instead, our attention is directed toward the ways in which culture influences the child rearing process.

Personality theorists who have attempted to tie together the nature of child rearing and later adult development generally have failed to appreciate the significant impact of the culture on this process. However, contemporary cross-cultural researchers are beginning to explore how the culture influences child development. Though personality theorists have included cultural determinants, no theorist of major significance has emphasized the culture as the *major* variable in determining personality. This is unfortunate, as cross-cultural studies can contribute to our understanding of personality development. As suggested by Thomae (1979), our knowledge can be enriched in the following ways: cross cultural studies (a) can provide information of life span consistencies and changes; (b) can connect personality to cultural variables and implicate their interaction in the developmental process; (c) can offer possible pan-cultural validity to Western derived theories; and (d) can call into question Western personality developmental models, encouraging other concepts and orientations.

Researchers who do study how the culture influences child development bring into play various perspectives, disciplinary viewpoints, theoretical orientations, and methodologies. For example, cross-cultural child development can be studied from an intra or inter-cultural perspective (e.g., Mexico and United States), from one disciplinary viewpoint or several (e.g., psychology and cultural anthropology), and/or interpreted from one societal or theoretical vantage point (e.g., Western or psycho-analytic) or many. Moreover, methods may include laboratory or field studies.

Researchers who have made major contributions to the field of cross-cultural child development have come from a variety of disciplines and utilized different methodologies in collecting data. Readers are referred to Table 1 for a listing of representative benchmark studies employing uni-, dual-, or multi-cultural populations.

Table 1
Representative Landmark Cross-Cultural Personality Studies

Uni-culture

Ainsworth's—*Infancy in Uganda* (1967).
Barker and Wright's—*Midwest and Its Children* (1955/1971)—U.S.
Fromm and Maccoby's *Social Character in a Mexican Village* (1970).
Spiro and Spiro's—*Children of the Kibbutz* (1958/1975).
Werner, Bierman and French's—*The Children of the Kauai* (1971).

Dual-Culture

Barker and Schoggen's—*Qualities of Community Life* (1973) England and U.S.
Bronfenbrenner's—*Two Worlds of Childhood—U.S. and U.S.S.R.* (1970).
Havighurst and Neugarten's—*American Indian and White Children* (1955).
Holtzman, Diaz-Guerrero and Swartz—*Personality Development in Two Cultures* (1975)—Mexico and U.S.

Multi-culture

Berry's *Human Ecology and Cognitive Style* (1976)—18 societies.
Minturn and Lambert's—*Mothers of Six Cultures* (1964).
Rohner's—*They Love Me, They Love Me Not* (1975)—101 societies.
Whiting's—*Six Cultures* (1963)—India, Kenya, Mexico, Japan, Philippines, U.S.
Whiting and Whiting's—*Children of Six Cultures* (1975).

Source: Based on recommendations of Tapp (1981).

Historical Context of Cross-Cultural Child Rearing Practices

Landmark studies in cross-cultural child-rearing practices were initiated by the Whitings and their colleagues in the 1940's and 1950's. Whiting and Child (1953) sent teams of trained anthropologists to various field settings to study parent-child interaction.

Their initial purposes were: (a) to widen the range of parental behaviors observed, (b) to determine whether the relationships between treatment by parents and the characteristics developed by children are universal, and (c) to study how variations in cultural history, the structure of the family, and politico-economic organization modify the processes and effects of parent-child interaction (Maccoby, 1980). Moreover, the Whitings began stressing the importance of reliable and valid observations, because they noted that their earlier research had depended on parent interviews which proved to be a source of inadequate data.

In the 1960's, the Whitings and their colleagues focused their interest on the third of these purposes. They noted that parent-child interaction is greatly influenced by factors such as: (a) whether the society is monogamous or polygamous, (b) whether the society has a pre-industrial or a more complex form of economic organization, (c) how work is distributed between men and women, and (d) whether there is a system of education available to all children. Further, the child rearing process was viewed as being embedded in a network of other social processes. Parents rear their children within a social system and therefore, child-parent interaction can only be understood within the context of society as a whole (Maccoby, 1980).

Increasingly, social science research is becoming more complex, and scientists are utilizing a wider range of approaches. First, current researchers are becoming increasingly aware of the impact of momentary situations on a child's behavior. This has forced researchers to observe in a number of different situations and at various times to determine the stable set of characteristics possessed by each individual child. Second, it is now widely accepted that developmental change is the rule rather than the exception (Maccoby, 1980). Therefore, children do not remain static, but undergo constant change as part of their developmental process. This view is best summarized by Maccoby who states:

> Considering these developmental transformations, it now seems unlikely that the parents' primary contribution to the child's long-range development comes from teaching specific behaviors.

Rather, the parents' most lasting influence probably comes through establishing modes of interacting with other people and teaching certain modes of adaptation to changing life circumstances. Recently, interest has revived in the parental contribution to the child's developing sense of identity or *self*. The assumption is that a coherent self-concept may function as a child's gyroscope, keeping the individual to a relatively steady course and producing long-term consistencies in behavior. (1980, p. 29)

Furthermore, contemporary studies in socialization are somewhat modest in scope than earlier studies, because researchers now understand that they are exploring a constantly changing relationship between parent and child. For example, parents influence the development of children, who in turn influence the behavior of their parents. Each influences the other in a series of feedback loops. Both parents and children are influenced by forces within the larger social context.

Figure 1 illustrates this concept and shows a schematic representation of the cultural influences on the young child. The culture has a direct impact on the physical and social environment of both parents and children. Within the social environment, values, socioeconomic status and degree of acculturation all influence the way in which instrumental competencies are defined. These competencies or requisite skills are those abilities that are deemed necessary by parents to inculcate in their children to ensure their survival within the context of the culture. These competencies are taught and modeled by parents. The nature of these competencies influence the child-rearing process and help structure the way in which parent-child interactions develop. These interactions are in constant flux as parents and children exert reciprocal influence on each other. All these forces (nurture) combined with the unique genetic endowment of each child (nature) influence the development and form of the psychological processes of each child. These psychological processes (i.e. cognition, memory, perception, motivation, language and emotion) can only develop within the context of the culture. Both the form and formation of these psychological processes help determine the self identity and behavior of the child. It should be understood that Figure 1 is an oversimplification of the entire process of child development. The point emphasized is that the culture has an overriding influence on the development of the young child, and that all the forces exerted during the course of development are interactive and interdependent.

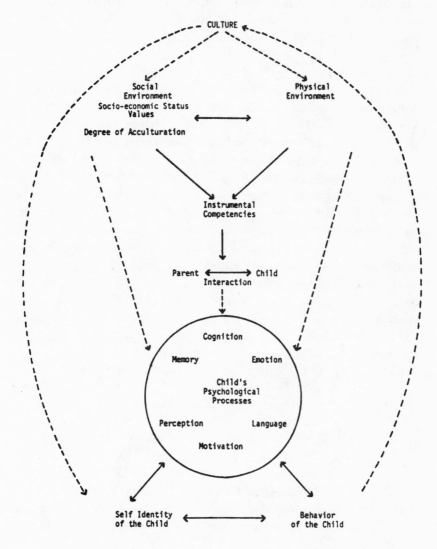

Figure 8-1. Cultural influences on the development of the young child.

The Significance of Neonatal Studies

Cross-cultural neonatal studies are of particular importance to those interested in multicultural influences on the development of the young child. Super (1980) emphasized the importance of studying social behavior in newborns since it may influence parental responses which may alter patterns of care, development, adult personality and culture. Super adds that the study of behavior in newborns poses the possibility that differences in behavioral disposition or temperament may have a genetic origin.

Cross-cultural research reports have illustrated how early environmental factors can influence behavior in the neonatal period. For example, nutrition and maternal health have been shown to be importance influences. Studies in Guatemala and Mexico show how economic and nutritional factors influence behavior (Brazelton, Tronick, Lechtig, Lasky, & Klein, 1977; Cravioto, Birch, De Licardie, Rosales, & Vega, 1969). Brazelton, Koslowski, and Tronick (1976) reported Zambian infants from low socioeconomic status families to be relatively quiet, inattentive, and irritable. Freedman (1971, 1974) proposes that gene pool differences account for the finding of relatively low irratability and an even disposition among newborns of Oriental background. This same phenomenon has been found with Navajo-Indian infants. Caudill and Weinstein's (1969) research in Japan and America along with later reports (Caudill, 1972; Caudill & Schooler, 1973) yielded a comprehensive picture of social interaction in the first six years of life. When observed in the home, Japanese mothers were seen to engage in a particularly close and solicitous relationship with their infants—soothing, pacifying, and calming them. The infants, in turn, were relatively quiet. Caudill compared this picture to the American mother who actively stimulated her baby, especially through lively vocalization. This coincides with the expected patterns of interaction in later years. Also it is consonant with two divergent folk theories. First, the need in the Japanese mother's mind to encourage social interaction and mutual interdependence, and second, the intent of the American mother to facilitate her baby's assertive individuality.

Growth of Competence

R. W. Le Vine (1967), Inkeles (1968) and Berry (1977) have suggested that child-rearing patterns of a culture may be influenced by the nature of its instrumental competencies required for adult economic, political, and social roles. Competency can be defined as the ability to perform the socially valued roles deemed important in a given society (Inkeles, 1968). According to Connolly and Bruner (1974), in any given society there are sets of skills which are essential for coping with existing realities. How an individual functions depends on the competencies (i.e. skills) required by these realities. It is generally agreed that competence is variously defined in different populations. Inkeles (1966) stated that the main task of childrearing in any culture is to train children to obtain the competencies that are socially valued in a specific culture in order to ensure survival.

Ogbu (1981) explained that in every relatively stable population, instrumental competencies have prior existence before individual families teach these competencies to their offspring through the process of childrearing. Child-rearing is thus the process by which children acquire prior existing competencies. Ogbu (1981) notes that "the study of the child-rearing process informs us of how the prior existing cognitive, linguistic, socialemotional, and practical competencies are transmitted and acquired" (p. 418).

Studies in competencies between members of two populations (e.g., middle class white and urban ghetto blacks) suggest that the nature of the instrumental competencies in a population determines the techniques parents and other child rearing agents employ to raise children, and influences how these children seek to acquire requisite skills as they grow older (Aberle, 1961; Barry, Child & Bacon, 1959; Inkeles, 1966, 1968; Kohn, 1969; R. W. Le Vine, 1967). Barry et al. (1959) provided a good example of how subsistence tasks determine personal attributes and how instrumental competencies appear to influence child-rearing practices. Barry et al. (1959) first described the personal attributes valued and rewarded in two types of societies distinguished by their levels of subsistence economy: low-food-accumulation societies of hunters vs. high-food-accumulation societies of pastoralists and farmers. The first type of society rewarded individualism, independence, assertiveness, and risk taking; whereas, the second type of society rewarded conscientious, compliant, responsible, and conservative adult behaviors. Instrumental competencies characteristic of each type of society were congruent with adult subsistence tasks. The authors suggested that these attributes tended to be generalized to everyday life.

Cohen (1965) studied child-rearing practices among the Kanuri of Nigeria. He observed that Kanuri parents utilize particular techniques to ensure that their children learn socially prescribed behaviors which are instrumental in helping their children attain high status when they reach adulthood. For example, the Kanuri male must demonstrate to those in power that he is loyal, obedient, and servile in order to acquire higher economic, political or social status. Thus, the qualities of loyalty, obedience, and servility are highly prized and are generalized to other relationships such as parent-child, teacher-student, and religious leader-followers, especially when status differentials exist. This example illustrates how the society's view of instrumental behaviors determines social competence, and how the latter influences child-rearing practices.

S. H. White (1973) recognized the linkage between subsistence strategies and instrumental competencies. He suggested that in modern societies subsistence strategies prepare children for adult life. He emphasized that one's participation in the economy determines one's subsistence, status and self-esteem. Miller (1971) explained that a job in American society is one of the most significant symbols of social status. It seems that people's participation in the economy is determined by the instrumental competencies acquired during childhood (Hunt, 1969; Schultz, 1961; Weisbrod, 1975). The acquisition of these instrumental competencies enable the individual to acquire the requisite training or education for suitable employment.

Ogbu (1981) explained that while all human populations respond to subsistence demands, "they do not all respond alike or with the same set of strategies because they do not occupy the same environment, because their environment does not contain the same resources, and because they have different histories of resource exploitation and of quest for protection" (p. 421). Different populations, therefore, seem to have evolved different strategies appropriate for their given circumstances. That is, parents learn best how to inculcate instrumental competencies in their children based on their knowledge of which strategies are effective in exploiting their resources. At first, trial and error approaches are used. Eventually, more effective techniques evolve which become "standardized and encoded in the people's customs and are transmitted like other aspects of their culture to subsequent generations" (Ogbu, 1981, p. 419). This transmission, both of skills and knowledge, ensures that parents and caregivers will share similar ideas concerning the instrumental competencies that children must learn to later become productive members of society.

Recent studies further contribute to our understanding of the linkage between competence and child-rearing. Frankel and Roer-Bornstein (1983) conducted an investigation to understand better the interaction between physical and social settings, cultural patterns of parenting, and the caretaker's ideology in two Israeli cultures undergoing modernization. The authors examined the parenting system of the Yemenite and Kurdish cultures. Mother/infant interactions were observed in nonstructured naturalistic settings. Yemenites traditionally have provided emotional support and encouraged intellectual growth for infants; whereas Kurdish people have encouraged motor and physical growth, autonomy, and self-sufficiency. Findings suggest that after 30 years of a common modernization, these two cultures exhibit significant differences in mother/infant interactions. These differences are correlated with traditional differences in infant rearing styles. Frankel and Roer-Bornstein conclude that culture and customs influence parenting behavior even in societies undergoing modernization.

Alston (1976) describes and analyzes observations of Chinese children from The People's Republic of China in 1975. Observations showed that Chinese infants displayed no anxiety when approached by strangers. Toddlers did not express the rebelliousness commonly associated with American children of the same age, even when asked to share toys or sit in chairs for long periods of time. It was noted that caretakers provided consistent affectionate physical stimulation. Within primary schools, children received group lessons and recitation whereas slow learners received out of class tutoring. School children appeared friendly, bright, spontaneous, but conforming. Their conformity was associated with the careful management of aggression in the school and society. The author concluded that (a) some developmental landmarks are culturally bound instead of universal, and (b) qualities such as liveliness, initiative and self-reliance are not eliminated by the control of competition, aggression and violence within a society. However, the management of aggression does appear to affect the development of individuality.

Ardila (1982) studies child-rearing practices in Colombia. He explained the development of the Colombian national character as the result of the social learning process acquired during infancy. Differences between different sectors of the population (e.g., geographical regions) are explained through the cultural process. He explained that through the cultural group and social class the child learns to understand the world in a culturally determined way. Children acquire values, attitudes and socially appropriate behavior that is integrated into their behavioral repertoire and forms the foundation for personality development, which in turn will be transmitted to future generations.

Parental Position in Society

As noted by Escovar and Lazarus (1982), a review of literature on child-rearing from a cross-cultural perspective reveals that social class frequently acts as a moderating variable. Social class or parental position in a society cuts across cultural groups in determining child-rearing practices. That is, there are some variations in child rearing that are strictly due to parental status and are not discrete, vertical cultural values (Geisman & Gerhart, 1968; Kohn, 1963).

Members of different social classes tend to view the world from different vantage points due to enjoying (or suffering) different conditions of life (Kohn, 1963). Social class can be defined as groupings of individuals who occupy broadly similar positions in society in terms of prestige. Social class is largely affected by occupational position, economic power and education. Social class is not homogeneous; variations in values occur within each class. Typically, class structure is categorized into four discrete classes:

(1) *lower class* consisting of unskilled manual workers,

(2) *working class* consisting of manual workers in semiskilled and skilled occupations,

(3) *middle class* consisting of white collar workers, managers and professionals, and

(4) *upper class* which is differentiated from the middle class in terms of lineage and wealth, more than by education or occupation. (See Table 2 for a description of the values associated with the working and middle classes.)

Table 2
Relationship Between High and Low SES Families and Child-Rearing Practices

Socioeconomic Status (SES)	Child-Rearing Practices
Lower Socioeconomic Status Working Class	— Stress obedience, respect, neatness, cleanliness, and staying out of trouble. Stress control, power assertive, authoritarian, arbitrary discipline, and physical punishment. Stress conforming to externally imposed standards — it is the overt act that matters.
Higher Socioeconomic Status Middle Class	— Stress happiness, creativity, ambition, independence, curiosity, self-control and self-direction. Democratic style, permissive or authoritative style of parenting. Stress open communication, reason with children, and use more complex language. Show more warmth and affection toward their children. It is the child's feelings and motives that matter.

Source: Based on findings of Hess (1970) and Kohn (1963).

Middle Class and Working Class Values. Kohn (1963) suggested that "class differences in parent-child relationships are a product of differences in parental values" (p. 471). He found that middle-class parents' values centered on self-direction, whereas working class parents' values focused on conformity to the external environment. These differences in values seem to be associated with differences in the conditions of life of the various social class groups. It appears that middle-class occupations require self-direction. In contrast, working-class occupations require that people follow rules set by authority figures.

In Kohn's seminal essay (1963), he interpreted these differences in values between working and middle class parents. First, working class individuals deal more with the manipulation of things, whereas middle class persons deal more with the manipulation of ideas, symbols and interpersonal relations. Second, working class parents are in occupations that stress conformity, standardization and direct supervision. In contrast, middle class occupations require self-direction. Third, getting advancement in working class occupations, especially union dominated industries, requires collective action; middle class occupations require more individual responsibility and self-initiative. It needs to be understood, however, that parents do not necessarily consciously train their children to meet future occupational demands. It is more probable that the parents' experience on the job have affected their own perception regarding desirable behavior for adults and children.

Lower Class Life and Economic Uncertainties. Other studies that examined class differences suggest that the economic uncertainties of lower-class life develop stressful situations that affect a mother's self-esteem, cognition and coping mechanisms (Bernstein, 1961; Hess & Shipman, 1967). The impact of life in impoverished environments affects the child in different ways: the mother/child interaction gets directly disrupted, and the child learns through observation the same modes of adaptation that the parents adopted. Lower class is usually associated with low income, crowded living conditions, insufficient resources to meet emergencies such as illness, accidents, etc. Anxiety and feelings of helplessness are often the results of poor living conditions. It seems that lower class life involves more stress for parents. These highly stressful conditions affect directly or indirectly the child-rearing practices of caregivers.

The Ghetto Environment. When examining the relationship between social class and child-rearing practices, it is certainly important to consider the child raised in a ghetto environment. Ogbu (1981) has applied a cultural-ecological model for studying child rearing in the urban black ghetto. He observed that urban ghetto blacks maintain a symbiotic relationship with the dominant white culture. Their environment is usually economically marginal and consists of a substantial amount of non-conventional resources, including the "street economy" (Bullock, 1973; Harrison, 1972). Many urban ghetto blacks are successful in finding conventional employment. However, for others, the job is menial, irregular, or worse—non-existent. Therefore, survival strategies become important. This could include hustling, pimping, drug dealing, and gambling, or more socially accepted occupations such as in sports or entertainment (Hudson, 1972; Newman, 1978; Valentine, 1979). Thus, models for success in the ghetto do not only include typical occupations.

Ogbu (1981) postulated that the ghetto theory of success is influenced by the aforementioned role models. However, the goals of the urban ghetto black are essentially the same as those of the middle class and include power, prestige, social recognition and self-esteem. The main difference depends on how these goals are realized. For example, ghetto blacks who have experienced a long history of racial barriers and economic oppression tend to believe less in the importance of education and tend to rely more on other alternatives in addition to schooling (Foster, 1974; Nobles & Traver, 1976).

It is suggested that the marginal participation of urban ghetto blacks in the conventional economy and their participation in the street economy influences child rearing practices. For example, marginal economic participation by the black male often makes it difficult for him to participate as the bread winning husband-father in the family. Ghetto parents often have to rely on relatives and friends for child care. These parents may have to apply for welfare or public assistance; this practice may require them to meet the demands of governmental agencies which may be perceived as ideologically alien to cherished values. Moreover, as noted by several researchers, parents who are actively involved in the street economy often have less stable family relationships than middle class parents (Ogbu, 1978; Stack, 1974; B. L. White, 1979). This lack of stability may drive their children at an early age into the street culture.

Ogbu (1981) suggested that in the post infancy period, the ghetto child is subject to inconsistent demands for obedience. Strong sanctions are applied that often create a relationship that becomes a contest between child and parent. The use of physical punishment and verbal rebuffs influence the development of the urban black child. Several theorists believe this type of child rearing practice fosters the development of functional competencies such as self reliance, ability to manipulate people and situations, mistrust of individuals in authority, ability to ward off attacks and strike back when necessary (Ladner, 1978; Nobles & Traver, 1976; Young, 1974).

In addition, ghetto rules for achievement and behavior are quite different than middle class rules. This relates to historical practices which prevented most blacks from obtaining the same careers goals open to whites. As stated by Ogbu, the ghetto rule is: "People should learn how to deal with white people—how to manipulate white people—and retain their own safety and identity, but not behave like white people" (1981, p. 125).

Parental Control

Cross cultural studies consistently show different patterns of parental control between cultures and across social classes. The amount, type and consistency of control exerted by parents have an important impact on the developing personality of the young child.

The concept of parental control has varied significantly from one study to another. Parental control can be defined as: (a) strictness-consistent enforcement of demands and rules, (b) restrictiveness—setting narrow limits on the child's activities, (c) demandingness—high level of responsibility expected, (d) authoritative—democratic enforcement of rules, requirements and restrictions, or (e) authoritarian—parents set rules, requirements and restrictions. A number of studies have suggested different effects as a result of parenting styles. Table 3 summarizes the results of the relationship between parental control and the effects upon their children.

Researchers have also studied differences in parental control between ethnic groups and social classes, and the interaction effect

Table 3

Relationship Between Parental Practices and Personality Development of the Young Child*

Strictness	Restrictiveness	Demandingness	Authoritative	Authoritarian
—Able to control aggressive impulses and not coercive toward parents (Patterson, 1976) —Adequately controlled (Block, 1971) —High in self-esteem at age ten or eleven (Coopersmith, 1967) —Able to approach new situations with confidence, to take initiative and persist in tasks once begun (Baumrind, 1967, 1971, 1977)	—Tend to lack empathy (Feshbach, 1974) —Obedience, orderliness, and lack of aggression (Baldwin, 1948)	*High Level of Demands:* —Low in aggression (boys) (Edward & Whiting, 1977) —Altruistic rather than egoistic (Whiting & Whiting, 1973, 1975) —Above average in competence (Baumrind, 1967, 1971, 1977) *Low Level of Demands:* —High aggression (Sears, Maccoby, & Levin, 1957) —Undercontrol of impulse (Block, 1971) —Immaturity (Baumrind, 1967)	—Competent, independent, cheerful, self-controlled, and socially responsible (Baumrind, 1967, 1971) —Planful, highly interactive with other children, dominant and fairly aggressive (Baldwin, 1948) —High in self-esteem (Coopersmith, 1967)	—Lacking in empathy (Feshbach, 1974) —Low in self-esteem (Coopersmith, 1967) —Poor in internalization of moral standards, oriented toward external rewards and punishments (Hoffman & Saltzstein, 1967) —Resistive, aggressive, cruel, lacking in spontaneity, affection, curiosity and originality, low in effective peer interaction (Baldwin, 1948) —Weak in establishing positive relationships with peers, frequently sad in mood, somewhat withdrawn (Baumrind, 1967, 1971, 1973, 1977) —Lacking independence (Baumrind, 1971)

*Results are not necessarily applicable to children in all cultures or different socioeconomic backgrounds. Findings are based on studies of North American children.

of these two variables. Within the United States today, Blacks and Hispanics are the largest minority group and have been studied extensively by cross-cultural researchers.

Cahill (1967) studied differences in child-rearing practices between lower socioeconomic ethnic groups (Puerto Rican, Black and White families). He found that Puerto Rican mothers were the most permissive, and that Blacks were the least permissive of the three groups. White mothers were the most anxious about child rearing and child dominance. Findings suggest that all three groups severely punished immodesty or sex play, all used physical punishment, all expected obedience, and none tolerated aggression toward parents.

Padilla and Ruiz (1974) noted that one of the main characteristics of the Hispanic family structure is the strong authoritarian role of the father. The mother maintains a submissive role in the family. The husband controls the family nucleus and tends to overprotect his daughters. However, the men expect much more independence for themselves.

Durrett, O'Bryant and Pennebaker (1975) studied child-rearing practices among White, Black and Mexican-American ethnic groups within the United States. They found clear differences among the three ethnic groups. White and Black parents reported themselves as being more authoritative than did Mexican-American parents. Fathers of both Black and White children appeared to encourage achievement and success more than Mexican-American fathers. Mexican-American parents placed less emphasis on individual responsibility; however, they were significantly more protective and stressed control of the emotions.

Minturn and Lambert (1964) compared child rearing across six cultures (U.S.A., Mexico, Philippines, Japan, India, Kenya). They noted that Mexican mothers maintain their children close to home and sometimes did not send them to school if the children had been bullied by more aggressive peers. They also found the Mexican parents tended to use physical punishment and verbal hostility more than parents of the other cultures studied. Anglo-American parents were less physical, and relied on verbal reprimand and logic in discipline.

Rusmore and Kinmeyer (1976) reported that Mexican-American

mothers maintained strict discipline and discouraged disagreements. Mexican mothers tried to exert absolute control over their children's decision-making and interactions. Mexican mothers encouraged their children to play at home with siblings rather than with friends in the neighborhood.

As previously emphasized, socio-economic status (SES) is an important moderating variable that cuts across cultures. Findings of Holtzman, Diaz-Guerrero and Swartz (1975) confirm the importance of social class distinctions in determining the use of parental control. For example, low SES mothers both in the United States and Mexico valued strict obedience, whereas high SES mothers stressed the democratic use of authority which is more consistent with their values of independence, tolerance and social concern.

Parental Warmth and Affection

Becker (1964) reviewed the literature on child-rearing practices that had been published up to early 1960's. He found that restrictive but warm parents developed polite, neat, obedient and non-aggressive children. However, restrictive but hostile parents produced children who were associated with a variety of neurotic symptoms, including withdrawal from social interaction with peers. Becker also found that the effects of permissiveness depended on the parents' warmth. Warm and permissive parents seem to foster socially outgoing, independent, active, creative, and domineering children, whereas hostile and permissive parents fostered the development of aggressive children or delinquents.

Baumrind (1967, 1971) also emphasized the importance of parental warmth. She found that permissive parents who were relatively warm, but lacked firm control, tended to have impulsive and immature children. Parents who combined warmth with firm control and open communication raised children who were self-controlled and unusually competent for their age.

Witkin, Dyk, Faterson, Goodenough, and Karp (1962) found that mothers represented the primary source of affection in the Hispanic family. Rusmore and Kinmeyer (1976) reported that these mothers usually fostered dependency relationships with their children, and they encouraged close and warm relationships with the family. Minturn and Lambert (1964) found Mexican mothers to be significantly higher in parental warmth than their Anglo-American counterparts.

Rohner (1975) documented a worldwide relationship between time spent as a sole caretaker of children and rejection. He analyzed ethnographic studies of 101 societies. He found that mothers who do not share child care responsibilities with anyone, especially a grandparent, tend to reject their children. The Hispanic mother, for example, usually places some of the child rearing responsibility on her extended family, thereby creating a more shared and affectionate environment. Whiting (1961) reported a similar relationship between infant indulgence and the number of adults living in the household. It seems that extended families tend to be more indulgent with their infants than nuclear families. Rohner (1975) noted more acceptance of children in households where fathers were present on a daily basis, regardless of culture.

Personality Development

Personality may be defined as the dynamic organization within the individual of those psychophysical systems that determine his or her unique adjustment to the world (Allport, 1937). As noted by Burton (1974), personality is not conceived of as something an individual has. Personality is more—it is a living, holistic entity, with goals, needs, purposes and meanings. As part and parcel of this dynamic process, the culture has a continuing impact on the way an individual organizes those psychophysical systems that ultimately determine personality.

In understanding personality development, it needs to be emphasized that the personality of the young child is in formation, it is developing (Palmer, 1970). It is the interaction and organization of functions—social, affective, motoric, perceptual and cognitive—that ultimately determine the identity of the child and constitute the core of personality. The interacting and organizational functions may best be perceived as *process* variables; whereas identity may be understood more as the *product*. This does not imply, however, a static system; the young child's identity is in constant flux and children, in the process of development, deal with conflicts which require successful resolutions. (Ludwig & Lazarus, in press; The interested reader is referred to Erikson's *Childhood and*

Society [1963] where he lays out the framework for his eight stages of human development, and the impact of their successful or unsuccessful resolution on personality formation.)

Self-Esteem

Within this section, discussion is limited to self-esteem because it is beyond the scope of the chapter to address all the psychological processes that make up the core of personality. The concept of self-esteem has received a great deal of attention in the cross-cultural child development literature. Coopersmith (1967) refers to self-esteem as the individual's personal judgment of worth. He found that people assess their own success in terms of *power* (ability to influence and control others); *significance* (the acceptance, attention, and affection of others); *virtue* (adherence to moral and ethical standards); and *competence* (successful performance in meeting demands for achievement). Felkner (1974) suggested that the self-concept serves three purposes: It maintains inner consistency, determines the interpretation of experiences, and provides expectations.

Padilla & Ruiz (1974) suggested that minority groups need to enhance their ethnic identity which appears to be an important source of self-esteem. Rosenberg and Simmons (1971) explained that the longstanding prejudice in American society against minorities has been interpreted as a threat to the self-esteem of minority group members. Individuals' self-attitude seems to be a product of reflected appraisals (Rosenberg & Simmons, 1971). Lewin (1948) suggests that members of the lower social strata are greatly influenced by the low self-esteem the majority project upon them. Gordon (1969) reviewed the literature of the 1930's through the 1960's and found that members of minority groups have been associated with: (a) self-hatred, (b) marginality, self-alienation, self-consciousness and self-disparagement, and (c) cognitive disparagement and discrimination. This has contributed to the stratification hypothesis: A person's level of self-esteem will evidence his or her ethnic group's social rank.

Rosenberg (1965) however rejects the stratification hypothesis, based on a comparison of 14 ethnic/racial groups in the United States. Rosenberg and Simmons (1971) compared 12 studies conducted between 1960 and 1968 and found that there are no significant racial differences in self-esteem between Blacks and Whites. Velasco-Barraza and Muller (1982) examined the development of self-concept, self-esteem and self-ideal in second, fourth, sixth and eighth graders from Chile, Mexico and the United States. Findings suggest substantial similarities in development of self-concept, self-esteem and self-ideal across national groups.

Recent cross-cultural studies do not support the existence of interethnocultural group differences in self-esteem. Nevertheless, it does suggest two situations that can affect self-esteem of minority group members: To live and/or work in a dissonant social situation, and experience conflict in cultural values (Rosenberg, 1962; Rosenberg & Simmons, 1971).

An example of a child at risk would be a Native American youngster attending an urban school where there are no peers of the same tribal group, and where the population is primarily Anglo-American. Researchers have consistently noted the value differences between Native Americans and Anglo-Americans (Burgess, 1980; Foerster & Little Soldier, 1974; Hynd & Garcia, 1979; Lazarus, 1982, Lazarus & Lavendera, 1981; Trimble, 1976; Zintz, 1963. See Table 4 where Zintz [1963, p. 175] provides a comparison of the Anglo-American and Pueblo cultures in terms of values).

Table 4
A Comparison of the Anglo-American and Pueblo Cultures in Terms of Values

Pueblo Values	Anglo American Values
Harmony with nature	Mastery over nature
Present-time orientation	Future time orientation
Explanation of natural phenomena	Scientific explanation of everything
Follow the old ways	Climb the ladder of success
Cooperation	Competition
Anonymity	Individuality
Submissiveness	Aggression
Work for present needs	Work to get ahead
Sharing wealth	Saving for future
Time is always with us	Clock watching
Humility	Win the first prize if possible
Win once, but let others win	Win all the time

Source: Based on Zintz (1963) findings.

If Native American children begin to assimilate Anglo-American values, it may have a detrimental effect on their self-esteem (Lazarus,

1982). When the Native-American child enters an Anglo-American school the youngster may begin to compare himself or herself unfavorably to the child of the dominant culture. Therefore, the Native American child in this setting would meet the previously mentioned risk criteria (Lazarus, 1982).

In contrast, Native American children who live and go to school on the tribal reservation would not be at risk. This is consonant with self-attitude formation theory. The theory postulates that an individual's self-evaluation is formed through perceived evaluation by significant others. Rovner (1981) explains that within most cultural groups, ethnocultural segregation is prevalent, therefore a child will compare himself or herself to peers of the same background. Although the dominant cultural group may downgrade a child from a minority group—in this instance, a Native American—this same child will most likely evaluate himself or herself with peers who are members of the same minority group. The Native American peers, rather than downgrade the child's self-esteem, will tend to enhance it. This theory also clarifies the failure to find inter-ethnic differences in self-esteem.

CULTURAL INFLUENCES ON PSYCHOLOGICAL DISORDERS IN CHILDREN

The last two decades have witnessed an increased concern in the relationship between culture and mental disorders. This interest has manifested itself across a variety of disciplines and has served as an impetus for the development of subdisciplinary specialties such as transcultural psychiatry (Kleinman, 1977; Marsella, 1979; Wittkower & Prince, 1974). Marsella (1979) noted that although there has been increased interest in the socio-cultural aspects of mental illness, few socio-cultural theories for understanding mental disorders have been advanced. The bulk of studies that have linked cultural influences to abnormal behavior have primarily been concerned with adults, and little emphasis has been given to the young child. As noted by Ludwig and Lazarus (in press), traditionally, there has been a belief that whatever advances were made in the field of psychopathology could be scaled down and applied to children. However, as Yule (1981) has so cogently emphasized: "Children are not merely smaller, less complex human beings. Their problems have to be evaluated within a developmental framework" (p. 5). Therefore, caution must be exercised when generalizing results to children from studies of adults.

As previously mentioned, the culture molds the family and the family molds the child (Sanua, 1980). Due to the lack of studies investigating cultural determinants of *childhood* psychopathology, it is best to look at the way that culture molds the family, and the familial antecedents of psychopathology. Leighton and Hughes (1961) theorized that the origin, course and outcome of psychiatric disorders is influenced by sociocultural factors and that certain child-rearing practices may foster mental impairment. Therefore, this section emphasizes the cultural influences and cultural stresses upon the family that may tend to foster childhood psychopathology — rather than direct studies of the child.

The Impact of Failures in Socialization

Sanua (1980) suggested that socialization is required for the child to face the demands of life. Therefore, childhood psychopathology may develop as a consequence of problems the child undergoes during this process. He suggested that problems in socialization may be viewed from two perspectives. First, psychopathology within the parents may make it impossible for the child to acquire the requisite competencies to deal with the complexities of life. Second, even if psychopathology is not evident within the family constellation, the child may be raised with certain incapacities or may fail to acquire the appropriate skills to deal with major life stresses. This second interpretation is similar to the viewpoint of Erikson (1963) who listed the developmental crises that must be resolved for the individual to emerge into adulthood psychologically healthy.

Palmer (1970) suggested that severe psychopathology in children is manifested when youngsters fail in their drive toward independence. If this drive is blocked during the socialization process, children may fail to develop emotionally. Therefore unless the family supports this drive towards independence, the child may seek to avoid the anxiety and stresses of maturation by regressing.

Leighton (1974) underscored the relationship between failures in socialization of the child and psychopathology. He believed that there is a strong relationship between sociocultural disorganization and mental illness. He evaluated communities according to a continuum from good to poor functioning; from sociocultural *integration* to sociocultural *disintegration*. Communities in the throes of disintegration produce more incidences of psychiatric disorders. He emphasized that failures in child-nurturing and child-rearing could result from economic breakdown within the social system. This would result in absent fathers, maternal deprivation and distorted relationships with peers. In communities undergoing disintegration there is a breakdown in the medical institutions. This can foster organic diseases due to an increase in unsanitary conditions; also, inadequate food resources can produce a host of medical diseases. Leighton (1974) also emphasized that stress from such conditions (from viewing the world as a series of frustrations and disappointments) leads to psychiatric disorders. Leighton's formula may be best expressed as: The greater the disintegration, the greater the stress, and the larger the incidence of mental disorders within the community.

The Impact of Stress

The impact of stress on the individual and the family has been underscored as a major etiological factor in precipitating mental disorders and medical diseases (e.g., Anderson, 1978; Brown, 1980; Friedman & Rosenman, 1974; Selye, 1974; Wolff, Wolf & Goodell, 1968). Moreover, the role of the culture as a stress inducer has been studied within the last two decades (e.g., Leighton & Hughes, 1961; Marsella, Kinzie & Gordon, 1973; Wittkower & Dubreuil, 1973). According to Marsella, "cultures vary with regard to both the amount and type of stress they induce in their members" (1979, p. 238). Marsella (1979) provided an extensive review of the literature on culturally related stresses and catalogued these stresses into seven major categories which are described in Table 5.

These seven types of stresses exert influences over the course and outcome of mental disorders, and have an impact as familial antecedents of psychopathology in children. However, it must be understood that each culture conditions certain patterns of behavior—which are termed acceptable—and that the definition of abnormality is only meaningful within the context of the culture. In addition, differences in personality vary across cultures. Individuals with particular personality characteristics may be more or

Table 5
Cultural Variations in Stress

Types of Stress	Precipitant Factors
Value Conflict Stress	Type of stress created by conflicting values in a given society
Social Change Stress	Stress develops as a consequence of the change and pressure generated by the process of urbanization or modernization
Acculturation Stress	Stress that occurs when different cultures come into contact with one another
Life Event Stress	Stress generated by events that require new adaptative responses. That is, events that require change in on-going patterns of adjustment
Goal-Striving Discrepancy Stress	Stress developed out of a large discrepancy between aspirations and achievements
Role Discrimination Stress	Stress related to social status
Role Conflict	Stress that occurs when the role that people play are in conflict with one another—Stress result as a consequence of the continual switching in role requirement and demands

Source: Based on Marsella (1979. p. 238–239).

less susceptible to cultural stresses due to their temperment, learned patterns of behavior, philosophies of life, coping style and biological predispositions (Marsella, 1978, 1979).

In conclusion, after reviewing the literature on cultural influences on psychopathology in children, it becomes evident that few theories help explain cultural differences in mental disorders of adults, let alone children. Therefore, one must be cautious in extrapolating results. Nonetheless, a recent surge of studies in this area may serve as a foundation for producing theoretical explanations. If a soundly researched sociocultural model is developed, it can provide a different vantage point for understanding psychopathology in children and augment psychodynamic, behavioral and biochemical theories of causation.

SUMMARY AND IMPLICATIONS

This chapter underscores the need to understand the multicultural factors that influence the course of child development. Not only do few theories exist that emphasize the role of cultural determinants in producing abnormal behavior in children; few personality theories stress the importance of the culture on normal child development. Though child development is a complex process that can be studied from many different vantage points, we highlighted the multicultural factors that influence the course of child development.

The major points emphasized in this chapter were:

- There is a need for more comparative cross-cultural research strategies for the assessment of both normal and abnormal personality formation in children,
- The course of child development can only be understood within the context of the culture.
- Child-rearing patterns of a culture are influenced by the nature of the instrumental competencies required for adult life and the main task of child rearing in any culture is to train children to acquire these requisite skills.
- Social class or parental position in society cuts across cultural groups in influencing the nature of the instrumental competencies, and in defining the values inculcated in children.
- Cross-cultural studies consistently show differences in parental control and parental warmth between cultures and across social classes.
- Recent evidence seems to support the assumption that different cultural groups foster the same level of self-esteem in their children.
- Cultures vary in the amount and type of stress they induce in their children.
- There is a strong relationship between socio-cultural disorganization and mental and physical illness in children.
- New theoretical models that stress the importance of the culture in personality formation — both normal and abnormal, need to be developed and evaluated.

In addition to these points, a few words for the concerned professional are in order. It is important that individuals in education and the mental health field be sensitive to cultural differences among children. Developing a knowledge base and a cultural frame of reference will enable practitioners to respond better to the needs of youngsters from different cultural groups. Today, the sociological theory of cultural pluralism is relevant to all new immigrants. Children are still being taught the instrumental competencies required to compete within society, however there is a new emphasis on children learning about their roots and preserving their cultural identity. Professionals should encourage this new emphasis, as it will foster self-esteem, instill pride and add a further dimension to a child's growing sense of self. Professionals continually need to be reminded that one culture is not superior to another. Each family reserves the right to raise their children in ways that seem consistent with their cultural norms, beliefs and values.

REFERENCES

Aberle, D. F. (1961). Culture and socialization. In F. L. K. Hsu (Ed.), *Psychological anthropology.* Evanston, IL: Dorsey.

Ainsworth, M. D. S. (1967). *Infancy in Uganda: Infant care and the growth of love.* Baltimore, MD: Johns Hopkins Univ. Press.

Alston, F. K. (1976, April). *Early childhood-rearing practices in the People's Republic of China.* Paper presented at the annual meeting of the American Educational Research Association, San Francisco, CA.

Allport, G. W. (1937). *Personality: A psychological interpretation.* New York: Holt, Rinehart & Winston.

Anderson, R. A. (1978). *Stress power: How to turn tension into energy.* New York: Human Sciences Press.

Ardila, R. (1982). *Pautas de crianza de los ninos en Colombia [Child-rearing practices of colombian children].* Unpublished report to COLCIENCIAS, Bogota, Colombia.

Baldwin, A. L. (1948). Socialization and the parent-child relationship. *Child Development, 19,* 127–136.

Barry, H., Child, I. L., & Bacon, M. K. (1959). Relation of child training to subsistence economy. *American Anthropologist, 61,* 51–63.

Barker, R. G., & Wright, H. F. (1971). *Midwest and its children: The psychological ecology of an American town.* Hamden, CT. Anchor Books. (Original Work published 1955).

Barker, R. G., & Schoggen, P. (1973). *Qualities of community life.* San Francisco: Jossey-Bass.

Baumrind, D. (1967). Child care practices anteceding three patterns of preschool behavior. *Genetic Psychology Monographs, 75,* 43–88.

Baumrind, D. (1971). Current patterns of parental authority. *Developmental Psychology Monograph, 4* (1, Pt. 2).

Baumrind, D. (1973). The development of instrumental competence through socialization. In A. D. Pick (Ed.), *Minnesota Symposium on Child Psychology* (Vol. 7). Minneapolis: Univ. of Minnesota Press.

Baumrind, D. (1977). *Socialization determinants of personal agency.* Paper presented at the biennial meeting of the Society for Research in Child Development, New Orleans.

Becker, W. (1964). Consequences of different kinds of parental discipline. In M. L. Hoffman & L. W. Hoffman (Eds.), *Review of child development research* (Vol. 1), New York: Russell Sage Foundation.

Bernstein, B. (1961). Social class and linguistic development: A theory of social learning. In A. H. Halsey, J. Floud, & C. A. Anderson (Eds.), *Economy, education and society.* New York: Free Press.

Berry, J. W. (1977). *Human ecology and cognitive style: Comparative studies in cultural and psychological adaptations.* New York: Halsted.

Block, I. H. (1971). *Lives through time.* Berkeley, CA: Bancroft Books.

Brazelton, T. B., Koslowski, B., & Tronick, E. (1976). *Journal of the American Academy of Child Psychiatry, 15,* 97–107.

Brazelton, T. B., Tronick, E., Lechtig, A., Lasky, R., & Klein, R. E. (1977). The behavior of nutritionally deprived Guatemalan infants. *Developmental Medicine and Child Neurology, 19,* 364–372.

Brislin, R. W., Lonner, W. J., & Thorndike, R. M. (1973). *Cross-cultural research methods.* New York: Wiley.

Bronfenbrenner, U. (1970). *Two worlds of childhood: U.S. and U.S.S.R.* New York: Russell Sage Foundation.

Bronfenbrenner, U. (1977). Toward an experimental ecology of human development. *American Psychologist, 32,* 513–531.

Brown, B. B. (1980). *Supermind: The ultimate energy.* New York: Bantam.

Bullock, P. (1973). *Aspirations vs. opportunity: "Careers" in the inner city.* Ann Arbor: Univ. of Michigan Press.

Burton, A. (1974). The nature of personality theory. In A. Burton (Ed.), *Operational theories of personality.* New York: Brunner/Mazel.

Burgess, B. J. (1980). Parenting in the Native-American community. In M. Fantini & R. Cardenas (Eds.), *Parenting in a multicultural society.* New York: Longman.

Butcher, J., & Pancheri, P. (1976). *A handbook of cross-national MMPI research.* Minneapolis: Univ. of Minnesota Press.

Cahill, I. D. (1967). Child-rearing practices in lower socioeconomic ethnic groups. *Dissertation Abstracts International, 27,* 3139 A. (Univ. Microfilms No. 67-2788).

Caudill, W. A. (1972). Tiny dramas: Vocal communication between mother and infant in Japanese and American families. In W. P. Lebra (Ed.), *Transcultural research in mental health: Vol. II. Mental health research in Asia and the Pacific.* Honolulu: Univ. Press of Hawaii.

Caudill, W. A., & Schooler, C. (1973). Child behavior and child rearing in Japan and the United States: An interim report. *Journal of Nervous and Mental Disease, 157,* 323–338.

Caudill, W. A., & Weinstein, H. (1969). Maternal care and infant behavior in Japan and America. *Psychiatry, 32,* 12–43.

Cohen, R. (1965). Some aspects of institutionalized exchange: A Kanuri example. *Cahiers d'etudes Africaine, 5*(3), 353–369.

Connolly, K. J., & Bruner, J. S. (1974). Introduction, competence: Its nature and nurture. In K. J. Connolly & J. S. Bruner (Eds.), *The growth of competence.* London: Academic Press.

Coopersmith, S. (1967). *The antecedents of self-esteem.* San Francisco: W. H. Freeman.

Cravioto, J., Birch, H. G., De Licardie, E., Rosales, L., & Vega, L. (1969). The ecology of growth and development in a Mexican preindustrial community: Report I. Method and findings from birth to one month of age. *Monographs of the Society for Research in Child Development, 34* (5, Serial No. 129).

Draguns, J. G. Culture and personality. (1979). In A. Marsella, R. G. Tharp & T. J. Ciborowski (Eds.), *Perspectives on cross-cultural psychology.* New York: Academic Press.

Durrett, M. A., O'Bryant, S., & Pennebaker, J. W. (1975). Child rearing reports of White, Black and Mexican-American families. *Developmental Psychology, 44*(6), 871.

Edwards, C. P., & Whiting, B. (1977). *Sex differences in children's social interaction.* Unpublished report to the Ford Foundation.

Erickson, E. (1963). *Childhood and society* (2nd ed.). New York: W. W. Norton. (Original Work published, 1950).

Escovar, P. L., & Lazarus, P. J. (1982). Cross-cultural child-rearing practices: Implications for school psychologists. *School Psychology International, 3,* 143–148.

Felkner, D. W. (1974). *Building positive self-concepts.* Minneapolis: Burgess.

Feshbach, N. D. (1974). The relationship of child-rearing factors to children's aggression, empathy and related positive and negative behavior. In I. de Wit & W. W. Hartup (Eds.), *Determinants and origins of aggressive behavior.* The Hague: Mouton Press.

Foerster, L. M., & Little Soldier, L. D. (1974). Open education and Native American values. *Educational Leadership, 34,* 41–45.

Foster, H. L. (1974). *Ribbin', jivin', and playin' the dozens: The unrecognized dilemma of inner city schools.* Cambridge, MA: Ballinger.

Frankel, D. G., & Roer-Bornstein, D. (1983, April). *Modernization: A case study of the interaction of setting, custom, and idealogy.* Paper presented at the biennial meeting of the Society for Research in Child Development, Detroit, MI.

Freedman, D. G. (1971). Genetic influences on development of behavior. In G. B. A. Stoelinga & J. J. Van der Werff Ten Bosch, *Normal and abnormal development of behavior.* Leiden, Germany: Leiden Univ. Press.

Freedman, D. G. (1974). *Human infancy: An evolutionary perspective.* Hillsdale, NJ: Erlbaum.

Friedman, M., & Rosenman, R. H. (1974). *Type A behavior and your heart.* New York: Knopf.

Fromm, E., & Maccoby, M. (1970). *Social character in a Mexican village: A socio-psychoanalytic study.* Englewood Cliffs, NJ: Prentice-Hall.

Geisman, L. L., & Gerhart, U. G. (1968). Social class, ethnicity, and family functioning: Exploring some issues raised by the Moynihan report. *Journal of Marriage and the Family, 30,* 480–487.

Gordon, C. (1969). *Looking ahead: Self-conceptions, race and family as determinants of adolescent orientation to achievement.* Washington, DC: The American Sociological Association. (Published for the Arnold N. and Caroline Rose Monograph Series)

Harrison, B. (1972). *Education, training and the urban ghetto.* Baltimore, MD: Johns Hopkins Univ. Press.

Havighurst, R. I., & Neugarten, B. L. (1955). *American Indian and white children: A sociopsychological investigation.* Chicago: Univ. of Chicago Press.

Hess, R. D. (1970). Social class and ethnic influence on socialization. In P. H. Mussen (Ed.), *Carmichael' manual of child psychology* (3rd ed.). New York: Wiley.

Hess, R. D. & Shipman, V. C. (1967). Cognitive elements in maternal behavior. In J. P. Hill (Ed.), *Minnesota Symposium on Child Psychology* (Vol. I). Minneapolis: Univ. of Minnesota Press.

Hoffman, M. L., & Saltzstein, H. D. (1967). Parent discipline and the child's moral development. *Journal of Personality and Social Psychology, 5,* 45–47.

Holtzman, W. H., Diaz-Guerrero, R., & Swartz, J. D. (1975). *Personality development in two cultures: A cross-cultural longitudinal study of school children in Mexico and the United States.* Austin: Univ. of Texas Press.

Hudson, J. (1972). The hustling ethic. In T. Kochman (Ed.), *Rappin' and stylin' out: Communication in urban black America.* Chicago: Univ. of Illinois Press.

Hunt, N. McV. (1969). *The challenge of incompetence and poverty.* Urbana, IL: Univ. of Illinois Press.

Hynd, G. W., & Garcia, W. I. (1979). Intellectual assessment of the Native American student. *School Psychology Review, 8,* 446–454.

Inkeles, A. (1966). Social structure and the socialization of competence. *Harvard Educational Review, 36*(3), 265–283.

Inkeles, A. (1968). Society, social structure and child socialization. In J. A. Clausen (Ed.), *Socialization and society.* Boston: Little, Brown.

Kleinman, A. (1977). Depression, somatization and the transcultural psychiatry. *Social Science and Medicine, 11,* 3–9.

Kluckhohn, C., & Murray, H. A. (Eds.), (1948). *Personality in nature, society, and culture.* New York: Knopf.

Kohn, M. L. (1963). Social class and parent-child relationships: An interpretation. *American Journal of Sociology, 68,* 471–480.

Kohn, M. L. (1969). Social class and parent-child relationships: An interpretation. In R. L. Coser (Ed.), *Life cycle and achievement in America.* New York: Harper & Row.

Laboratory of Comparative Human Cognition. (1979). Cross-cultural psychology's challenges to our ideas of children and development. *American Psychologist, 34,* 827–833.

Ladner, I. A. (1978). Growing up black. In J. H. Williams (Ed.), *Psychology of women: Selected writings.* New York: Norton.

Lazarus, P. J. (1982). Counseling the Native American child: A question of values. *Elementary School Guidance and Counseling, 17,* 83–88.

Lazarus, P. J., & Escovar, P. (1981, June). *Hispanic child rearing practices.* Paper presented at the Inter-American Congress of Psychology, Santo Domingo, Dominican Republic.

Lazarus, P. J., & Lavendera, L. (1981, June). *The implementation of a transcultural model in the development of school psychological services for Indians in the United States.* Paper presented at the Inter-American Congress of Psychology, Santo Domingo, Dominican Republic.

Leighton, A. H. (1974). Social disintegration and mental disorder. In S. Arieti & G. Caplan, (Eds.), *American handbook of psychiatry.* New York: Basic Books.

Leighton, A., & Hughes, J. (1961). Culture as causative of mental disorders. In *Causes of mental disorders: A review of epidemiological knowledge.* New York: Milbank Memorial Fund.

Le Vine, R. A. (1970). Cross-cultural study in child development. In P. H. Mussen (Eds.), *Carmichael's manual of psychology* (Vol. 2, 3rd ed.). New York: Wiley.

Le Vine, R. A. (1973). *Culture, behavior, and personality.* Chicago: Aldine.

Le Vine, R. A. (1979, March). *Anthropology and child development.* Paper presented at the meeting of the Society for Research in Child Development, San Francisco.

Le Vine, R. W. (1967). *Dreams and deeds: Achievement motivation in Nigeria.* Chicago: Univ. of Chicago Press.

Lewin, K. (1948). *Resolving social conflicts: Selected papers on group dynamics.* New York: Harper & Row.

Looft, W. R. (1973). Socialization and personality throughout the life span: An examination of contemporary psychological approaches. In P. B. Baltes & K. W. Schaie (Eds.), *Life-span developmental psychology: Personality and socialization.* New York: Academic Press.

Ludwig, R. P., & Lazarus, P. J. (in press). Psychological evaluation of children and adolescents with severe emotional handicaps. In P. J. Lazarus & S. Strichart (Eds.), *Psychoeducational evaluation of children with low incidence handicaps.* New York: Grune & Stratton.

Maccoby, E. E. (1980). *Social development: Psychological growth and the parent-child relationship.* New York: Harcourt Brace Jovanovich.

Manaster, G. J., & Havighurst, R. J. (1972). *Cross-national research: Social psychological methods and problems.* Boston: Houghton Mifflin.

Marsella, A. J., Kinzie, D., & Gordon, P. (1973). Ethnocultural variations in the expression of depression. *Journal of Cross-Cultural Psychology, 4,* 435–458.

Marsella, A. J. (1978). Thoughts on cross-cultural studies on the epidemiology of depression. *Culture, Medicine, and Psychiatry, 2,* 343–357.

Marsella, A. J. (1979). Cross-cultural studies of mental disorders. In A. J. Marsella, R. G. Tharp & T. J. Ciborowski (Eds.), *Perspectives on cross-cultural psychology.* New York: Academic Press.

Minturn, L. & Lambert, W. (1964). *Mothers of six cultures: Antecedents of child-rearing.* New York: Wiley.

Miller, H. P. (1971). *Rich man, poor man.* New York: Crowell.

Munroe, R. J., & Munroe, R. H. (1975). *Cross-cultural human development.* Monterey, CA: Brooks/Cole.

Newman, D. K. (1978). *Protest, politics, and prosperity: Black Americans and white institutions, 1940–1975.* New York: Pantheon.

Nobles, W. W., & Traver, S. (1976). Black parental involvement in education: The African connection, *Child Welfare and Child Development: Alton M. Childs Series.* Atlanta, Georgia: Atlanta Univ. School of Social Work.

Ogbu, J. U. (1978). *Minority education and caste: The American system in cross-cultural perspective.* New York: Academic Press.

Ogbu, J. U. (1981). Origins of human competence: A cultural-ecological perspective. *Child Development, 52,* 413–429.

Padilla, A. M., & Ruiz, R. A. (1974). *Latino mental health: A review of the literature.* (DHEW Publication ADM) Washington, D.C.: U.S. Government Printing Office.

Palmer, J. O. (1970). *The psychological assessment of children.* New York: Wiley.

Patterson, G. R. (1976). The aggressive child: Victim and architect of a coercive system. In L. A. Hamerlynck, L. C. Handy & E. J. Mash (Eds.), *Behavior modification and families.* New York: Brunner/Mazell.

Price-Williams, D. R. (1974). Psychological experiment and anthropology: The problem of categories. *Ethos, 2,* 95–114.

Price-Williams, D. R. (1975). *Explorations in cross-cultural psychology.* San Francisco: Chandler & Sharp.

Rosenberg, M. (1962). The dissonant religious context and emotional disturbance. *American Journal of Sociology, 68,* 1–10.

Rosenberg, M. (1965). *Society and the adolescent self-image.* Princeton, NJ: Princeton Univ. Press.

Rosenberg, M. & Simmons, R. (1971). *Black and white self-esteem: The urban school child.* Washington, DC: The American Sociological Association. (Published for the Arnold M. and Caroline Rose Monograph Series).

Rovner, R. A. (1981). Ethno-cultural identity and self-esteem: A reapplication of self-attitude formation theories. *Human Relations, 34,* 427–434.

Rohner, R. P. (1975). *They love me, they love me not: A worldwide study of the effects of parental acceptance and rejection.* New Haven: HRAF Press.

Rusmore, J. T., & Kinmeyer, S. L. (1976). *Family attitudes among Mexican-American and Anglo-American parents in San Jose, California.* Paper presented at the 56th annual meeting of the Western Psychological Association, Los Angeles, CA.

Sanua, V. D. (1980). Familial and sociocultural antecedents of psychopathology. In H. C. Triandis & J. G. Draguns (Eds.) *Handbook of cross-cultural psychology* (Vol. 6). Boston: Allyn & Bacon.

Sears, R. R., Maccoby, E. E., & Levin, H. (1957). *Patterns of child-rearing.* Evanston, IL: Row Peterson.

Selye, H. *Stress without distress.* (1974). Philadelphia: Lippincott.

Schultz, T. W. (1961). Investment in human capital. *American Economic Review, 5*(1), 1–17.

Spiro, M. E., & A. Spiro. (1958). *Children of the Kibbutz: A study in child training and personality.* Cambridge, MA: Harvard Univ. Press, (Rev. ed., 1975).

Stack, C. B. (1974). *All our kin: strategies for survival in black urban community.* New York: Harper & Row.

Super, C. M. (1980). Behavioral development in infancy. In R. L. Munroe & B. B. Whiting (Eds.), *Handbook of cross-cultural human development*. New York: Garland Press.

Tapp, J. L. (1981). Studying personality development. In H. C. Triandis & A. Herox (Eds.), *Handbook of cross-cultural psychology* (Vol. 4). Boston: Allyn & Bacon.

Thomae, H. (1979). Personality development in two cultures: A selective review on research aims and issues. *Human Development, 22,* 296–319.

Triandis, H. C. (in association with Vassiliou, V., Vassiliou, G., Tanaka, Y., & Shanmugam, A. V.) (1972). *The analysis of subjective culture*. New York: Wiley-Interscience.

Triandis, H. C., Malpass, R. S., & Davidson, A. R. (1972). Cross-cultural psychology. *Biennial Review of Anthropology, 7,* 1–84.

Triandis, H. C., Malpass, R. S., & Davidson, A. R. (1973). Psychology and culture. *Annual Review of Psychology, 24,* 355–378.

Trimble, J. E. (1976). Value differences among American Indians: Concerns for the concerned counselor. In P. Pederson, J. Draguns, W. Lonner & J. Trimble (Eds.), *Counseling across cultures*. Honolulu, HI: Univ. Press of Hawaii.

Valentine, B. (1979). *Hustling and other harkwork: Life-styles in the ghetto*. New York: Free Press.

Velasco-Barraza, C. R., & Muller, D. (1982). Development of self-concept in Chilean, Mexican, and United States school children. *Journal of Psychology, 110*(1), 21–30.

Weisbrod, B. A. (1975). Education and investment in human capital. In D. M. Levine & M. J. Bane (Eds.), *The "inequality" controversy*. New York: Basic.

Werner, E. E., Bierman, J. M., & French, D. (1971). *The children of Kauai: A longitudinal study from the prenatal period to age ten*. Honolulu: Univ. of Hawaii Press.

White, B. L. (1979). *The origins of human competence: The final report of the Harvard preschool project*. Lexington, MA: Heath.

White, S. H. (1973). *Federal programs for young children: Review and recommendations. Vol. I. Goals and standards of public programs for children*. Washington, D.C.: U.S. Government Printing Office.

Whiting, B. B. (Ed.) (1963). *Six cultures: Studies of child rearing*. New York: Wiley.

Whiting, B. B., & Whiting, J. W. (1973). Altruistic and egoistic behavior in six cultures. In L. Nader & T. W. Maretzki (Eds.), *Cultural illness and health: Essays in human adaptation*. Washington, D.C.: American Anthropological Association.

Whiting, B. B., & Whiting, J. W. (1975). *Children of six cultures: A psychocultural analysis*. Cambridge, MA: Harvard Univ. Press.

Whiting, J. W. (1961). Socialization process and personality. In F. L. Hsu (Ed.) *Psychological anthropology*. Homewood, IL: Dorsey Press.

Whiting, J. W., & Child, I. L. (1953). *Child training and personality*. New Haven, CT: Yale Univ. Press.

Witkin, H., Dyk, R., Faterson, I., Goodenough, D., & Karp, S. (1962). *Psychological differentiation.* New York: Wiley.

Wittkower, E., & Dubreuil, G. (1973). Psychocultural stress in relation to mental illness. *Social Science and Medicine, 7,* 691–704.

Wittkower, E. D., & Prince, R. (1974). A review of transcultural psychiatry. In S. Arieti & G. Caplan (Eds.), *American handbook of psychiatry* New York: Basic Books.

Wolff, H. G., Wolf, S. G., & Goodell, H. (1968). *Stress and disease.* Springfield, IL: Charles C Thomas.

Young, V. H. (1974). A black American socialization pattern. *American Ethnologist, 1*(2), 415–431.

Yule, W. (1981). Epidemiology of child psychopathology. In B. B. Lahey & A. E. Kazdin (Eds.), *Advances in clinical child psychopathology,* (Vol. 4). New York: Plenum.

Zintz, N. V. (1963). *Education across cultures.* Dubuque, IA: Brown.

CHAPTER 9

TECHNOLOGICAL ADVANCES AND THE YOUNG CHILD
Television and Computers

DOUGLAS H. CLEMENTS

S ince the advent of television, and more recently the personal computer, there has been much interest in technology and its impact on young children. This chapter will examine what is known about how technological advances affect children. Scientific knowledge is growing at an ever-increasing rate; if we wish to avoid being "condemned to repeat history," we need to look at ways media have been both used and studied since the first technologies were invented.

HISTORICAL PERSPECTIVES ON MEDIA RESEARCH: THE MORE THINGS CHANGE, THE MORE THEY REMAIN THE SAME

In 1913, Thomas Edison stated that within ten years, books would be obsolete, to be replaced by motion pictures. Nearly 50 years later, similar pronouncements were made about television (Griffin, 1983). In the present day, advocates of the educational potential of computer technology predict another impending "revolution." What impact will the new technologies have on children; their development and education?

In deciding how to view the new technologies that each year brings us, it is important first to look to earlier media innovations— radio and cinema were advanced technology just a few decades ago! Hindsight reveals that there is a standard progression of research questions as each new innovation is adopted by society (Wartella & Reeves, 1983). As the medium is being developed, researchers examine how much and in what ways it is being used. Attention then shifts to the possibly deleterious effects of the medium on physical and emotional health. Finally, the effects of the *content* on values, attitudes, and behavior become the dominant concerns.

The first wave of research is motivated by concerns expressed by parents and educators about the supposedly inordinate amount of time children occupy themselves with the new medium. Researchers usually confirm what is popularly accepted: The new innovation displaces previous occupations, including earlier media, and consumes a large part of children's time. This concern turns the focus of attention to the quality of this time.

Physical and emotional health effects are often the next topic of concern and investigation. In the first decades of this century, there was concern about children viewing films in dark, possibly unsanitary, movie houses. There was concern that listening to radio would affect children's hearing. Television, and more recently computer screens, have been accused of causing bad eyesight, and of emitting harmful radiation. In each case, it is shown that there is no basis for these warnings, and concern moves to emotional health (Wartella & Reeves, 1983). Finally, society and researchers have focused their attention on the effects of the media's content upon children's morality—"gangsterism" on radio, sex and violence on films, and so on.

THE EFFECTS OF TECHNOLOGICAL MEDIA ON YOUNG CHILDREN'S DEVELOPMENT

Television

Viewing

One basic indicator of the influence of television (TV) on children is the amount they view it. By this criterion, its influence may be considerable—children spend more time engaged in watching TV than in any other waking activity. By the time they leave high school, they will have spent 11,000 hours in classroom and 22,000 hours viewing TV. The heaviest consumers are preschoolers (Doerken, 1983). According to one study, by the time children are three or four years old, they are averaging four hours of viewing per day, with a range of 2 hours to 72 hours per week (Singer & Singer, 1981). Reviews of several studies indicated that preschoolers typically watch 21.5 to 34.2 hours a week. In that time, it can be reasonably estimated that they view about 2052 violent incidents per week and store 555 in memory (Braithwaite & Holman, 1981; Comstock, Chaffee, Katzman, McCombs, & Roberts, 1978).

How soon does this habit start? Hollenbeck and Slaby (1979) found that some children are already watching TV for one and one-half hours each day by nine months of age. However, children do not become systematic viewers until the preschool years. By the age of three, children are already experienced viewers and evidence a consistency in the frequency and pattern of viewing (Singer & Singer, 1981). It seems that habits are already well established by preschool age.

To measure actual viewing time more accurately, Anderson (1983) put video cameras in volunteers' houses. His study indicated that, compared to a national average of preschoolers' viewing of 3.8 hours a day, the time these children actually spent with TV was 2.2 hours, and the time they actually watched it was 1.3 hours a day. He warned that data reported by parents are probably unreliable and constitute overestimates. Importantly, he found that children do not just stare at TV, instead, TV becomes a backdrop for toy play and other activities. Co-viewing peers influence each other in a synchronous fashion; when one child looks at the television or displays overt involvement, others tend to do the same thing. Thus, viewing television is a transactional process among the viewer, the TV, and the TV-viewing environment (Anderson, Lorch, Smith, Bradford, & Levin, 1981). Children do not become systematic TV viewers until about two and one-half years of age.

What is Viewed?

Most people decide first to watch *television*, then decide on the program (Comstock et al., 1978). However, as soon as they begin viewing, children have definite preferences as to what to view.

Although children predominantly watch child-oriented shows, especially cartoons and situation comedies (Comstock et al., 1978), they also view every type of programming, including a sizable proportion of adult programs (Singer & Singer, 1981). In fact, between the hours of 11:30 pm and 2 am every night, there are 2 million viewers ages 2 to 11 years (Postman, in Callaway, 1982). In addition, the quality of children's television has come under attack. Melody (1973) has described the factory-line, production techniques which quickly produce standardized products at minimal cost and risk, using and re-using low-quality animation.

Attention to and Comprehension of Television Content

Even very young children respond to TV. In one study, 6-month-old infants were presented with a televised adult model repeating either a novel phoneme pattern or an adult conversation from typical daytime programming. Infants exposed to the model of the phoneme pattern altered their vocalization pattern, whereas the others did not (Hollenbeck & Slaby, 1982).

Comprehension.

The level of children's comprehension of content is not only interesting in and of itself, it also is pertinent to the potential social impact of television. For example, adults use perceptions of motives as the bases for evaluating the behavior of characters; however, children do not always use such cues. Young children recall less of what they view, and more of what they *do* recall is only peripheral to the situation (Collins, 1979). Thus, their evaluation of social portrayals may be difficult to predict. It has been shown that children as old as 8 years have limited understanding of such portrayals, knowing significantly less of the information that mature raters characterize as central to comprehension of the plot. Not only do they have poor memory for explicit content, but they are unlikely to integrate this information across time (e.g., tying aggressive acts to motives). This is important, as information about an aggressive model's motives has been found to moderate the likelihood that children will be affected by whatever they see (Collins, 1979).

Three factors seem to affect how children process television content. The first is familiarity with certain exposition forms, such as story plots. Young children's poor recall of details may be attributable to inadequate structures which might serve as a framework on which to hang these details. The second is knowledge and experience of the social world. While children of all ages recognize common-knowledge sequences, only older viewers recognize events that deviate from common expectations, and therefore only they would note their possible importance. Third is an understanding of the formal features of television (Collins, 1981).

Formal Features of Television.

Wright and Huston (1983) have conducted a series of investigations concerned with this aspect of television; that is, how its *form* (its codes, conventions, and formats) interacts with children's social and cognitive development. Formal features of television can be described independently of content and include auditory and visual production and editing techniques. It was found that commercially produced programs for young children, such as Saturday morning shows, were characterized by high action, fast pace and numerous special effects, all of which are perceptually salient features. Correspondingly, they contained relatively little dialogue. Educational programs included more long zooms, singing, moderate action levels, slower pacing, and dialogue, all of which present more contextual information. Thus, although programs such as *Sesame Street* include many visually salient techniques, these are distinctly different from those used in commercial programs in that the former promote reflection.

Formal features such as animation, character voices, and sound effects elicit and maintain young children's attention to TV. However, the reason for this probably is not just due to the stimulation these features provide; rather, they may signal to children that the content of the program is going to be comprehensible and interesting to them (Wright & Huston, 1983). Younger children gain information from attention to nonverbal auditory features, which apparently call attention to child dialogue, a symbolic feature they can understand. Children who *ignore* adult dialogue are *more* likely to understand television content (Calvert, Huston, Watkins, & Wright, 1982).

Older children are increasingly guided by the information provided by these features. They use these as markers to understand the structure of the program and to differentially address their attention to specific segments of the program. Development of these skills is facilitated by television content that is related to children's knowledge, and that demands cognitive skills just above the children's present level of functioning. It is also aided by commentary made in an informal way by an adult companion. Thus, research findings contradict the popular notion that young children's attention is captured by superficial production features. Comprehensibility, promoted by such features as understandable dialogue, is crucial in maintaining children's attention (Anderson, Lorch, Field, & Sanders, 1981). It would not seem that children are mesmerized by the screen regardless of their understanding of its contents, in contrast to the claims of many (e.g., Lesser, 1977; Winn, 1977). However, there does seem to be a phenomenon of "attentional inertia"—the longer the child views, the more he or she is likely to continue viewing.

Another hypothesis that has received some support alleges that exposure to certain forms of media themselves can cultivate the development of specific mental skills. For example, young children typically have difficulty with part-whole relationships. It has been shown that exposing children to close-ups significantly improves their mastery of the ability to relate parts to wholes, probably by activating this skill (Salomon, 1979). The children most affected, however, are those who initially have a fair mastery of the skill. Those with poorer initial ability are not so affected. Would a different type of exposure be helpful? Interestingly, the use of zoom shots, which specifically *model* the operation of relating parts-to-wholes, can serve as models for observational learning. Children who are initially unskilled learn to use this mental skill when it is modeled for them in this way (Salomon, 1979). It is not known to what extent these skills will transfer to other media and other situations. As shall be discussed later, there is some disagreement as to whether these formal features are unique to specific media.

The results of several investigations have disproved the popular notion that television viewing is passive. Children need to select important content, integrate events, and infer conditions, motives, and events not shown. Formal features can help children know "where to look" (Wright & Huston, 1983).

Advertising.

There has been much debate as to the ethicality of directing advertising to young children, especially because they view 20,000 TV commercials a year. Do preschoolers recognize commercials for what they are? Do commercials affect them? In one study, children's ability to correctly identify videotaped TV segments as either programs or commercials improved with age (3 to 5 years), but they responded above chance level at each age. They used both auditory and visual cues in making the identification. Apparently, it is not necessary to separate children's programming from commercials with special devices; rather, children should be educated on the purpose and evaluation of commercials (Levin, Petros, & Petrella, 1982).

Exposure to TV is not enough to allow children to comprehend it. Children whose families emphasize television, whose mothers are less imaginative, and who have less regular bedtime routines and more power-assertive discipline are less likely to grasp plot details and understand commercials (Singer & Singer, 1983). Even children in fourth grade often do not understand the intent of commercials (Feshbach, Feshbach, & Cohen, 1982). Thus, in both regular programming and advertising, young children may not comprehend significant aspects of television programs and their intent, leading to the possibility of harmful effects.

Children do remember commercial products; furthermore, this memory goes beyond specific brands and generalizes to products that are members of the same class. So advertisements have implicit, diffuse messages (Stoneman & Brody, 1983). Education concerning commercials is therefore warranted.

Effects on Achievement and Cognition

Instructional Television.

Major reviews of the research on instructional television have provided a number of important generalizations (Chu & Schramm, 1968; Murray, 1980).

1. Under favorable conditions, children learn efficiently from instructional television. It can teach any subject matter where one-way communication will contribute to learning. There seem to be few differences between learning from television and learning from conventional teaching.
2. If students are given immediate feedback as to whether they responded correctly, they will learn more.
3. Supplementary activities or related adult co-viewing will significantly increase the effectiveness of instructional television for young children.
4. The use of certain production techniques such as humor, games, or brief dramatizations may enhance learning for young children, whereas these techniques do not consistently aid learning for older students.
5. There is insufficient evidence that color will improve learning, although it may bring about more favorable attitudes. In addition, irrelevant, attention-gaining cues may have a negative impact on learning.
6. Liking instructional television is not always correlated with learning from it.
7. Instructional television works best when it is made an integral part of instruction; when it is applied to a problem of sufficient size to justify its use; and when its use grows out of attention to the basic requirements of good teaching.

Can educational TV make a contribution to *young* children's learning? Evaluations consistently show that *Sesame Street* and *The Electric Company* are effective in developing readiness skills in young children (Ball & Bogatz, 1973; Bogatz & Ball, 1971; Minton, 1975). Younger preschool children appear to gain the most. However, *Sesame Street's* effectiveness may be limited to skills specifically programmed into the show, and to lower-level tasks involving specific knowledge and skills such as alphabet naming, matching forms, and naming numbers.

In addition, critics have maintained that *Sesame Street* may be considerably less effective than these reports indicate. After reviewing the reports, Lesser (1977) suggested that other forms of instructional television are needed for the preschool child, including emphases on socialization, "thinking out loud," the ability to monitor one's thinking, generally "learning how to learn," and so on. Is this possible?

Some training studies have failed to develop cognitive abilities in preschool children, often leading the authors to conclude that Piagetian theory is supported (this theory posits that active manipulation with a concrete environment is necessary to the development of certain cognitive operations), and that television cannot train these operations (e.g., Hoffman & Flook, 1980). However, other studies have shown highly significant training effects through televised modeling of Piagetian operations such as seriation and number conservation (Henderson, Swanson, & Zimmerman, 1975; Raeissi & Wright, 1983).

Thus, television has demonstrated the ability to educate young children in important and cost effective ways. However, it has been criticized for its limitations—that children become passive viewers rather than active learners; that only low-level cognitive abilities are taught; and that it replaces other more worthwhile and creative activities (Winn, 1977). Some have hypothesized that the production techniques of programs such as *Sesame Street* engender hyperactivity, short attention spans, and lack of interest in classroom work which is slower paced and less visually appealing (e.g., Lesser, 1977). More research is needed, but it seems that educational programs which use production techniques involving fast pacing and relatively high action levels do not produce hyperactivity (Wright & Huston, 1983), although amount of viewing of commercial TV is significantly related to measures of impulsivity (Anderson & Maguire, 1978). However, slow-paced, repetitively-structured programs such as *Mr. Roger's Neighborhood* may result in more learning.

It would seem that, properly designed, television can positively affect young children's cognition. What about programming *not* so designed?

Commercial Television.

Critics argue that young viewers of commercial TV will not achieve well in school. There seems to be some evidence validating this claim. Huston et al. (nd) found that, even at young age, heavy viewers were less interested in books. Salomon (1981) hypothesizes that television does not demand as strong an amount of invested mental effort as does reading, and therefore may not contribute as well to learning. In several studies, more television viewing was correlated with lower grades in reading (Gunter, 1982; Neuman & Prowda, 1982; Ridley-Johnson, Cooper, & Chance, 1983).

Yet, some studies have revealed that second and third grade avid TV watchers are also avid readers (e.g., Busch, 1978). It may be that television begins displacing reading most strongly in the intermediate grades. Furthermore, the type of program viewed may be significant: Research shows that viewing educational programs is related to increased academic grades, whereas viewing adult comedies and action-adventure programs is associated with decreased academic performance (Gunter, 1982; Murray, 1980). An extensive review of the research indicated that television may indeed displace verbal activities, with a resultant decrease in creative verbal fluency and reading (Murray, 1980).

Other studies have not found significant relationships between television viewing and achievement (e.g., Anderson & Maguire, 1978; Neuman, 1980). In one review of 23 research efforts, an overall correlation between the hours of viewing and achievement was negative, but quite small (this indicates that as hours of viewing increases, there is a slight tendency for achievement to decrease). This effect was not consistent across the range of viewing times — the relationship was slightly positive up to 10 hours per week of viewing, and increasingly more deleterious until 35–40 hours per week was reached, beyond which additional viewing time had little effect. Females and children with high IQs were more adversely affected (Williams, Haertel, Haertel, & Walberg, 1982). TV may also affect creativity. Preschoolers who watch the least television are reported to have a more developed imagination at 8 years of age (Singer & Singer, 1983).

The weakness of correlational data is that a *causal* connection cannot be made. There is, however, evidence that restricting TV viewing can benefit children. Gadberry (1980) matched 6-year-olds for sex, age, pretest IQ, and TV viewing time, and assigned them, for experimental purposes, to either a restricted or unrestricted TV viewing group. Results suggested that TV restriction enhanced performance IQ, reading time, and impulsive-reflective cognitive style scores. Children of parents who set rules for watching television had higher IQs than other children, although the relationship between viewing and IQ is not seen to be strong (Ridley-Johnson, Cooper & Chance, 1983).

Of course, other variables must be considered. One study suggested that the best predictor of reading comprehension emerges from a *combination* of (a) familial factors such as positive discipline techniques, the mother's self-description as resourceful, and orderly household routines with more hours of sleep, and (b) television variables such as fewer hours of viewing during the preschool years (Singer & Singer, 1983).

Even infants respond to television by altering their behavior. How will such response to such non-responsive stimulation affect their development? Will they learn or fail to learn cognitive skills or to achieve control over their social environment? Little evidence is available, although amount of viewing has been shown to be negatively correlated with two measures of language growth (Nelson, 1973).

It appears that continued governmental, private, and public support for worthwhile educational television programs for young children is warranted. Judicious use of salient formal features is probably effective in gaining attention; however, overuse may have negative effects on behavior. Other techniques which do not involve perceptually salient cues are also effective and deserve more consideration, such as readily comprehensible content, stories with attractive themes, and humor (Wright & Huston, 1983). Those responsible for the care of young children should probably monitor the amount and type of commercial TV viewed.

Effects on Behavior and Socio-emotional Development

Violence and Aggression.

The question of the impact of viewing violence on young children has generated more research and public concern than any other question dealing with the effects of television. Yet even scholarly reviews of the *same* research have come to quite different conclusions. On one hand, that media do not have any significant effect on the level of violence in society, and, on the other, that a causal link has been established between violence viewing and aggression.

The major initial studies on the influence of television or film violence were those of Bandura (1978). A protocol for these studies would have a young child presented with a film, projected from the back onto a television screen, in which an adult model displayed unusual aggressive behaviors toward an inflatable doll. Afterwards, the child was moved to a playroom with the doll and his or her aggressive behavior toward the doll or other objects were recorded. Children who had viewed the aggressive film were more aggressive than the control children. Bandura claimed that these results substantiated the "social learning theory of aggression." Yet, the experiments have been criticized for being too different from typical television programming and for using invalid measures of aggression.

A study conducted for the Surgeon General's research report attempted to address these criticisms (Liebert & Baron, 1972). Following the viewing of a violent television program, young children were more willing to hurt another child than were children who had viewed an equally stimulating but non-violent program. Children who evidenced facial expressions of pleasure while watching the violence were more likely to hurt others. Other studies of this *experimental* type have not shown such effects, or have provided evidence that other background variables must be taken into account (Murray, 1980). For example, children who are exposed to more violent television are more likely to chose an aggressive mode of resolving conflict situation; however, they and their mothers also watch more television.

Thus, the social learning theory of aggression posits that television can have four different effects: (a) it teaches aggressive styles of conduct; (b) it alters restraints over aggressive behavior and legitimizes violence; (c) it desensitizes and habituates people to violence; and (d) it shapes people's images of reality upon which they base many of their actions (heavy viewers are less trustful of others and overestimate their chances of being victimized).

Some correlational studies have also been conducted with young children. These studies usually agree that there is a relationship between viewing, or preference for viewing aggressive television content, and aggressive behavior and attitudes. Singer and Singer (1981) provided evidence of a "television-aggressive factor." Children, especially boys, who watched a great deal of television would be more likely to be more aggressive and less cooperative. Recent research continues to show that early heavy television viewing by preschoolers relates to measures of aggressive behavior in the second and third grades (Singer & Singer, 1983).

Correlation studies, however, cannot indicate whether viewing violence *causes* aggression. In fact, it might be that violent people may simply prefer to watch violence. Causal connections can be inferred from the aforementioned experimental studies; however, ethical considerations put a limit on how closely the experimental situation can mirror reality. For example, children in these studies often push a button they are told will hurt a child in another room. One study attempted to ameliorate these problems. Measures of aggression and preferences for various types of television, radio, and reading matter were obtained at age 8. Ten years later, measures of aggression and television program preferences were obtained from the same subjects. Preference for television violence at age 8 was significantly related to aggression at age 8 (that is, as this preference increases, so did aggressive behavior), but this relationship did not hold at age 18. A *larger* correlation was obtained between preference at age 8 and aggression at age 18. Just as important, there was little or no relationship in the opposite direction (Eron, 1982; Eron, Huesmann, Brice, Fisher, & Mermelstein, 1983). This suggests that preference for watching violent television in third grade contributes to aggressive habits. In fact, the single best predictor at age 8 of whether a child will be aggressive at age 18 is the amount of violent television he is watching. Evidence indicates that third grade may be a period during which a number of factors converge and make children particularly susceptible to the effects of television (Eron, 1982).

Finally, field studies have been conducted within more natural environments, such as kindergartens. These generally support the hypothesis of cumulative effect of exposure to television violence (Comstock et al., 1978; Murray, 1980). One study revealed that preschool children who viewed *Batman* and *Superman* shows became significantly more aggressive, while those who watched the prosocial *Mr. Rogers' Neighborhood* became more cooperative (Friedrich & Stein, 1973). In another study, the initial level of television viewing was more likely to predict later aggression than the initial level of aggression was to predict later viewing of television (Singer & Singer, 1981).

In opposition to this view is the position that viewing violence might serve as a *cathartic,* by purging aggressive impulses. One study with older children found that boys who watched nonviolent programs were more aggressive (Feshbach & Singer, 1971). The study has been criticized on methodological grounds (e.g., the validity of the measures; use of untrained raters who were not naive to children's assignment to treatment condition); furthermore, some children assigned to the nonviolent group were allowed routinely to watch violent programs; those not allowed may have been frustrated by this. Other problems with the catharsis theory are that it requires an intense emotional involvement not present in television viewing, and that there is little evidence from other studies which support it (Murray, 1980). There is some indication that catharsis may occur if viewed violence is stylized, rather than realistic, and the victim is unseen (Lesser, 1977).

Another possible process might account for the relationship between violence-viewing and aggression. The viewing may simply stimulate children, arousing them to aggressive acts which may then be reinforced. There is some evidence this phenomenon may occur during the viewing of high-salience commercials (i.e., high action, rapid change of scene and character, frequent use of cuts and pans; Greer, Potts, Wright, & Huston, 1982).

Longitudinal research data indicate that the following combination of factors puts a child at risk for behavior problems at early elementary school age: (a) uncontrolled television viewing in those homes with the least evidence of books and musical instruments or records (these parents consistently report it is the *child* who controls the television set); (b) heavy preschool viewing; (c) recent heavy viewing of violent programs; (d) parents who emphasize physical force in discipline, who are rejecting, and whose self-descriptions do not emphasize creativity or imagination; (e) low popularity and intellectual ability; (f) belief that the shows are an accurate portrayal of life; and (g) identification with the aggressive characters (Eron, 1982; Huesmann, Lagerspetz, & Eron, in press; Singer & Singer, 1981; Singer & Singer, 1983).

Is this violence necessary to capture viewers? Although violence is used by television producers to maintain attention, it has been found that violent content was not associated with visual attention independently of its association with formal features such as fast paced movement, and special effects. It is these later features which elicit attention, rather than the violence. Whether it is these features or the violent content which stimulate aggression is not as clear. High rates of salient formal features can, in certain situations, stimulate aggression, but cues available in the child's postviewing environment seem to play a major role (Wright & Huston, 1983).

It can safely be concluded that although for some children in some situations viewing television violence may serve as a cathartic; while for most children in most situations it increases aggressive behavior and attitudes. Although the causal relationship between violence-viewing and aggression is probably circular, with each affecting the other (Huesmann et al., in press), there is strong evidence that viewing increases aggression, both through modeling and through alteration of beliefs and attitudes about aggression. Preschoolers are more influenced by television violence and can learn new aggressive behaviors from as little as a single exposure; furthermore, aggressive behavior appears particularly likely to be learned (Comstock et al., 1978).

Imaginative Play.

Another concern is that television, with its pre-packaged, low-demand entertainment, might stultify imaginative play, an essential resource with which children learn to cope with the cognitive and socioemotional demands of development. There is limited evidence that this is true (Singer & Singer, 1981).

Prosocial Television.

If viewing violence promotes violent behavior, might viewing cooperation promote cooperative behavior? In recent years more researchers have begun to address this question. Several of their studies, most measuring the effects of *Mr. Rogers' Neighborhood,* have indicated that this is indeed the case (Coates, Pusser, & Goodman, 1976; Friedrich & Stein, 1973; Sprafkin, Liebert, & Poulos, 1975). This work has found increases in prosocial behaviors such as cooperation, empathy, helping, and sharing. In addition, this program has been shown to increase creativity and imaginativeness of play (Singer & Singer, 1981). Viewing constructive solutions to conflict in a plot from commercial television programming has also increased prosocial responding (Collins & Getz, 1976). After being exposed to inserts of nonwhite children at play, 3- to 5-year-olds showed a strong preference for play with minority children; a control group showed no such preference (Gorn, Goldberg, & Kanungo, 1976). At least in certain situations, prosocial programming can increase children's subsequent prosocial behavior (Comstock et al., 1978).

Interventions.

It is clear that television either can be detrimental or beneficial, both in its formal features and its content. How can it best be used? Postman (in Callaway, 1982) stated that TV does *not* complement what goes on in school—it opposes it, competes with it, and is antagonistic to it. He advises teachers not to copy TV, but to develop language, the ability to *ask* questions, and an historical sense. One of the most reliable research findings is that a co-viewing adult significantly aids children's comprehension of, and learning from, television (Collins, Sobol, & Westby, 1981; Watkins, Calvert,

Huston-Stein, & Wright, 1980; Wright & Huston, 1983). Many other authorities agree that educators teach *about* TV. It has been shown that such attempts can be successful (Feshbach, Feshbach, & Cohen, 1982; Singer & Singer, 1983).

There is also evidence for the effectiveness of long-term interventions (Eron, 1982; Eron et al., 1983; Huesmann, Eron, Klein, Brice, & Fischer, 1983). A treatment was based on the theory that children behave aggressively because they perceive TV violence as realistic, they identify with the television character, and they believe that society accepts aggression. When primary grade children were directly taught that watching television violence was not desirable and it should not be imitated, their attitudes became altered. In addition, children were rated as less aggressive. Although they still watched violence, apparently they did not use it as a model for their own behavior. Another approach with some evidence of success involves the provision of training in affection-like behaviors, which can buffer the occurrence of television-provoked aggression (Marton & Acker, 1981).

Consciousness-raising sessions designed to induce parents to reduce their children's television viewing are not always successful. The baby-sitting function of TV may be too attractive. More successful is the training of parents to lead children in developing imaginative play and cognitive skills (Singer & Singer, 1983).

As teachers we are *not* helpless. Children in school must learn about television. Several pertinent suggestions have been offered (Doerken, 1983; Morrow, 1977; Singer, Singer, & Zuckerman, 1981; White, 1983; Winick & Wehrenberg, 1982). For those interested in such suggestions, a list has been compiled (see Appendix A).

COMPUTERS

Computer Assisted Instruction.

Can computers teach? Computer assisted instruction (CAI) involves the use of computers to provide tutorials, drill and practice, instructional games, and the like. The following sections report what research has to say about the effects of the computer application on students' achievement.

What Does the Research Say Generally?

Several extensive reviews and meta-analyses of the research concerning the effectiveness of computer assisted instruction have been conducted (Billings, 1983; Bracey, 1982; Chambers & Sprecher, 1980; Foreman, 1982; Kearsley, Hunter, & Seidel, 1983; Visonhaler & Bass, 1972). Most of them combine results from all grade levels; however, they provide directions for early childhood education. There is general agreement on the following points:

1. Computers can be used to make instruction more effective; the use of CAI either improves performance or shows no difference when compared to traditional classroom approaches. This is regardless of the types of CAI, computers, or measurement instruments used. It is approximately equivalent to individual tutoring.
2. CAI usually yields these results in less time.
3. Computers can make the learning experience more exciting, satisfying, and rewarding for learner and teacher. Students have a positive attitude toward CAI, frequently accompanied by increased motivation, attention span, and attendance.
4. Students given CAI lessons may not retain as much information.
5. Computers do not stifle the creative process, nor are they dehumanizing.
6. None of these benefits are inherent in CAI; rather, they depend on the abilities of the professionals involved—CAI is most effective when it is used as an adjunct under the control of the classroom teacher.
7. It is still not known *why* CAI is effective, or *how* to individualize instruction or maximize the positive effects.
8. Teacher training must be radically altered and updated to accommodate the preparation of teachers in the new technology.
9. There is a dire need for quality courseware and new instructional design methodologies for technological media.

10. Computers have dramatically changed the entire field of education and educational research, and yet the potential of CAI has only begun to be realized.

How Does CAI Affect the Development of Reading and Other Language Arts Skills?

Positive effects of the technology on children's reading abilities have been reported for more than a decade. O. K. Moore's "Talking Typewriter" was shown to increase significantly young children's scores on alphabet recognition and verbal ability tests (e.g., Israel, 1968). Atkinson and Fletcher (1972) taught first grade children to read with computer programs emphasizing letter recognition and recall, sight words, spelling, phonics, and sentence and word meanings. They reported that the CAI group gained 5.05 months over a control group and maintained a 4.9 month gain for over a year. The theoretical foundation and practical implementation of both these projects are still worthy of serious study by those interested in young children and CAI reading.

More recent work also provides encouraging evidence. Young children exposed to CAI materials have been shown to have developed reading readiness concepts (Piestrup, 1981; Smithy-Willis, Riley, & Smith, 1982; Swigger & Campbell, 1981) and reading skills (Lavin & Sanders, 1983; Ragosta, Holland, & Jamison, 1981). These studies have utilized drill-and-practice CAI. While some people despair of this emphasis on low-level skills, there is evidence that there is a causal relationship between decoding (including rapid word recognition) and comprehension in beginning readers. Therefore, computerized practice of information-processing components of reading can make an important contribution to reading success. Several developmental projects along these lines exist, and some have generated evidence supporting their efficacy (Lesgold, 1983; Perfetti, 1983).

Another application involves using a computerized text editor, or word processor, to facilitate writing. This application takes advantage of the interrelatedness of the language arts, the active processing that writing involves, and the fact that writing implies comprehension. Research is only beginning to accumulate, but researchers and practitioners tend to agree that writers using computers: write more; are less worried about making mistakes;

take increased pride in their writing because the text looks better; have fewer fine motor control problems; give more attention to finding errors; and revise more, correcting punctuation and spelling (Daiute, 1982; Watt, 1982). These beneficial effects seem to transfer to later paper and pencil work. Children make twice as many deletions and eight times as many insertions in later pencil compositions. Children who have the most difficulties in writing may benefit the most. Disadvantages have been noted, too. Word processors are expensive and not portable, and they are complicated. The size of the screen limits the amount of text that writers can see at one time (so text coherence may negatively be affected). Finally, the attraction of "gadgetry" may distract some writers. Other programs which integrate reading and writing are evidencing considerable success (Martin, 1981).

How Does CAI Affect the Development of Mathematics?

In a meta-analysis of the research on CAI and mathematics achievement covering grades 1–12, Burns and Bozeman (1981) concluded that:

1. A mathematics program supplemented with CAI was more effective in significantly fostering student achievement.
2. CAI drill and practice was more effective at all levels with highly achieving and disadvantaged students as well as with students whose distinct ability levels were not determined by researchers; however, the achievement of average level students was not significantly enhanced.
3. There was no evidence that results were an artifact of experimental design features.

Studies with young children have substantiated these results (Lavin & Sanders, 1983; Ragosta et al., 1981).

Computer Programming.

One popular argument is that learning to program ("teach the computer" rather than being taught by the computer) will increase children's achievement and ability to solve problems. Much of this research has focused on teaching the computer language Logo, which has been designed to be accessible to young children (Papert, 1980). Children draw by directing the movements of a graphic "turtle," a small triangular pointer that can move around the display screen, leaving traces of its path (lines on the computer screen), in response to messages sent it by the programmer. Initial messages usually include directions for turning right or left and moving forward and backward. Logo is procedural — problems can be divided into small pieces, and a separate procedure written for each piece. In this way children can "divide and conquer" problems as they begin to see, in a concrete fashion, how tasks can be broken down into procedures, how procedures can be combined to form superprocedures, and how procedures interact. This illustrates that Logo is extensible — children can "teach" the computer new words.

Some research has been conducted to measure the affects of Logo programming on the knowledge states of older children. Case studies appear to indicate that children exposed to programming profit intellectually (Papert, 1980; Papert, diSessa, Watt, & Weir, 1979). However, Howe and O'Shea (1978) reported that mathematics test results revealed no significant differences between groups of low achieving 12-year-olds with and without computer programming experience. Research (Pea, 1983) indicates that children who learned Logo for a year still possessed fundamental misunderstandings concerning the workings of the language, and that few mastered important aspects of Logo's "powerful ideas," such as the concept of a variable and recursion.

Seymour Papert, a leading exponent of the use of computer programming to expand children's intellectual power, based his ideas on the theories of Piaget, with whom he studied. Papert (1980) has argued that the most beneficial learning is what he calls "Piagetian learning," or "learning without being taught." He has proposed that computer programming environments can create conditions under which intellectual models take root; where young children can master notions formerly thought too abstract for their developmental level. Computers can make the abstract both concrete and personal as they help improve children's learning by making their thinking processes conscious. By programming the computer to do what they want it to do, children must reflect on how one might do the task oneself, and therefore, on how they themselves think. The computer programming environment holds the promise of being an effective device for cognitive process instruction—teaching *how*, rather than *what*, to think (Lochhead & Clement, 1979).

The research evidence, however, is contradictory. Gorman (1982) reported that third-grade children who worked for one hour a week on Logo programming performed significantly better on a test of rule learning than those with 30 minutes a week programming experience. Seidman (1981) found no significant gains on tests of conditional reason abilities for fifth grade children trained in the Logo language. One researcher taught fifth graders either Logo or BASIC, another popular computer language which is more linear and does not include procedural thinking or drawing with a turtle. This study produced limited evidence in favor of Logo over BASIC (e.g., students working with the former reported greater independent judgment), but the overall pattern failed to support the hypothesis of cognitive benefits from programming. Some positive and generalized effects were found in the motivational domain for each programming language and for a CAI treatment (Milojkovic, 1983). Pea (1983) found that in two classes of 25 children, after a year's experience in programming in Logo, did not display greater planning skills than a matched group. Pea expressed deep doubts about the current optimism concerning the cognitive benefits of computer programming. Most of these studies have been conducted with intermediate grade or older children.

One study, conducted with first graders, tends to have more positive implications. Clements and Gullo (in press) provided instruction and exploratory activities in the Logo computer language to nine randomly selected first grade children and, for an equal period of time, CAI exposure to nine other children. Posttesting revealed that the programming group scored significantly higher on measures of reflectivity and on two measures of divergent thinking (figural creativity), whereas the CAI group showed no significant pre- to posttest differences. The programming group outperformed the CAI group on measures of meta-cognitive ability (realizing when you don't understand) and ability to describe directions. No differences were found on measures of cognitive development. Thus, evidence was provided that computer programming does not change children's basic cognitive *ability*. Rather it may affect their cognitive *style*—the way in which they utilize the cognitive abilities they possess, putting them in touch with and in command of these abilities.

Effects of Behavior and Socio-Emotional Development.

It already has been noted that children prefer social use of computers to isolated use, and that computers can effectively promote positive social and emotional development (Clement, 1981; Swigger, Campbell, & Swigger, 1983). Some teachers say that the greatest impact of computers in the classroom is that children tend to share more (Center for Social Organization of Schools, 1983).

Children who program in Logo are significantly more likely to collaborate with each other when they work with computers, by comparison with their interaction during other classroom tasks. In addition, the computer context is the one where children more consistently identify certain of their peers as resources for help (Hawkins, Sheingold, Gearhart, & Berger, 1982).

Children tend to talk to each other more about their work when they are doing programming tasks than when they are doing noncomputer tasks (Hawkins, 1983). In addition, children engage in more collaborative activity with computer tasks. Children do talk to each other when working on other classroom tasks (e.g., math), but their conversations are often not related to what they are doing. In a similar vein, White (in Callaway, 1982) reported that children socialize and ask more questions while working with computer three times as often as they do working in the classroom.

There is evidence that playing violent video arcade games arouses aggressive behavior in much the same way that watching violent television does. No support for the catharsis explanation has been found (Silvern, Williamson, & Countermine, 1983).

SPECIAL EDUCATION

Technological advances hold much promise for exceptional children. Apparently, they use most media as much as other children; for example, deaf children watch more TV than hearing children (Liss & Prince, 1981). However, the value of commercial TV for many exceptional children is questionable (e.g., Ahrens & Singh, 1977). Special programming may be necessary.

Microprocessors *are* being applied in special ways to aid special children, as compensatory and instructional devices. For example, computer technology is quickly becoming the most powerful prosthetic device, compensating for a wide range of disabilities. Computers have been connected to devices which tactually present words on the abdomen for deaf children. Similar technology allows the blind to read by translating letters passed under a camera to braille or spoken output. Possibly an even more powerful function is in helping disabled children to control their environment, including doors, typewriters, telecommunications, and so on, so that even those with severe mobility handicaps can become independent and employable (Schofield, 1981).

Computers can also serve an instructional function. Although the research is not extensive, there is support for the use of CAI with the mentally retarded (Lally, 1981; Williams, Thorkildsen, & Crossman, 1983) and the deaf (Prinz, Nelson, & Stedt, 1982). Telecommunications technology has been used to educate severely handicapped preschoolers (birth to age 6) whose physical disabilities or geographic location make attendance in school impossible (Aeschleman & Tawney, 1978). Some children demonstrated learned visual discrimination rapidly. Kleiman, Humphrey, and Lindsay (1983) found that hyperactive and other attention deficient children benefited from working with computer programs providing drill in arithmetic.

Case studies give positive reports of the effects of working with computer-based exploratory learning systems. For example, computer programming in Logo, or language programs enable a child to identify a noun and a verb and see a dramatization based on his or her selection (Goldenberg, 1979; Weir & Watt, 1983).

MEDIA COMPARISON STUDIES

Which media help children learn the best? What is the relative achievement of groups who receive instruction on similar subject matter from different media? Although these questions have been the focus of most media research since the beginning of this century, the results of these studies can be summed up simply: No significant difference. There *have* been isolated studies where the introduction of media have increased learning; however, it is usually possible to explain the results in terms other than the effects of the medium. For example, the introduction of media often is accompanied by a change of curriculum or teaching strategy (Clark, 1983).

Small differences may relate to the specific aspects of the medium. One study showed that, compared to television, radio elevated the use of knowledge unrelated to the story for inferences by young children (Beagles-Roos & Gat, 1983). Television may reduce attention to expressive language, whereas radio may induce children to go beyond story content to substantiate information. Television, on the other hand, may augment knowledge of visual story details, ability to sequence pictures, and ability to make inferences based on action.

Another study taught children to construct a three-dimensional toy under three conditions: videofilm, pictures, and non-instruction. The film markedly increased the performance of 4-year-olds, whereas the pictures were of relatively little help to this group. Pictorial teaching was effective for children 5 years and older (Murphy & Wood, 1982). Note that it was the *mode* of presentation that was varied.

If factors *other* than media, such as content, mode of presentation, teaching strategy, and situation, are varied, one cannot conclude that the media made the difference. But if all other variables have been controlled, what is there left to study?—only a delivery device. However, research indicates that the same kind of teaching is similarly effective with or without various technological aids (Wilkinson, 1980).

> The best current evidence is that media are mere vehicles that deliver instruction but do not influence student achievement any more than the truck that delivers groceries causes changes in our nutrition. (Clark, 1983, p. 445)

Are there certain things specific media can do that cannot be duplicated in other situations? It is possible that computer programming in child-appropriate languages, or interacting with an artificially intelligent machine, will deliver instructional environments which cannot be duplicated without this technology. However, the benefits of environments such as these remain to be assessed.

Media Attribute Research

In addressing these limitations of media comparison research, many investigators turn to the study of the attributes of different media and suggest that these attributes are an integral part of media and provide for the cultivation of cognitive skills. However, Clark (1983) argues that media are also mere vehicles for these attributes, just as they are vehicles for the delivery of instruction. In addition, while there is evidence that the presence of these attributes may be sufficient for learning to occur, it has not been shown that they are *necessary* conditions for the learning of these skills. Other methods of instruction may be just as effective, as long as they contain the critical cognitive process features which underlie the development of instructional theory (Clark, 1983). It may be that among the important variables to investigate are people's *beliefs* and attributions concerning media.

There are other essential questions, including the cost and distribution of instruction. The caveat is that we do not lose sight of what we are comparing, and for what purpose we are comparing different media.

Too many studies have used summative, either/or research designs. There is a need for more formative research, or research which takes place while programs are being developed (Barbatsis, 1978). With television and CAI especially, there needs to be more concern with the development and improvement of the media for the instruction of children. Instruction will be more effective if (a) it is integrated into the traditional instructional program; (b) it utilizes a systems approach; and, (c) teachers have received specific training in its utilization (Chu & Schramm, 1968; Wilkinson, 1980).

VISTAS

White (1983) has described electronic learning as developing in three stages: The television stage; the computer stage; and finally, the electronic environment for information, for work, and for entertainment. What elements will this last environment have? For young children especially, speech synthesis and speech recognition will greatly extend the quality and quantity of computerized material with which they can interact. Adequate speech synthesis is presently affordable, and quality educational materials are being produced in increasing numbers. Recognition of speech is a much more difficult technological program; however, expensive systems are already available.

Another major advance will be in interactive video, in which computer programs control videodisk technology to allow numerous high-quality video pictures and sound to be accessed quickly under CAI or student control. Electronic communication will allow children to access information from virtually anywhere in the world and communicate with children and adults with similar interests. Even more exotic devices, such as brain-wave sensors to analyze children's attention and involvement in a computerized dialog, have been suggested. Some such devices already exist; for example, one computer system presents foreign language sentences and, if the readers *eyes* linger too long on a word, translates that word automatically.

Perhaps the most promising and most stimulating advances will come from the developing field of artificial intelligence—the study of the "machine that thinks." While arguments continue regarding the ultimate potential of computers to simulate human intelligence, it is true that systems have already been invented that can solve problems, several of which no person had solved before. Similarly, computer tutors which "understand the student"—at least on a limited basis— have been constructed (Burton & Brown, 1979). This brings up an interesting question: Should we work to *simulate* intelligence or *stimulate* intelligence? Or will the two pursuits merge in the future?

Are these advancements economically feasible? There is a limit on technological solutions to educational problems. In less than a decade we will have less real fiscal resources for equipment than we have presently (Dede, 1980). Education must find a less expensive way of teaching. The costs of CAI are decreasing 5% per year, with a 10% increase per year in productivity. So, within a decade, machines will be three times as productive at half the cost; and for what machines do well, people are not economically competitive (Dede, 1980).

> The question, can children learn new knowledge from video technologies?, is vapid. Yes, children will learn new things from these video technologies! Useful questions are not how can we teach children their abc's better through video technologies but rather what potential range of content of media can most fruitfully expand the range of experiences for children. (Wartella & Reeves, 1983, p. 9)

If we want to see what children can learn, we must go beyond traditional school achievement tests in our measurement of what children learn. We must go beyond traditional visions of technological advances and their use with young children.

REFERENCES

Aeschleman, S., & Tawney, J. (1978). Interacting: A computer-based telecommunications system for educating severely handicapped preschoolers in their homes. *Educational Technology, 18*(10), 30–35.

Ahrens, M. G., & Singh, N. N. (1977). Television viewing habits of mentally retarded children. *Australian Journal of Mental Retardation, 4,* 1–3.

Anderson, D. R. (1983). *Home television viewing by preschool children and their families.* Presented at the biennial meeting of the Society for Research in Child Development, Detroit, MI.

Anderson, D. R., Lorch, E. P., Field, D. E., & Sanders, J. (1981). The effects of TV program comprehensibility on preschool children's visual attention to television. *Child Development, 52,* 151–157.

Anderson, D. R., Lorch, E. P., Smith, R., Bradford, R., & Levin, S. R. (1981). Effects of peer presence on preschool children's television viewing behavior. *Developmental Psychology, 17,* 466–453.

Anderson, C. C., & Maguire, T. O. (1978). The effect of TV viewing on the educational performance of elementary school children. *The Alberta Journal of Educational Research, 24,* 156–163.

Atkinson, R. C., & Fletcher, J. D. (1972). Teaching children to read with a computer. *Reading Teacher, 25*(4), 319–327.

Ball, S., & Bogatz, G. A. (1973). *Reading with television: An evaluation of The Electric Company* (PR-74-15). Princeton, NJ: Educational Testing Service.

Bandura, A. (1978). Social learning theory of aggression. *Journal of Communication, 28*(3), 12–29.

Barbatsis, G. S. (1978). The nature of inquiry in analysis of theoretical progress in instructional television from 1950 to 1970. *Review of Educational Research, 48,* 399–414.

Beagles-Roos, J., & Gat, I. (1983). Specific impact of radio and television on children's story comprehension. *Journal of Educational Psychology, 75,* 128–137.

Billings, K. (1983). Research on school computing. In M. T. Grady & J. D. Gawronski (Eds.), *Computers in curriculum and instruction* (pp. 12–18). Alexandria, VA: Association for Supervision and Curriculum Development

Bogatz, G. A., & Ball, S. (1971). *The second year of Sesame Street: A continuing evaluation* (PR-71-21; 2 vols.). Princeton, NJ: Educational Testing Service.

Bracey, G. (1982, November/December). What the research shows. *Electronic Learning,* pp. 51–54.

Braithwaite, V., & Holman, J. (1981). Parent observed behaviors of preschool television viewers. *Australian Journal of Psychology, 33,* 375–382.

Burns, P. K., & Bozeman, W. C. (1981). Computer-assisted instruction and mathematics achievement: Is there a relationship? *Educational Technology, 21,* 32–39.

Burton, R. R., & Brown, J. S. (1979). An investigation of computer coaching for informal learning activities. *International Journal of Man-Machine Studies, 11,* 5–24.

Busch, J. S. (1978). TV's effect on reading: A case study. *Phi Delta Kappan, 59,* 668–671.

Callaway, J. (Moderator). (1982). *The new media and the American family* [Cassette Recording]. Racine, WI: The Johnson Foundation.

Calvert, S. L., Huston, A. C., Watkins, B. A., & Wright, J. C. (1982). The relation between selective attention to television forms and children's comprehension of content. *Child Development, 53,* 601–610.

Center for Social Organization of Schools (1983, June). *School uses of microcomputers: Reports from a national survey* (Issue No. 2). Baltimore, MD: John Hopkins Univ. Press.

Chambers, J. A., & Sprecher, J. W. (1980). Computer assisted instruction: Current trends and critical issues. *Communications of the ACM, 23,* 332–342.

Chu, G. C., & Schramm, W. (1968). *Learning from television: What the research says.* Washington, DC: NAEB.

Clark, R. E. (1983). Reconsidering research on learning from media. *Review of Educational Research, 53,* 445–459.

Clement, F. J. (1981). Affective considerations in computer-based education. *Educational Technology, 21,* 28–32.

Clements, D. H., & Gullo, D. F. (in press). Effects of computer programming on young children's cognition. *Journal of Educational Psychology.*

Coates, B., Pusser, H. E., & Goodman, I. (1976). The influence of "Sesame Street" and "Mister Rogers' Neighborhood" on children's social behavior in the preschool. *Child Development, 47,* 138–144.

Collins, W. A. (1979). Children's comprehension of television content. In E. Wartella (Ed.), *Children communicating: Media and development of thought, speech, understanding* (pp. 21–52). Beverly Hills: Sage.

Collins, W. A. (1981). Schemata for understanding television. In H. Kelly & H. Gardner (Eds.), *Viewing children through television* (pp. 31–45). San Francisco: Jossey-Bass.

Collins, W. A., & Getz, S. K. (1976). Children's social responses following modeled reactions to provocation: Prosocial effects of a television drama. *Journal of Personality, 44,* 488–500.

Collins, W. A., Sobol, B. L., & Westby, S. (1981). Effects of adult commentary on children's comprehension and inferences about a televised aggressive portrayal. *Child Development, 52,* 158–163.

Comstock, G., Chaffee, S., Katzman, N., McCombs, M., & Roberts, D. (1978). *Television and human behavior.* New York: Columbia Univ. Press.

Doerken, M. (1983). *Classroom combat: Teaching and television.* Englewood Cliffs, NJ: Educational Technology.

Daiute, C. (1982, March/April). Word processing. Can it make good writers better? *Electronic Learning,* pp. 29–31.

Dede, C. J. (1980). Educational technology: The next 10 years. *Instructional Innovator, 25*(3), 17–23.

Eron, L. D. (1982). Parent-child interaction, television violence, and aggression of children. *American Psychologist, 37,* 197–211.

Eron, L. D., Huesmann, L. R., Brice, P., Fisher, P., & Mermelstein, R. (1983). Age trends in the development of aggression, sex typing, and related television habits. *Developmental Psychology, 19,* 71–77.

Feshbach, S., Feshbach, N. D., & Cohen, S. E. (1982). Enhancing children's discrimination in response to television advertising: The effects of psycho-educational training in two elementary school-age groups. *Developmental Review, 2,* 385–403.

Feshbach, S., & Singer, R. D. (1971). *Television and aggression: An experimental field study.* San Francisco: Jossey-Bass.

Forman, D. (1982). Search of the literature. *The Computing Teacher, 9*(5), 37–51.

Friedrich, L. K., & Stein, A. H. (1973). Aggressive and prosocial television programs and the natural behavior of preschool children. *Monographs for the Society for Research in Child Development, 38*(4, Serial No. 151).

Gadberry, S. (1980). Effects of restricting first graders' TV viewing on leisure time use, I.Q. change, and cognitive style. *Journal of Applied Developmental Psychology, 1,* 45–57.

Goldenberg, E. P. (1979). *Special technology for special children.* Baltimore, Maryland: Univ. Park Press.

Gorman, H., Jr. (1982, August). The Lamplighter project. *Byte,* pp. 331–332.

Gorn, G. J., Goldberg, M., & Kanungo, R. (1976). The role of educational television in changing the intergroup attitudes of children. *Child Development, 47,* 277–280.

Greer, D., Potts, R., Wright, J. C., & Huston, A. C. (1982). The effects of television commercial form and commercial placement on children's social behavior and attention. *Child Development, 53,* 611–619.

Griffin, W. H. (1983). Can educational technology have any significant impact on education? *T.H.E. Journal, 11*(3), 96–99.

Gunter, B. (1982). Does television interfere with reading development? *Bulletin of The British Psychological Society, 35,* 232–235.

Hawkins, J. (1983). Learning Logo together: The social context. In *Chameleon in the classroom: Developing roles for computers* (Tech. Rep. No. 22) (pp. 40–49). New York: Bank Street College of Education, Center for Children and Technology.

Hawkins, J., Sheingold, K., Gearhart, M., & Berger, C. (1982). Microcomputers in schools: Impact on the social life of elementary classrooms. *Journal of Applied Developmental Psychology, 3,* 361–373.

Henderson, R. W., Swanson, R., & Zimmerman, B. J. (1975). Training seriation responses in young children through televised modeling of hierarchically sequenced rule components. *American Educational Research Journal, 12,* 479–489.

Hoffman, R., & Flook, M. A. (1980). An experimental investigation of the role of television in facilitating shape recognition. *Journal of Genetic Psychology, 136,* 305–306.

Hollenbeck, A. R., & Slaby, R. G. (1979). Infant visual and vocal responses to television. *Child Development, 50,* 41–45.

Hollenbeck, A. R., & Slaby, R. G. (1982). Influence of a televised model's vocabulary pattern on infants. *Journal of Applied Developmental Psychology, 3,* 57–65.

Howe, J. A. M., & O'Shea, T. (1978). Learning mathematics through Logo. *ACM SIGCUE Bulletin, 12*(1).

Huesmann, L. R., Eron, L. D., Klein, R., Brice, P., & Fischer, P. (1983). Mitigating the imitation of aggressive behaviors by changing children's attitudes about media violence. *Journal of Personality and Social Psychology, 44,* 899–910.

Huesmann, L. R., Lagerspetz, K., & Eron, L. (in press). Intervening variables in the television violence-aggression relation: Evidence from two countries. *Developmental Psychology.*

Huston, A. C., Wright, J. C., Kerkman, D., Seigle, J., Rice, M., & Bremer, M. (nd). *Family environment and television use by preschool children.* Unpublished manuscript, Department of Human Development, Univ. of Kansas, Lawrence, KS.

Israel, B. L. (1968). *Responsive environment program: Brooklyn, N.Y.: Report of the first full year of operation. The talking typewriter.* Brooklyn, NY: Office of Economic Opportunity. (ERIC Document Reproduction Service No. ED 027 742)

Kearsley, G., Hunter, B., & Seidel, R. J. (1983). Two decades of computer based instruction projects: What have we learned. *T.H.E. Journal, 10*(4), 88–96.

Kleiman, G., Humphrey, M., & Lindsay, P. (1983). Microcomputers and hyperactive children. In D. Harper & J. Stewart (Eds.), *Run: Computer Education* (pp. 227–228). Monterey, CA: Brooks/Cole.

Lally, M. (1981). Computer-assisted teaching of sight-word recognition for mentally retarded school children. *American Journal of Mental Deficiency, 85,* 383–388.

Lavin, R., & Sanders, J. (1983, April). *Longitudinal evaluation of the C/A/I Computer Assisted Instruction Title 1 Project: 1979–82.* Chelmsford, MA: Merrimack Education Center.

Lesgold, A. M. (1983). A rationale for computer-based reading instruction. In A. C. Wilkinson (Ed.), *Classroom computers and cognitive science* (pp. 167–181). New York: Academic Press.

Lesser, H. (1977). *Television and the preschool child.* New York: Academic Press.

Levin, S. R., Petros, T. V., & Petrella, F. W. (1982). Preschoolers' awareness of television advertising. *Child Development, 53,* 933–937.

Liebert, R. M., & Baron, R. A. (1972). Short-term effects of televised aggression on children's aggressive behavior. In J. P. Murray, E. A. Rubinstein, & G. A. Comstock (Eds.), *Television and social behavior (Vol. 2): Television and social learning.* Washington, DC: United States Government Printing.

Liss, M. B., & Price, D. (1981). What, when, and why deaf children watch television. *American Annals of the Deaf, 126,* 493–498.

Lochhead, J., & Clement, J. (Eds.). (1979). *Cognitive process instruction: Research on teaching thinking skills.* Philadelphia: Franklin Institute Press.

Martin, J. H. (1981). On reading, writing, and computers. *Educational Leadership, 39,* 60–64.

Marton, J. P., & Acker, L. E. (1981). Television provoked aggression: Effects of gentle, affection-like training prior to exposure. *Child Study Journal, 12,* 27–43.

Melody, W. (1973). *Children's television: The economics of exploitation.* New Haven: Yale Univ. Press.

Milojkovic, J. D. (1983). *Children learning computer programming: Cognitive and motivational consequences.* Doctoral dissertation, Stanford Univ.

Minton, J. H. (1975). The impact of Sesame Street on readiness. *Sociology of Education, 48*(2), 141–151.

Morrow, J. (1977). *Media & kids: Real-world learning in the schools.* Rochelle Park, NJ: Hayden Book Co.

Murphy, C. M., & Wood, D. J. (1982). Learning through media: A comparison of 4–8 year old children's responses to filmed and pictorial instruction. *International Journal of Behavioral Development, 5,* 195–216.

Murray, J. P. (1980). *Television & youth: 25 years of research and controversy.* Boys Town, NE: The Boys Town Center for the Study of Youth Development.

Nelson, K. (1973). Structure and strategy in learning to talk. *Monographs of the Society for Research in Child Development, 38*(1–2, Serial No. 149).

Neuman, S. B. (1980). Listening behavior and television viewing. *Journal of Educational Research, 74,* 15–18.

Neuman, S. B., & Prowda, P. (1982). Television viewing and reading achievement. *Journal of Reading, 25,* 666–670.

Papert, S. (1980). *Mindstorms: Children, computers, and powerful ideas.* New York: Basic Books.

Papert, S., diSessa, A., Watt, D., & Weir, S. (1979). *Final report of the Brookline Logo Project: Project summary and data analysis.* Logo Memo 53, MIT Logo Group.

Pea, R. D. (1983). Logo programming and problem solving. In *Chameleon in the classroom: Developing roles for computers* (Tech. Rep. No. 22) (pp. 25–33). New York: Bank Street College of Education, Center for Children and Technology.

Perfetti, C. A. (1983). Reading, vocabulary, and writing: Implications for computer-based instruction. In A. C. Wilkinson (Ed.), *Classroom computers and cognitive science* (pp. 145–163). New York: Academic Press.

Piestrup, A. M. (1981). *Preschool children use Apple II to test reading skills program.* Portola Valley, CA: Advanced Learning Technology. (ERIC Document Reproduction S

Prinz, P., Nelson, K., & Stedt, J. (1982). Early reading in young deaf children using microcomputer technology. *American Annals of the Deaf, 127,* 529–535.

Raeissi, P., & Wright, J. C. (1983, April). *Training and generalization of number conservation by television for preschoolers.* Paper presented at the meeting of the Society for Research in Child Development, Detroit, MI.

Ragosta, M., Holland, P., & Jamison, D. (1981). *Computer-assisted instruction and compensatory education: The ETS/LAUSD study.* Princeton, NJ: Educational Testing Service.

Ridley-Johnson, R., Cooper, H., & Chance, J. (1983). The relation of children's television viewing to school achievement and I.Q. *Journal of Educational Research, 76,* 294–297.

Salomon, G. (1979). Shape, not only content: How media symbols partake in the developmental abilities. In E. Wartella (Ed.), *Children communicating: Media and development of thought, speech, understanding* (pp. 53–82). Beverly Hills: Sage.

Salomon, G. (1981). Introducing AIME: The assessment of children's mental involvement with television. In H. Kelly & H. Gardner (Eds.), *Viewing children through television* (pp. 89–102). San Francisco: Jossey-Bass.

Schofield, J. M. (1981). *Microcomputer-based aides for the disabled.* London, England: Heyden & Son Ltd.

Seidman, R. H. (1981). *The effects of learning a computer programming language on the logical reasoning of school children.* Paper presented at the Annual Meeting of the American Education Research Association, Los Angeles, CA, April 14, 1981.

Silvern, S. B., Williamson, P. A., Countermine, T. A. (1983, April). *Aggression in young children and video game play.* Paper presented at the biennial meeting of the Society for Research in Child Development, Detroit, MI.

Singer, J. L., & Singer, D. G. (1981). *Television, imagination, and aggression: A study of preschoolers.* Hillsdale, NJ: Erlbaum.

Singer, J. L., & Singer, D. G. (1983). Psychologists look at television: Cognitive, developmental, personality, and social policy implications. *American Psychologist, 38,* 826–834.

Singer, D. G., Singer, J. L., & Zuckerman, D. M. (1981). *Teaching television.* New York: The Dial Press.

Smithy-Willis, D., Riley, M., & Smith, D. (1982, November/December). Visual discrimination and preschoolers. *Educational Computer Magazine,* pp. 19–20.

Sprafkin, J. N., Liebert, R. M., & Poulos, R. W. (1975). Effects of a prosocial televised example on children's helping. *Journal of Experimental Child Psychology, 20,* 119–126.

Stoneman, Z., & Brody, G. H. (1983). Immediate and long-term recognition and generalization of advertised products as a function of age and presentation mode. *Developmental Psychology, 19,* 56–61.

Swigger, K., & Campbell, J. (1981). Computers and the nursery school. *Proceedings of the National Educational Computing Conference.* Iowa City, Iowa: National Educational Computing Conference.

Swigger, K. M., Campbell, J., & Swigger, B. K. (1983, January/February). Preschool children's preferences of different types of CAI programs. *Educational Computer Magazine,* pp. 38–40.

Visonhaler, J. F., & Bass, R. K. (1972). A summary of ten major studies on CAI drill and practice. *Educational Technology, 12,* 29–32.

Wartella, E., & Reeves, B. (1983.) Recurring issues in research on children and media. *Educational Technology,* 23, 5–9.

Watkins, B., Calvert, S., Huston-Stein, A., & Wright, J. C. (1980). Children's recall of television material: Effects of presentation mode and adult labeling. *Developmental Psychology, 16,* 672–674.

Watt, D. (1982, June). Word Processors and writing. *Popular Computing,* pp. 124–126.

Weir, S., & Watt, D. (1983). Logo: A computer environment for learning-disabled students. In D. Harper & J. Stewart (Eds.), *Run: Computer Education* (pp. 214–222). Monterey, CA: Brooks/Cole.

White, M. A. (1983). Toward a psychology of electronic learning. In M. A. White (Ed.), *The future of electronic learning* (pp. 51–62). Hillsdale, NJ: Erlbaum.

Wilkinson, G. L. (1980). *Media in instruction: 60 years of research.* Washington, DC: Association for Educational Communications and Technology.

Williams, J., Thorkildsen, R., & Crossman, E. K. (1983). Application of computers to the needs of handicapped persons (pp. 228–238). In D. Harper & J. Stewart (Eds.), *Run: Computer Education.* Monterey, CA: Brooks/Cole.

Williams, P. A., Haertel, E. H., Haertel, G. D., & Walberg, H. J. (1982). The impact of leisure-time television on school learning: A research synthesis. *American Educational Research Journal, 19,* 19–50.

Winick, M. P., & Wehrenberg, J. S. (1982). *Children and TV II: Mediating the medium.* Washington, DC: Association for Childhood Education International.

Winn, M. (1977). *The plug-in drug.* New York: Viking Press.

Wright, J. C., & Huston, A. C. (1983). A matter of form: Potentials of television for young viewers. *American Psychologist, 38,* 835–843.

APPENDIX A

HELPING CHILDREN BENEFIT FROM TELEVISION

Viewing television can be helpful or harmful to young children. Research has indicated that there are many things teachers and parents can do to maximize the positive effects of television and minimize any negative influences. The following list contains those suggestions which research indicates are effective in helping children benefit from television.

1. Watch what children watch (with your children, if you are a parent). Adults help children make inferences and connections which they are unlikely to make on their own.
2. Help children distinguish reality from fantasy.
3. Encourage older children to evaluate programs for stereotypes, use of language, handling of plot and these, artistic style, motivation and development of characters, and so on.
4. Keep a TV log—then discuss it objectively. Encourage children to be active viewers, by first reading about programs, selecting the best, and forming opinions about the worth of shows.
5. Analyze the images that advertisements give of our society. Have children compare this image to their own opinions. Analyze mass persuasion techniques.
6. Inculcate values that TV mocks, for example, reverence for the old.
7. Teach children not to generalize about minority groups as stereotypically portrayed on TV.
8. Emphasize that violence should not be imitated.
9. Children primarily attend to television visually; but classroom learning is primarily auditory and children may not recognize the cues which tell them when to attend. Teachers should develop a set of cues that are classroom-oriented.
10. Create a classroom resource area in which surveys of viewing are posted; children critique shows; special shows are highlighted on a bulletin board, put in world context with maps; and so on.

11. Teach how TV programs are made.
12. Involve children in the active production of media, from simple stages and skits, to cartoons, to video tape productions, as a natural way to learn school subjects and learn about the fantasy aspect of TV.
13. Teach children to be discriminating viewers and consumers.

CHAPTER 10

SOCIAL AND PERSONAL ECOLOGY INFLUENCING PUBLIC POLICY FOR YOUNG CHILDREN
An American Dilemma

VALORA WASHINGTON

G enerations of American Presidents, both Democratic and Republican, have pronounced the importance of children and the family for a strong government. For example, Lyndon B. Johnson (1967) observed: "The family is the cornerstone of our society. More than any other force it shapes the attitudes, the hopes, the ambitions, and the values of the child" (p. 130). Richard Nixon (1972) affirmed a "national commitment to providing all American children an opportunity for a healthful and stimulating development during the first five years of life" (p. 1174–1187). As a Presidential candidate, Jimmy Carter (1978) stated: "There can be no more urgent priority for the next administration than to see that every decision our government makes is designed to honor and support and strengthen the American family" (p. 463, 464).

Yet, there is little in American social policy, aside from the public school, which commits the resources of the United States to fulfill these lofty promises for children and families. Indeed, care for children, and family support, has generally been considered a private matter.

This contrast between political rhetoric and actual policy poses the American dilemma which surrounds public policy toward young children. A distinction must be made between a general cultural piety about the family, and specific social policies directed to family concerns. The two need not be complementary; most often, in American experience, they are in conflict (Moynihan, 1973).

Nevertheless, this dilemma raises a myriad of questions for

public consideration: Should we routinely provide for the care of young children using public resources? Should public care be targeted to particular groups, such as the poor or handicapped? Should care be preventative or rehabilitative? How can our government reconcile our laissez-faire traditions toward children with increasing calls for comprehensive policies for all children?

This chapter presents an overview of America's public response to the dilemma surrounding its policies affecting young children. The chapter is organized into five sections. The first section presents the social ecology, those historical variables which form the context for children's policy; generally this context reveals a deeply-rooted American tradition of reluctance to involve public policy in the "private" domain of child and family life. Of course, many policies for children and families do exist. The second section illustrates the personal ecology which typically forms the basis for "exceptions" to America's noninterventionist stance. The third section is a review of children's policies and programs. Section four discusses the increasing calls for a comprehensive, universal, and developmental approach to child and family policy. The final section explores the future of children's policy and illustrates ways in which parents, educators, and child advocates are working to create solutions to this American dilemma.

SOCIAL ECOLOGY: AMERICAN TRADITIONS AND CHILDREN'S POLICY

In any country, societal taboos and beliefs influence the quality of life and shape the ecological perspectives of young children. In the United States, the societal posture has been one of restraint and nonintervention. The care of children is considered to rest in the private domain of the family. Gilbert Steiner (1976), a noted analyst of child and family policy, calls child rearing "the least regulated important aspect of American life" (p. 1).

The American tradition toward restraint in family matters has its roots in the eighteenth century liberal or "laissez-faire" philosophies. The doctrines of Adam Smith, John Locke and others stressed individual freedom and free-enterprise in a truly competitive market. Thus, the best government was the one that governed least. In the 1980's, such beliefs are labelled "conservative," yet they are still rooted in the notion that individuals can, in the prevailing social order, provide for their own needs through work, savings, investments, and acquisitions of property (Gil, 1976; Keniston et al., 1977).

Property rights have been ascendant in American values, and historically children have been considered the property of their parents. Thus, Condry and Lazar (1982) claim that when policy decisions raise a conflict between property rights and the needs of children, property has usually won. As an example, they observe that pressure toward developing and enforcing strict federal day care standards in the 1970's was reduced because these standards would have increased the cost to private day care providers.

The tendency to insist on parental rights over children's needs (Sponseller & Fink, 1982) may also be related to the multiethnic character of our country. America's multiplicity of cultures and religious values lead to alternative child rearing styles. It would be difficult, at best, to "choose" from among the alternatives.

Further, suggestions that the government might provide general services to children and families have often been viewed with alarm. There is a historical tendency to fear "big government" as an invasion of the privacy and the sanctity of the individual family.

The primacy of the family in our country is such a strong ideological view that attempts to develop non-educational policies affecting children are subject to intense political attacks. For example, President Richard Nixon (1972), when vetoing proposed legislation, echoed the sentiments of millions of Americans when he asserted that "for the federal government to plunge headlong financially into supporting child development would commit the vast moral authority of the National Government to the side of communal approaches to child rearing and against the family centered approach" (p. 1174–87).

Politicians however, are not the only source of public reticence toward public policy for children (Cohen & Connery, 1967; Greenblatt, 1977; Kamerman & Kahn, 1978). Many professionals in early childhood education also fear that social action might disrupt the parent-child bond or might infringe on family rights (Sponseller & Fink, 1980). Thus, some educators have a propensity to exhort parents, rather than advocate for societal policies which might conflict with parent practices and the cultural norms. Bettye Caldwell (1977) also has observed that educators sometimes discount studies indicating that children's attachment to parents is not harmed by out-of-home care, while citing authors who point to the dangers in this child care arrangement.

Nevertheless, Americans have not been hesitant to adapt its social ecology around childhood during national emergencies. During the Depression of the 1930's, for example, day care centers were established under the federal government's Works Progress Administration. During World War II, the Lanham Act provided funds for day care and extended school services to facilitate women's participation in war-related industries; these Lanham child care centers were closed at the end of the war (Condry & Lazar, 1982; Steiner, 1976).

The historical record converges to create a society in which it has not been politically feasible nor, in some cases, desirable to develop children's policy. Against this backdrop, child advocates have had difficulty in developing or implementing acceptable public policies targeted to young children.

PERSONAL ECOLOGY: "ABNORMAL" DEVELOPMENT AS THE CORE OF CHILDREN'S POLICY

The non-interventionist tradition in American policy is not absolute. For the most part, however, aside from national emergency, economic disaster or a health crisis, American tradition holds that a family should, and will, care for its own children without public assistance. Although experts differ in their approaches, they share the basic assumption that families, as self-sufficient entities, are responsible for their children's welfare (Keniston, et al., 1977).

A variety of child-serving policies have evolved, nonetheless. Government policy consistently has enacted programs or procedures to protect all children from catastrophic and preventable conditions such as polio or blindness. However, in contrast with

Presidential oratory on societal commitment to all children, often children and their families must exhibit a dysfunctional range of personal characteristics in order to qualify for public assistance. Indeed, the ecology surrounding program-eligibility is based on a personal deficit model. Child-oriented policies and programs are typically targeted toward those children considered to be "abnormal" by virtue of their social or physical handicaps.

Federal policy which allows for the care of "special needs" children (such as those who have dead, absent or abusive parents) does not, in any fundamental way, threaten the noninterventionist posture of American tradition. Rather, by limiting policy to crises in poor or dysfunctional families, the tradition is preserved (Steiner, 1981). Indeed, public policy as a response to human "deficiencies" has the benefit of appearing indicative of a mature and humane society.

The "normal" development of a child tends to exclude him or her from most federal policy which affects young children. Legislative actions and policies have focused primarily on children identified as needy (Verr, 1973). If individual deficiencies would cease to exist, then so would child and family policy. "If we want less government," stated President Jimmy Carter (1978), "we must have stronger families. For government steps in by necessity when families have failed" (p. 463, 464).

Justifying federal programs as a response to the individual's personal failure has been a vital part of the development of policy aimed at children. Rooted in English Poor Law, America's deficit model of the poor partly reflects the Victorian attitude that poverty is the result of individual handicaps and deficiencies. Steiner (1981) observes that a large part of the interest in family policy would disappear if there were no indigent families requiring assistance. Certainly, proponents of child policies inevitably depend on indicators of inadequate income and dysfunctional behavior as their rationale. Consequently, federal policies aimed at specific groups implicitly or explicitly define the groups as inadequate (Keniston, et al., 1977).

This focus on personal deficiencies and abnormalities does not occur without costs. Labelling, stigma, categorization, and contempt of the poor necessarily follow this deficit philosophy

(Mandell, 1975). Families which do not attain self-sufficiency are subject to "blame." The public response is to remediate or uplift the family through "parent education," or through "rehabilitation and opportunities" programs, which focus on changing individuals (Bowler, 1974; Keniston, et al., 1977).

A REVIEW OF CHILDREN'S POLICIES AND PROGRAMS

Despite the legitimate concerns of critics of social programs (Anderson, 1978; Koldin, 1971) the deficit assumptions of public assistance overlooks the fact that young children are "typical" welfare recipients. Children are more likely to be poor than any other group in America. One in five American children is poor, a rate twice as high as in 1965 when the War-on-Poverty began. In addition, younger children are more likely to be poor than are older children (CDF, 1983a; USDC, 1981a; USDL, 1980).

For members of the various racial groups, the picture is even more bleak. For example, half of all poor Black Americans are children (CDF, 1983a). Black children are more than three times more likely to be poor than white children (USDC, 1981a). Relief for poor children is not occurring. Approximately half of the additions to the poverty rolls in 1980 were children (USDC, 1981a; USDL, 1980). Since 1980 alone, more than 2.5 million children have fallen into poverty (CDF, 1983a).

A variety of policies and programs have evolved to address the needs of poor children. These programs provide income support, health care, protection from abuse, nutritional assistance, and child care.

Income Support and "Means" Tests

Critics charge that these "special programs for special people" (or poor programs for poor people) stigmitize their recipients and commonly subject them to special investigations, tests, requirements, and restrictions (Keniston, et al., 1977; Steiner, 1981).

Aid to Families With Dependent Children (AFDC) is an example of the special requirements surrounding public assistance. AFDC is the only federal program aimed explicitly at protecting poor children by providing income support to their families. Sixty-eight percent of all AFDC recipients are children; forty-five percent of them are Black, half are eight years or younger. Over 42 percent of AFDC families have only one child (CDF, 1983a).

Receiving AFDC requires the child's family to pass several eligibility and "means" tests. For decades in some states, these requirements included "man-in-the-house" and "morality" rules. Today, some of the tests are as follows: the family's gross income minus work related expenses must be below the amount of money each state determines is necessary to meet a minimal standard of living for each family size. Families must meet an "asset test" which is also specified by the state, subject to a federal outer limit (CRS, 1981). Also, all able-bodied recipients, including mothers whose youngest child is at least six-years-old, must register for training and employment services. A parent, without children under age three, may be required to participate in a community work experience program (CWEP) if child care is available (American Public Welfare Association, 1982).

Health Care

Health care is provided through three programs: Medicaid, Maternal and Child Health Program, and Community Health Centers. Over 10 million poor children depend on Medicaid for health screening, diagnosis, and treatment; children rely on Medicaid more than any other age group. In 1980 the Maternal and Child Health and Crippled Children's Program reached nearly 12 million children and mothers. In one community health program, the Childhood Immunization Program, 16.6 million doses of no-cost vaccines were provided for over six million children in 1981 (CDF, 1983a).

Abused, Neglected, Homeless and Disturbed Children

Programs aimed at the problems of abused, neglected, homeless, and emotionally disturbed children include the Child Abuse Prevention and Treatment Act, the Adoption Assistance and Child

Welfare Act of 1980, Title XX Social Services Program, and the Mental Health Block Grant (CDF, 1983a).

Food and Nutrition Programs

Food programs sponsored by the federal government include food stamps, the School Breakfast and School Lunch Programs, the Child Care Food Program, the Special Supplemental Food Program for Women Infants and Children (WIC), and the Summer Food Service Program. School Lunch serves 23 million children, half of whom are from low-income families. School Breakfast serves 3.4 million children, 90 percent of whom are poor. The Summer Food Service program continues the School Lunch Program in primarily low-income areas during the summer months. The Child Care Food Program helps defray the cost of meals to children being cared for in day care centers or in family day care homes; 800,000 children are served, about 70 percent of whom are low-income. About half of all people participating in the food stamps program are children. The Special Supplemental Food Program For Women, Infants and Children reaches about 2.3 million people who are low income and determined by a medical professional to be a risk of illness due to inadequate nutrition (CDF, 1983a).

Child Care

Child Care services are provided through Title XX services, the Child Care Food Program, AFDC, the Child Care Tax Credit and Project Head Start. In 1980, Title XX paid for all or part of care costs for 750,000 low and moderate-income children. AFDC provides child care by allowing families to be compensated for child care costs up to $160 a month per child. The Child Care Tax Credit, enacted in 1976, is the largest federal expenditure for child care; it is claimed by 4.2 million families, primarily those in the middle and upper income brackets. Project Head Start, perhaps the most successful War-on-Poverty program, serves 395,800 children, 90 percent of whom are economically disadvantaged. Two-thirds of Head Start children are members of minority groups (CDF, 1983b).

Other Benefits

Children also benefit indirectly by a number of other federal programs, such as the Low-Income Home Energy Assistance Program, the Unemployment Compensation Program, and the Job Training Partnership Act. About half of the families in subsidized housing have children. Social security pays a stipend to widow(ers) and their dependent children. Unemployment insurance and workmen's compensation provides benefits without regard to an income test, although benefits are tied to past earnings.

Limits To Assistance For Children

Yet, despite the wide array of programs which assist children, there are many Americans, including children, who do not receive support. Although the USA's overall spending on social welfare benefits (services and transfer payments) doubled between 1965 and 1972, this increase had little effect on the children of poor and near-poor families. Rather, most of the increased government spending for the poor goes to other groups, particularly the aged. While these other beneficiaries certainly merit help, it is unfortunate that policies have neglected the needs of poor children (Keniston et al, 1977).

Examples of the continuing inadequacies of social programs abound in every category of aid. While children represent 48 percent of the total Medicaid population, they account for only about 19 percent of the Medicaid expenditures; in general, Medicaid income standards for mothers and children are lower than those for aged, blind or disabled adults (U.S. House of Representatives, 1982). Because states define the criteria for need in the AFDC program, benefits vary widely; as of July 1981, 22 states made maximum payments that left recipients needy by their own standards (CRS, 1981). In food and nutrition programs, about 6 million women, infants and children are eligible for the WIC program but do not receive it (USDC, 1981a). In child care, only about 15 percent of Head Start eligible children can participate in the program (CDF, 1983b; Rivlin & Timpane, 1975). More than one in eight children lives in substandard housing; about one in four Black and Hispanic children lives in substandard housing (USDH, 1980).

Budget cuts since 1980 have further slashed benefits to children. About 1.5 million children have lost their AFDC benefit eligibility. About 290,000 children have lost health services as a result of funding cuts to community health services. Free and reduced price lunches have been taken from 1.1 million low income children. About one million people have had their food stamps eliminated, and about four million others have had their benefits reduced (CDF, 1983a).

Thus, while needy children are targeted for a wide array of programs, many of these services are either unavailable or now available only on a limited basis. In addition, when they are available, the provision of services is fragmented (Keniston, et al., 1977).

CHANGING SOCIAL ECOLOGY: UNIVERSAL BENEFITS

Partly as a result of the proliferation of fragmented programs, the deficit model for public assistance recipients is gradually being replaced by a growing awareness that many of the stresses facing children and families are beyond their control. Rather than being the "cause" of their problems, families are typically subject to broader social and economic forces. The Depression of the 1930's, from which many social programs emerged (including AFDC) emerged, helped to trigger the evolution of the principle that poverty and social catastrophe are not necessarily the result of individual deficiencies (Moroney, 1976). Indeed, "adequate" families, contrary to the myth of self-sufficiency, are not insulated from outside pressures (Keniston et al., 1977).

While not necessarily critical of programs aimed at the poor, there is a growing literature which asserts that this narrow target no longer is appropriate. Policy which focuses on deprivation is said to ignore the impact of outside forces on *all* families. The Carnegie Council on Children (Keniston et al., 1977) warns that American families are generally weakening under the force of societal pressures, and that these families are harmed by the historical posture to insulate family matters from public policy. Supportive and helping services are needed by average, ordinary families faced with the growing complexities and stresses of daily living (Kamerman & Kahn, 1978). Families with children, it is argued, have dramatically changed their functions and powers, especially in their ability to raise their children unaided (Keniston, et al., 1977).

It is suggested that policies which focus on deprivation fail to recognize the unmet needs of millions of children who may not be poor or handicapped. For example, in the USA there are about 19 million children under the age of six and 31 million between the ages of six and fourteen (USDC, 1981b). Census Bureau figures indicate that almost seven million children have no known source of day care (USDC, 1976). The number of births to unmarried women has been steadily increasing for many years, with about 44 percent of these births being to adolescent women (USDC, 1981c). Many children are in homes lacking the support system and structure which traditional nuclear households are presumed to provide.

Largely as a consequence of these changes in the family lives of the nonpoor, the societal principle of nonintervention for children has been challenged by the women's movement, child development specialists, teachers, and parents' groups. Rather, it is argued that America needs a universal and developmental philosophy of care for children. It is not enough to protect children against abuse, abandonment, abject poverty, or dramatic conditions such as polio and blindness, although these activities should not be forsaken. In addition, the government has a responsibility to insure the *development* of *every* child, according to his or her potential (Steiner, 1976, 1981).

Sponseller and Fink (1980, 1982) state that there has been little commitment to rhetoric or action on behalf of the needs of *all* children. Many advocates now express the view that "services for all who need them must be the first principle for publically provided social services" (Keniston et al., 1977, p. 142). Keniston and his colleagues argue that it is in the public interest to insure that services are available without regard to the race, income, place of residence, or language of the child. Kamerman and Kahn (1978), in a review of policy in fourteen countries, cite the need for comprehensive family policy at the highest levels of government.

Universal access is also expected to have benefits for the poor. As with the public school example, universal access may stimulate equality by the very fact that the government organizes, provides, and pays for services to all in need (Keniston et al., 1977). It is contended that substituting a routine benefit for a discretionary one will obscure the dependency status, and thus the stigma for poor families (Steiner, 1981). Sponseller and Fink (1980, 1982) argue that it is the *lack* of commitment to *all* children that may put in jeopardy services to those children who are most in need. Advocating for the concept of universal entitlement, Keniston, et al., states that special programs for the poor may remain necessary, but that the long-range goal of family policy should be to include their recipients in programs that are universal (1977). Such advocates support a revised range of comprehensive and universally accessible public services to support and strengthen, not to replace, families in the rearing of their children.

Programs Approaching Universality

Despite the focus on deprivation there has gradually been an increase in the number of child-serving programs which approach universal eligibility. In terms of the *number* of programs, Keniston et al. (1977) found that seventy-five percent of the federal programs for families and children existing in 1972 were not intended primarily for the poor, and nearly 36 percent of these were completely unrestricted and meant to benefit all children and families. Even programs targeted to the "disadvantaged" often define the term broadly enough to include non-needy children and non-poor children. For example, the Appalachian Child Development Program helps all children in a disadvantaged region of the country. Chapter I (then Title I) of the Elementary and Secondary Education Act helps low-achieving students in economically deprived areas regardless of parental income. Also, ten percent of Head Start children can be non-poor. Food Stamps, too, approaches universal accessibility; the program provides a minimum floor and is not abruptly cut off when income rises above an arbitrary figure but rather tapers off gradually (Keniston et al., 1977).

Child health is another issue that has had universal applicability.

Steiner (1976) argues that when its focus is on those health issues that cut across class and race, child health generally gains a receptive ear from politicians—as in the case of mandating the use of silver nitrate to protect neonates from blindness, or in outreach programs to identify and serve crippled children. But, argues Steiner, modern preventative health medicine has sharply limited the number of child health causes that derive strength from their democratic character. Rather, immediate issues in child health— for example, medical screening for disadvantaged children—are more divisive. Indeed, there is no mechanism in place for formulating a comprehensive child health policy.

The subsidized school lunch program has become a social benefit that is almost universally available (Steiner, 1976). Federal expenditures, however, have been increasingly directed toward the children of poor families. Despite efforts by Presidents Johnson and Ford to limit benefits to the poor, many believe, as did Senator Hubert Humphrey "that every boy and girl is entitled to at least one nutritious lunch per day as they attend our schools under the laws of compulsory education" (Humphrey, 1973, p. 396). In the fall of 1983, the House of Representatives voted overwhelmingly to restore the budget reductions it had approved in the National School Lunch Act and the Child Nutrition Act in 1981 as part of President Ronald Reagan's programs. Yet, complaints about helping "well-heeled families" remain:

> Some of us Neanderthal types have a problem in justifying the school lunch and nutrition programs at all. We recollect that no such programs were operating in the pit of the depression, and we cannot recall that millions of children keeled over from rickets, spavins, or tapeworms. (Kilpatrick, 1983).

Opposition To Universal Eligibility

The notion of universal eligibility is not accepted among all child advocates. While there are legitimate needs and interest for non-poor children, there are many valid reasons for the social history of restraint and nonintervention in child and family life. First, what society has to offer children often been has not always been an improvement over the family; the history of the foster care system, for example, is lucid with examples of societal neglect and inadequate care. Second, as Steiner (1976) points out, children's minimum needs elude measurement. There is no way to monitor provision of minimum services to children in private families in the fashion that wages, hours, and occupational safety and health are monitored routinely in the private work place. Third, America's emphasis on tolerance of religious and cultural diversity lead to recognition that ethnic groups vary in their perception of "acceptable" and appropriate child-rearing practices. The literature on child abuse show examples of this.

Nathan Glazer feels that the lack of family policy may be because social programs that come about as a consequence of a weakening social structure, inevitably further weaken the social structure (Steiner, 1981). Steiner (1981) suggests that the absence of a family policy agenda may be due to the widespread deviations from the traditional model of family. Though many deplore the deviations, others applaud them, thus making it foolhardy for a politician to become involved in social manipulation.

The principle of public responsibility has evolved, but there is far from universal acceptance of this principle (Moroney, 1976). Indeed, how the government could address this "responsibility" remains ambiguous at best. As Steiner (1976, 1981) points out, child and family policy is "infinitely flexible." It can be argued that day care policy, for example, is both *pro*-family and *anti*-family. Further, there is no way to turn ideals about such policy into legislation or administrative regulation without making some judgments about specifics. Hierarchies of society priority will continue to exist. Although the debasing means-test of the English Poor Law era has faded, it is now replaced with a "needs test" as a rationing device (Moroney, 1976). Such judgments will inevitably mean that a "comprehensive, universal policy" will become selective (Steiner, 1981).

Recognizing that government cannot provide services to fill all the needs of all the nation's families, Keniston and his colleagues (1977) concede that, in practice, priority will most often be given to lower-income families. It is suggested that when services are in short supply, priority should be given to children with special developmental, emotional, or educational needs.

Priority to needy children is also more likely to receive a favorable consideration by policymakers. President Carter, when attempting to formulate family policy without regard to conditions of poverty and race, did not find it easy to break the traditional focus on the needy. Sensitive to the tradition of family privacy, a focus on deprivation is most likely to receive serious consideration because it addresses identifiable problems (Steiner, 1981).

Nevertheless, the social ecology of the United States continues to indicate that policy for children addresses personal deficits without an equally strong or concurrent recognition of the impact of social forces on individuals. Personal characteristics of children and their families are key variables used to define eligibility for public programs. Furthermore, the "floor" for eligibility appears to be dropping as the commitment to America's children becomes reduced. An immediate answer to calls for universal access also appears unlikely due to the philosophical objection that the family is the last bastion of privacy in an already overregulated and overorganized society (Steiner, 1981). Dysfunction and deficit remain the passwords which open the door to public assistance.

CHILDREN AND PUBLIC POLICY: PERSONAL AND SOCIAL ACTION

Part of the American dilemma toward children—political piety coupled with the absence of policy—is nowhere more evident than in the issue of universal benefits. There are defensible bases for providing universalistic, continuous, and developmentally-based care for all American children. Yet, in a restrictive economy it is more difficult to serve the needs of poor and needy children to whom a federal "commitment" has already been formulated.

Laosa (1983) points out that much policy affecting poor children was created during the War-on-Poverty during a time of "affluence and optimism." It was an era of rapid growth, high spirit, and excitement focused on the policy-making process as a means of solving social inequalities. Public concern about children was subsequently accompanied by an unprecedented expan-

sion in government support of social service programs and social/
behavioral science research.

This atmosphere does not exist today. Indeed, we are in a era of
restrictive growth, reflection, and skepticism about the role of
public policy in the lives of children and families. Intense ideological debates shroud the issues of child development and public
policy. Moroney (1976) observes that the historical pattern over
the past decades suggests that ideological disagreements have a
tendency to become more important in times of economic crisis.
Fundamental differences may seem relatively unimportant in an
expansionary period but tenuous consensus on issues is readily
reversed in poor economic situations. As societies are moving
from accelerated to slow growth, there has been an abrupt retrench-
ment of existing public programs and a mass alienation from big
government coupled with a resurgence of the laissez faire or
libertarian outlook (Veroff, Douvan, & Kulka, 1981). Therefore,
the sustained commitment that should be made to all children is
not evident even for those groups of children who do have primary needs and major continuing problems (Sponseller & Fink,
1980). Steiner (1976) encapsulates the history of children's policy
by simply stating that comprehensive child development legislation,
child-care centers, and child-welfare services have floundered.

In this environment, difficult choices must be made. The
Children's Defense Fund (1983a) has brilliantly drafted a Children's
Survival Bill which trades military "frills" for children's services.
Realistically, however, choices between intercontinental ballistic
missiles and food stamps are not likely to be seriously debated in
the Congress at the present time.

In such an atmosphere it seems unlikely that comprehensive
and universal benefits can be attained. Such benefits, generally
expanding services to better-educated and politically astute Americans, possibly could be enacted at the expense of the relatively
poor, politically unorganized population. Until the safety net
around the most needy of children can more adequately be secured,
universal benefits do not seem feasible.

One must recognize that cherished beliefs and ideals surround
the "deficit" orientation of child policy—an orientation that is
unlikely to be changed in a comprehensive fasion. If it was accepted

that the government should promote child development, reasonable people would have fundamental disagreements about the best way to ensure that goal. Is development enhanced by out-of-home early education? Does development require the provision of nutritionally balanced meals in a school setting? Evidence, and political muscle toward changing the traditional American principle to unregulated family life is not, in the public mind, compelling. Child development and the frequently advocated out-of-home care are not synonymous. Ideological differences between specific groups of child advocates also make agreement on specific proposals for action difficult to achieve (Sponseller & Fink, 1982).

Child advocates, parents and educators must continue to hope, and work for, the realization of a time when the United States, as the richest nation in the world, will realign its priorities in ways which would better serve the children of America. Many alternatives for children have been proposed:

First, consistent with the high value that Americans place on giving parents maximum control over how they raise their children, Keniston et al., (1977) suggest that the long term goal of the country should be to enable families themselves to choose and pay for the services they want. Second, there are many groups established for the purpose of advocacy on behalf of children. The National Black Child Development Institute since 1970 has been particularly concerned with influencing both the philosophy and orientation of programs for the poor. Similarly, The Children's Defense Fund has closely monitored the impact of federal budget cuts on children, particularly those children who are most in need.

Third, and most recently, three organizational structures have been implemented in the Congress to observe, report, and act on the status of children: The Select Committee on Children Youth and Families (authorized in February 1983); the Senate Children's Caucus (formed June 9, 1983); and the Senate Family Caucus (formed June 8, 1983).

Fourth, academic communities are also becoming increasing involved in the preparation of students for policy roles. Noted examples are the three "Bush Centers on Child and Family Policy" which offer predoctoral and professional fellowships at the University of North Carolina at Chapel Hill, The University of Michigan, and Yale University. The Society for Research in Child Development sponsors a postdoctoral Congressional Science Fellowship program which aims to bridge the gap between research and policy. The Institute for Child and Family Psychiatry in Silver Springs, Maryland, offers internships to undergraduate and graduate students to learn the practical and technical skills needed to relate to the complexities of child policy.

Fifth, public concern is also evident. A three day symposium, "America's Children Need Powerful Friends," was sponsored primarily for high-level state officials in the summer of 1983. Since 1980, several states have published reports of childhood indicators (Children's Policy Research Project, 1980, 1983; Lash, Segal, & Dudzinski, 1980).

Sixth, many groups feel that parent advocacy is the key to social programs for children. The Carnegie Council on Children argues that responsible parents must become public advocates for children's interests, and that cause must be interpreted broadly. Today, there are countless parent support groups concerned with adoption, foster care, child abuse, and drug abuse.

Whether action for children is stimulated by academicians or parents, increasingly it will be important to recognize the greater role of the state and the private sector in addressing gaps in children's needs. States do bear direct responsibility for the health and education of children. However, Robert Haggerty, President of the William T. Grant foundation, warns that states cannot fulfill this function without federal support.

For decades there has been little disagreement that the government should function as the primary social institution to protect and promote the general welfare of its members. Controversy arises when determining which policies and approaches would best achieve that goal. An overall policy need, however, is to have a realistic understanding of contemporary families rather than concepts of "the family" which are outmoded or may have never existed (Moroney, 1976).

Observers have proclaimed the twentieth century as "the century of the child" (Halsey, 1978). Indeed, reflecting this emphasis on children, 1979 was declared "The International Year Of The

Child." Despite the rhetoric, how we will reconcile our laissez-faire traditions toward children with increasing calls for comprehensive policies remains to be seen.

REFERENCES

American Public Welfare Association. (February, 1982). *Memorandum W-5. The FY 83 budget proposals for Aid to Families with Dependent Children.* Washington. D.C.: APWA.

Anderson, M. (1978). *Welfare: The political economy of welfare reform in the United States.* Stanford, CA.: Hoover Institution Press.

Bowler, M. K. (1974). *The Nixon guaranteed income proposal.* Cambridge, MA.: Ballinger.

Bronfenbrenner, U. (1975). *Influences on human development.* Hillsdale, Ill.: Dryden Press.

Caldwell, B. M. (1977). Child development and social policy. In M. Scott and S. Grimmet (Eds.), *Current issues in child development.* Washington, D.C.: National Association for the Education of Young Children.

Carter, J. (1978). A Statement in New Hampshire. *The presidential campaign, 1976, (Vol. 1).* Washington, D.C.: Government Printing Office.

Children's Defense Fund. (CDF). (1983a). *A children's defense budget: An analysis of the president's FY 1984 budget and children.* Washington, D.C.: CDF.

Children's Defense Fund. (CDF). (1983b). *Give more children a head start: It pays.* Washington, D.C.: CDF.

Children's Policy Research Project. (1980). *The state of the child.* Chicago, Ill.: The School of Social Service Administration, Univ. of Chicago.

Children's Policy Research Project. (1983). *Children of the state.* Chicago, Ill.: The School of Social Service Administration, Univ. of Chicago.

Cohen, N. E. & Connery, M. F. (1967). Government policy and the family. *Journal of Marriage and the Family, 29,* 6–17.

Condry, S. M., & Lazar, I. (1982). American values and social policy for children. In W. M. Bridgeland and E. A. Duane (Eds.), *Young children and social policy.* Beverly Hills, CA.: Sage.

Congressional Research Service. (CRS). (September 1981). *Need and payment levels in the program of Aid to Families with Dependent Children (AFDC): Legislative history and current state practices.* Report number 81-149 EPW. Washington, D.C.: CRS.

Gil, D. G. (1976). *Unravelling social policy.* Cambridge, MA.: Schenkman Publishing Company.

Greenblatt, B. (1977). *Responsibility for child care.* San Francisco, CA.: Jossey-Bass.

Halsey, A. H. (1978). *Change in Brittish society.* London: Oxford University Press.

Humphrey, H. (1973). *Federal food program — 1973, hearings before the Senate Select*

Committee on Nutrition and Human Needs, Washington, D.C.: Government Printing Office.

Johnson, L. B. (1967). To fulfill these rights, Howard University, June 4, 1965. In L. Rainwater & W. L. Yancy (Eds.), *The Moynihan report and the politics of controversy* Cambridge, MA.: M.I.T. Press.

Kamerman, S. B., & Kahn, A. J. (Eds.). (1978). *Family policy: Government and families in fourteen countries.* New York: Columbia Univ. Press.

Keniston, K., & The Carnegie Council on Children. (1977). *All our children: The American family under pressure.* New York: Harcourt, Brace, Jovanovich.

Kilpatrick, J. J. (1983, November 22). Even well-heeled children helped by school lunches. *Durham Morning Herald.*

Koldin, L. C. (1971). *The welfare crisis.* New York: Exposition Press.

Laosa, L. M. (in press). Social policies toward children of diverse ethnic, racial and language groups in the United States. In H. W. Stevenson and A. E. Siegel (Eds.)., *Child development and social policy,* Univ. of Chicago Press.

Lash, T., Segal, H., & Dudzinski, D. (1980). *The state of the child: New York City II.* New York: Foundation for Child Development.

Mandell, B. R. (Ed.). (1975). *Welfare in America.* Englewood Cliffs, N.J.: Prentice-Hall Inc.

Moroney, R. M. (1976). *The family and the state.* New York: Longman Group Limited.

Moynihan, D. P. (1973). *The politics of a guaranteed income.* New York: Random House.

Nixon, R. (1971, December 9). *Veto message,* as reported in the Public Papers for 1972, pp. 1174–87.

Rivlin, A. M., & Timpane, P. M. (Eds.). (1975). *Planned variation in education.* Washington, D.C.: Brookings Institution.

Sponseller, D. B., & Fink, J. S. (February 1980). Early childhood education: A national profile of early childhood educators' views. *Education and urban society, 12*(2), pp. 163–173.

Sponseller, D. B., & Fink, J. S. (1982). Public policy toward children: Identifying the problems. In W. M. Bridgeland & E. A. Duane (Eds.), *Young children and social policy.* Beverly Hills, CA.: Sage.

Steiner, G. Y. (1976). *The children's cause.* Washington, D.C.: The Brookings Institution.

Steiner, G. Y. (1981). *The futility of family policy* Washington, D.C.: The Brookings Institution.

U.S. Department of Commerce. Bureau of the Census. (USDC). (October 1976). *Current population reports, Series P-20, No. 198, Daytime care of children: October 1974 and February 1975.* Table 1. Calculations by Children's Defense Fund. Washington, D.C. Government Printing Office.

U.S. Department of Commerce. Bureau of the Census. (USDC). (August 1981a). *Current population reports, Series P-60, No. 127, Money income and poverty status of families and persons in the United States: 1980 (Advance data from the March 1981 Current Population Survey)* Washington, D.C.: Government Printing Office

U.S. Department of Commerce. Bureau of the Census. (USDC). (October 1981b). *Current population reports, Series P-20, No. 365, Marital status and living arrangements: May 1980.* Washington, D.C.: Government Printing Office.

U.S. Department of Commerce. Bureau of the Census, (USDC). (1981c). *Statistical abstract of the United States 1981,* Washington, D.C.: Government Printing Office.

U.S. Department of Housing and Urban Development. (USDH). Office of Policy Research and Development. (August 1980). *Housing our families,* Washington, D.C.: Government Printing Office, p. 52.

U.S. Department of Labor. (USDL). Employment and Training Administration. (1980). *Employment and training report of the President 1980, Table G-9.* Washington, D.C.: Government Printing Office.

U.S. House of Representatives, Subcommittee on Oversight of the Committee on Ways and Means, and Subcommittee on Health and the Environment of the Committee on Energy and Commerce, (March 3, 1982). *Impact of budget cuts on children.* Washington, D.C.: Government Printing Office.

Veroff, J., Douvan, E., & Kulka, R. A. (1981). *The inner American: A self portrait from 1957 to 1976.* New York: Basic Books.

Verr, V. (1973). One step forward—two steps back: Child care's long American history. In P. Roby (Ed.), *Child care: Who cares?* (pp. 157–171). New York: Basic Books.

PART III

IMPLICATIONS AND CONCLUSIONS

CHAPTER 11

EVALUATING THE ECOLOGY
OF THE YOUNG CHILD:
INTERNAL AND EXTERNAL ENVIRONMENTS

CAVEN S. MCLOUGHLIN

E legant research designs are prerequisites for investigations in modern social science to be considered exemplary or simply acceptable. Yet the rigor available in educational and psychological research is typically a poor cousin to that expected, available and required by the physical sciences. Where child developmentalists have attempted to emulate these strict experimental methodologies, some perhaps to gain a credibility as quasi "hard" scientists, all too frequently the context in which the results were gained has been ephemeral, artificial, unlikely or unfamiliar, or otherwise contrived. This statement should not be construed as mocking those attempts at empirical investigation of a complex and dynamic arena, it is simply that some matters are "knowable" only in the context in which they occur. Where that context is changed, even if only subtly or slightly by the manner of the investigator, then although the results can be reliable they may be invalid.

Urie Bronfenbrenner (1977) made this point forcefully by stating that the majority of contemporary research in child and developmental psychology was involved in "the science of the strange behavior of children in strange situations with strange adults for the briefest possible periods of time" (p. 513). For this chapter, which deals with the evaluation of *the child, the child's context*, and the *child-in-context*, a fundamental point is that this task of evaluation cannot be done with any assurances of validity without considering the corollary of Bronfenbrenner's thesis.

The corollary is that the strange behaviors of children (or for that matter the behavior of *strange* children) simply cannot be considered as typical or usual for children in general. Equally, the setting in which the behavior is recorded and the stimuli to which the child is reacting are also of concern to anyone who wishes to understand fully the child's behavior. Without a recognition of these variables the contextual meaning of the child's behavior is uncertain. It is generally well accepted that:

> Most developmental research has little to say about children and their daily lives.... American developmental psychology ... has tended to emphasize laboratory studies in which the child performs an unfamiliar task in a strange situation with a strange adult. It has tended to neglect the study of social settings in which children live and the persons who are central to them emotionally. (Skolnick, 1975, 52–53)

If the dilemma must be one of choice between rigor or relevance, for this chapter the costs associated with extreme rigor must take a second place to the benefits of relevance (to use Bronfenbrenner's, [1977] terminology). There is little benefit in knowing with absolute and finely detailed accuracy something of marginal import. For this reason the admittedly blunt tools of evaluation will here be sharpened on the whetstone of reality.

As to the matter of why studies of child development involving observational methodologies are the least typical and possibly least favored (in terms of their incidence in prestigious periodicals; Larson 1975), a cynic might retort that it is because they are so difficult to complete and evaluate. To this end the second theme of this chapter is more of an acknowledgement than a focus: whereas it is possible to gather evaluation data in a brief period, its value is generally directly proportional to the care and effort involved in the gathering.

Notwithstanding that in actuality the *preferred* is often a compromise for the *ideal*, a third theme of this chapter is that optimally the examiner should cause as little change as is possible to the behaviors which are the focus of the data collection. The purpose of the evaluation is to learn something of the target child, and not of the individual who gathered the information.

INTERNAL AND EXTERNAL ENVIRONMENTS

To recognize the meaning of a child's particular behavioral repertoire requires more than simply considering in isolation the *child* and the *behavior in action*. It demands that the child's internal and external environments be evaluated, and that the interplay between these forces be assessed. External environments include the total social context in which the child's significant others are functioning. Thus, to a degree the examiner must feel and act as a social, economic, psychological, educational and even political investigator for the child and the child's immediate context. Assessment is most appropriately conceived as "the process of understanding the performance of (children) in their current ecology" (Salvia & Ysseldyke, 1978, p. 4).

Understanding the child's internal environment also means knowing something of the physiology and anatomy of the human condition. How can an examiner recognize the significance of lassitude and apathy if unable to recognize the symptoms of acute fatigue brought about by chronic ill health? For example, the examiner who knows nothing of the incidence and prevalence of middle-ear and upper respiratory tract infections in children from particular social settings, will miss the significance of some children's "I don't know" answers, and apparent disinterest upon questioning.

In a similar way the pervasive effects of social class differences (the most well known and all encompassing of external environments) have a clear impact on the child's general and specific levels of functioning. It is well established, for example, that lower socioeconomic status is generally associated with reduced scores on measures of language ability (Arnold & Reed, 1976; Johnson, 1974). External environment refers to the surround in which the child is developing, and it is the assessment of this mutual interdependency or adaptation between child and surroundings which is the tenuous element which needs to be captured. Brim (1975) located in model form one notion of the child's environment. He typified the environment as being a nested arrangement of micro-, meso-, and macro-systems.

The micro-structure refers to the immediate setting of the child, including those who care for the child. The meso-setting refers to societal agencies and programs that function at the community level, as well as informal social networks and relationships.

The macro-setting relates to the encompassing cultural milieu in which the child is geographically, socially, and politically located. This latter element also includes the means of transmission of information and beliefs across generations. Many traditional child examiners shy away from looking evaluatively at social policies, cultural thrusts, political influences and similar "subjective" criteria. Yet, to fully understand the child's perspectives, possibilities and existence requires a sensitivity for such forces. This awareness makes the difference between a simplistic individual analysis of the child, and a more comprehensive and dynamic consideration of the child in all contexts.

The child is in continual and creative adaptation with the environment. This process is dynamic, progressive and evolving. At any one time the observations of a child are gathered as if taken from a single frame excised from a length of movie film. The standard adage is that data collected on a child as the result of an examination are valid descriptors *only* for that particular slice of examination time. Clearly, this is a pertinent reminder for all involved in evaluation. However, it misses the main point of evaluation, which is involved less in the gathering of "historically" relevant information, and is more related to the creation of predictive and prognostic statements.

It is, of course, most important to keep accurate records. However, the archival purpose of child evaluation, typically involving report preparation or record keeping, is one of the least important functions for serving the diagnostic or prescriptive needs of the child. Rather, preparing reports is usually done to meet the needs of investigator to prepare a child-*description*. Even those child reports which were designed exclusively as archival records have a responsibility to anticipate the child's future. The sole legitimate justification for evaluating young children is the intention of providing remediation for any discovered deficits (Keogh & Becker, 1973).

Prior to evaluating young children there are numerous evaluation-related issues that need consideration, whether *direct* (eg. What is the earliest age for measuring skill-mastery with an acceptable level of predictive validity?) or *indirect* (eg. Should pre-kindergarteners ever be tested on "academic" content?). Procedural matters are intimately involved in such questions (eg. Can strangers-as-examiners ever be efficient examiners? Where should examinations occur? Can instruments custom-designed by the examiner ever approach the psychometric standards of those published?). Such practical matters have all been cited as sources of potential test violation (Kiernan & Du Bose, 1974; Mcloughlin, 1983; Simmeonsson, Huntington, & Parse, 1980). Answers to the questions implicit in these concerns generally rely on an analysis of the psychometric properties of the evaluation device or procedure, in addition to considering the cost-effectiveness of the enterprise. At this point the psychometric properties and some related problems of any assessment format will be discussed.

ERROR, RELIABILITY, VALIDITY AND BIAS

A brief consideration is appropriate of some basic concepts relevant to anyone involved in measurement and evaluation. Whether one is administering a "standardized test" or gathering anecdotal observations from a third-party, the issues of reliability and validity are central. The results of any test (and for this purpose a test will be considered as *any* form of data gathering) are only a sample of the domain of experiences, deficits and attributes of a child. Thus, the evaluation of results must take into account the degree to which the sample of behavior or persons (or both) reflects reality.

Whereas the statistical computation of error estimates is beyond the scope of this chapter, a consideration of the concept is central. The amount of error in a test score relates to the degree of discrepancy between what is measured and the true score or reality. Thus, error deals with the relative reliability or accuracy of the data gathering. Error is inevitable, for we can never evaluate the sum total of a child's experiences. The point is that if error is inevitably present we must have as accurately as possible an estimate of its impact.

Reliability refers to the extent to which a measure is free from random error, and the consistency that a test measures a given attribute or behavior. To be perfectly reliable a test would need to produce exactly the same result every time that it measures a particular variable. Any score consists of two elements: the random, which reflects chance events, and the systematic. Methods for creating an estimate of the reliability of a measure typically involve the study of the consistency of scores (or observations) on a single occasion, or their stability over two or more occasions. Two types of reliability are typically cited: *test-retest* and *inter-examiner.*

Test-retest reliability refers to the stability that test scores have over time. This means, for example, the amount of fluctuation that is noticed between two administrations of a single test two weeks apart. It does, however, assume that there is no reason to attribute any observed changes that are noticed either to the child's increased learning that came solely from the earlier test administration, or to any other intervening instruction. Inter-examiner reliability indices are derived from a comparison of scores obtained from alternative evaluators. At its simplest this gives a measure of the degree to which characteristics of the examiners' or test-scorers' themselves have affected results. This sort of reliability is of crucial importance for those instruments that demand observation and categorization of child-behaviors by an adult. Those responses that are recorded may be extremely idiosyncratic to a particular observer, and may tell more about the biases of the observer (intended or not), than of the child. Inter-examiner reliability is also relevant for determining how much the presence or even the demeanour of the examiner contributes to the child's test scores (McCauley & Swisher, 1984).

Validity, which was first conceptualized psychometrically by Binet and Henri (1895, 1896), relates to the extent to which a test measures what it purports to measure—that is, the degree to which the results are supported or justified by evidence. A test is valid only to the degree that it does that job accurately. If performance on a test of one skill is concurrently influenced by another ability then the test's validity for its intended purpose is compromised. So, validity is not an absolute quality independent of the intended function. A handyman analogy on the use of another sort of tool might be that whereas a chisel *can* be used to drive a screw into wood, a purpose-made screwdriver will do the job with a better finish, and the screw will more likely appear in the intended position. Test validity is an embedded characteristic, there is nothing a user can do to enhance the validity of a test once it has been constructed.

While reliability is concerned with the precision of a procedure, validity refers to what the test measures, and not how well the procedure makes that assessment. Reliability of results enters only indirectly into the evaluation and determination of validity. However, while a necessary component, reliability is an insufficient condition to establish validity (Reynolds, 1983). Support for the validity of a measure has traditionally been gathered from the perspectives of criterion, content, and construct.

Criterion validity relates to a test's use as a predictor of criterion performance (Anastasi, 1982). The examination of this feature involves collecting empirical evidence that test scores are related to some other measure of the target behavior. Bias in this case would refer to an inaccuracy in predicting, for example, academic achievement based on a preschool child's knowledge of color names. Generally, two forms of criterion validity are considered important: *concurrent* and *predictive* validities. The concurrent type is determined by assessing how close a child's score relates to a criterion measure that is taken at about the same time. For example, comparing a child's age score on a test of expressive language with a developmental psychologist's judgment would constitute a measure of concurrent validity. The assumption, then, is that the test is measuring the same attributes as the expert judge. The predictive validity of an instrument is assessed by the degree to which a young child's score on a test can be used to predict future performance.

Where a test is used to evaluate a child's performance in a specified content area, then the test's capacity to sample from the total domain is of concern. This issue is one of content validation. Usually someone with particular expertise in the target behavior examines the characteristics and coverage of individual items and their total complement.

Construct validity is applicable when test scores are used to typify a child's relation to a hypothesized characteristic or theoretical construct; at issue is the degree to which the score represents the construct. This latter form of validity is of overiding importance, and recent discussions have proposed that all other validities should be made subordinate to construct validity (Cronbach, 1980; Messick, 1975, 1980).

Matters of bias are fundamentally matters of validity. Yet, even for those instrumentations with established forms of validity, some test critics suggest that any procedures supporting biological determinism (for example, those which evidence ability differences between racial groups, or those which draw attention to the deficits of handicapped persons) should be outlawed (cf. Jensen, 1980). Whether or not democratically correct, this is scientifically unacceptable; for, science studiously attempts to avoid predisposing results. Predeigning the outcome of an investigation is the real nature of bias.

Validity relates to the soundness of all the possible interpretations for the results of a test (Cronbach, 1971). Where differences in scores exist between individuals, the bias-question concerns whether these differences accurately reflect *actual* variations in the characteristics being evaluated. A synonym for the term valid is *accurate,* and the antonym is *biased.*

The possibility of bias in evaluation has, in the last two decades, become of interest not only to scholars and test publishers but also to the legal community (Cole, 1981; Bersoff, 1981; Reschly, 1983). Bias does not have to be intentional for it to trigger litigation, and simply that there was no premeditation is not cause for us to be less concerned. Legal scrutiny, inevitably, has made everyone more sensitive to both social and scientific concerns over testing (Cronbach, 1975; Haney, 1981; Mcloughlin & Koh, 1982). This is particularly true for the issue of testing linguistic minorities. Litigation which began with *Hobson v. Hansen* in 1969, and latterly culminated in the contradictory decisions of *Larry P. v. Riles* (1979) and *PASE v. Hannon* (1981), has focused on condemning those classificatory means which have used group assessment to track less able children. Such tracks have almost always been found to encompass a greater proportion of ethnic minority children than their actual number would suggest, and this has been reason for challenge. Initially it was the *content* of the education in these tracks which was the focus of litigation, more recently it has been the tests used to place the children in these educational "dead-ends" that have been of concern (*Larry P. v. Riles,* 1979).

PROBLEMS AND PROCEDURES
IN ASSESSING YOUNG CHILDREN

The criteria of reliability and validity are pertinent to the measurement of all populations, however the evaluation of young children brings particular problems to the accuracy and meaning of the obtained information. This is particularly apposite when assessing young children with handicapping conditions. It is to these issues that this section will be addressed.

Young children are *generally* difficult to evaluate. They require particularly careful establishment of rapport prior to testing, and some care as to the order of test administration. For example, it is rarely appropriate to begin with test content that requires high verbal performance. This will probably cause greater anxiety (and raise the likelihood of refusal), than an "action" or nonverbal test. The younger the child, the greater will be the effect of the child's age upon test performance (Graham & Berman, 1961).

Young children's level of cooperation reflects their limited social skills. Their concentration span can be severely restricted and often they do not have well developed verbal abilities. Coincidentally, the young child may not recognize the peculiar social expectation that the examinee is expected to acquiesce to the demands of the examiner! Thus, those who have attempted to evaluate a young child outside of the caretaker's presence have all too often found themselves learning more of the child's crying or distress repertoire than they had bargained for.

Not surprisingly, in the pursuit of both accuracy and convenience, the evaluation methods-of-choice have become observational approaches, checklists, work sample reviews, play techniques and questioning caretakers through rating forms. Since children's behavior can be highly variable from moment to moment (Vane & Motta, 1978), it is this which makes indirect rating measures preferable to those taken directly. Such information usually includes a wide range of developmental milestones summarized on informal checklists. For example, questionnaires have been constructed to assess parental desires, aspirations and expectations; measure satisfaction with existing services, and obtain parents' estimates of their children's developmental functioning, with or without a comparative reference point.

There is particular concern that young children not be labelled (Hobbs, 1975). In part, the reticence for making prognostications on infants has focused on infant tests' poor predictive levels. This, in turn, may be attributed to an overuse of norm referenced scales to the virtual exclusion of criterion referenced instruments (cf. Brown & Mcguire, 1976). However, even the criticism that traditional scales are poor predictors of later intellectual functioning (eg. Bayley, 1970; Honzik, 1976; Lewis, 1973; Stott & Ball, 1965; Yang & Bell, 1975) itself has been empirically questioned (Illingworth, 1970; Knobloch & Pasamanick, 1974). What may confidently be stated is that norm-referenced developmental scales are certainly reliable monitors of current child functioning (MacTurk & Neisworth, 1978), and particularly so for developmentally delayed youngsters (Bagnato & Neisworth, 1979, 1980; Bricker & Bricker, 1973; Du Bose, 1977, 1981a, 1981b).

The greater the degree of corroboration by informants from the widest variety of possible settings, the better will be the data pool (Cross, 1977; Frankel, 1979; Honzik, 1976). Yet, the credibility of parent reports is generally and *wrongly* considered severely suspect by professionals (Mcloughlin, 1981), who themselves judge parents' expectations about their child's performance as likely to be inflated. While this latter determination is generally correct (for parents typically are optimistic about their children's skills), it should remind that if a parent thinks that there is a problem then their worry merits serious consideration. Professionals' information and opinions tend to be overrepresented in the accumulated data pool. It is the professional who typically records progress in norm terms, while the parent makes progress statements in the form "he can do this now, though he couldn't do it a month ago." This is a clear example of a criterion referenced statement. With parents and professionals using different yardsticks to measure the same performance, albeit the performance of the *same* child, there is little wonder that both can come to differing conclusions.

Norm-referenced instruments compare the child's performance

with that of comparable others'. While these approaches are measures of *inter-individual* differences, criterion referenced measurement deals with *intra-individual* differences—a comparison of a specific attribute of the child with the child's own total repertoire, or profile (Hambleton, Swaminathan, Algina, & Coulson, 1978). By comparison to norm referenced measurement, criterion measurement has a brief history of about two decades, and is generally traced to papers by Glaser (1963), and Popham and Husek (1969). A third source of information on a child's functioning has to do with comparing the child's performance on one occasion in one setting, with the child's later performance, either in the same or in a different setting. Regardless of the apparent stability and integrity of a single measure, Goodwin and Driscoll (1980) state that only with supplementary information from many sources can the picture be complete. Whatever is the relative individual utility of these various approaches it is generally agreed that the most advanced designs involve collection with multiple measures across several settings (Airasian, 1974; Hamilton & Swan, 1981).

SELECTING THE MEASUREMENT REFERENCE

The appropriate antecedent to evaluation is a determination of the purposes of the endeavor. Assessment, typically, has one or two purposes: identification for placement, and planning for intervention (Coulter & Morrow, 1978). For the former, selected normative-standardized and criterion-referenced tests are generally appropriate, for the latter the measures will likely reflect those behaviors and concepts which are targetted during programming. Such instruments are generally criteria or objectives referenced.

In order to determine which of the alternatives: norm-reference, criterion reference, or child-performance, is most appropriate for the common forms of child appraisal, one needs to consider the various possible matches. The typical measurement purposes for meeting the needs of young children include: Screening, Diagnosis, Instruction, and Program Evaluation. These purposes and the preferred evaluation mode for each will be considered in turn.

Screening: When constructing a device to identify a child's eligibility for an intervention program the typical comparison is with the performance of others on the same measure—normative comparisons. In this case the relative position of the child is made evident from the scores of others'. The task of screening is to evaluate whether there is a practically significant discrepancy, between the obtained score and the expected score, to warrant further investigation. Most screening devices are simply compendia of samples of critical developmental behaviors. A lack of a significant number of these behaviors, either in the child's spontaneous form or when prompted, is taken to signify a significant deficit.

Due to the time consuming alternative of individual assessment, which will typically require an investment of eight hours of a professional's time, screening is often the approach-of-choice. Notwithstanding the convenience of the indirect approach of group administered measurement, there are few redeeming features for the group assessment of children younger than six years (that is, excepting ease of data collection), for until that age children do not develop the application necessary to perform optimally. Virtually all available individual and group screening tests may be reviewed in Buros' *Mental Measurement Yearbooks* and *Tests in Print* (1974, 1978). The efficacy of screening measurement may further be investigated in Gerken (1979), Kaufman and Kaufman (1977), Reynolds (1979, 1981) and Stangler, Huber and Routh (1980).

Screening alone should never be sufficient to warrant a child's inclusion in any special program. Screening is solely a measure of *quantity* of discrepancy, it tells nothing of the *qualities* of any shortcoming. An in-depth analysis of the deficits will always be required prior to beginning an intervention; for, prescription is never possible from the outcome of a true screening test. Screening can be comprehensive, in exactly the same way that diagnostic-prescriptive testing can be comprehensive. Yet, whereas diagnosis focuses on depth, screening has as its goal, breadth.

The validity of a screening device relates to its ability to correctly identify children in need (Reese, Howard & Reese, 1978). Of course, it is always preferable to have an instrument which slightly *overincludes* at each cutoff score, since it is preferable to find out in subsequent evaluation that a child was incorrectly considered at-risk, than it is to miss a child who is in actual need. The possible outcomes of screening can be depicted as a matrix which contrasts the actual incidence of a handicapping condition with the screening instrument's determination. The four options are depicted in Figure 1. The proportion of hits to false-alarms is determined by the cut-off criterion. A high cutoff results in a high number of false-alarms (i.e., overinclusion of children whose "screening" says they are handicapped when in fact they are not). A conservative cutoff criterion limits the number of "misses" (i.e., children who are assumed non-handicapped but who actually are).

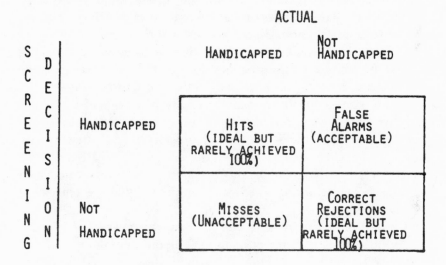

Figure 11-1. The Screening Matrix.

Diagnosis: Hamilton and Swan (1981) describe a three Phase model for the the diagnostic process. In phase One there is verification that the screening procedure correctly identified the child as in need of intervention, and a norm-referenced determination of the child's abilities and aptitudes in multiple domains. Additional measures, some taken across varying contextual settings, may involve informal reference to the child's levels of psychosocial skill functioning. Phase Two incorporates a specific focusing, through criterion-referenced evaluation, of those areas of functioning previously found deserving of attention. Finally, "the diagnostic process aims at determining what the child can and cannot do within very specific skill areas" (p. 45) constitutes Phase Three.

The direction of investigation at each juncture is from the general to the specific. For example, in Phase One the investigator might be interested in the child's general accomplishments with respect to communication. Whereas in Phase Two the child's *receptive* and *expressive* language skills might be of concern. In the final Phase the child's ability to discriminate letters in an alphabet sequence could be the diagnostic target.

Instruction: Measurement within the instructional phase of an intervention has as its task a determination of the on-going efficacy of the instruction. Since the instructor's responsibility is to move the child to a superior level of functioning, any tracking procedure which enhances the monitoring of increased competency or mastery, increases the efficiency of the instruction. Yet, whereas in prior stages the measurement has been *directly* of the child, in this latter stage all measurement is *indirect*. It focuses on testing which of the instructional objectives have successfully been accomplished. Criterial methods are most typically incorporated for this purpose, but rarely are they more sophisticated than simple checklists noting whether or not the task has been mastered by the child.

Child-referenced measurement is used whenever there is intra-individual investigation across time. The most common example is pre- and post-testing of the child, that is, testing the child before and after a specific unit of instruction. Here the focus is upon the target child, yet it is a measure of mastery which implicates confounding variables. Both the child's ability to learn and the capacity of the material to teach is being questioned.

There are numerous objections forwarded by those, particularly professionals in education, who see pragmatic problems with merging evaluation into instruction. Teachers complain frequently that instruction is their primary concern, and state that observation and regular data collection is difficult (if not impossible) within the classroom. While the sentiment is understandable, this comment must be considered educationally illogical and invalid. The very hallmark of efficient instruction is that it is built upon feedback of results to the instructor. Kozloff (1971) reviewed some of these objections and offered counterarguments. Without observation and the measurement of behavior, instruction cannot be effective in producing learning (Halle & Sindelar, 1982).

Teachers who terminate the process of evaluation following the administration and analysis of an assessment instrument have an incomplete measure of a child's functioning. Clearly, evaluation is essential to, and inseparable from, effective instructional intervention. Once an instructional program has been prescribed on the basis of an evaluation, then it is important to regularly continue measuring so that instructional progress can be monitored and changes incorporated into the program as necessary.

Program Evaluation: The fourth level of interest to those involved in measuring the performance of young children involves judging the merit of combinations of instruction, which we typically know as a "program." Since often the program is simply a compilation of related instructional material and experience, which individually and corporately aim to advance the child, there are clear parallels between "instructional" and "programmatic" evaluation. Whether the child (or a group of children) is to be compared with comparator-samples, or whether the programmatic gains are being matched against those from an alternative regime, the prime concern is the validity of the chosen benchmark. It is, unfortunately, all too easy to set up a "straw-man" index as a comparison in a biased attempt to display an alleged "superiority" for a particular program or intervention.

Program evaluation is reasonably considered a functional responsibility of administrators, but should equally be assumed by those who implement the procedures, whether preschool teachers or parents. Research on preschool ecologies has investigated both regular (Wachs, 1979) and special-class settings (Krantz & Risley, 1977; Olds, 1979; Rogers-Warren & Wedel, 1980) through both program and environmental evaluation. Yet, it is a sad indictment of the paucity (and the "armchair" nature) of research about classroom design that Rogers-Warren could write in 1982:

Environmental arrangement has a rich folklore of common-sense suggestions shared formally (in textbooks) and informally through generations of teachers. Many of these suggestions are excellent; however, few are data based. (p. 21)

AN HISTORICAL PERSPECTIVE ON
INFANT AND PRESCHOOLER ASSESSMENT

The previous quotation reminds us that there is a generated heritage even to the assessment of young children. Since the *modern* history of psychometry is so relatively brief some mention of its development will be given here.

There were formal examinations for governmental officers in China as early as 1115 B.C. They were sensitive even then to the needs for test objectivity, subject and examiner anonymity, controlled and uniform testing conditions, and score rank ordering (see Du Bois, 1966; Kelley & Surbeck, 1983). It was not until the mid nineteenth century (A.D !) that the Western world became involved in psychometry (see Goodenough, 1949). For example, it was 1890 when Cattell first coined the term "mental tests." The modern intelligence testing movement, which is generally credited to the work of Francis Galton (1869, 1883) in England, and which developed both in continental Europe and in the USA, evolved from investigations of normal children's behavioral repertoires. Thus was the developmental scale born.

Over the last century—almost the total history of modern psychometry—numerous scales have been developed. Some of the most important landmarks are noted in Appendix A. The earliest modern developmental scale on record, and one apparently unknown to test developers who immediately followed (Garwood, 1982), was prepared by Dr. S. E. Chaille, a physician at the Tulane University Medical School. Eighteen years prior to the publication of Chaille's work (*Infants: Their Chronological Process;* 1877), Charles Darwin's famous evolutionary treatise (*The Origin of the Species,* 1859) was published. However, it was most probably Darwin's *Expression of the Emotions in Man and Animals* (1872) which caught Chaille's particular interest, wrath and scorn; for this later work intimated that the early behaviors of young children might offer clarification on the ontogenesis of human development. Apparently Chaille wished to counter Darwin's thesis and assert the impact of

environment upon development, by his descriptions of "the progress which should be expected of the average baby" (p. 894).

Chaille demonstrated that he was alert to the problems of prog-
nosticating from a less than representative data base: "I have
attempted to record specially the average baby only, and not the
exceptional one" (p. 855). The first baby biographies, aimed at
both popular and scholarly audiences, attempted to chart the
typical sequences of early development (eg. Darwin, 1877; Preyer,
1882; Shinn, 1900; Stern, 1914; discussed in greater detail by Kelley
& Surbeck, 1983). This was a major shift from the immediate
earlier foci of attention on the patently atypical (eg. Esquirol,
1838; Seguin, 1866).

It was the 30 item scale developed by Alfred Binet and Theodore
Simon in their native French language (1905; second edition,
1908) which first incorporated an order-of-difficulty arrangement.
Yet, not until Terman (1916) published the the Stanford version of
the Binet test following the translations of Goddard (1908, 1910),
did that test and the term "intelligence quotient" become widely
used. Kuhlmann (1914) attended to the assessment of young children in a limited way, yet it was a few years until the preschool
child was more fully considered (Burt, 1921; Yerkes & Foster, 1923).

From 1916 the pediatrician Arnold Gesell at the Yale Clinic of
Child Development was involved in measuring the developmental growth of normal preschoolers and in developing the first
multi-domain maturational sequence of normal development
(Gesell, 1925, 1928) Subsequent incorporation of his item pool by
other test-authors has been sufficiently frequent for Gesell's work
now to be considered the benchmark against which measures are
compared.

From the earliest days of psychometry to contemporary times
the purposes for testing have encompassed the charting of individual differences. Whether these differences have been noted between
individuals or between groups the essence has been the same,
noting the *relative* standing of individuals. Oftentimes these differences have been measured against a common denominator relative
to the group, which we have come to term the "norm." In all cases
the task of determining intra- or inter-individual differences results
in some persons (or in the case of intra-individual differences, some

skills) being determined as inferior and some as superior. It is the matter of discrimination which is the topic of the following section.

DISCRIMINATION: THE TASK OF THE TEST

Standardized tests are becoming increasingly popular devices to determine the effectiveness of instructional programs partly as a result of moves towards professional "accountability." Yet, standardized tests have long been used as indices of intellectual and achievement performance of children. Since the advent of federal legislation (eg. PL 94-142) to determine children's eligibility for special educational services *on the basis of their performance on standardized tests' results* there has been increased momentum for testing with norm-based standardized instruments. Guidelines which specify acceptable standardization procedures and reliability and validity levels, have been prepared by joint committees of the American Psychological Association, the American Educational Research Association and the National Council on Measurement in Education (*Standards for Educational and Psychological Tests*, 1974). A revised set of these guidelines, which are anticipated to be rather more stringent than previously, are expected to be published in 1985.

Tests are intentionally created to be discriminatory devices. This is an outcome of any procedure which plans to identify which members of a group have mastered a set of skills. Thus, it is an educationally illogical stance to suggest that tests should *not* be used *because* they are discriminatory. However, particular tests or content items are inappropriate for some of the uses to which they are put. For example, responses may be required that are inconsistent with the goals of instruction, or the test may appear to be tapping one domain while in fact it produces an estimate of skills or attributes from another. In both of these cases the test is inappropriate, but nevertheless it may be adequately standardized. Even a test which has been scrupulously standardized may lead to consistently poorer results from an identifiable subgroup of the population. This is not necessarily prima facie evidence for the invalidity of a test (although it may demonstrate invalidity for the purpose then being used). The relatively poorer outcome may in fact (and psychometrically *should*) be an actual reflection of skill-differences across groups.

With care, standardized instruments can be sophisticated vehicles for better understanding a child and the impact that instruction has upon the child's development. All tools are open to abuse whether intentionally or inadvertently misused. Thus, there are cautions and limitations to be considered in any discussion of testing devices. At several points in this chapter a suggestion has been offered that the instructor continue gathering progress reports during the course of the prescribed intervention. However, most standardized tests do not easily lend themselves as repeated measures. This is because children can become "test-wise" about the specific content. Test protocols are simply *samples* of the domain that is being tested. Unless there are equivalent alternative forms it may be impossible to administer the same test on multiple occasions within a relatively brief time-frame.

The results of an evaluation need to be understood in the dual contexts of the assessment situation and the child's other characteristics (Ramey, Campbell & Wasik, 1982). Children should not, and are not, adequately described solely on the basis of a test's global standard score. This is true regardless of the psychometric properties of the selected instrument. Additionally, these scores are essentially measures of an *outcome* (the "what"), whereas the educator might prefer information on the *process* (the "how") used by a child. While outcome variables may be important indices for noting the efficiency of a child's processing, generally they shed little understanding on the particular way that a child arrived at an answer (Lahey, Vosk, & Habif, 1981).

Developmental scales have a long history (see Appendix A) and clearly established utility in describing the status of the normally developing child. However, there are problems in transferring this information to an understanding of developmentally delayed children. Although a particular test may originally have been intended to be used as a norm referenced measure it might be used as an index of criterial functioning instead. This is particularly so for those tests where an author gathered a compendium of developmental milestones, then validated the order of the items, and finally collected evidence of when children typically master those skills. In fact, such an instrument is often most appropriately thought of as a normed and empirically validated criterial measure. Such a combination may, in fact, reflect the best of the worlds of criterion and norm-referenced measurement.

DOMAIN EVALUATIONS

Of specific importance in domain evaluation for young children are: sensory integrity; intellectual or cognitive functioning; language; social, emotional and adaptive behavior; and, motor ability (including gross and fine control, and perceptuo-motor abilities). Each of these domains will be considered in turn with a brief overview of some pertinent measurement issues. What follows will be a necessarily brief overview of some pertinent but very selected measurement issues.

Sensory Integrity. In its technical meaning, sensation is the capacity to experience stimulation through the sense organs. Clearly, any abberation in development of the sense organ (generally occuring during fetal development) or injury at any time to the relevant sensory system, can make the sense associated with that organ nonfunctional. Damage to the nervous system, specifically the neural pathways which transmit the message for higher-level interpretation or "perception," can result in a perfectly healthy sense organ which is rendered nonfunctional due to the lack of a linkage with the central nervous system (CNS). For example, the child's ear mechanism may be totally undamaged and fully capable of receiving messages from the environment, yet damage to the auditory nerve pathways causes the child to be thought of as profoundly deaf.

Whether the deficit is in the receptor or expressor organ, or whether in the afferent (*to* the CNS) or efferent (*from* the CNS) neural pathway, the outcome may appear exactly the same—a dysfunctional (inefficient rather than absent) recognition of sensory stimuli. Since information provided by outcome data cannot diagnose with any degree of confidence the cause of the sensory deficit, then the task of evaluation becomes especially complex. Few sensory deficits can be confidently diagnosed by educators alone or without the confirmatory assistance of other relevant professionals, who may include medical doctors, speech pathologists, audiologists, and opthalmologists.

Diagnosis brings one set of problems. Following diagnosis comes another task which is at least as problematical, that of prescription. Sensory deficits generally cannot entirely be remediated, in that only rarely can they be cured. However, palliative measures such as prescription hearing and vision aids, often have enabled those with sensory dysfunctions to become more efficient in recognizing sensory stimuli. Truly nonfunctional systems only rarely are open to remediation, despite the advances of modern medical science.

What is not conveyed by a developmental scale is the peculiar portfolio of disabilities for the child handicapped by hearing impairment or deafness, or by partial sight or blindness. Examiners must be sensitive to the need for improvising on standard evaluation procedures so as to avoid penalizing the sensorially impaired child. There is nothing to be gained by steadfastly retaining test-integrity by keeping to the exact instructions in the test manual if the child is automatically placed at a disadvantage. Test authors and publishers provide standardized administration procedures to follow for those occasions when the test is is given in a *standard* manner. Nonstandard children require nonstandard administrations and appropriate allowances. This concept is neatly encapsulated by Cohen in the title of his book: *There Are No Standardized Children — Only Standardized Tests* (1977).

Deafness, for example, brings its greatest impact to language development. Since verbal language is the primary means of communication in our society, and typically the only means for the very young, there are concomitant delays to social skill developments. In most cases motor development is not affected by deafness. Neither are there necessarily any delays to cognitive development, yet most tests of this domain rely heavily on verbal instructions and demand oral responses and consequently penalize the deaf child. Specific qualitative as well as quantitative differences in learning are typical in the child with problems in hearing.

Similar complications are evident for the child with any degree of significant vision impairment. Blindness most severely impacts skill acquisition. Affected are gross and fine motor development, perceptual schemes such as awareness of spatial relationships and object permanence, social skills (particularly self-care), and to a minor degree both language and cognitive skills. Inputing the expressed intent of others from both verbal and nonverbal messages is a particularly problematical enterprise for the vision-impaired socially-naive young child. This sort of information is a minimally essential base for the evaluator of a sensorially deprived child. Knowing that the existence of a sensory problem loss has a multiplicative rather than simple additive effect will help the examiner tread sensitively and sympathetically when drawing conclusions about the nature of the expressed learning difficulty.

Intellectual or Cognitive Functioning. Some educators are fearful of "subjecting" a child to an intellectual evaluation. This may be due to a concern that a determination of sub-average performance will lead invariably to stigmatizing, and to a lowering of the child's self concept and associated negative effects of "labelling". Reynolds and Clark (1983) reviewed these claims in the highly recommended text *The Psychoeducational Assessment of the Young Child* (Paget & Bracken, 1983) and concluded that "these criticisms . . . do not seem to hold, as cogent arguments against early identification and remedial programming" (p. 164; see also Reynolds, 1979).

Considerations about the advisability of group versus individual measurement, screening procedures for young children, and the concomitancy of intellectual with other associated handicapping conditions may be found earlier in this chapter. Additionally, the reader is directed to Chapter 2 of this book for a discussion of developmental changes in children's thinking.

Language. Language is the primary currency of thinking, and the most potent vehicle for the efficient mastery of our environment. A language delay is the most prominent signal (and universally considered an indicator among early childhood professionals) of an *overall* developmental delay. Excepting the relatively few children with specific sensory deficits which alone contribute to sub-average language functioning (eg. hearing impaired children, discussed earlier), most children with language delays have the parallel involvement of cognitive delay.

Chapter 3 of this book has additional observations on the place of language and communication in the life of the young child. For readers wishing to review published discussions and annotated bibliographies of language-related tests the following suggestions are offered: Bernthal and Bankson, (1981, pp. 205–219); Bloom and Lahey (1978, pp. 354–356); Darley (1979); and, Salvia and Ysseldyke (1981, pp. 387–429).

Social, Emotional and Adaptive Behavior. Developing from early infancy comes social skill acquisition, which includes growth in gender role interpretation, cultural identification, self-help skills, ethical development, emotional growth and self-concept development. The conventional wisdom is that infants and pre-schoolers are so egocentric that their "socializing" is all self-directed and internally fantasized. Yet, some studies have generated data that shows some infants as young as 18 months prefer the play company of age mates to their own mother's company (Eckerman, Whatley, & Kutz, 1975; Rubenstein & Howes, 1976), and that two and half year old toddlers can be as sociable as older preschoolers (Cooper, Schillmoeller, & Le Blanc, 1975). Intriguing new evidence on this topic are described in Chapter 2 which suggests that young children may "grow out" of their egocentricity earlier than had previously been assumed.

Sociability is an early emerging trait which is maintained by the environment. Crucial to general mental health and even to later academic successes, early social development is particularly critical. For, there is a high level of prediction for social awareness and concern-for-others from children's development in preschool to later life.

Motor Ability. Motor development is reliant upon sensory capacity and the central nervous system's efficiency at coordinating and integrating the sensory input. As the child's neuro-physiological capacity matures then the more complex the motor repertoire can be, and greater will be the child's ability to generalize what has been mastered to new situations.

SOME TENTATIVE CONCLUSIONS

There is no clear concensus among early childhood educators that the identification of young children's problems is either feasible or warranted (eg. Escalona, 1968; Flapan & Neubauer, 1970; Hobbs, 1975; Keogh, 1970; Keogh & Becker, 1973; Shipe & Miezitis,

1969). Nevertheless, there are numerous advocates for early identification and remediation who proffer evidence that problems
remediated *early* are problems remediated *easily* (e.g., Bangs, 1968;
Ilg, 1965; Ingram, 1969). What can be said with confidence is that
the evaluation of young children is a complex exercise, made
more difficult by the child's particularly dynamic rate of development in the earliest years.

The weak levels of prognostic confidence possible from infants'
tested IQ's to adult functioning complicates immensely questions
about the utility of assessment (Knobloch & Pasaminich, 1974;
McCall, Hogarty, & Hurlbert, 1972). Also disturbing is the knowledge that "no single parameter of early functioning can be used to
securely predict later difficulty" (Lidz, 1977, p. 130). Some repu-
table child developmentalists believe that norm-referenced measurement is so flawed that it is cannot be supported for any
evaluation objective (e.g., Muma, 1981; Muma, Lubinski, & Pierce,
1982). Others assert that even a full battery of instruments,
approaches and procedures are insufficient to reflect the "whole
child" (Cohen, 1977; Sigel, 1975; Takanishi, 1979). Another group
of investigators, including Ross (1976), call for dispensing alto-
gether with assessment in its formal guise, by replacing it with a
structured monitoring of teaching: "when the question is 'how
does this child learn and how best can she be taught?' the best way
of answering it is by teaching her something under controlled
conditions, using a variety of teaching formats, and comparing
their effectiveness" (p. 10).

Several of these concerns are magnified when one considers
the threefold task commonly expected of infant and preschool
assessment:

- To provide guidance for the child's instructor by suggesting
  prioritized prescriptions.
- To comprehensively acknowledge the multitude of variables
  interacting to affect the child's capacity to complete the developmental assessment tasks, and provide an accurate appraisal
  of the child's current functioning (which, it is hoped, will
  have some positive correlation to future functioning).
- And, determine the efficacy of an intervention.

There is, perhaps, little wonder that with such a comprehensive bill of fare evaluation does not fulfill some peoples' expectations. The screening-programming-evaluation notion requires a highly professional scientific-objective approach, and it is perhaps understandable that some educators consider that it falls outside of the realm of *instruction.* Yet teachers (and for that matter parents), can tailor-make educational plans for children, focus on specific goals, creatively interpret curriculum so that it matches a child's needs, and concurrently collect data to support their implicit assertion that the child is making progress. At its most basic, that is the kernel of the nut we call evaluation.

There are, admittedly, problems associated with the collection of data on a young child. Not the least of which include, self-fulfilling prophecies in labelling, abuses of confidentiality, superficial evaluation resulting from evaluation-by-"strangers," severely limited data input, bias of all varieties, and instrumentations of questionable psychometric underpinning. This latter point, which relates to the inadequacy of the available measures of young children's functioning, has less to do with our ability to conceptualize a domain or skill and more to do with our ability to directly measure that construct.

The psychometric properties of most tests for young children are correctly considered notorious. For example, a recent psychometric review conducted by McCauley and Swisher (1984), of 30 of the most popular language and articulation tests for preschoolers, found them to be seriously lacking. The tests were checked against ten psychometric criteria focusing on the adequacy of their standardization samples, evidence of reliability and validity, and the internal statistical integrity of the results reported by the test manual. Half of the reviewed tests met no more than two criteria and all but three of the tests were deficient in at least half of the criteria. This is an uncomfortable confirmation that the tests used to measure young children's language skills are less-than-perfect. However, it is worth noting here that most failures of the tests to meet particular criteria came from an absence of sought-after information rather than the result of reported poor performance. It may be that test publishers deem it insufficiently important to reveal this crucial information in the manuals because they (perhaps correctly?) judge that *most* test-users either will not refer to it, or even understand the information.

There are clear side-effects to testing, yet all is not lost. Screening routinely alerts parents and educators to children who are in need of supportive or compensatory services. Without testing this need would, perhaps, have gone unnoticed. There are children for whom an evaluation resulted in a reduction or removal of parents' (or even their own) unwarranted fears about specific problems or developmental delay. Moreover, the fundamental measure is that evaluation, in the long run, can do more good than harm.

This brief discussion of testing and evaluation in early childhood, like the proverbial stone, only has skimmed the surface and touched down here-and-there. The field is now sufficiently mature to have given rise to complete books devoted to this topic (eg. Goodwin & Driscoll, 1980; Paget & Bracken, 1983). The focus of such books, and of this chapter, is that it is to the child's immediate and lasting benefit if weaknesses are recognized early, and decisions are made about the most appropriate remediation.

REFERENCES

Airasian, P. W. (1974). Designing summative evaluation studies at the local level. In W. J. Popham (Ed.), *Evaluation in education: Current application.* Berkeley: McCutchan.

Alpern, G. D., & Boll, T. J. (1972). *Developmental profile.* Indianapolis, IN: Psychological Development Publications.

American Psychological Association, American Educational Research Association, National Council on Measurement in Education. (1974) *Standards for education and psychological tests.* Washington, D.C.: Author.

Arnold, K., & Reed, L. (1976). The Grammatic Closure subtest of the ITPA: A comparative study of black and white children. *Journal of Speech and Hearing Disorders, 41,* 477–485.

Bagnato, S. J. & Neisworth, J. T. (1979). Between assessment and intervention: Forging an assessment/curriculum linkage for the handicapped preschooler. *Child Care Quarterly, 8*(3), 179–195.

Bagnato, S. J. & Neisworth, J. T. (1980). The intervention efficiency index (IEI): An approach to preschool program accountability. *Exceptional Children, 46*(4), 264–269.

Bangs, T. (1968). *Language and learning disorders of the preacademic child.* Englewood Cliffs, NJ: Prentice-Hall.

Barnes, K. E. (1982). *Preschool screening: The measurement and prediction of children at-risk.* Springfield, IL: Charles C Thomas.

Bayley, N. (1933). *The California First Year Mental Scale.* Berkeley, CA: University of California Press.

Bayley, N. (1969). *Bayley Scales of Infant Development.* New York: Psychological Corporation.

Bayley, N. (1970). Development of mental abilities. In P. H. Mussen (Ed.), *Carmichael's manual of child psychology,* (3e, Vol. 1). New York: Wiley.

Bernthal, J., & Bankson, N. (1981). *Articulation disorders.* Englewood Cliffs, NJ: Prentice-Hall.

Bersoff, D. N. (1981). Testing and the law. *American Psychologist, 36*(10), 1047–1056.

Binet, A., & Henri, V. (1895). La memoire des phrases. *L'Annee Psychologique, 1,* 24–59.

Binet, A., & Henri, V. (1896). La psychologie individuelle. *L'Annee Psychologigue, 2,* 411–465.

Binet, A., & Simon, T. (1905). Methodes nouvelles pour le diagnostic du niveau intellectuel des anormaux. *L'Annee Psychologigue, 11,* 191–244.

Binet, A., & Simon, T. (1908). Le development de l'intelligence chez les enfants. *L'Annee Psychologigue, 14,* 1–94.

Bloom, L., & Lahey, M. (1978). *Language development and language disorders.* New York: Wiley.

Bricker, D., & Bricker, W. A. (1973). *Infant, toddler, and preschool research and intervention project: Report-year #3* (IMRID Behavioral Science Monograph, #23). Nashville, TN: George Peabody College.

Brigance, A. (1978). *Brigance inventory of early development.* Massachusetts: Curriculum Associates.

Brim, O. G. (1975). Macro-structural influences on child development and the need for childhood social indicators. *American Journal of Orthopsychiatry, 45,* 516–524.

Bronfenbrenner, U. (1977). Toward an experimental ecology of human development. *American Psychologist, 32*(7), 513–531.

Brooks, J., & Weinraub, M. (1976). A history of infant intelligence testing. In M. Lewis (ed.), *Origins of intelligence.* New York: Plenum Press.

Brown, W. R. & McGuire, J. M. (1976) Current psychological assessment practices. *Professional Psychologist, 7,* 477–484.

Buros, O. K. (Ed.) (1974). *Tests in print* (2nd ed.). Highland Park, NJ: Gryphon Press.

Buros, O. K. (Ed.) (1978). *The eighth mental measurements yearbook.* Highland Park, NJ: Gryphon Press.

Burt, C. L. (1921). *Mental and scholastic tests.* London: King.

Cattell, J. (1890). Mental tests and measurement. P. *Mind, 15,* 373–381.

Cattell, P. (1940). *The measurement of intelligence of infants and young children.* New York: Psychological Corporation.

Chaille, S. E. (1887). Infants: Their chronological process. *New Orleans Medical and Surgical Journal, 14,* 89–902.

Cohen, D. (1977). *There are no standardized children — only standardized tests.* New York: Bank Street College of Education.

Cole, N. S. (1981). Bias in testing. *American Psychologist, 36*(10), 1067–1077.

Compton, C. (1980). *A guide to 65 tests for special education.* Belmont, CA: Pitman Learning.

Cooper, A. Y., Schilmoeller, K. J., & Le Blanc, J. M. (1975, April). A comparison of the effects of teacher attention and special activities for increasing cooperative play of a heterogenous group of normative and developmentally limited children. Paper presented at the Biennial Meeting of the Society for Research in Child Development, Denver, CO.

Coulter, A., & Morrow, H. (1978). *The concept and measurement of adaptive behavior.* New York: Grune & Stratton.

Cronbach, L. J. (1971). Test validation. In R. L. Thorndike (Ed.), *Educational Measurement, 10,* 237–255.

Cronbach, L. J. (1975) Five decades of public controversy over mental testing. *American Psychologist, 30,* 1–14.

Cronbach, L. J. (1980). Selection theory for a political world. *Public Personnel Management, 9,* 37–50.

Cross, L. (1977). Diagnosis. In L. Cross & K. Goin (Eds.), *Identifying handicapped children: A guide to casefinding, screening, diagnosis, assessment and evaluation.* New York: Walker.

Cross, L., & Johnson, S. (1977). A bibliography of instruments. In L. Cross & K. Goins (Eds.), *Identifying handicapped children: A guide to casefinding, screening, diagnosis, assessment and evaluation.* New York: Walker.

Darley, F. (Ed.) (1979) *Evaluation of appraisal techniques in speech and language pathology.* Reading, MA: Addison-Wesley.

Darwin, C. (1859). *The origin of the species.* London: Murray.

Darwin, C. (1872). *Expression of the emotions in man and animals.* New York: Appleton.

Darwin, C. (1877). A biographical sketch of an infant. *Mind, 2,* 285–294.

DuBois, P. (1966). A test dominated society: China, 1115 BC.–1905 AD. In A. Anastasi (Ed.), *Testing problems in perspective: Twenty-fifth anniversary volume of topical readings from the invitational conference on testing problems.* Washington, D.C.: American Council on Education.

Du Bose, R. F. (1977). Predictive value of infant intelligence scales with multiply handicapped children. *American Journal of Mental Deficiency, 81,* 388–390.

Du Bose, R. F. (1981 a). Assessment of severely impaired children: problems and recommendations. *Topics in Early Childhood Special Education, 1*(2), 9–18.

Du Bose, R. F. (1981 b). *Final performance report. Innovative diagnostic training: Preparation of diagnostic personnel to serve severely handicapped children.* (USOE–BEH Report #G007701304). Nashville, TN: George Peabody College.

Eckerman, C. O., Whatley, J. L., & Kutz, S. L. (1975). Growth of social play with peers during the second year of life. *Developmental Psychology, 11,* 42–49.

Escalona, S. (1968). *The roots of individuality.* Chicago: Aldine.

Escalona, S. K., & Corman, H. (1969). *Albert Einstein Scales of Sensorimotor Development.* New York: Albert Einstein College of Medicine of Yeshiva Univ.

Esquirol, J. (1838). *Des maladies mentales considerees sous les rapports medical, hygenique et medico-legal.* Paris: Bailliere.

Fillmore, E. A. (1936). Iowa Tests for Young Children. *Univ. of Iowa Studies in Child Welfare. 11*(4).

Flapan, D., & Neubauer, P. B. (1970). Issues in assessing development. *Journal of the American Academy of Child Psychiatry, 9*(4), 669–687.

Frankel, R. (1979). Parents as evaluators of their retarded youngsters. *Mental Retardation, 9*(2), 75–85.

Frankenberg, W., & Dodds, J. (1968). *Denver Developmental Screening Test.* Denver, CO: Univ. of Colorado Medical Center.

Furuno, S., O'Reilly, K. A., Hosaka, C. M., Inatsuka, T. T., Allman, T. L., & Zeisloft, B. (1979). *Hawaii Early Learning Profile.* Palo Alto, CA: VORT Corporation.

Galton, F. (1869). *Hereditary genius.* London: Macmillan.

Galton, F. (1883). *Inquiries into human faculty and its development.* London: Dutton.

Garwood, S. G. (1982). (Mis)use of developmental scales in program evaluation. *Topics in Early Childhood Special Education. 1,*(4), 61–69.

Gerken, K. (Ed.) (1979). Services to preschoolers and children with low incidence handicaps. Special issue of the *School Psychology Digest, 8*(3).

Gesell, A. (1925). *The mental growth of the preschool child: A psychological outline of normal development from birth to the sixth year.* New York: Macmillan.

Gesell, A. (1928). *Infancy and human growth.* New York; Macmillan.

Gilliland, A. R. (1948). The measurement of the mentality of infants. *Child Development, 19,* 155–158.

Glaser, R. (1963). Instructional technology and the measurement of learning outcomes. *American Psychologist, 18,* 519–521.

Goddard, H. H. (1908). The Binet and Simon tests of intellectual capacity. *Training School, 5,* 3–9.

Goddard, H. H. (1910). A measuring scale of intelligence. *Training School, 6,* 146–155.

Goodenough, F. L. (1926) *Measurement of intelligence be drawings.* Chicago:World Book.

Goodenough, F. L. (1949). *Mental testing.* New York: Rinehart.

Goodenough, F. L., Maurer, K. M., & Van Wagenen, M. J. (1940). *Minnesota Preschool Scales: Manual of instructions.* Minneapolis: Educational Testing Bureau.

Goodwin, W., & Driscoll, L. (1980). *Handbook for measurement and evaluation in early childhood education.* San Francisco: Jossey-Bass.

Graham, F. K., & Berman, P. W. (1961). Current status of behavior tests for brain damage in infants and preschool children. *American Journal of Orthopsychiatry, 31,* 713–727.

Griffiths, R. (1954). *The abilities of babies.* London: Univ. of London Press.

Halle, J. W., & Sindelar, P. T. (1982). Behavioral observation methodologies for early childhood education. *Topics in Early Childhood Education, 2*(1), 43–45.

Hambleton, R. K., Swaminathan, H., Algina, J., & Coulson, D. B. (1978). Criterion-referenced testing and measurement: A review of technical issues and developments. *Review of Educational Research, 48*(1), 1–47.

Hamilton, J. L. & Swan, W. W. (1981). Measurement references in the assessment of preschool handicapped children. *Topics in Early Childhood Special Education, 1*(2), 41–48.

Haney, W. (1981). Validity, vaudeville, and values: A short history of social concerns over standardized testing. *American Psychologist, 36*,(10), 1021–1034.

Hobbs, N. (1975). *The futures of children.* San Fransisco: Jossey-Bass.

Hobson v Hansen (1969). 269F. Supp. 401 (D. D. C. 1967), *aff'd sub nom.* Smuck v. Hobson, 408 F. 2d. 175 (D. C. Cir. 1969).

Honzik, M. P. (1976). Value and limitations of infant's tests: An overview. In M. Lewis (Ed.), *Origins of intelligence: Infancy and early childhood.* New York: Plenum.

Ilg, F. L., & Ames, L. D. (1965). *School readiness.* New York: Harper and Row.

Illingworth, R. D. (1970). *The development of the infant and young child: Normal and abnormal.* London: E. & S. Livingstone.

Ingram, T. T. (1969). The early recognition of handicaps in childhood. *Journal of Learning Disabilities, 2*(5), 252–255.

Jensen, A. R. (1980). *Bias in mental testing.* New York: The Free Press.

Johnson, D. (1974). The influences of social class and race on language test performance and spontaneous speech of preschool children. *Child Development, 45,* 517–521.

Johnson, K., & Kopp, C. (undated). *A bibliography of screening and assessment measures for infants: Project REACH.* Unpublished manuscript, Univ. of California, Los Angeles, Graduate School of Education.

Kaufman, A. S., & Kaufman, N. L. (1977). *Clinical evaluation of young children with the McCarthy Scales.* New York: Grune and Stratton.

Kelley, M. F., & Surbeck, E. (1983). History of preschool assessment. In K. D. Paget and B. A. Bracken (Eds.), *The psychoeducational assessment of preschool children.* New York: Grune and Stratton.

Keogh, B. K. (1970). Early identification of children with learning problems. (Ed.), *Journal of Special Education, 40*(3), 307–363.

Keogh, B. K., & Becker, L. D. (1973). Early detection of learning problems: Questions, cautions, and guidelines. *Exceptional Children, 40,* 5–11.

Kiernan, D., & Du Bose, R. F. (1974). Assessing the cognitive development of preschool deaf-blind children. *Education of the Visually Handicapped, 6,* 103–105.

Knobloch, H. & Pasamanich, B. (1974). *Gesell and Armatruda's developmental diagnosis.* Hagerstown, MD: Harper & Row.

Kozloff, M. A. (1971). *Measuring behavior: Procedures for recording and evaluating behavioral data.* St. Ann, MO: CEMREL.

Krantz, P., & Risley, T. R. (1977). Behavior ecology in the classroom. In K. D.

O'Leary & S. G. O'Leary (Eds.), *Classroom management: The successful use of behavior modification* (2e). New York: Pergamon Press.

Kuhlmann, F. (1914). *A handbook of mental tests.* Baltimore, MD: Warwick and York.

Lambert, N. (Ed.) (1981) *Special education matrix.* Monterey, CA: McGraw-Hill CTB.

Lahey, B. B., Vosk, B. N., & Habif, V. L. (1981). Behavioral assessment of learning disabled children: A rationale and strategy. *Behavioral assessment, 3,* 3–14.

Larry P. et al. u Wilson Riles (1979). U. S. District Court, Northern District of California, Case #C-71-2270 RFP, 1974, 1979. Appeal docketed, #80-4027 (9th Cir., Jan. 17, 1980).

Larson, M. T. (1975). *Current trends in child development research.* Greensboro, NC: University of North Carolina, School of Home Economics.

LeMay, D., Griffin, P., & Sanford, A. (1977). *A Learning Accomplishment Profile Examiner's Manual.* Chapel Hill, NC: Chapel Hill Training-Outreach Project.

Lewis, M. (1973). Infant intelligence tests: Their use and misuse. *Human Development, 16,* 108–118.

Lidz, C. S. (1977). Issues in the psychological assessment of preschool children. *Journal of School Psychology, 15*(2), 129–135.

MacTurk, R. H. & Neisworth, J. T. (1978). Norm-referenced and criterion based measures with preschoolers. *Exceptional Children, 45*(1), 34–39.

McCall, R. B., Hogarty, P. S., & Hurlbert, N. (1972). Transitions in infant sensorimotor development and the prediction of childhood IQ. *American Psychologist, 27,* 728–748.

McCauley, R. J., & Swisher, L. (1984). Psychometric review of language and articulation tests for preschool children. *Journal of Speech and Hearing Disorders, 49,* 34–42.

Mcloughlin, C. S. (1981). Evaluation of self-instructional parent training by parent and others' reports. *Dissertation Abstracts International, 42,* 2580-B. (Univ. Microfilms No. 8125902).

Mcloughlin, C. S. (1983). An annotated bibliography of 30 selected tests for preschoolers. *Psychological Documents, 13*(2), 2223 (Abstract), MS #2578.

Mcloughlin, C. S., & Koh, T. H. (1982). Testing intelligence: A decision suitable for the psychologist? *Bulletin of the British Psychological Society, 35,* 308–311.

Messick, S. (1975). The standard problem: Meaning and values in measurement and evaluation. *American Psychologist, 30,* 955–966.

Messick, S. (1980). Test validity and the ethics of assessment. *American Psychologist, 35,* 1012–1027.

Muma, J. (1981). *Language primer for the clinical fields.* Lubbock, TX: Natural Child Publishing.

Muma, J., Lubinski, R., & Pierce, S. (1982). A new era in language assessment: Data or evidence. In N. Lass (Ed.), *Speech and language: Advances in basic research and practice* (Vol. 7). New York: Academic Press.

Olds, A. R. (1979). Designing developmentally optimal classrooms for children with special needs. In S. J. Meisels (Ed.), *Special education and development.* Baltimore, MD: Univ. Park Press.

Paget, K. D., & Bracken, B. A. (1983). *The psychoeducational assessment of preschool children.* New York: Grune and Stratton.

(PASE) Parents in Action on Special Education u Joseph P. Hannon (1980). U. S. District Court, Northern District of Illinois, Eastern Division, #74-3586.

Popham, W. J., & Husek, T. R. (1969). Implications of criterion referenced measurement. *Journal of Educational Measurement, 6,* 1-9.

Preyer, W. (1882). *The mind of the child.* New York: Appleton.

Ramey, C. T., Campbell, F. A., & Wasik, B. H. (1982). Use of standardized tests to evaluate early childhood special education programs. *Topics in Early Childhood Special Education, 1*(4), 51-60.

Reese, E. P., Howard, J., & Reese, T. W. (1978). *Human behavior: Analysis and applications* (2e). Dubuque, IA: William C. Brown.

Reschly, D. R. (1983). Legal issues in psychoeducational assessment. In G. W. Hynd (Ed.), *The school psychologist: An introduction,* New York: Syracuse Univ. Press.

Reynolds, C. R. (1979). Should we screen preschoolers? *Contemporary Educational Psychology, 4,* 175-181.

Reynolds, C. R. (1981). Screening tests: Problems and promises. In N. Lambert (Ed.), *Special education assessment matrix.* Monterey, CA: CTB/McGraw Hill.

Reynolds, C. R. (1983). Foundations of measurement in psychology and education. In G. W. Hynd (Ed.), *The school psychologist: An introduction,* New York: Syracuse Univ. Press.

Reynolds, C. R., & Clark, J. H. (1983). Assessment of cognitive abilities. In K. D. Paget and B. A. Bracken (Eds.), *The psychoeducational assessment of the preschool child.* New York: Grune and Stratton.

Rogers, S. J., & D'Eugenio, D. B. (1977). *Developmental programming for infants and young children: Assessment and application.* Ann Arbor, MI: Univ. of Michigan Press.

Rogers-Warren, A. K. (1982). Behavioral ecology in classrooms for young, handicapped children. *Topics in Early Childhood Special Education, 2*(1), 21-32.

Rogers-Warren, A. K., & Wedel, J. W. (1980). The ecology of preschool classrooms for the handicapped. *New Directions for Exceptional Children, 1,* 1-24.

Ross, A. O. (1976). *Psychological aspects of learning disabilities and reading disorders.* New York: McGraw-Hill.

Rubenstein, J., & Howes, C. (1976). The effects of peers on toddler interaction with mother and toys. *Child Development, 47,* 597-605.

Salvia, J., & Ysseldyke, J. E. (1978). *Assessment in special and remedial education.* Boston, MA: Houghton Mifflin.

Seguin, E. (1866). *Idiocy: Its treatment by the physiological method.* New York: Columbia Univ. Press.

Shearer, D. (1972). *Portage guide to early education.* Portage, WI: Cooperative Educational Service Agency, (#12).

Shinn, M. (1900). *The biography of a baby.* Boston, MA: Houghton Mifflin.

Shipe, D., & Miezitis, S. (1969). A pilot study in the diagnosis and remediation of special learning disabilities in preschool children. *Journal of Learning Disabilities,* 2(11), 579–592.

Shirley, M. (1931). The sequential method for the study of maturing behavior patterns. *Psychological Review, 38,* 507–528.

Sigel, I. (1975). The search for validity, or the evaluator's nightmare. In R. Weinberg and S. Moore (Eds.), *Evaluation of educational programs for young children: The Minnesota round table on early childhood education,* Vol. 2, Washington, DC: The Child Development Consortium.

Simmeonsson, R. J., Huntington, G. S., & Parse, S. A. (1980). Assessment of children with severe handicaps: Multiple problems – multivariate goals. *American Journal of Mental Deficiency, 63,* 696–698.

Skolnick, A. (1975) The limits of childhood: Conceptions of child development and social context. *Law and Contemporary Problems, 39,* 38–77.

Southworth, L. E., Burr, R. L., & Cox, A. E. (1981). *Screening and evaluating the young child: A handbook of instruments to use from infancy to six years.* Springfield, IL: Charles C Thomas.

Stangler, S. R., Huber, C. J., & Routh, D. K. (1980) *Screening, growth and development of preschool children.* New York: McGraw Hill.

Stern, W. (1914). *Psychology of early childhood up to the sixth year of age.* New York: Henry Hall.

Stott, L. H. & Ball, R. S. (1965). Infant and preschool mental tests: Review and evaluation. *Monograph of the Society for Research in Child Development, 30,* (3, Serial #101).

Stutsman, R. (1931). *Mental measurement of preschool children.* New York: World Books.

Takanishi, R. (1979). Evaluation of early childhood programs: Towards a developmental perspective. In L. Katz, (Ed.), *Current topics in early childhood education,* Vol. 2. Norwood, NJ: Ablex.

Telzrow, C. F., Ellison, C. L., & Bohmer, D. S. (1981) *A model for comprehensive delivery for preschool handicapped children.* Maple Heights, OH: Cuyahoga Special Education Service Center.

Terman, L. M. (1916). *The measurement of intelligence.* Boston, MA: Houghton.

Uzgiris, I. C., & Hunt, J. McV. (1966). *An Instrument for Assessing Infant Psychological Development.* Chicago: University of Illinois, Psychological Development Laboratries.

Vane, J. R. & Motta, R. W. (1978). Test response inconsistency in young children. *Journal of School Psychology, 18,* 25–33.

Wachs, T. (1979). Proximal experience and early cognitive-intellectual development: The physical environment. *Merrill-Palmer Quarterly, 25,* 3–41.

Walls, T. D., Werner, T., Bacon, A., & Zane, T. (1977). Behavior checklist. In J. Cone & R. Hawkins (Eds.), *Behavioral assessment: New directions in clinical psychology.* New York: Brunner/Mazel.

Yang, R. K. & Bell, R. Q. (1975). Assessment of infants. In P. McReynolds (Ed.),

Advances in psychological assessment (Vol. 3). San Francisco: Jossey-Bass.

Yerkes, R. M., & Foster, J. C. (1923) *A point scale for measuring mental ability.* Baltimore, MD: Warwick and York.

APPENDIX A

A BRIEF HISTORY OF ASSESSMENT
FOR INFANTS AND PRESCHOOLERS

(Prepared by Caven S. Mcloughlin —
References may be found at the end of Chapter 12)

This listing is not intended to be comprehensive, and the exclusion of an instrument from this selection should not be construed as reflecting upon its worth or importance to this historical perspective. Annotated bibliographies of test materials suitable for administration to normally developing and handicapped young children, some including critical summations, may be of use to the reader wishing to widen this brief perspective (see Barnes, 1982; Compton, 1980; Cross & Johnson, 1977; Johnson & Kopp, undated; Lambert, 1981; Mcloughlin, 1983; Salvia & Ysseldyke, 1982; Southworth, Burr & Cox, 1981; Telzrow, Ellison & Bohmer, 1981; Walls, Werner, Bacon, & Zane, 1977). For reviews and perspectives specifically on some of the earlier instruments, particular attention is drawn to work by Brooks and Weinraub (1976), and Stott and Ball (1965).

The Chronology

Chaille's *Infants: Their chronological process* (1887)
Binet-Simon Scale (1905, 1908)
Kuhlman's *Handbook of Mental Tests* (which incorporated test content for infants; 1914)
Gesell's "Mental growth of the preschool child: . . . birth to the sixth year" (1925)
Goodenough Draw-a-Man Test (Goodenough, 1926)
Shirley's Motor Scale (1931)
Merrill-Palmer Scale of Mental Tests (Stutsman, 1931)
California First Year Mental Scale (Bayley, 1933)
Iowa Tests for Young Children (Fillmore, 1936)
Minnesota Preschool Scale (Goodenough, Maurer, & Van Wagenen, 1940)
Infant Intelligence Scale (Cattell, 1940)

Northwest Infant Intelligence Scale (Gilliland, 1948)

Mental Development Scale (Griffiths, 1954)

Instrument for Assessing Infant Psychological Development (Uzgiris & Hunt, 1966)

Denver Developmental Screening Test (Frankenberg & Dodds, 1968)

Albert Einstein Scales of Sensorimotor Development (Escalona & Corman, 1969)

Bayley Scales of Infant Development (Bayley, 1969)

Portage Guide to Early Education (Shearer, 1972)

Developmental Profile (Alpern & Boll, 1972)

Learning Aptitude Profile (LeMay, Griffin, & Sandford, 1977)

Developmental Programming for Infants and Young Children (Rogers, & D'Eugenio, 1977)

Brigance Inventory of Early Development (Brigance, 1978)

Hawaii Early Learning Profile (Furuno, O'Reilly et al, 1979)

CHAPTER 12

FACILITATING THE DEVELOPMENT OF THE YOUNG CHILD*

Nicholas J. Anastasiow

INTRODUCTION

The title of this chapter can be read to mean that development is a natural unfolding process that requires facilitation. Development is usually defined as moving from a globally undifferentiated state to one of finer and finer differentiation of functions. Developmental psychologists seek the processes underlying the change from the global state of the infant to the sophisticated functioning of the adult. Psychologists seek these processes within the individual. They also study what effects the practices and customs of child rearing, used by persons in the individual's environment, have on development.

The intent of this chapter is to present the rationale that development is natural, and based in nature or genes. However, development requires that the environment provide the stimulus to set these processes in motion. Environments can be facilitative and enhance development; alternatively, environments can be debilitating, so that the individual does not achieve his or her genetic possibilities. In essence, development is based on genes as potentials to be realized in environments.

To be sure, some genetic potentials are so strongly based in evolution (canalized in Waddington's 1957 term) that it takes major

*Portion of N.J. Anastasiow's work is supported by Grant #444687 from the Office of Special Education Programs. Acknowledgement is given to University of Hawaii Press for permission to quote from E. E. Werner, J. M. Bierman, and F. E. French (1971). *The Children of Kauai.* Honolulu, Hawaii. Special thanks to Ann Ngai for her important contribution to the preparation of the manuscript.

313

disruptions to the central nervous system to alter their course of development. Measles in the third trimester of pregnancy is one such disruption which can result in infant blindness, deafness, and/or mental retardation. Sexual maturation is so deeply rooted in evolutionally planned development that, unless death intervenes, even seriously damaged multihandicapped individuals (deaf-blind, retarded, emotionally disturbed) will reach sexual maturity during the adolescent period. However, maturation is the name of the process of maturing and is not an explanation of the how, when, or what of development.

The term development is perceived to be a probability statement (Gottlieb, 1976). As J. Hunt (1979) states, it is very likely or probable that all but a small proportion of the world's children will develop into normal adults. Although, we can make that statement with confidence, the term development does not explain individual differences within socio- and ethnocultures, nor does it explain the differences in individuals across cultures.

What will be discussed in the sections that follow are the questions: What capacities does the infant possess at birth that can be identified as potentials for development, and how do caretakers facilitate these capacities? Also, Do caretakers assist in developing capacities not present at birth by knowledge and skills which require environmental input and social learning?

A PSYCHO-NEUROLOGICAL POINT OF VIEW

The position put forth in this chapter is that psychological processes are built upon biological predispositions. It proposes that the brain is structurally organized to some degree at birth to operate in a predictable and planned fashion, out of which the individual is able to construct a sense of self and a sense of others, as well as acquire processes of higher-order thinking.

If readers at this point suspect that Gall is being resurrected, they are correct (see Fodor, 1983). The modular notion of the brain organization is currently an accepted idea at least for perceptual processes, which includes language. Whether there are molar and/or mini modules is a hotly debated point, but not necessary to pursue for the development of this chapter (see Gardner, 1983 for a discussion of these issues, particularly the note section at the end of the book concerning chapter 3).

Infants are born with a range of perceptual capacities which, given environmental events, will develop into sophisticated perceptual systems. The evidence indicates that these infants' perceptual systems are prewired and act independently of each other, as well as follow their own course of early development. Lecours (1975) has demonstrated that the areas of the brain related to gross motor, vision, hearing, touch, and taste are sufficiently developed in the first two to three months of life to be able to function. Thus, infants can see, hear, taste, smell, and feel and are oriented toward hearing, seeing, and responding to the touch of humans. Infants look at human faces, listen to human voices, respond to human touch (Bruner, 1977; Schaffer, 1977). Infants also respond to pleasant tastes (sweet) and odors (banana, strawberry and vanilla) with smiles, and to unpleasant tastes (bitter) and odors (spoiled fish and rotten eggs) with grimaces and head withdrawal (Lipsitt, 1979). Specific odor preferences appear to be learned, and infants six to ten days of age can recognize their mothers through olfactory cues (Werner & Lipsitt, 1981). Vision and hearing have assumed dominance in higher mammals, particularly humans.

It should be stressed that these perceptual systems are not under the control of the infant but act much like reflexes. They operate independently in the presence of an environmental stimuli. Unlike reflexes (e.g., startle, fear moro, grasping), however, they do not disappear but rather develop into more complex systems and, as the brain develops, become connected to higher cortical functions and under some control of the individual. The word "some" was used to indicate that there are mini-module functionings, such as face recognition, that operate whether the individual desires it or not (Carey & Diamond, 1980). The turning point in infant development at which the emerging self begins to recognize internal and external stimuli and to exercise some control is about seven to nine months, the period Zelazo (1976) refers to as the "dawn of consciousness" (p. 77).

At least two other sets of factors operate in infancy which are implicated in the course of development. The first is the notion of plasticity. The brain, before full maturation, is able to "restructure" itself to some degree. That is, neurons, which in most humans may play a similar role, will with brain damage assume other roles. The most dramatic example is the disorder of Sturge-Weber syndrome which requires the removal of the entire cortical hemisphere of the infant (Dennis, 1980). These infants develop the skills that are usually associated with the hemisphere in spite of its removal. Thus, in the earliest periods of life the nervous system can adapt to some severe injuries.

In addition, the nervous system can flexibly adapt to variations in human culture. Language, as a perceptual system, stores in words and images and can communicate images through words from individual to individual. As I write, I see out my window gently falling wet snow covering my azaleas, which can be written down or described in words, interpreted, and "seen" by the reader who has experienced soft snow and recognizes azaleas. The flexibility of the language module is that it is capable of great plasticity. Any infant can learn any language of the world given the appropriate environmental experience and early input. Thus, plasticity is involved in the ability to develop in a range of human environments and to acquire the shapes, sounds, smells, tastes (as in food preferences), and movements of the home and culture in which the infant is born.

The second factor is the notion of critical periods. They appear to be critical times for the realization of the sensory systems. For full development of the sensory systems, stimuli or experiences must occur in the infant's environment early in life before full maturation of the brain. Infants must hear a language in order to speak it, they must experience objects in patterned light in order to detect vertical and horizontal lines, curves, moving objects, and so on. There are few reported cases of infants deprived of normal experience but there are ample animal research studies to support the notion of critical periods. The work of Hubel and Wiesel (1979) with kittens has elegantly documented that seeing in light by three to five weeks of life is necessary for normal visual system development. Kittens with normal visual systems who do not experience light by this period behave as if they are genetically blind. Hubel and Wiesel have mapped out the visual system of the cat so as to be able to describe which portion of the eye and visual pathways must be stimulated (experience seeing) for the development of horizontal line detectors, vertical line detectors, and so on (The August 1979 issue of *Scientific American* has excellent articles on brain development, including that cited by Hubel and Wiesel).

Fortunately, we do not experiment with humans in the same manner, but there are some experiments of nature in the case of sensory impaired infants. Deaf/blind infants who do not perceive sound or light can develop fully if the sensory system of touch is used and used early in life, supporting both the notions of plasticity and critical period. If extra stimulation through touch is not supplied during the critical time of three to seven months, deaf/blind children may develop behaviors usually associated with emotional disturbances: swaying, avoidance of humans, and bizarre finger and body gestures (Fraiberg, 1977). However, through the physical stimulations of handling and touch, normal cognitive and affective development can be obtained in deaf/blind children in spite of the enormous loss of two sensory systems (Meshcheryakow, 1979). Goldman's (1976) work with monkeys strongly suggests that the critical time for early experience is before the brain is fully mature. For the human brain the course of development is highly varied, with some portions of the brain maturing early and the "higher order cognitive system" sections maturing later, some well into the second decade of life. There is much to be learned about these later developments; however, Luria's (1973) work suggests that the areas of the brain, related to the self and planning, reach full maturation at the mid- to late-adolescence period.

One additional factor remains in our genetic base of development, which relates to the fixed behavior patterns that occur at regular intervals in the course of maturation, and that require experiences to be maintained. These fixed behavior patterns appear universally in infant behavior across all cultures. The first well-documented pattern occurs at two to three months with the appearance of babbling and the social smile (Emde, Gaensbauer, & Harmon, 1976). Blind infants will smile, but in the absence of seeing smiles will stop smiling. Deaf infants will babble, but in the absence of hearing human language will stop babbling. Both cases support the existence of the universal nature of the fixed action pattern.

The genetic purpose of the fixed action pattern at two to three months is perceived by some researchers as stimuli to evoke the environment to care for the infant (Bell, 1968). To Bowlby (1969) the evolutionary purpose of the smile is to evoke the caregivers' formation of attachment, and babbling is to encourage the caregivers' production of the language of that culture. The latter point of view is taken in this chapter and later will be elaborated.

Bowlby's position is a blending of psychoanalytic and ethnological viewpoints that gives greater emphasis to biological predispositions which can be shaped by cultures than does the Piagetian theory. Piaget proposes that infants make sense out of the world through their reflexes, sensory perceptions, and physical actions. Through these activities, sensorimotor intelligence is developed and mental operations are built through the interiorization of actions. Following the early stage, the interiorization of actions is modified into the capacity for symbol use, with the later period of development influenced by the experiencing of objects and environments, which leads into reasoning about the world of objects (concrete operations) and, last, the world of symbols themselves (abstract reasoning). The course of Piagetian universal stages appears to be accurate for individuals who live in Western cultures and attend Western type schools (Cole & Scribner, 1974). Piagetian theory is particularly useful for understanding the acquisition of the laws of physics and chemistry (logical-mathematical deductive reasoning). It is less able to account for the influence of the development of attachment, and for the development of other intelligences such as music, spatial, and person (Gardner, 1983). In addition, Piaget's theory does not give as much credence to the influence of parenting practices on development, nor does the theory give as much attention to the different courses and results of development across contexts (Zimmerman, 1983).

Recent research in cognitive psychology suggests that Piaget was perhaps in error to propose deductive reasoning as natural or genetically based. Individuals who do not attend Western type schools, do not use deduction but rather induction as a mode of reasoning (M. Hunt, 1982; Cole and Scribner, 1974). M. Hunt's is an excellent summary of the issues concerning deductive and inductive reasoning which suggests that humans are excellent inducers who seek rules and order in their environment by using natural and realistic concepts based on their own direct experience. The use of deduction appears to be a product of education.

Piaget observed, for example, that children discover the laws of conservation through their own experimentations and actions upon the environment. Piaget's conclusion that children do so by deduction appears to be in error. The laws appear to be discovered by induction and good guesses about how things in the world work. As M. Hunt (1982) states, "That we are right more often than wrong is the miracle of the human intellect" (p. 188).

To M. Hunt (1982), what is clear is that the infant brain is genetically prewired to respond to the experience of gravity, three-dimensional space, time, quantity, and causality in a very vague way in which become increasing complex as the brain matures and the infant experiences. It is a transaction of continuous interaction between brain maturation and emerging potentials gained from experience (M. Hunt, 1982; see Chapter 6 in particular).

This chapter takes the position that Bandura's (1977) social learning theory is a powerful tool for explaining the impact and effectiveness of teaching and learning strategies. There are, in addition, human dispositions which are learned easily because they are genetically based (Garcia & Levine, 1976). The timing of developmental acquisitions is related to neurological maturations of the brain (Epstein, 1974a & b; Lecours, 1975). This point of view is psychoneurological rather than purely epigenetic. Further, whereas Piagetian theory stresses logical-mathematical reasoning as a hallmark of human achievement, this chapter stresses the development of the affect system (emotions) as the foundation underlying mental health and cognition, with affect as the dominant system and cognition subordinate to it.

THE EARLY COMMUNICATION SYSTEM: EMOTIONS

Recent work on emotional development has supported Darwin's (1973, originally published in 1872) earlier speculations that emotions are innate and appear in a regular fixed pattern in all humans across all cultures (Campos, Barrett, Lamb, Goldsmith, & Stenberg, 1983; Ekman, 1980; Izard, 1977). The newest conception is to perceive emotions as a primary communication system which communicates internally to the individual. States of joy, pleasure, fear, discomfort are communicated externally to others through facial expressions, cries, and gestures (Campos, et al, 1983). There is good evidence that the facial expressions of emotions are biologically prewired, and that one can "read" the face and receive the emotion it is communicating (Ekman, 1980). Later in life, display-rules concerning emotions are learned, and adults learn to control the external communications of emotions to fit the cultural norm.

Facial expressions, cries, and gestures are not under the control of the infant but have communication power for the adult, who can infer the infant's internal state from the expressions and cries. Interestingly, other infants respond to infant crying by themselves crying.

To Bruner (1977), spoken language develops out of the early emotional communication system. From an evolutionary perspective, emotions probably serve as the basic communication system among humans, and it was only later with the invention of spoken language, based on an arbitrary system of sounds, that spoken language became the dominant system. To Gazzaniga and LeDoux (1981), the language system in the adult operates as a central system for the interpretation of internal feelings and external communication, playing a dominant role in human behavior.

Be that as it may, the infant is basically an affective behavior system (Scarr-Salapatek, 1976). The infant is motivated toward perceiving aspects of humans in the environment and seeks to reduce pain, fear, and discomfort and to continue pleasant, comfort-arousing situations (Schaffer, 1977). Erickson (1950) built his sense of basic "trust," and Bowlby (1969) his notion of "attachment" out of the manner in which humans in the environment respond to the infant-initiated communications of pain and pleasure. In the course of establishing basic trust or secure attachment, the infant becomes a young child with a sense of *autonomy* and *competence* (Wertheim, 1975a, b, c, d). Autonomy is defined as the child developing into a separate individual who can act on his or her own without adult guidance. Competence is defined as the child's ability to perform the tasks culturally associated with the skills and knowledge appropriate to the child's chronological age. Once a secure attachment is made, the infant develops cognitively and acquires the language spoken in his home environment. In less secure attachments, the child may acquire cognition and language but manifest social problems associated with the emotions. Scroufe's (1983) excellent summary indicates that securely attached children can individuate, relate to others, develop concepts of self and self control, and move into autonomous behavior and master the requirements of the environment. Poorly or anxiously attached children will display behavioral disorders which can be detected through the course of childhood in expressions of dependency, aggression, negative acting-out, and noncompliance. To Scroufe, the development of the personality does not reside in inborn qualities, but in the nature of the caregiver/child interaction, and the manner in which attachment is established and autonomy and competence are developed. How these two global states are accomplished is examined in the rest of the chapter.

FUNCTIONAL MATERNAL INTELLIGENCE

The number of factors that have been identified as facilitating children's development have come to be grouped under the term functional maternal intelligence. The term probably should be called functional basic caregiver intelligence or parental intelligence, for it is the basic caregiver who has major impact on the child's development and this person may or may not be the child's biological mother. For most children in the world, it is the biological mother who serves as the basic caregiver. However, the findings discussed below are believed to apply to any basic caregiver, whether fathers as Lamb (1981) reports in Sweden, grandmothers, older siblings, or "Kith, Kin, and Hired Hands" (Werner, 1984). What is clear is that what the basic caregiver does in home with the infant can facilitate the child's attainment of a stable personality capable of solving problems when confronted with them. Alternatively, the caregiver's parenting strategies can have an effect more traumatic than breech birth and/or anoxia, two conditions known to have strong relationships to handicapping conditions (Broman, Nichols, & Kennedy, 1975). There are known strategies associated with the facilitation of development just as there are known factors that can be grouped as various forms of neglect (overindulgence, physical neglect, and physical punishment) (Axelrad & Brody, 1978).

There have been many studies which have identified sets of variables that are correlated to later success in life, usually measured as IQ scores or verbal functioning or teacher's perceptions of success. Each will be discussed below.

SOCIAL CLASS

Social class has been implicated in most studies as an important variable in predicting positive child functioning (Clarke-Stewart, 1973; Deutsch, et al, 1967; Laosa, 1981). However, social class is a set of variables which includes child-rearing attitudes and practices as well as economic settings with or without sufficient health care, housing, clothes, and so on. Globally, more children with school problems can be found from the lower social classes than from the middle class. What is masked in this economic and social hierarchy of class are the attitudes and values held by one class which are also held by the dominant culture. Basically, middle-class children of almost all ethnic and racial groups tend to do well in school, whereas about one-half of lower-class children do not. Why they do not has been attributed by Jensen (1969) to racial characteristics and lower intelligence. Jensen's argument has been largely discounted by the recent data of intervention programs (Garber & Heber, 1981; Lazar, Hubbell, Murrary, Rosche, & Royce, 1977; Stedman, Anastasiow, Dokecki, Gordon, & Parker, 1972). In addition, Shipman, McKee, & Bridgeman (1976) have shown that lower-class parents who value achievement have children who do better in school. Ogbu (1974) states that most lower-class parents want their children to achieve in school, so their children's lower performance is not due to lack of motivation to succeed. What Heath (1983) demonstrates is that while valuing school achievement, both poor Black and White populations do not practice the parenting skills that lead to school success. In contrast, the middle class Whites who lived in the city (or "mainstream-middle class" in Heath's terminology) prepares their children effectively for school success, and this training begins in infancy.

Heath's (1983) two economically disadvantaged poor populations produced children who were verbal, but who had difficulty with indirect questions used by teachers in schools, and who did not use language in the ways the school expected. Blank, Rose, and Berlin (1978) found similar problems in the language use of the poor. Black parents who were economically poor did not, in Heath's study, expect their children to be information givers or conversational partners. According to Heath, they expected their children to "pick up" knowledge by being immersed in the conversation of adults. They encouraged their girls to practice "fussing," a talent the adults perceived to be useful as mothers. Similarly, they encouraged their boys to be aggressive and self-protective. Both *talents* were perceived by the school as negative behaviors.

In addition, the Black adults in Heath's study modeled and encouraged verbal games that were boastful and verbal "put downs" or ritualized insults. Girls developed verbal "put down" songs in jump rope rhythms and songs. Labov (1972) found similar ritualized verbal insult games in New York where adolescents practiced "playing the dozens," a game in which the winner is the master insulter. These games and songs are rich in metaphoric language but, cast in the "impolite" insult form, are rejected by the middle-class school and are not perceived as language talents. These children have higher-order language skills, the form of which is not valued by the middle-class-dominated school although it is valued in the home community. One of Heath's Black mothers stated: "We don't talk to our children like you (White) folks do" (p. 84). The children are not asked questions about what they know but are asked accusative questions about what they may have done, for example, "What did youse do?" (p. 81).

Heath's economically disadvantaged White families provide a different home environment for their children than do the poor Blacks, but their children are equally unproductive in school settings. White parents buy toys for their children and raise them in what Heath calls, "a world of colorful, mechanical, musical, literary (nursery rhymes), based stimuli" (1983, p. 116). However, communication content by the caregiver is directed to the child or to the caregiver's needs, where the caregiver gives all of the information without expecting an interaction from the child. If the child does talk, the information is passed over and the child and caregiver continue in parallel, not interactive, exchanges. The assumption in Heath's interpretation is that if the child listens, the child will learn. As with Black children who reside in poverty, their White counterparts may be "more polite," but they too fail to understand the questioning mode of the school or the function of the inquiry in general. What appears to be a major loss (i.e., mental retardation) is simply the failure to make the kind of middle-class cognitions and language gains that come from caregiver-child interactions. Children who reside in poverty, both White and Black, have very different notions of truth and the language appropriate for school.

Tough's (1977) work in England with working-class children produced findings that are consistent with Heath's work. Tough found that the working-class child tends to use language in ways that differ from the ways desired by the school. These children tend to overuse pronouns and be oriented toward the present and future. Middle-class children can also use language to explain their needs and desires, as well as to explore and understand their own behavior. Although Tough did not have specific data from the home, she believes that the model of language used by the parents in the home provides the model that the child adopts. The model which the middle-class parent presents is isomorphic with the ones the teacher use, whereas the working-class child learns and practices strategies that are not successful in school. More extensive review of the literature dealing with children who reside in poverty can be found in Anastasiow, Hanes, and Hanes (1982).

In general, both Heath and Tough find that the middle-class parents utilizes child-rearing strategies that lead to school and societal success. When these practices are used by the lower-class parent, they also lead to success. The lower-class mother who tends to value the strategies of the middle class is likely to produce a child who is successful in the school environment (Bradley & Caldwell, 1978). Conversely, the middle-class mother who uses the more demanding and restricting techniques typical of the lower class tends to produce children who have serious speech disorders (Wulbert, Kriegsman, & Mills, 1975).

The differentiating factor with the class differences appears to be about eleven years of education (Laosa, 1981); eleven years of education produces caregivers who use the more facilitative practices. As Laosa states, "schooling is a powerful force in cultural evolution (p. 161)." Years of mother's education was found to be the positive predictor of children's IQ in the collaborative study (reported by Broman, Nichols, & Kennedy, 1975).

Parenting practices grow out of values, and not all subcultures in the United States share the same orientation toward what are the important key values. Papajohn and Spiegel (1975) have identified four key value domains:

1. Activity: Action as measured by *Doing:* Some standard of achievement; *Being:* Action expresses personality; *Being in Becoming:* Action for developing the whole self.
2. Relationship: *Individuality:* Roles based on individual experience; *Collaterality:* Roles based on groups; *Lineality:* Roles hierarchically arranged.
3. Time: *Future:* Planning for what is to be; *Present:* Planning for immediate goals; *Past:* Emphasis on tradition.
4. Man-Nature: *Mastery:* Overcome and control nature; *Subjugation:* Efforts cannot control nature; *In-Harmony:* Efforts on coexistence.

Table 1 presents the major differences of how social classes relate to these themes.

Table 1
Relative Position of Value Themes for the Lower Class and Middle Class

Value	*Lower Class*	*Middle Class*
	Themes	*Themes*
Activity	Being > Doing > Being-in-becoming	Doing > Being > Being-in-becoming
Relationship	Collaterality > Lineality > Individuality	Individuality > Collaterality > Lineality
Time	Present $\geq$ Past > Future	Future > Present > Past
Man-Nature	Mastery $\leq$ Subjugation $\geq$ In-Harmony	Mastery > Subjugation > In-Harmony

The middle-class home is an expression of the Judeo-Christian ethnic seen in the Puritan ethnic of the United States, and the

Togagawa ethic of the Japanese (Werner, Bierman, & French, 1971). The lower-class themes presented in Table I hold for most socio- and ethnic groups of the lower class and are themes also held by some other cultural groups, for example, the Spanish surname (Laosa, 1981) and the Hawaiian cultures (Werner & Smith, 1982).

In Papajohn and Spiegel (1975), an individual becomes successful in the dominant middle-class society to the extent that the major value system is adopted. Laosa (1981) has demonstrated that it may take three generations for Spanish surname families to adopt the mainstream values. In adopting the values, the individual not only buys into a particular view of the world but adopts codes of how-to-act and how-to-prepare children to function in that world.

The nature of the child-rearing variables that prepare children to function successfully in the middle-class world, particularly the schools, is examined next.

THE POSITIVE FACTORS: RESPONDING TO INFANTS' REQUESTS

Responding to the child's initiated requests is viewed as an underlying structural variable by which the child learns to "trust" the environment (Brinker & Lewis, 1982; Emde & Harmon, 1981; Lewis & Brooks, 1980). The infant can be observed to cry and then pause as if listening. If the infant "hears" or has learned to recognize the caregiver's approach, crying will cease. In the case of the lack of caregiver's responsiveness, the infant will continue to cry, and continued lack of responsiveness leads to infant anger, frustration, and ultimately to withdrawal, failure to thrive and in extreme cases, death. Thus, in the context of satisfying the infant's needs or following the infant's requests, a sense of trust and basic attachment is formed.

In this context, one finds a host of correlated variables demonstrated by the responding caregiver:

Warmth: Picking up the infant, cuddling the infant, speaking soothing, comforting tones and words; psychological warmth has been found to be a positive facilitating variable in most studies of parent-child interaction research (see Martin, 1975, for an excellent summary).

Transactions: Reciprocal Interactions—Besides the physical involvement, these caregivers talk and interact with the infant. The infant cries, the mother picks the child up and says, "Oh, my baby's crying," waits for the child to either stop or pause. The mother then picks up the beat and talks some more. The infant will look and respond. Eye contact will be made. Smiles will be exchanged and the child and caregiver will transact in a mutually rewarding reciprocal relationship (see Bower, 1974; Schaffer, 1977).

Stimulation: In these settings, the caregiver provides verbal interchanges as well as provides food and comfort or pain relief. The caregiver also involves the child in pointing out objects in environment, calling attention to a pet, or commenting on the colors of a mobile. The caregiver does so by speaking in simple, redundant sentences in a high pitched voice, which is often referred to as "Motherese" (e.g., "See the doggie, nice doggie, it's a baby's doggie"). Sentences are filled with questions which the caregiver answers and elaborates upon. It is a process of "listening to them and talking to them" (Cooper & Anastasiow, 1981; Snow & Ferguson, 1977).

Push to Achieve: The caregiver increases the complexity of her language as the child develops. The caregiver encourages the child to acquire more complex language, just as she encourages the child to master motor milestones (Bloom & Lahey, 1978). For example, once the child can master head control, the caregiver encourages control of head, neck, and upper torso. From that point, free sitting without support is encouraged and, later, crawling, walking, stair climbing, running, catching, and so on. Effective caregivers encourage their children to make the next developmental accomplishment once the lower-level one has been attained. This push is in a context of encouragement and psychological support (Werner & Smith, 1982).

FREEDOM AND ENCOURAGEMENT
TO EXPLORE AND OBJECTS TO EXPLORE

Once the child is physically able to move, the effective caregiver allows the child freedom to explore a safe environment. Children will look to the basic caregiver for reassurances that it is all right to move ahead, what Campos (1983) refers to as *maternal referencing*. That is, the child will move toward an object, look toward mother, and if mother smiles or nods, the child will continue to explore. If the mother frowns or expresses concern, the securely attached infant will back away from the perceived danger. Campos purposes that infants learn how to avoid the large number of environmental hazards by the technique of maternal referencing rather than by directly experiencing each.

Conversely, children learn how the environment works through their own direct interaction of objects. Infants shake and drop objects and learn that things rattle, bounce, or roll. These early learnings of the basic characteristics of objects, and how they are learned, is what Piagetian theory so elegantly describes (Piaget, 1983).

As Bradley and Caldwell (1978) found, children need objects to explore and the objects we give children to explore are called toys. Toys need not be commercially prepared, they may be pots and pans or cans and utensils. What is important is that age-appropriate objects are provided to young children if they are to develop.

The caregiver who takes the child out of the home on frequent trips to the store or neighborhood has a child who is a faster language-learner. These mothers tend to be low television watchers, and in all likelihood spend more time interacting with their children (Nelson, 1973).

REASONING–DISTRACTING
VERSUS PHYSICAL PUNISHMENT

There can be no place for the use of physical punishment before a child is mobile. As we have seen, children under seven to nine months are not in control of their emotions and physical needs and cannot control their expressions. Physical punishment to stop these uncontrolled behavioral expressions is not only useless but ludicrous. As Bijou (1983) reports, punishment and strict discipline lead to escape avoidance behaviors. When the child is mobile and does not respond to maternal referencing to avoid danger, removing the object or distracting the child usually stops the undesired actions. If the child persists, for example in running across a four-lane highway, physical punishment may stop the behavior. The problem is that pain breeds mistrust, and the pain of physical punishment may interfere with the establishment of attachment.

As the child matures, reasoning or giving reasons can supplement distraction. Schachter (1979) has two protocols in her "Everyday Talk with Children," which bear on this point and contrast social-class differences. A lower socio-economic class mother says, "Take your fingers out of your mouth," a demand which is repeated several times. When it fails the child is physically punished. A middle-class mother who does not want her child to spill or waste the bubble water cautions her child, reasons, elaborates, gives examples and alternatives before taking the bubble water away. She says the bubble water is not ordinary water, it is not like playing in the bath tub, or pouring from one container to another. She reminds her child that it has to be bought at the store and that last time the child wasted it and was sorry.

Wertheim (1975a, b, c, d) summarizes the negative effects that physical punishment has on the child's mastery of autonomy and competence. The data are substantial to implicate the negative impact of physical punishment in the child's affective, social, and cognitive development. Other studies have shown similar findings. Clarke-Stewart (1973) found positive effects in mother's use of reasoning, affection, helping, responsiveness, explaining, sharing, expanding language, low punishment and restrictions, and conversing with the child in an atmosphere of psychological warmth and praise.

Conversely, Clark-Stewart found negative effects on the child in mother's use of strict control, coaxing, commanding, threatening, and physical punishment. Henderson (1981), in summarizing the facilitating aspects of parent-child interactions, lists: academic press, language model, range of environmental stimuli, parental modeling, activeness of the family, intellectuality of the home, work habits of the family, and well-established routines. Henderson (1981), states that it is the specific characteristics of the home environment which account for the social-class variations in intellectual performance. In essence, Henderson is saying that measured differences in IQ scores can be attributed to social-class differences in uses of language rather than to genetic potential.

Scarr and Weinberg (1980), when further clarifying the role of the environment in achievement, point out that making pottery can foster conservations of quantity as an aspect of logical-mathematical thinking; weaving develops symbolic representation; tailoring can enhance mathematical skills; and, rice farming facilitates mastery of estimation of quantity. All these activities have functional adaptational value. Thinking is developed in culturally relevant activities.

Siegel (1984) found that the nature of the home environment influenced development. In her study children who had normal developmental progress at one year of life but were delayed at three years of age were raised in non-facilitating home environments. Conversely, the child who was delayed at one year of age functioned normally at three were raised in facilitating homes. The home environment has a powerful influence on development, and a set of enriched experiences is powerful in the development of the normal child and the remediation of the damaged child. As Rutter (1981) found, brain damaged children placed in an enriched environment, where they are free to act and experience sets of extrinsic experiences, will have a nutritive trophic impact on the brain, even to the point of reactivation of damaged neurons through regeneration of axons (p. 93).

In the classic, elegant longitudinal study conducted on the island of Hawaii by Emmy Elizabeth Werner and her colleagues, summarized by Werner and Smith (1982), we find operating the facilitating sets of variables described above. The researchers followed all reported pregnancies for the years 1955–56 for all socio- and ethnocultures in Kauai island until the children's adolescent period. What they found can be best stated in the outcomes of four groups of children, in their own words (Werner, Bierman, & French, 1967; pp. 80–81).

Group 1, the children *without perinatal stress* who grew up in homes rated *favorable in environmental stimulation and emotional support,* had 10-year IQs in the superior (128) to average (101) range. No child had achievement problems in school, and all except one had gained IQ points since the two-year follow-up—*an average gain of 13 points,* with a range from 2 to 28 points.

Group 2, the children who had suffered *severe perinatal stress* but grew up in homes rated *favorable in educational stimulation and emotional support,* had 10-year IQs ranging from 125 to 96, from the superior to the average range. One-fourth of these children had some achievement problems, but the overwhelming majority functioned adequately in school. One-sixth had significant physical problems. All children on whom Cattell test scores were available had *gained an average of 13 IQ points,* an increase similar to the group without perinatal stress which was exposed to a favorable environment.

Group 3, the children *without perinatal complications* who grew up in homes rated *unfavorable in educational stimulation and emotional support,* had 10-year IQs ranging from 123 to 70. More than half of these children had IQs below 85, in the "slow learner" or "educable mentally retarded" range. *Intelligence quotient point changes from two to 10 years were erratic,* ranging from +37 to −20, *with an average loss of four IQ points.* With one exception, all of the children in this group had serious achievement problems in school; four-fifths also had behavior problems. Nearly two-thirds of the children had verbal subtest scores significantly lower than performance test scores, indicating a serious language disability. Only two children had significant physical defects.

Group 4, the children who had suffered *severe perinatal stress* and also grew up in *homes rated unfavorable,* had a very wide range of IQs at age 10, from 117 to 30. One-half of the children in this group were either "slow learners" or mentally retarded; four-fifths had serious achievement problems; one-fourth had serious behavior problems; and one-fourth had perceptual problems. *All but three of the children who had Cattell test scores reported a loss in IQ points* since the two-year follow-up. One third had significant physical defects of the central nervous and the musculoskeletal systems. (emphases added)

Thus, the facilitating strategies of these American-Hawaiian and other multiethnic group mothers not only facilitated the development of the normal child but, in most all cases, assisted the child damaged at birth to achieve normality.

SUMMARY

Putting It Together

Parenting strategies facilitate the development of the basic perceptual systems by providing environmental stimuli and allowing the child to experiment (i.e., play) with objects. Furthermore, positive parenting strategies facilitate the child's mastery of the language of the home environment, social roles, and how to use language to inquire and reason. Humans possess the ability to reason inductively as part of their genetic make up. What the caregiver as teachers (and typical teachers in Western schools) do is to teach the child how to use language to think, and to reason deductively about the world. What has been stated above about differences between social-class members and different ethnic groups is that whereas all groups tend to provide opportunities for some language learning, not all groups model or instruct children to reason deductively and how to use language to do so.

Development is not a uniform or singular process. As we have seen, perceptual systems develop more or less independently of each other and require environmental experiences to realize what is genetically programmed. What is developed is a product of genetic predispositions and genetic potentialities which are realized through the transactions of the individual and the caregiver. The caregiver operates in an ecological setting which has both constraints and opportunities. The values of the culture may prepare the caregiver to facilitate the acquisition of skills that operate well in middle-class, Western-type societies. Alternatively, they may prepare the child toward different sets of goals which, although valued and valuable, are not the prized roles of the middle-class Western society.

Supporting evidence for the long term effects of facilitative child rearing strategies described in this chapter can be found in Valliant (1977). He followed men from their entrance into Harvard in 1942–1943 to their fifty-fifth birthday. The men who were deemed as successful were those who had prestigious occupations and were economically secure. Valliant found that the successful men had childhoods which resembled the ones described here. Men who had bleak childhoods were unable to play as adults. Men who satisfactorily established their own identity (usually apart from their mothers) were able to maintain feelings of autonomy and competence through to middle age. Most of the unsuccessful men had not resolved their identity crises and had insecure attachments, and many unsuccessful men still lived with their mothers.

Unfortunately, those adults who suffer bleak childhoods with various forms of neglect and abuse tend to repeat these patterns in adulthood with their own children. To prevent this from being a continuous cycle, attention must be given to preparing future generations in the knowledge and skills of facilitating children's development. Perhaps a book such as this can serve as background information for those who train.

REFERENCES

Anastasiow, N. J., Hanes, M. L., & Hanes, M. L. (1982). *Language and reading strategies of poverty children.* Baltimore, MD: Univ. Park Press.

Axelrad, S., & Brody, S. (1978). *Mothers, fathers and children.* New York: International Univ. Press.

Bandura, A. (1977). *Social learning theory.* Englewood Cliffs, NJ: Prentice-Hall.

Bell, R. Q. (1968). A reinterpretation of the direction of effects in studies of socialization. *Psychological Review, 75,* 63–72.

Bijou, S. W. (1983). The prevention of mild and moderate retarded development. In F. J. Menolascino, R. Neman, and J. A. Stark (Eds.), *Curative aspects of mental retardation.* Baltimore, MD: Paul Brookes.

Blank, M., Rose, S. A., & Berlin, L. J. (1978). *The language of hearing.* New York: Grune and Stratton.

Bloom, L. & Lahey, M. (1978). *Language development and language disorders.* New York: Wiley.

Bower, T. G. R. (1974). *Development in infancy.* San Francisco: Freeman.

Bowlby, J. (1969). *Attachment and loss* (Vol. 1, Attachment). New York: Basic Books.

Bradley, R. H., & Caldwell, B. M. (1978). Screening the environment. *American Journal of Orthopsychiatry, 48*(1), 114–130.

Brinker, R. P., & Lewis, M. (1982). Discovering the competent handicapped infant: A process approach to assessment and intervention. In Fewell, R. R. (Ed.), *Topics in Early Childhood Special Education.* Gaithersburg, MD: Aspen.

Broman, S. H., Nichols, P. L., & Kennedy, W. A. (1975). *Preschool IQ.* Hillsdale, NJ: Erlbaum.

Bruner, J. (1977). Early social interaction and language acquisition. In H. R. Schaffer (Ed.), *Studies in mother-infant interaction.* New York: Academic Press.

Campos, J. J., Barrett, K. C., Lamb, M. E., Goldsmith, H. H., & Stenberg, C. (1983). Socioemotional development. In P. H. Mussen (Ed.), *Handbook of child psychology* (Vol. 2, pp. 783–916). New York: Wiley.

Carey, S., & Diamond, R. (1980). Maturational determination of the development course of face encoding. In D. Caplan (Ed.), *Biological studies of mental processes.* Cambridge, MA: MIT Press.

Clarke-Stewart, K. A. (1973). Interactions between mothers and their young children. *Monographs of the Society for Research in Child Development, 38*(6–7, Serial No. 153).

Cole, M., & Scribner, J. (1974). *Culture and thought.* New York: Wiley.

Cooper, G., & Anastasiow, N. (1981). *Moving into skills of communication.* Denver, CO: LADOCA Publishing.

Darwin, C. (1973). *The expressions of the emotions in man and animals.* Chicago: Univ. of Chicago Press.

Dennis, M. (1980). Language acquisitions in a single hemisphere. In D. Caplan *Biological studies of mental process.* Cambridge, MA: MIT Press.

Deutsch, M., Laosa, L., & Clarke-Stewart, K. A. (1967). *The disadvantaged child.* New York: Basic Books.

Ekman, P. (1980). *The face of man.* New York: Garland STPM Press.

Emde, R. N., Gaensbauer, T. J., & Harmon, R. J. (1976). *Emotional expression in infancy.* New York: International Univ. Press.

Emde, R. N., & Harmon, R. J. (1981). *Attachment and affiliative systems: Neurobiological and psychobiological aspects.* New York: Plenum Press.

Epstein, H. T. (1974a). Phrenoblysis: Special brain and mind growth periods. Part I: Human brain and skull development. *Developmental Psychobiology, 7*(3), 207–216.

Epstein, H. T. (1974b). Phrenoblysis: Special brain and mind growth periods. Part II: Human mental development. *Developmental Psychobiology, 7*(3), 217–224.

Erikson, E. H. (1950). *Childhood and society.* New York: Norton.

Fodor, J. A. (1983). *The modularity of mind.* Cambridge, MA: MIT Press.

Fraiberg, S. (1977). *Insights from the blind.* New York: Basic Books.

Garber, H., & Heber, R. (1981). The efficacy of early intervention with family rehabilitation. In M. Begab, H. Garber, & H. C. Haywood (Eds.), *Psychosocial influences in retarded performance* (Vol. 2: Strategies for improving competence). Baltimore, MD: Univ. Park Press.

Garcia, J., & Levine, M. S. (1976). Learning paraligms and structure of the organism. In M. R. Rosenzweig and E. L. Bennett (Eds.), *Neural mechanism of learning and memory.* Cambridge, MA: MIT Press.

Gardner, H. (1983). *Frames of mind: A theory of multiple intelligences.* New York: Basic Books.

Gazzaniga, M. S., & LeDoux, J. E. (1981). *The integrated mind.* New York: Plenum Press.

Goldman, P. S. (1976). The role of experience in recovery of function following orbital prefrontal lesions in infant monkeys. *Neuropsychologia, 14,* 401–411.

Gottlieb, G. (Ed.). (1976). The roles of experience in the development of behavior and the nervous system. In G. Gottlieb (ed.), *Studies on the development of behavior and the nervous systems* (Vol. 3, Natural and behavioral specifically). New York: Academic Press.

Heath, S. (1983). *Way with words.* London: Cambridge Univ. Press.

Henderson, R. (1981). *Parent-child interaction.* New York: Academic Press.

Hunt, J. Mc.V. (1979). Psychological development: Early experience. In M. R. Rosenzweig and L. W. Porter (Eds.), *Annual review of psychology.* Palo Alto, CA: Annual Reviews, *30,* pp. 103–143.

Hunt, M. (1982). *The Universe Within.* New York: S & S Press.

Hubel, D. H., & Wiesel, T. N. (1979). Brain mechanism of vision. *Scientific American, 241*(3), 150–162.

Izard, C. E. (1977). *Human emotions.* New York: Plenum Press.

Jensen, A. R. (1969). How much can we boost IQ and scholastic achievement? *Harvard Review, 39,* 1–123.

Labov, W. (1972). *Language in the inner city: Studies in the black English vernacular.* Philadelphia, PA: Univ. of Pennsylvania Press.

Lamb, M. E. (Ed.). (1981). *The role of the father in child development.* Hillsdale, NJ: Erlbaum.

Laosa, L. (1981). Maternal behavior: Sociocultural diversity in family interactions. In Henderson, R. W. (Ed.), *Parent-child interaction.* New York: Academic Press.

Lazar, I., Hubbell, V. R., Murrary, H., Rosche, M., & Royce, J. (1977). *The persistence of preschool effects* (OHDS, 78-30129). Department of Health, Education, and Welfare Publications.

Lecours, A. R. (1975). Myelogenetic correlates of the development of speech and language. In E. H. Lenneberg and E. Lenneberg (eds.), *Foundations of language development: A multidisciplinary approach* (Vol. 1). New York: Academic Press.

Lewis, M., & Brooks, J. (1980). *The origins of the concept of self.* New York: Plenum Press.

Lewis, M., & Rosenblum, L. A. (1978). *The development of affect.* New York: Plenum Press.

Lipsitt, L. P. (1979). The newborn as informant. In R. B. Kearsley and I. E. Sigel, (Eds.), *Infants at risk: Assessment of cognitive functioning.* Hillsdale, NJ: Erlbaum.

Luria, A. R. (1973). *The working brain.* New York: Basic Books.

Martin, B. (1975). Parent-child relations. In Horowitz, F. D. (Ed.), *Review of child development research* (4th Ed.). Chicago: University of Chicago Press.

Meshcheryakow, A. (1979). *Awakening to life.* Moscow: Progress Publishers.

Nelson, K. (1973). Structure and strategy in learning to talk. *Monographs of the Society for Research in Child Development, 38* (1–2, Serial No. 149).

Ogbu, J. V. (1974). *The next generation.* New York: Academic Press.

Papajohn, J., & Spiegel, J. (1975). *Transactions in families.* San Francisco: Jossey-Bass.

Piaget, J. (1972). Intellectual evolution from adolescence to adulthood. *Human Development, 15,* 1–12.

Piaget, J. (1983). Piaget's theory. In P. H. Mussen (Ed.), *Handbook of child psychology* (Vol. 1), W. Kessen (Ed.), *History, theory, and methods.* New York: Wiley.

Rutter, M. (1981). Psychological sequelae of brain damage in children. *Journal of American Psychometric Association, 32,* 1553–1554.

Scarr, S., & Weinberg, R. A. (1980). Calling All Camps! The war is over. *American Sociological Review, 45,* 859–865.

Scarr-Salapatek, S. (1976). An evolutionary perspective on infant intelligence: Species patterns and individual variations. In M. Lewis (Ed.), *Origins of intelligence.* New York: Plenum Press.

Schachter, F. F. (1979). *Everyday mother talk to toddlers: Early intervention.* New York: Academic Press.

Schaffer, H. R. (1977). *Studies in mother-infant reaction.* New York: Academic Press.

Scroufe, L. A. (1983). Infant caregiver attachment and patterns of adaptation in preschool: The roots of maladaptation. In M. Perlmitter (Ed.), Development and policy concerning children with special needs. *The Minnesota Symposium on Child Psychology* (Vol. 16). Hillsdale, NJ: Erlbaum.

Shipman, V. C., McKee, J. D., & Bridgeman, B. (1976, December). Notable early characteristics of high and low achieving black low SES children. *Educational Testing Service* (PR-76-21).

Siegel, L. S. (1984). Biological and environmental variables as predictors of intellectual functioning. In S. Harel and N. J. Anastasiow (Eds.), *The at risk infant.* Baltimore, MD: Paul Brookes Publishing.

Snow, C. E., & Ferguson, C. A. (1977). *Talking to children: Language input and acquisition.* Cambridge, MA: Cambridge Univ. Press.

Stedman, D. J., Anastasiow, N. J., Dokecki, P. R., Gordon, I. J., & Parker, R. K. (1972, October). *How can effective early intervention programs be delivered to potentially retarded children?* A report for the Office of the Secretary of the Department of Health, Education and Welfare.

Tough, J. (1977). *The development of meaning.* New York: Wiley.

Vaillant, G. E. (1977). *Adaptation to life.* Boston, MA: Little-Brown.

Waddington, C. H. (1957). *The strategy of genes.* London: Allen and Unwin.

Werner, E. E., Bierman, J. M., & French, F. E. (1971). *The children of Kauai.* Honolulu: Univ. Press of Hawaii.

Werner, E. E., & Smith, R. (1982). *Vulnerable but invincible.* New York: McGraw Hill.

Werner, E. E. (1984). *Kith, Kin and Hired Hands.* Baltimore, MD: Univ. Park Press.

Werner, J. J., & Lipsitt, L. P. (1981). The infancy of human sensory systems. In E. J. Gollen, *Developmental plasticity.* New York: Academic Press.

Wertheim, E. S. (1975a). Person-environment interaction: The epigenesis of autonomy and competence: I. Theoretical considerations (normal development). *British Journal of Medical Psychology, 48,* 1–8.

Wertheim, E. S. (1975b). Person-environment interaction: The epigenesis of autonomy and competence: II. Review of the developmental literature (normal developmental). *British Journal of Medical Psychology, 48,* 95–111.

Wertheim, E. S. (1975c). Person-environment interaction: The epigenesis of autonomy and competence: III. *British Journal of Medical Psychology, 48,* 237–256.

Wertheim, E. S. (1975d). Person-environment interaction: The epigenesis of autonomy and competence: IV. *British Journal of Medical Psychology, 48,* 391–402.

Wulbert, M. S., Kriegsman, E., & Mills, B. (1975). Language delay and associated mother-child interactions. *Developmental Psychology, 2*(1), 61–70.

Zelazo, P. R. (1976). From reflexive to instrumental behavior. In L. Lipsitt (Ed.), *Developmental psychobiology.* NJ: Lawrence Earlbaum.

Zimmerman, B. J. (1983). Social learning theory: A contextualist account of cognitive functioning. In C. Brainerd (Ed.), *Recent advances in cognitive development.* New York: Springer.

INDEX